On Sociology

On Sociology

Numbers, Narratives, and the Integration of Research and Theory

John H. Goldthorpe

OXFORD

UNIVERSITY PRESS

OXFORD

UNIVERSITY PRESS

Great Clarendon Street, Oxford OX2 6DP

Oxford University Press is a department of the University of Oxford.
It furthers the University's objective of excellence in research, scholarship,
and education by publishing worldwide in

Oxford New York

Athens Auckland Bangkok Bogotá Buenos Aires Calcutta
Cape Town Chennai Dar es Salaam Delhi Florence Hong Kong Istanbul
Karachi Kuala Lumpur Madrid Melbourne Mexico City Mumbai
Nairobi Paris São Paulo Singapore Taipei Tokyo Toronto Warsaw
and associated companies in Berlin Ibadan

Oxford is a registered trade mark of Oxford University Press
in the UK and certain other countries

Published in the United States
by Oxford University Press Inc., New York

British Library Cataloguing in Publication Data

Data available

Library of Congress Cataloging in Publication Data
Goldthorpe, John H.
On sociology: numbers, narratives, and the integration of research and theory/
John H. Goldthorpe.
Includes bibliographical references and index.
1. Sociology. 2. Sociology—Philosophy. 3. Sociology—Research. 4. Social action.
5. Social classes. I. Title.
HM585.G65 2000 301—dc21 00-021359

ISBN 0-19-829571-5
ISBN 0-19-829572-3 (Pbk)

1 3 5 7 9 10 8 6 4 2

Typeset by Best-set Typesetter Ltd., Hong Kong
Printed in Great Britain
on acid-free paper by
Biddles Ltd
Guildford and King's Lynn

PREFACE

During my career as a sociologist I have been fortunate in having a series of able and congenial collaborators, in the company of whom research has, even in its most tiresome phases, proved a rewarding experience. Working alone, I have found, is not only more demanding in itself but provides far less opportunity for incidental entertainment. In writing the essays collected in this volume, which was in the main a solitary task, I have therefore more than usually felt the need for support and conviviality. But in this regard, too, I have been fortunate in my association with a number of individuals and institutions.

I have continued to benefit greatly from the privilege of my Fellowship at Nuffield College, Oxford, and from my membership of the Sociology Group there. I am especially appreciative of the unfailing help and encouragement that I have received from David Cox, both as Warden of the College and after his retirement, and from Gordon Marshall. In recent years I have assumed the office of Fellow Librarian, but I shall not let this prevent me from saying that the College Library is one of quite outstanding quality, for it is well known that all credit for this rests with the Librarian, James Legg, his predecessor, Christine Kennedy, and the Library staff, to all of whom I would like to give my thanks for their excellent professional services and for many kindnesses over and above the call of duty.

Beyond Nuffield, it is the ties that I have formed over the years with sociologists in various European countries that have been of chief importance for me. It gives me particular pleasure to record here the great intellectual advantage—and enjoyment—that I have gained from my friendships with Karl-Ulrich Mayer, Walter Müller, and Robert Erikson (the last also a long-term collaborator), which date back to the early 1970s; and I have more recently benefited in similar ways from coming to know and work closely with Richard Breen. Others who have regularly provided inspiration, guidance, and constructive criticism include Hans-Peter Blossfeld, Raymond Boudon, Peter Hedstrom, Janne Jonsson, Aage Sørensen, and Wout Ultee. Conferences organized by the European Consortium for Sociological Research have been the setting for several highly rewarding exchanges. I should also note that personal relationships have in several cases led on to institutional connections, whether of a formal or an informal kind, that I much value: in particular, with the Swedish Institute for Social Research in Stockholm, the Max Planck Institute for Human Development in Berlin, the Economic and Social Research Institute in Dublin, and the Interuniversity Centre for Social Science Theory and Methodology in the Netherlands.

Finally, I would like to acknowledge the many ways in which my wife, Rhiannon, through her courage, patience, and very practical help, has made my work on this book far less stressful and more pleasurable than it would otherwise have been.

J. H. G.

The Barbican, London
September 1999

CONTENTS

1

Introduction

OVER RECENT decades, a state of crisis in sociology has been so frequently proclaimed, and on so many different grounds, that to do so yet again can have little dramatic impact. I can, however, only report that, as the end of the twentieth century has approached, I have come to believe with ever greater conviction that sociology is indeed in a condition that cannot for much longer continue without seriously adverse, and possibly quite disastrous, effects ensuing. It is then this intensifying belief that has primarily motivated these essays—all written within the last ten years—and their collection in this volume. It might, of course, be thought that little more is here involved than a bad case of *fin-de-siècle* apocalyptic gloom. Before introducing the essays themselves, I therefore try to explain why I regard the present state of sociology as giving cause for such concern and also to indicate how in general I would think it best to respond.

The Background

In the course of the twentieth century, and especially in the last thirty or forty years, sociology has succeeded rather well in establishing itself as a 'discipline' in an institutional sense. In most nations of the world in which university systems exist these now include departments and chairs of sociology; and, at least in economically more advanced societies, arrangements are also in place through which sociological research, as conducted within both universities and other centres, receives public support, financial and organizational. There has also been a widespread development of professional associations of sociologists, on both a national and an international basis, together with the standard accompaniments of journals, research networks, conferences, honours, etc. However, if sociology is viewed from an intellectual rather than an institutional standpoint, a very different picture presents itself, and 'discipline' is scarcely the first word that would spring to mind. The intellectual state of contemporary sociology could in fact only be described as one of general, and steadily worsening, disarray. Three indications of this disarray, which I would regard as having cumulative significance, are the following.

First, there is a manifest lack of integration of research and theory—the 'scandal of sociology', as I have called it elsewhere (Goldthorpe 1997*a*). In this regard, sociology has for long fallen short of the standards of other social and human sciences, such as, say, economics or psychology, even though these standards are not in fact all that demanding. But what is yet more disturbing at the present time is that this lack of integration is now less often *seen* as a scandal. Rather than strenuous efforts being made to bring research and theory into a closer relationship, arguments are in fact advanced that appear to be aimed at justifying their 'separate development'.

Here, I believe, chief responsibility has to lie with theorists and, above all, with proponents of what has become known as 'general' theory. In usual scientific parlance—and this would be the case in social and human sciences such as economics and psychology as well as in the natural sciences—theories are bodies of ideas that provide a systematic basis for the *explanation* of phenomena of interest. A theory of wages, say, offers a basis for explaining how wages are determined, why they vary across different occupations, or how they are related to the level of unemployment; a theory of attitudes offers a basis for explaining how attitudes are formed, how they are reinforced or modified, or how they influence or are influenced by behaviour. However, in sociology today what is notable is that those who would represent themselves as general theorists are reluctant to see an increased capacity for the explanation of social phenomena as being the main objective of their work, and indeed appear anxious to establish understandings of theory that would in fact largely exonerate them from responsibility in this regard.

For example, Alexander (1998: 165) openly acknowledges that, 'In order to defend the project of general theory, it must be accepted that sociological arguments need not have immediate explanatory pay-offs to be scientifically significant.' And in a similar fashion Giddens (1984: p. xviii) seeks to 'distance' himself from the position that what is essential to sociological—or, as he would prefer to say, 'social'—theory are explanatory propositions 'of a generalizing type'. For Alexander (1998: 165–70), theory in sociology has to be recognized as a form of 'discourse' that involves arguments 'that do not have immediate reference to factual or explanatory concerns' but that pertain rather to the differing 'background assumptions', 'supra-empirical considerations', and 'criteria of truth' that characterize the competing 'traditions and schools' into which sociology is inevitably divided. For Giddens, it would seem, theory should be directed not towards explanation but simply conceptualization. Social theory 'has the task of providing *conceptions* of the nature of human social activity and of the human agent' or, again, of 'reworking *conceptions* of human being and human doing, social reproduction and social transformation' (Giddens 1984: pp. xvii, xx; emphasis added).

Thus, whatever view one may take of the intrinsic value of these attempts at redefining the nature and purpose of theory, it can scarcely be denied that, to the extent that they are adopted, the connection of theory to research, in the sense of empirical enquiry, is necessarily weakened. If theory is understood as providing a basis for explanation, theory is thereby linked to research in quite specific ways. On the one hand, theories are open to evaluation in terms of the adequacy of the explanations of research findings to which they lead and also in terms of the validity of these explanations when exposed to further empirical testing. On the other hand, research is open to evaluation in terms of its relevance to theory, whether through the process of testing or of assessing the relative explanatory power of rival theories or, say, through the further empirical investigation of instances where, apparently, all extant theory fails. In contrast, with alternative understandings of theory of the kind that are suggested by Alexander and Giddens, the nature of the relationship between theory and research becomes obscure and, so far as one can see, highly tenuous. Thus, Alexander (1998: 32) talks of a 'scientific continuum' in sociology 'ranging from abstract, general, and metaphysical elements on the one end to the concrete, empirical, and factual on the other'. But just what is supposed to happen along this continuum—the actual mode of interaction that is envisaged among its constituent elements—is not spelled out. Giddens claims (1984: p. xvii) that the concepts that it is the 'task' of social theory to provide are then to be 'placed in the service of empirical work'. But no indication is given of what criteria might be applied in determining whether these concepts are of any use in such work. Indeed, in regard to his own 'structuration theory', Giddens appears to change tack somewhat and speaks (1984: 327) of 'the tasks of social research informed by structuration theory'. The question of whether, in pursuing its tasks, this research might in fact lead to the conclusion that the theory is mistaken—or, perhaps, devoid of content—is not taken up.[1]

It is indeed difficult here to avoid the judgement that what general theorists would wish to see, and are in fact aiming to bring about, is a situation in which theory construction and development, or, one might better say, 'writing about' theory, can go on in large part without serious reference to empirical enquiry. As van den Berg has put it (1998: 205–6), general theory does not seek 'to formulate coherent accounts of things happening "out there"' but rather 'to become a sub-discipline in its own right, and one with

---

[1] In the work cited in the text Giddens seeks to illustrate the implications of 'structuration theory' for empirical research by reference to a number of studies 'that have mostly been undertaken outside any immediate influence of the concepts I have elaborated' (1984: 327). The crucial issue to be addressed, one might then have thought, is that of *what is gained* if these studies are re-examined in the light of Giddens's concepts. But Giddens offers very little specific commentary in this regard. And indeed, while the exercise in which he engages may help to clarify somewhat the previous, highly abstract, presentation of 'structuration theory', it is difficult to see how, conversely, the concepts he would introduce are in fact in any way more illuminating than those originally used in the studies. Giddens's virtual equation of concepts and theory—of proposals about how we might view the social world with proposals about how it really works—is sadly reminiscent of later Parsons: in effect, highly complex conceptual preparations are made for a theoretical journey that never seems to get started. On the matter of the excessive importance that sociologists tend to attach to conceptualization as opposed to theory construction *per se*, see Popper's apt observations on 'rampant verbalism' (1976b: 18–31) and more generally on 'the myth of the framework' (1994).

its own apparent criteria of utility and relevance that seem wholly divorced from the needs and concerns of practising sociological researchers.[2']

Moreover, as a scarcely surprising reaction, many researchers, and especially among those working in a quantitative style, have formed strongly negative views of general theory[3]—and have then, by an unfortunate and unwarranted extension, tended to become dismissive of theory in general. This attitude they express less in explicit critique than in assumptions implicit in their practice: for example, the assumption that research findings can largely 'speak for themselves' without need of theoretical explanation, and that where data are given quantitative form causal relationships can in any event be determined directly from statistical analysis. Thus, as van den Berg further observes (1998: 206), the 'autonomization' of theory here finds its equivalent in the autonomization of technique, and in a way that is 'no less absurd or damaging to the discipline as a whole'.

Secondly, and in large part underlying the lack of integration of research and theory, one can identify a collective failure on the part of sociologists to decide just what kind of discipline sociology is or ought to try to be. And in this regard, too, the situation would appear to be deteriorating. In the middle decades of the twentieth century it was widely accepted that sociology should aim to establish itself as a social science, drawing inspiration from the model—or rather models—provided by the natural sciences, although with due regard for distinctive features of the phenomena and problems with which it was concerned. However, this position became strongly challenged in the context of the so-called *Positivismusstreit* (see Adorno *et al.* 1976), which began in Germany in the later 1960s and was protracted, chiefly by opponents of what was labelled the 'orthodox consensus', for twenty years or more.

While the controversy was from the first seriously confused, not least over just what 'positivism', whether in sociology or more generally, should be taken to mean, one concern of its critics was evident enough. That is, to reject 'methodological monism' or, in other words, the idea of the unity of scientific method across all fields of its application, and to maintain that even if sociology were to be regarded as a social science, it must still rest on a methodology fundamentally different from that of the natural sciences. The grounds on which this argument was advanced varied a good deal, but what was usually entailed was some appeal back to the distinction, central to German debates over scientific and scholarly methods in the later nineteenth century,

---

[2] van den Berg could have found striking confirmation for this claim in the distinction explicitly made by C. G. A. Bryant (1995: 152–4) between 'theorists' theory' (i.e. theory *à la* Alexander and Giddens) and 'researchers' theory'. For Bryant, the problem with the latter, as pursued, for example, by Coleman (1990), is that it is 'impervious to the linguistic turn, the double-hermeneutic and the preoccupations of post-empiricist philosophy of science'. It is seemingly beyond Bryant's comprehension that not everyone is as impressed as he by the intellectual cogency of these developments; and that what, in any event, must remain of crucial importance for researchers is the explanatory power of theory in relation to the substantive problems with which they grapple.

[3] e.g. 'a goopy mess of (deceptive) intellectual history, a healthy dollop of ideology, and a Chinese menu of "schools", "approaches", and buzzwords' (Davis 1994: 184).

between *Geisteswissenschaften* and *Naturwissenschaften*, and to the claim that the former were decisively set apart from the latter by the 'hermeneutic imperative': that is, by the need, where social or cultural phenomena were studied, to go beyond objective explanation to an ultimate 'subjective understanding' of their human meaning. From this standpoint, therefore, sociology could be represented as having a closer affinity with the humanities than with the natural sciences and in particular with literary criticism and theory where issues of 'interpretation' were crucial.[4]

As might then be expected, general theorists, with their concern to play down the link between theory and explanation, took a leading part in the assault on positivism and on the unity of method in particular. But also prominent were those favouring various forms of qualitative research in sociology, ranging from micro-level ethnography through to macro-level historical analyses, for whom the possibility of replacing explanatory with interpretative approaches—even if of widely differing kinds—appeared attractive. In consequence, positivism became to a large extent equated, for polemical purposes at least, with quantitative research and, especially, with that based on sample survey methodology. However, criticism arising out of the *Positivismusstreit* proved to have remarkably little impact on such research. Few practitioners were motivated to respond to it (though see Marsh 1982). In part, this was because the criticism was widely regarded as ill-informed; but perhaps more important was the fact that sociologists engaging in, or using the results of, quantitative research tended to have quite different intellectual orientations and reference groups from those who found it important to maintain the 'reaction against positivism' at a high level of intensity.

For example, sociologists involved in more applied fields, such as education, management, criminology, demography, or social medicine, often worked with survey methods and associated techniques of quantitative data analysis alongside colleagues from different disciplinary backgrounds for whom the debate over positivism held little interest and for whom, too, the idea of 'human sciences' tended to override, implicitly if not explicitly, any supposed distinction between *Geisteswissenschaften* and *Naturwissenschaften*. Moreover, if for these researchers and other quantitative sociologists any major methodological watershed *had* to be recognized, this would in fact be a quite different one: namely, that lying between the experimental and the non-experimental sciences. And, thus, in so far as more philosophical questions were taken up, these were much less likely to relate to explanation versus understanding than to the problem of how far, in fields where experimenta

---

[4] I would, however, agree with Frisby (1976) that in the *Positivismusstreit* issues of method were actually subordinate to those of historicism and value freedom. It is certainly these latter issues that are central to the initial debates between Adorno and Habermas, on the one side, and Popper and Albert, on the other (Adorno *et al.* 1976). I would also suggest that it ought to be much clearer to sociologists today than it was in the socio-political climate that prevailed at the time of these debates that Popper and Albert have by far the better of the exchanges.

tion was precluded on practical or ethical grounds, statistical analysis could serve as substitute.

However, even though quantitative sociologists tended simply to ignore attempts to undermine the idea of the unity of method and pressed on with their research regardless, this did not mean that these attempts went unchallenged. At a relatively early stage in the *Positivismusstreit* Popper contended (1972: 183–6) that 'labouring the difference' between the natural sciences, on the one hand, and the social sciences or the humanities, on the other, had become 'a bore', and charged those who continued to do so with a lack of knowledge of the *actual* methods of the natural sciences and of the ways in which these too involved forms of 'understanding'. Although Popper recognized that techniques of enquiry and strategies of explanation should, and indeed did, vary according to the nature of the phenomena studied—and *within* the natural sciences just as much as between them and other kinds of discipline—still, he argued, at the most basic level the *same* method, that of problem solving or 'the method of conjecture and refutation', was in fact practised: 'It is practised in reconstructing a damaged text as well as in constructing a theory of radioactivity.'[5] Subsequently, other authors, whether writing as philosophers or more specifically as sociologists—for example, Elster (1983*a*) or Runciman (1983)—have maintained a broadly similar position, and with certainly no less sophistication and cogency than is shown by those who would urge that the *Geisteswissenschaften* and *Naturwissenschaften* are to be set sharply apart. The essential claim is that, once the various possible modes of 'understanding' are more clearly differentiated than is usually the case, then, in Runciman's words (1983: 55, 221), 'there is no special problem of explanation in the sciences of man' nor any requirement for social scientists 'to adopt different criteria of validity' from those that apply in other sciences in testing explanations.[6]

The issue of the nature of sociology as a discipline, which was reopened by the debate over positivism, remains, therefore, without any effective resolution. Sociologists have quite different, and indeed in certain respects quite incompatible, ideas about the goals that they should pursue and about the methodologies that would best help them to attain these goals. Moreover, from this situation there then arises the third, and perhaps most disturbing, indication of the current intellectual disarray of sociology. That is, the fact that there is yet further—what might be called 'second-order'—disagreement over how the disagreement over the nature of sociology should itself be viewed.

[5] A further valuable aspect of Popper's contribution to the debate (see also 1994: esp. ch. 8) was his clarification of the respective parts played by 'general laws', 'theories', and 'models' in both the natural and the social sciences and his arguments to show that, although there are in this regard important differences of degree, these are by no means such as to set up an unbridgeable gulf in method.

[6] It is further of interest—and especially in the light of n. 4—that Runciman (1983: 42) at least (and Elster too, I suspect) would at the same time reject the idea, accepted by 'general theorists' as a matter of course, that 'the social sciences are not and cannot be value-free'.

In this regard, the most common response, at all events within university departments of sociology and professional associations, is that of an appeal to 'pluralism'. Sociology, it is held, should be recognized as being, in Ritzer's convenient phrase (1975), 'a multiple paradigm science'; the quest for an orthodoxy or mainstream is misguided in principle and likely to be damaging in practice. Such a response, it may be noted, is highly congenial to those theorists who would believe that the main task of theoretical writing is not that of providing a basis for more successful explanations but indeed of expounding, analysing, and 'discursively' criticizing the variety of traditions and schools that sociology comprises. For a vista is thus opened up of books being written out of books, with little need for empirical enquiry, that extends indefinitely. But it has, of course, also to be recognized that the invocation of pluralism has a larger attractiveness. It can be taken to express a wide-ranging intellectual and academic tolerance and a concern to avoid any restrictive dogmatism, which, especially in times of great uncertainty and turmoil, would seem evident virtues. None the less, and despite the clear risks of misrepresentation that are involved, the rhetoric of pluralism has in fact been called into question; and the argument can furthermore be made that, over the recent past, the importance of so doing has increased rather than diminished.

For example, in an early paper, prompted in fact by the first exchanges of the *Positivismusstreit*, Klima (1972) sought to distinguish between 'genuine pluralism' within a scientific field and mere 'pseudo-pluralism'. The precondition of genuine pluralism, he maintained, is that it should be accompanied by a vigorous, indeed often mortal, competition of ideas. Conversely, pseudo-pluralism is characterized by the fact that 'the confrontation of standpoints' is not organized as such a competition, either because rival schools are able to protect themselves against 'foreign' attacks or because their 'approaches' are so formulated as to be largely immune to criticism of any kind. Genuine pluralism thus has clear limits. There can be diversity in theories and in research strategies and styles but there must at the same time be an ultimate methodological consensus that determines the ground rules and the standards of achievement according to which the competition of ideas is conducted. In sociology, Klima then argued, such methodological consensus was lacking and therefore no more than pseudo-pluralism was possible. Rather than sociology being a 'multiple paradigm science', it was better seen as a field still in its 'pre-paradigmatic' stage, in which, to quote Kuhn (1962: 48), 'frequent and deep debates over legitimate methods, problems and standards of solutions . . . serve rather to define schools than to produce agreement'.

The position represented by Klima has remained minoritarian. Perhaps not surprisingly, sociology departments and associations have recoiled from the implication that they might uphold pluralism not as a serious moral and scientific ideal but rather as the only means of preserving a minimum of socio-political cohesion in the face of intellectual anarchy—and with the aim, perhaps, more of avoiding than of promoting open but potentially self-destructive debate. However, the need to examine closely what passes for pluralism has of late been underlined by the increasing popularity within sociology of the philosophy of 'postmodernism'.

The chief significance of postmodernism (understood as a philosophical movement rather than as a theory of contemporary societal change) is that it seeks to subvert what Searle (1993; see also 1995) has characterized as 'the Western rationalist tradition' of scholarly and scientific enquiry. In essence, this tradition could be said to suppose the following: that a world exists 'out there', independently of the ideas about it that any particular scholar or scientist may hold; that it is possible to use language in order to make statements about this world that may be regarded as being true in the degree to which they accurately represent or 'correspond to' it; and that the attempt to determine their truth, or otherwise, can be carried out through various procedures grounded in a generally valid logic governing the linkage of evidence and argument. Postmodernism appears to challenge this position at virtually every point. What is maintained is something on lines such as these. There is no world 'out there' existing independently of our representations of it or, that is, of the ways in which we socially construct it through our language; thus, the criterion of the truth of statements cannot be correspondence with such an independent world; truth is not discovered but is rather *made*, and is made, moreover, in many different ways, and always with a moral and political intent; thus, all truth is 'local' and 'contextual'; there is no knowledge that can claim a privileged, objective, and universal status by virtue of the methods through which it is secured, only 'knowledges' that are specific to particular communities, cultures, and so on, and that serve their purposes.[7]

In a postmodernist perspective, therefore, a remarkable reversal of Klima's argument becomes possible. What he would see as genuine pluralism could exist only as a sham: if the methodological consensus that is required were to be constructed, this could have no rational foundation, only a socio-political one as in fact a form of intellectual oppression. Correspondingly, what Klima would regard as pseudo-pluralism is the only authentic basis on which a scholarly or scientific field can be organized: different 'standpoints' *have* simply to 'confront' each other, and which prevails will be determined

---

[7] Since postmodernism thus represents (cf. Gellner 1992) an extreme expression of the doctrine of cognitive (or 'epistemic') relativism, it is important that its reception by sociologists should be seen against the background of clear *pre-existing* tendencies within sociology in this same direction, most notably, perhaps, in the form of the post-Mertonian 'strong programme' in the sociology of science. For those who, like myself, would agree with Gellner that the doctrine of cognitive relativism is not only self-defeating but also manifestly wrong in that 'The existence of trans-cultural and amoral knowledge is *the* fact of our lives' (1992: 54), it is entirely apt, and congenial, that the reaction against postmodernism now building up should comprise forceful attacks on the 'strong programme'. See e.g. Gross and Levitt (1994), Gross et al. (1996), Sokal and Bricmont (1997), and Koertge (1998). Of particular significance are critiques that bring out not only the philosophical difficulties but further the simple empirical inadequacy of much work claiming to exemplify this programme.

not on rational grounds but by the exercise in some way or other of socio-political power.

When, as a response to radical disagreements over the nature of sociology as a discipline, appeals to pluralism are made, it cannot then be thought that these are in themselves able to offer some kind of resolution of the underlying problem. Rather, such appeals are likely to carry very different implications, which, once spelled out, only display second-order disagreement in its full extent. For those who would still adhere to the Western rationalist tradition, pluralism in the sense of a free but fierce competition of ideas appears as vitally important as a way to the truth but requires some significant amount of prior agreement: that is, on basic methodological issues. For those persuaded by postmodernism, in contrast, to think of pursuing truth in such a way must be quite nonsensical, for, if our ideas about what is true are plural, then so too must be truth itself; pluralism can, therefore, only mean rejecting any attempted discrimination among these ideas via a spurious foundationalism. Between these positions compromise is scarcely possible.

To summarize the foregoing, sociologists are at the present time seriously divided over the relationship of their two basic activities, research and theory; further, over what sort of scholarly or scientific enterprise sociology is, or might aim to become; and, finally, over how they should interpret and respond to their divided—indeed fragmented—state. The question that cannot then be avoided is that of how far this intellectual disarray is likely to undermine the degree of institutional success that sociology has attained. One possibility is, of course, that the disarray continues to worsen until, as a discipline, sociology simply collapses from within and the resulting debris is assimilated elsewhere.[8] However, even if the disarray turns out to have some equilibrium point or can be internally managed, as, say, on the basis of 'pluralism', it has still the potential to expose sociology to external threat, and increasingly so, it might be thought, under conditions of intensifying competition for resources within higher education and research. Two closely related problems can in this regard be identified.

First, as Huber (1995) has observed, sociology cannot in its present state lay claim to any well-defined disciplinary 'core' in the sense of an agreed body of knowledge and expertise that any competent sociologist should possess. A good indicator of the existence of such a core would be a consistent set of requirements across the graduate courses provided by different university departments of sociology, since these courses are presumably intended,

---

[8] Such a collapse could conceivably come about through a series of 'secessions'. For example, some university departments of sociology have already become in effect departments of 'cultural studies', and this could then prompt sociologists committed to quantitative analysis and 'theory-for-explanation' to seek new homes within social-science faculties that would allow them to work more closely with economists, political scientists, demographers, or social statisticians. However, what chiefly militates against such a scenario is sociology's previous institutional success and the very fact that sociology departments do now exist. Changing the disciplinary organization of a university is, as a colleague once remarked, 'like moving a cemetery'.

among other things, to maintain the academic succession.[9] The importance
of a disciplinary core, Huber argues (1995: 203), is that it represents 'what
must be retained if the discipline is to continue to exist'. Thus, in situations
of shrinking resources, university departments representing disciplines with
a weak core will be particularly vulnerable to financial cutbacks and reductions in size, since these departments may not find it possible to formulate a
coherent case about what they would regard as essentials.

   Secondly, the fact that there is no agreement on the basic methodology of
sociological research, nor on the purposes that sociological theory should
serve, means that it is difficult to have any established criteria for judging the
quality of sociological work and, in particular, criteria of excellence. This is
then an obvious weakness when, in competition for funds for research, fel-
lowships, endowments, and so on with disciplines that have taken on a more
'paradigmatic' character, sociology is called upon to cite notable examples of
what it has achieved. This can, in effect, be done only at the cost of some,
more or less evident, hypocrisy.[10] Moreover, sociology is placed at a yet greater
disadvantage in so far as it is implied—or, perhaps, from a postmodernist
standpoint, openly contended—that criteria of the kind in question are illusory. For, as Huber (1995) again has pointed out, postmodernist arguments
have achieved only limited influence within academe and are unlikely to
impress many representatives of other social sciences, let alone natural scientists or, most seriously of all, university or foundation administrators and
civil servants. Indeed, such arguments may well open up the question of why
sociological research should receive any support at all, or at least from the
public purse. As Hammersley has recognized (1999: 581), with sociological
ethnography specifically in mind, postmodernist tendencies would appear 'to
breach the implicit contract which underlies the public funding of social
science'. Academic freedom is one side of this contract, but the other is that

---

[9] Huber recounts how, when President of the American Sociological Association, she set
up a task group to review graduate teaching programmes in university departments of sociology. The report of the group confirmed that no core components could be identified. When,
however, the report was submitted to the ASA Council, it was neither approved nor circu-
lated to the membership. Huber's worries over the lack of rigour and the 'smorgasbord cur-
riculum' of American programmes would certainly apply in the British case. Most notably,
the Economic and Social Research Council, which has clear responsibility and powers in
regard to the standards of research training provided by graduate courses in sociology, has
so far manifestly failed to meet its own objective of ensuring that all such courses for which
it provides accreditation should include effective teaching and examination in quantitative
methods.
[10] The same problem does, of course, arise where evaluations have to be made *within* the
discipline. For example, the sociology committees set up by the UK Higher Education Funding
Council for purposes of its Research Assessment Exercises have been made up of individuals
who, in the light of their published views on the nature of sociology, could not conceivably
reach any genuine intellectual consensus on what should count as achievement in the field.
In other words, the gradings of departments at which they have arrived could only be the
outcome of some kind of 'political' compromise—as, say, on the lines of 'you don't say what
you really think about my kind of sociology and I won't say what I really think about yours'—
and, of course, of the numerical support for differing positions. An interesting question is
whether HEFC officials are aware of this situation; and a still more interesting question is
how, if they are aware of it, they would envisage responding to it.

social science should produce reliable knowledge of relevance to public concerns and public policy. Thus 'Denying that such knowledge is possible, or redefining *knowledge* to mean *illuminating fictions* or *partisan perspective*, represents a flouting of that obligation as generally understood, and the contract is unlikely to be renegotiable'.

Such grounds for fearing that the intellectual disintegration of sociology may presage its institutional decline cannot, I believe, be dismissed as implausible. In both the USA and Europe a significant number of cases have been recorded over recent years of university departments of sociology being threatened with closure or in fact closed, of foundations winding up their sociological research programmes, and of sociology receiving a diminishing share of the budgets of national organizations with general responsibility for scientific training and research. While it would be clearly wrong to suppose that all such developments can be accounted for in similar terms, they should none the less be taken, I would argue, as clear warning signs that the present state of the discipline may not be sustainable and that the future of sociology, both intellectually *and* institutionally, is indeed problematic.

It would be easy to say that the remedy for sociology's ills must then be the creation of a new disciplinary core—of a new sociological mainstream—that would bring research and theory into a vital relationship, express a clear consensus on the nature of sociology as a social science, and thus provide a basis for a genuine rather than a spurious pluralism to flourish. I would myself see precisely this as being the long-term goal. However, it is obvious enough that nothing of such a kind could be accomplished simply by *fiat* and, further, that the existing intellectual disarray, which did not after all come about by accident, itself constitutes a major barrier. In such circumstances, I would suggest, the best that can be done by those who would wish to see a more coherent sociology eventually emerge is to attempt to identify the elements in the fragmented discipline of today that would appear to hold out most promise as components of a new core; and then to make out the case for believing that a sociology built up around such a core could hope to be significantly more successful intellectually, and in turn more secure institutionally, than is sociology in its present state. Given the prevailing situation, any such endeavour must expect to meet with a critical response. But, if nothing else, a sharper focus should in this way be achieved in the continuing debates in and about sociology and in turn a clearer understanding of just what is centrally at issue. In this volume my underlying aim is to pursue a strategy on lines indicated, although, since I have written a series of essays and not a treatise, I necessarily do so in a rather indirect and piecemeal way

The Essays

The essays are grouped as follows. The first three (Chapters 2–4) are primarily critical, the next three (Chapters 5–7) are primarily programmatic, while the next four (Chapters 8–11) could perhaps best be described as illustrative in that they represent attempts to put some of the previous preaching into practice. There is then a concluding essay (Chapter 12) of a historical character. In introducing the essays, in this same order, I aim to set them against the background that I have described above and also, in the case of those published some years ago, to make some observations on their reception.[11]

As I remarked earlier, the reaction against positivism in sociology developed in such a way that by the 1970s and 1980s its main critical focus had come to rest on quantitative, survey-based research—even though to no very great effect. In this period I was myself heavily engaged in such research, and while not, as I hope will become apparent, entirely blind to its difficulties and weaknesses, I none the less shared in the general indifference of its practitioners to criticism that appeared often to show a very inadequate understanding of the methodology that it called into question. What, however, I did find provoking was the counterposing to 'positivist' quantitative research of various kinds of qualitative research, which, it was claimed or implied, were free of the major defects of the former and, for one reason or another, more appropriate to the central concerns of sociology. It appeared to me that these favoured alternatives did in fact run into many of the same problems as quantitative research, that in addition they often had some distinctive ones of their own, and, most seriously, that they were not to the same extent as quantitative research associated with methodological traditions within which their procedures could be reviewed and problems identified and grappled with. In this regard, then, I was led into a 'reaction against the reaction' against positivism, of which the first three essays in this collection are the product.

The essays relate, in turn, to historical sociology, to 'case-oriented' as opposed to 'variable-oriented' approaches in comparative macrosociology, and to sociological ethnography. My purpose, I must emphasize, is not to dismiss these versions of qualitative sociology out of hand. It is rather to raise, in regard to each alike, methodological issues that have, I believe, been so far inadequately treated and that call for serious attention. I also show how in each case proponents of these styles of enquiry, even while inveighing against positivism in an often rather imprecise way, have, paradoxically, themselves been led into positions that are in fact 'positivist' in quite basic and well-established senses. This, I believe, provides further grounds for supposing that, in retrospect, the *Positivismusstreit* will increasingly be seen not only as itself a confused, but also as a thoroughly confusing, episode in the history of sociology.

---

[11] The essays previously published have been only lightly edited. I have made a few alterations in the interests of terminological clarity and consistency, restored some changes to my text made by previous sub-editors, cited some more recent literature, added various cross references, and so on. However, I have not attempted to rewrite the essays in any way that would change their original structure. There are, therefore, a number of repetitive passages in regard to which I can only appeal to the well-known theory that redundancy aids communication.

The first essay, 'The Uses of History in Sociology: Reflections on Some Recent Tendencies', starts from a rejection of the view advanced by Abrams (1980), following Giddens (1979), that 'history and sociology are and always have been the same thing'. In the essay, I focus on one particular, methodological difference between the two disciplines, which, I argue, is of a highly consequential kind: namely, that, while historians have to rely solely on evidence in the form of what I call 'relics'—that is, the physical remains of the past of one kind or another—sociologists, in so far as they work in present-day societies, have the further possibility of using various kinds of research procedure in order to generate evidence that did not exist before. I then discuss the implications of this difference for sociologists' research strategies and the more specific problems that it raises for the practice of historical sociology. I conclude with a critique of what I call 'grand historical sociology': that is, historical sociology that usually aims to deal with large macrosociological issues and that is written on the basis not of relics themselves—or, in other words, of 'primary' sources—but rather on the basis of the pre-existing work of historians. I seek to show how, in thus using 'secondary' (or yet more derivative) sources as their main empirical materials, grand historical sociologists are led, willy-nilly, into accepting what historians themselves have for long recognized and criticized as a 'positivist' conception of historiography, and, in turn, into various formidable methodological difficulties that they have so far largely failed to appreciate, let alone resolve.

This essay produced two main reactions that differed markedly in their nature and quality. The first came in the form of four critical comments by Bryant, Hart, Mann, and Mouzelis that appeared in the *British Journal of Sociology* in 1994, three years after my essay first appeared. These proponents of grand historical sociology seemed chiefly motivated by sorrow or anger that I had seen fit to question the methodological foundations of this genre, and thus to show disrespect to such apparently iconic works as Barrington Moore's *The Social Origins of Dictatorship and Democracy* (1966). I cannot, however, see that their criticism itself carried any great force, not least because so much of it was based either on rather gross misrepresentations of my position or on attacks on my own 'positivist' survey-based work that, whether valid or not, were quite irrelevant to the matters under debate. I have therefore little to add here to the reply that I made (1994) to the comments, although there is one point on which I might briefly elaborate, since it bears directly on an issue that arose earlier and that will indeed recur.

One of the main problems resulting from grand historical sociologists' reliance on secondary sources is that of how they should decide which source or sources to follow where, as is often the case, historians are in disagreement on the accounts that they give (on the basis of primary sources) of events, situations, causal processes, and so on. Both Bryant and Mann claim that the solution to this problem lies in 'theory': where secondary sources are in conflict, grand historical sociologists can resort to theory to enable them to choose those accounts that carry the greatest sociological plausibility. What, then, must be emphasized is that, if this argument is to get off the ground, the theory involved must have strong explanatory, if not predictive, power. It cannot be 'general' theory in the sense of Alexander's 'discourse' or Giddens's 'conceptualization' or 'conceptual reworking', which have no explanatory ambitions, nor yet can it be the inductively developed 'grounded theory' of Glaser and Strauss (1967), as is advocated in Hart's comment, since with such theory all empirical possibilities can be, and indeed have to be, equally well accommodated. Unfortunately for the persuasiveness of their argument, neither Bryant nor Mann shows himself ready to give any indica-tion of just what kind of theory it is that they do have in mind, let alone any illustration of how it might be applied in the way that they would propose.

The second reaction to my essay came from a far less obvious quarter— American political scientists with comparative interests in such topics as state formation and regime transition. Most notably, Lustick (1996; cf. Katznelson 1992/3; Collier 1998) follows the *BJS* commentators in concentrating on my attack on grand historical sociology but with a much more secure grasp of the issues that I raised. Lustick in fact formulates these issues in a way that I hinted at but did not develop as fully as I might have done: that is, as being the expression, in the context of studies based on secondary historical sources, of the more general problem of 'selection bias' in data that occurs in one form or another across virtually the whole range of sociological research. Lustick's main critical—and factually correct—observation on my essay is then that, having identified the key issue of how grand historical sociologists should choose among rival or contradictory sources without undue bias, I do not offer any solution to it; and, he speculates (1996: 610), with reference to the *BJS* comments, that this is why my essay has led to responses 'that have been so defensive and so nearly, in some cases, hysterical'. For unless some intellectually satisfying solution can be provided, 'the whole field is vulnerable'.

Lustick goes on to suggest (1996: 613–15) that at least the beginnings of a solution might be found if researchers dependent upon secondary historical materials were to be more explicitly concerned with 'patterns within histori-ography', as distinct from 'patterns within History', and ready to treat each possible secondary source as a 'data-point' that is subject to error, whether random or biased, in just the same way as any other kind of data. I would regard this as a proposal that should certainly be taken further. To do so would at all events serve to bring discussion of the methodology of grand historical sociology into a recognized tradition, even if some difficulties with the pro-posal would then rather quickly be apparent.[12] I would also note that the

---

[12] Most obviously, a problem would arise in that it would often be difficult to regard the 'data points' represented by different secondary sources as being independent of each other. Lustick's response does, however, compare favourably with that of an American sociologist, Calhoun (1996), who has also commented briefly on my essay. I find Calhoun's attempt to reassert the inseparability of history and sociology highly unconvincing (and marred by the raising of curiously irrelevant matters, such as which individuals should be labelled as a soci-ologists and which as historians); but what I would chiefly note is that he manages almost

problem of selection bias does in fact occur at two different levels, as Lustick appears at one point to acknowledge: that is, not only at the level of the researcher's choice of secondary sources but further at the deeper level of the 'natural' selection of primary sources during the passage of time. And the extreme, though not uncommon, case that here arises is where relics from the past of the kind that would be necessary for making certain inferences have simply not survived to any adequate extent. In such instances, the only solution possible, though not perhaps one that would commend itself to grand historical sociologists, is well expressed by a favourite philosopher of the anti-positivist reaction in a remark of his more relevant than most to the practice of sociology: 'wovon man nicht reden kann, darüber muss man schweigen'.

In the second critical essay, 'Current Issues in Comparative Macrosociology', I intervene in a long-standing debate in this field between proponents of qualitative or 'case-oriented', and quantitative or 'variable-oriented', approaches. Specifically, I seek to challenge the idea that certain methodological problems that are well known to arise with the latter approach—what I label as the small N, the 'Galton', and the black-box problems—can in fact be avoided or more readily handled with the former. These problems, I argue, are just as serious in qualitative as in quantitative work, although quantitative researchers tend to recognize them more clearly and attempt to modify and develop their procedures accordingly. In contrast, the distinctive methods supposedly available to the case-oriented approach not only fail to deliver but also, like the standard procedures of grand historical sociology, often carry wider implications that, if more fully appreciated, could scarcely be welcome to their proponents. Most seriously, perhaps, attempts to overcome the small N problem (the problem of 'too many variables and not enough cases') by resort to logical as opposed to statistical methods of analysis must rest on the—strongly positivist—assumption that the social world is deterministic rather than probabilistic in character and can be studied on this basis: an assumption, I suspect, that very few sociologists would, on due reflection, be inclined to accept.

The essay was published in a special number of *Comparative Social Research* in 1997, together with comments by Abbott, Goldstone, Ragin, Rueschemeyer and Stephens, Teune, and Tilly, to which I then responded. Of the many interesting points that arise, there are two that it would seem of particular relevance to pick out here.

First, my criticisms of case-study methods are linked by more than one commentator to those previously made by King, Keohane, and Verba (1994), and by Lieberson (1992, 1994), and are thus construed as part of a concerted attack

entirely to avoid the central question of grand historical sociologists' choice of sources, arguing simply (1996: 312) that what I have to say on this question could 'largely be rephrased as useful advice' to the latter to 'take care' over evidence. Unlike Lustick, Calhoun has then nothing whatever to suggest to grand historical sociologists about just what methodological approaches and procedures they might actually pursue by way of exercising such 'care'.

on qualitative research as such. I would indeed largely underwrite the methodological arguments of the authors in question. But it is important further to note that King (1986) and Lieberson (1985) have *also* been trenchant critics of various common practices and associated assumptions in quantitative social research, and that in this regard too I am sympathetic to the positions they take up (cf. Erikson and Goldthorpe 1992*a*: ch. 12; Breen and Goldthorpe, forthcoming). What in fact I share with these authors is not a principled hostility to qualitative research but rather a commitment to the view that there is 'one logic of inference' (King *et al.* 1994: p. ix), that it is this that is expressed in the underlying unity of scientific method, and that the particular procedures followed in qualitative and quantitative research *alike* must be subject to it.

Secondly, a general—and welcome—agreement emerges that, once empirical regularities have been established (whether by statistical or logical methods), theory is then required as a basis for explaining these regularities: that is, in order to overcome the black-box problem of otherwise merely 'mindless' correlations, and associations. However, differing notions of the form that theory should take are at the same time apparent. As I would see it, several commentators, in emphasizing the explanatory importance in macrosociology of historical sequences, paths, turning points, and so on, do not sufficiently distinguish between narratives of a historical and a causal kind; or, that is, do not see the force of Teune's blunt observation (1997: 77) that 'a story is no theory'. Thus, while Rueschemeyer and Stephens, for example, are ready to acknowledge that any causal explanation must involve 'theoretical claims' that 'transcend' historical particularities, it tends none the less to be left unclear exactly what the source of such claims might be. In this regard, I would then concur with criticisms made by authors such as Kiser and Hechter (1991, 1998; see also Levi 1997) of the unduly weak nature of the theory that prevails in qualitative macrosociology—and grand historical sociology likewise. And I would, furthermore, share in the view of these critics that what chiefly creates this weakness is a tendency for theory development to be carried out in a too inductive mode—often under the pernicious influence of the idea of 'grounded theory'—and for the empirical testing of theory not then to be recognized as a process that is to be separately and, as far as possible, independently undertaken.[13]

The third critical essay, 'Sociological Ethnography Today: Problems and Possibilities', which is here published for the first time, can be seen as closely

---

[13] It is in this regard of interest to note that in the most sustained response that has so far been made to Kiser and Hechter's criticisms, Somers (1998) in effect rejects their espousal of what I have referred to as the 'Western rationalist tradition' and resorts to a position of cognitive relativism appealing to a 'historical epistemology', supposedly—but in fact very questionably—derived from Kuhn. What this proposes is 'that all our knowledge, our logics, our presuppositions, indeed our very reasoning practices, are indelibly (even if obscurely) marked with the signature of time' (Somers 1998: 731). It would be difficult to provide a better example of how the prevailing intellectual condition of sociology removes the possibility of a genuine pluralism and indeed of any kind of meaningful dialogue.

parallel to the second. I start off from current debates among ethnographers occasioned by the reception of postmodernist ideas, but my main concern is again to question, this time in regard to ethnographic case studies, the effectiveness of methods that can, apparently, transcend the logic of inference and that—as some would see it—offer the possibility of sociological ethnography establishing itself as a radical alternative to 'positivist' (namely, survey-based and quantitative) forms of research. I argue that, as applied to widely recognized problems of what I call variation within and variation across the locales of ethnography, such methods do not work. The problems in question are again ones ultimately of potential selection bias, and solutions to them are only likely to be found through ethnographers adapting to their own purposes the logic of sampling as this has been developed within the survey tradition. Further, I once more illustrate how efforts to avoid recourse to what is deemed to be positivist methodology can in fact lead to the adoption of *ur*-positivist positions: that is, where attempts to justify generalizations from ethnographies of unknown representativeness turn out to depend upon a conception of theory as providing certain knowledge of deterministic, lawlike relations. Finally, though, I argue that sociological ethnography, in a methodologically enhanced form, could take on an important role in the *testing* of theory and in particular in testing for the presence of causal processes that are specified at the micro-level of individual action and interaction. In this way, ethnography might be brought into both a complementary and a revealing competitive relationship with survey-based research.

If the critical essays in this collection are ones motivated by what seemed to me especially irritating aspects of the reaction against positivism, the programmatic essays are inspired by what I would take to be the two most hopeful developments, in research and in theory, that have been apparent in sociology over recent decades—even as its general intellectual condition has steadily declined.

On the side of research, notable advances have been made in quantitative work and, in particular, in the analysis of large-scale data sets obtained from surveys of increasingly diversified design.[14] In the course of the 1970s, at the very time that the reaction against positivism was reaching its peak, more sustained interaction between sociologists and statisticians than had previously occurred (cf. Clogg 1992) transformed the possibilities for quantitative sociology to an extent that seems not always to be fully appreciated—even by practitioners themselves. Sociologists were in effect freed from a historical dependence on techniques originating in biometrics, psychometrics, and econometrics and were provided with ones far better suited to the kinds of

---

[14] Critics of survey-based sociological research ritually characterize it as static or 'presentist' and as 'atomistic' in character. This is simply to ignore the rapid development over recent decades, on the one hand, of longitudinal or 'diachronic' survey work, whether based on the repeated sampling of populations, the collection of retrospective life-history data or panel designs, and, on the other hand, of surveys producing 'hierarchical' data sets that comprise both individual-level data and data relating to a series of supra-individual entities in which respondents are or have been involved.

data and problem with which they are typically concerned. Thus, for example, loglinear modelling and related techniques allowed for the powerful analysis of categorical data, as, say, in investigating multi-way associations among different attributes of individuals, such as gender, ethnicity, education, marital status, employment status, social class, religious affiliation, or political partisanship. Techniques of event-history analysis could be effectively applied in the study of the transitions made by individuals, or other entities, over series of discrete states, as occurs in educational, occupational, or criminal 'careers' or in the formation and dissolution of families or organizations. And the development of multi-level modelling enabled sociologists for the first time reliably to separate out the effects of variation in social contexts from those of variation in individual attributes, as is crucial in the study of, say, classroom or school effects on educational performance or of community effects on ethnic exogamy or voting or of the effects of macrosocial inequality on personal health.

The general result of the application of these new techniques has then been the demonstration, in a wide range of substantive fields, of empirical regularities, whether over time or space, that can only be regarded as revelatory. By this I mean that these regularities are not ones that could conceivably be apparent to the lay members of a society in the course of their everyday lives: for example, regularities in class and gender differentials in educational attainment, in relative rates of intergenerational social mobility or of class voting, in the dependence of hazard rates of entry into marriage or divorce on different time dimensions, or in contextual effects on political involvement and party support. Such regularities became apparent to sociologists themselves *only when* they had access to the kinds of data and technique adequate to disclose them and, in addition, had developed appropriate concepts—'class differentials', 'relative rates', 'hazard rates', 'contextual effects'— at some remove from those of lay members. Moreover, the further significance of the regularities that have been established is that they pose clear theoretical challenges; or, that is, they do so to those sociologists for whom the first requirement of theory is that it should have explanatory potential. For these regularities are ones that for the most part remain essentially *opaque* in character: the explanation of just how they are created and sustained or, in some instances, modified or disrupted is far from evident.[15]

---

[15] Research results of the kind referred to in the text are also challenging in another way. They call directly into question the arguments advanced by 'general theorists' and their supporters that, in consequence of the linguistic turn, the double hermeneutic, the post-empiricist philosophy of science, and so on, we should recognize that sociology is not in fact capable of producing findings of a revelatory and cumulative character, so that, instead of being concerned with relevant explanatory theory, we have to settle for sociology as 'discourse'. Such 'impossibilists'—C. G. A. Bryant (1995) is a good example—remind one of those (perhaps apocryphal) physicists who demonstrated, with great theoretical elaboration, that bumble bees cannot fly. The particular question of the relation between sociologists' concepts and theories and those of lay actors is in fact in need of much clearer and more discriminating treatment than is provided by Giddens's discussion of the double hermeneutic. For example, his claims that 'All social science . . . is parasitic upon lay concepts, as a logical

On the side of theory, no advance comparable to that achieved in research could be claimed. What can, however, be observed, from the 1980s onwards, is the seemingly final collapse of structural-functionalism in both its liberal and its Marxist forms—*fonctionnalisme rose* and *fonctionnalisme noir*—and, correspondingly, a revival of what Boudon (1987) has called the 'individualistic' theoretical tradition or paradigm: that is, one in which the explanation of social phenomena is sought not 'macro-to-micro' in terms of the functional or teleological exigencies of 'social systems', but rather 'micro-to-macro' in terms of the conduct of individuals and of its intended and unintended consequences. This revival has, moreover, been most marked, and, in my view, pursued to best effect, in that version of methodological individualism in which the emphasis is placed on individual *action* rather than *behaviour* and, further, in which the attempt is made as far as possible to treat such action as being in some sense *rational,* so that it may ultimately be not only explained but also rendered intelligible.[16]

In the first programmatic essay, 'The Quantitative Analysis of Large-Scale Data-Sets and Rational Action Theory: For a Sociological Alliance', my aim then is, as the title indicates, to argue that the proponents of these two more promising concerns of contemporary sociology, labelled as QAD and RAT, could with mutual advantage enter into a closer relationship. QAD, I maintain, needs RAT. It is now clear that, as various critics have insisted, statistical techniques, no matter how powerful in revealing social regularities, cannot at the same time be used to crank out causal explanations of these regularities. A theoretical input is essential, and on several counts causal narratives grounded in RAT would in this regard seem an especially attractive proposition. Conversely, RAT needs QAD. As critics have also pointed out, for the explanatory capacity of RAT to be more convincingly demonstrated than hitherto, it needs to be seen at work in other than apparently hand-picked and often 'data-poor' cases. Probabilistic yet wide-ranging regularities of the kind that QAD can establish would then appear as highly appropriate *explananda* in relation to which the full range of application of RAT (and at the same time its eventual limits) could be shown up.

The essay first appeared in the *European Sociological Review* in 1996 as the lead item in a special number in which various authors considered the prospects for the kind of alliance that I suggest, and it was then reprinted in a collective volume on the same theme, edited by Blossfeld and Prein (1998).

---

condition of its endeavours' and further that its findings are therefore always likely to appear 'banal' (Giddens 1987: 19, 21, 71) seem demonstrably false, unless both 'parasitic' and 'banal' are understood in some way well beyond normal usage. Nor is it necessary, or in many instances even at all likely, that sociological concepts will become 'constitutive of what we do' in our daily activities. A much better starting point to take would be Schutz's essay 'The Social World and the Theory of Social Action' (1960)—which in fact sets out a position in many respects significantly different from that usually ascribed to Schutz in the secondary literature.

[16] The alternative behavioural version itself comes in two different forms: that grounded in psychological behaviourism and represented most directly by Homans (1961) and the more implicit and diffuse 'social behaviourism' that is forcefully criticized by Coleman (1986a).

I am appreciative of the attention that the essay thus received and encouraged by the fact that I am evidently not alone in believing that, through building on the successes of QAD and the potential of RAT, a substantial component of a new disciplinary core for sociology could in fact be created. At the same time, though, commentary on, or prompted by, my essay leaves me under no illusions about the resistance still to be overcome if such a project is to make headway, and resistance even among those who would in principle at least view the project with favour, to say nothing of those who would react to it with horror as positivism *redivivus*.

Thus, among proponents of QAD there are, I suspect, not a few who still have difficulty with the idea of taking theory seriously. Establishing social regularities is, they would believe, the real business of sociology—or at any rate is what sociologists can claim to do well; and even if empirical facts cannot speak for themselves, they can always be given a reasonable, commonsense 'interpretation' in one way or another. Correspondingly, among proponents of RAT there seems often to be an underlying feeling that what really counts as an intellectual achievement is producing an elegant model that resolves some theoretical 'puzzle'. It is not then seen as altogether fair that they should be expected to take as *explananda* regularities that just happen to have been produced by QAD, and, perhaps, on the basis of research guided by quite atheoretical—for example, administrative or policy—concerns.[17] I would agree with Hechter (1998: 289–90) that the main difficulty here is not so much basic intellectual conflicts as differences in 'comparative advantage' arising out of tendencies towards specialization in either empirical research or theory that are, unfortunately, increasingly marked in sociology today. None the less, such a difficulty could well prove persistent and troublesome.[18]

The second and third programmatic essays are aimed, in different ways, at elaborating on the first. In the second, 'Rational Action Theory for Sociology', I start from the observation that RAT comes in fact in a range of different versions, and I attempt to analyse these by reference to three criteria: the strength of the rationality requirements that are imposed; whether the focus is on situational or procedural rationality; and whether the ambition is to provide a theory of action of a special or a general kind. On this basis, I then try to identify in exactly which form RAT would seem to hold out most promise for

---

[17] As well as examples of both orientations being found in papers in the collection edited by Blossfeld and Prein, the latter orientation is also well illustrated in several papers in what can in many ways be seen as a complementary collection edited by Hedström and Swedberg (1998c). None the less, these two collections together do, I believe, serve well to bring out the possibilities as well as the problems in efforts to overcome the long divorce of research and theory in the practice of sociology. It is also noteworthy, and of some possible significance for the future, that the contributors to them are predominantly European rather than American.

[18] Hechter remarks on the lack of 'switch-hitters' in sociology and urges the need for team projects in which specialist researchers and theorists would collaborate. I would myself stress the importance—to shift from a baseball to a cricketing metaphor—of having far more good all-rounders: sociologists who can combine a solid average as empirical batsmen with a high strike rate as theoretical bowlers (and it would help if they could cut off a lot of the flashy nonsense going past gully as well).

sociology, and especially for use in conjunction with QAD. I conclude that sociologists are likely to be best served by RAT that draws on a conception of subjective rather than objective rationality and in turn imposes rationality requirements of 'intermediate' strength; that has a strong emphasis on explaining action in terms of its situational rationality (or, in Popper's phrase, its 'situational logic'); and that seeks to be only a special theory of action although one that is still in various ways privileged.

The general objective that I had in writing the essay was to counter the tendency, widespread among sociologists, to equate RAT, or indeed the entire individualistic theoretical tradition, with the particular versions of such theory, or the particular expressions of this tradition, that are to be found in economics or in 'rational-choice' or 'public-choice' styles of political science, and thus to see RAT as in some way alien and threatening to the very nature of the sociological enterprise. It is scarcely surprising that this misunderstanding should prevail, since it is one that theory textbooks determinedly perpetuate (as recent examples, see Barnes 1995: ch.1; Baert 1998: ch. 7). However, what is in this way missed is precisely RAT of the kind that I would wish to highlight and that in fact has deep roots in the history of sociology: consider only the continuities that can be readily traced back from the work of a contemporary RAT theorist such as Boudon to that of Popper, of Max Weber and Simmel, and of Tocqueville. It is, moreover, a crucial feature of such RAT—indeed the main basis of its claim to privilege as a theory of action—that it offers the possibility of transcending the supposedly radical division between 'understanding' and 'explanation' that was so strenuously insisted upon in the course of the *Postivismusstreit*. For, as I seek to show, the category of rationality can effectively serve *both* as that through which the subjective understanding of social action is achieved *and* as that in which the ultimate explanation of such action is grounded.

The third programmatic essay, 'Causation, Statistics, and Sociology', then takes up a topic which, it seems to me, has been somewhat avoided: that of how the idea of causation might best be applied in the context of sociological analysis. I distinguish three different understandings of causation deriving chiefly from the work of statisticians. The first, 'causation as robust dependence', is that associated with attempts to make causal inferences through statistical technique alone, without theoretical or other 'subject-matter' input. The second, 'causation as consequential manipulation', is that associated with experimental designs, and especially in applied sciences, where attention centres on assessing the effects of (given) causes—that is, 'treatments' or other interventions—rather than on determining the causes of effects. The first understanding is, I argue, by now outmoded in sociology, and the second, although capable of powerful technical elaboration, is not well suited to a subject in which research must for the most part be non-experimental and, moreover, in which the concept of action is central. The third understanding of causation that I identify, that of 'causation as generative process', I find far more attractive. In this case, the key idea is that

advancing a causal explanation of phenomena that are taken to be evident
in a set of data means giving an account of some 'underlying' process, or
mechanism, that would in fact be capable of bringing the phenomena into
being: that is, a process operating at a deeper or more micro-level than that
at which the relevant data are themselves observed.

This understanding of causation obviously fits well with the micro-to-macro
style of sociological explanation that is upheld in the individualistic tradition, and I then take it as a basis for proposing an approach to causal analysis that would seem especially appropriate for use in the context of a
QAD–RAT alliance. This approach can be represented schematically as a three-
stage sequence. The first stage is that of establishing the phenomena: that is,
of demonstrating the social regularities that constitute the *explananda*, with
statistical techniques here being used in an essentially descriptive mode. The
second stage is that of hypothesizing generative processes at the level of
action that have explanatory adequacy and that are of a theoretically
grounded kind—as, say, in the form of RAT-based narratives. And the third
stage is that of testing the actual validity of the explanations that are thus
advanced, using as wide a range of strategies, direct or indirect, and of research
methods and analytical techniques, quantitative or qualitative, as can be
effectively brought into play.[19]

The approach outlined does in fact encapsulate the main arguments that
are developed in the programmatic essays: that is, the case for the centrality
of both numbers and narratives in sociological work. In this way, a bridge
is then created to the four illustrative essays that follow. The purpose of the
latter is essentially to show the approach being pursued in particular
instances, with an emphasis on the second stage of drawing on theory—that
is, RAT—in order to provide accounts of generative processes that are adequate to explain observed regularities. The substantive issues treated in these
essays are drawn from the field of social stratification in which my own
research experience and expertise chiefly lie. [20]

The first and second of the illustrative essays are concerned with regularities that have been demonstrated in class, and also in gender, differentials in

[19] It has been objected to the idea of such a sequence that theory must be involved already
at the first stage, since all empirical observations are necessarily 'theory laden'. I would accept
that all observations must take place within some *conceptual* scheme, and it might in turn
be argued that all such schemes have at least an implicit theoretical basis. However, in so far
as theory is in *this* way involved in the establishment of social regularities, it does not follow
that circularity must then arise in the empirical testing of generative processes that are
hypothesized. Furthermore, it should not be supposed that adopting one conceptual scheme
rather than another will always radically change what is observed. For example, the regularities in class differentials in educational attainment or in relative rates of intergenerational
class mobility that are considered in Chapters 8, 9, and 11 below are revealed with varying
degrees of sharpness and detail when differing conceptualizations of class are used, but in
no case do they disappear totally from view.
[20] It might be helpful to note here that in the course of these essays I do in fact use 'theory'
in two rather different ways: sometimes, and more properly, to refer to the general basis of
the explanatory accounts that I offer—that is, in effect, to RAT—but sometimes too to refer
to these accounts themselves, as being 'theories of' something. While this double usage is
not very tidy, it is, I think, innocuous.

educational attainment. Despite the expansion of educational provision and increases in general levels of attainment that are apparent in all modern societies, class differentials have in most cases remained rather little altered over many decades: that is, young people of less advantaged class origins have not succeeded in 'closing the gap' in attainment relative to their counterparts from more advantaged origins. In contrast, however, gender differentials in educational attainment in favour of males have in recent years tended to narrow sharply and indeed instances of their reversal are not uncommon. In the first essay, 'Class Analysis and the Reorientation of Class Theory: The Case of Persisting Differentials in Educational Attainment', I outline a RAT-based account of how the general failure of class differentials to diminish might be explained: that is, an account that aims to show how this aggregate outcome results from central tendencies in educational decision-making by children and their families in different class situations that can be understood as rational, given the differing nature of the opportunities and constraints that characterize these situations. I also indicate how this account may be appropriately extended to the most obviously 'deviant' case, that of Sweden, where a decline in class differentials in educational attainment is well established.

In the second essay, 'Explaining Educational Differentials: Towards a Formal Rational Action Theory', which is co-authored with Richard Breen, the account is then developed, especially in regard to gender differentials, and, as the title indicates, is given a more formal—that is, mathematical—expression. Such formalization is still rather rare in sociology and is here undertaken in a largely experimental spirit. Formalization can, however, undoubtedly serve to bring out the full implications of a theoretical argument and thus to increase both the coherence with which it is stated and the extent to which it becomes open to empirical test. In the present case, for example, we were helped to see and to spell out more clearly the crucial part that is played in our explanation of persisting class differentials by the idea that some degree of perceived risk attaches to children continuing in education rather than leaving or, more generally, in making more rather than less educationally ambitious choices and, further, that this risk tends to be greater in the case of children from less rather than more advantaged class backgrounds.

Two responses to these essays may be noted, which form an instructive contrast. Devine (1998), in a paper concentrating on the first essay, criticizes RAT in principle—in a way that exemplifies the tendency I noted earlier not to discriminate sufficiently among its different versions—and then, more specifically, objects that the explanation of persisting class differentials that I offer is too narrowly conceived in neglecting the part played by class-linked cultural and normative factors. This I can only regard as a rather stunning case of begging the question. Although Devine misconstrues the explanation advanced in certain respects, she is, of course, quite correct in observing that the autonomous influence I give to cultural values and social norms is sharply restricted: that is indeed the very point of a RAT-based causal narrative. However, whether this is to be regarded as a weakness, or as a strength, is not something that can then be settled by the kind of 'discursive' criticism (as Alexander might call it), focusing on 'underlying assumptions', 'non-empirical considerations', and so on, in which Devine exclusively engages. It is a matter that can be decided only by consideration of the adequacy of the explanation in relation to the phenomena it addresses and of its validity in the light of the empirical testing of the further implications that it carries.

While these issues are disregarded by Devine, they are of chief concern in a contribution by Need and De Jong (1999) in which they take the formal-ized statement of the second essay and, using data from a panel survey, then investigate how far the causal processes that are hypothesized would appear to differentiate the educational choices of students in Dutch secondary schools regarding their participation in higher education. The results reported are subject to various limitations of the data, but do generally point to the fact of these processes being at work in creating class differentials, although not always in the case of gender differentials. Need and De Jong's research is still in progress and their findings are not yet in their final form; but theirs is the kind of response, I would argue, with which attempts at putting theory to explanatory use should in fact meet.[21] It is the fate of all such attempts that they will, sooner or later, be shown to have difficulties: at worst, they will turn out to be quite mistaken, at best to require refinement, qualifica-tion, or extension. But matters can be advanced only through further enquiry, not through critique that lacks any empirical reference.

The regularities that mark the starting point of the third illustrative essay, here published for the first time, were established in a somewhat unusual way: that is, through various efforts made to check the criterion validity of a 'class schema' that I have developed, with various colleagues, for the purposes of empirical research and that has by now become widely used. The conceptual basis of the schema is the definition of class positions in terms of employ-ment relations, but it is actually implemented through information on indi-viduals' employment status and occupation. The question of criterion validity is that of how far the schema does then capture those differences in employ-ment relations that, conceptually, it is supposed to capture. In fact, analyses of survey data indicate that it performs rather well in this respect.[22] What this

---

[21] While this volume has been in press, I have learnt of several other attempts at testing the 'Breen-Goldthorpe model'. Davies, Heinesen and Holm (1999) is one notable preliminary report.

[22] Following similarly encouraging results from tests of its construct validity, the schema was taken over by the Office of National Statistics as the basis for its new Socio-Economic Classification, designed to replace the Registrar General's Social Classes for use in official stat-istics (see further Rose and O'Reilly 1998) and is presently being considered as the possible basis for a new European classification. I see this as an encouraging example of how con-ceptual thinking in sociology, *when seriously linked to considerations of actual research proced-ures and their validity*, can prove of practical as well as of academic value.

means, therefore, is that an association exists between individuals' employment status and occupation, on the one hand, and, on the other, the kind of employment relations in which they are involved as indicated by form of payment, perquisites, control of working time, security, promotion opportunities, and so on.

Why then should this be so? Why, especially in the case of employees, should those in different occupational groupings have their employment regulated in systematically differing ways? I suggest an answer in terms of employers' rationally motivated attempts to deal with problems of the employment contract as these arise in the case of employees engaged in different kinds of work and, specifically, with problems of work monitoring and human asset specificity. Although, ideally, employers might wish to reduce all employment contracts to simple money-for-effort spot contracts—or in effect to 'commodify' labour—I seek to show that, with other than rather basic forms of labour, such contracts are unlikely to meet the needs of organizational effectiveness; and that, in the case of professional, administrative, and managerial employees, contracts with a quite different rationale are typically required. This leads then to the prediction that the differentiation of employment contracts will continue on its present pattern to a far greater extent than much fashionable discussion of 'the future of work' would suggest. In developing a RAT-based explanation here, I am more influenced than elsewhere by current theory in economics—but chiefly of a kind that shows divergences from orthodox utility theory and in ways that in fact bring it closer to RAT in the form that I would see as especially appropriate for sociology.

The fourth illustrative essay (again not previously published) is, like the first two, concerned with regularities that point to remarkably persisting social inequalities. A substantial body of research by now exists to show that relative rates of intergenerational class mobility—which could be taken as an indicator of equality, or inequality, of opportunity—are characterized by a high degree of constancy over time within most modern societies and, further, by a notable commonality in their pattern across these societies. Drawing in various ways on theoretical arguments developed in the preceding essays, I try to account for these regularities as being conditioned by the nature of the class structures of modern societies and in particular by the systematic inequalities in resources that they create, but as in fact resulting more directly from the nature of the mobility strategies that are typically pursued by individuals from differing class origins. While understandable as rational adaptations to prevailing opportunities and constraints, these strategies tend to have the overall effect of maintaining the state of intergenerational 'class competition' for more or less desirable class positions largely unaltered. An implication of this account is, therefore, that inequality of *opportunity*, as reflected in relative rates of mobility, is only likely to show significant temporal change or cross-national variation in association with corresponding change or variation in inequalities of *condition* among the members of different classes.

This implication, I argue, is borne out by the results of research in national cases in which mobility regimes do show deviation from generally prevailing patterns, such as Hungary during the Communist era and, again, Sweden; and I in turn take it as the basis for venturing a further prediction. That is, that, in so far as trends towards greater class inequalities in income, as are now evident in the UK, the USA, and elsewhere, continue, and social welfare provision is at the same time cut back, the general stability in relative rates of class mobility will break down and here too greater inequality will be seen.

I would then hope that these illustrative essays, although necessarily limited in the range of substantive topics with which they deal, may serve to show that a sociology on the lines indicated in the programmatic essays is viable and is indeed capable of addressing problems that are of generally recognized importance from both a sociological and a socio-political standpoint. Moreover, to revert to issues raised in the first part of this chapter, such a sociology evidently involves a very close integration of research and theory, offers a way of bridging conceptions of sociology that derive from differing exemplars in the natural sciences and the humanities, and can thus make strong claims to represent a central element in the formation of any new disciplinary core or mainstream within which a genuine rather than a spurious pluralism would be possible. As I earlier recognized, it would be quite unrealistic to expect any quick or large agreement to this (or any other) proposal for reducing the extent of the prevailing intellectual disarray in sociology. But at all events a challenge is thus laid down to those who would dissent: that is, either to argue for alternative bases on which greater coherence might be sought or to produce a more convincing case than presently exists—and convincing to those who provide the resources that sustain sociology institutionally—to show why no effort to move beyond the prevailing situation need be made.

The final and specially written essay in the collection, 'Sociology and the Probabilistic Revolution, 1830–1930: Explaining an Absent Synthesis', then takes up a particular problem that may well have occurred to readers at some earlier stage. If a sociology of the kind that I argue for and seek to illustrate does hold out the potential that I would like to suppose, why has it taken so long to emerge? In the history of sociology the concerns to advance the quantitative study of social phenomena and to elaborate and apply a theory of social action have for the most part been pursued in isolation from each other. One can indeed readily perceive the origins of the separation of research and theory and of the sharply differing understandings of the nature and purpose of sociology that are so prominent today. Does then this historical experience reflect some inherent incompatibility between these two concerns that I have simply overlooked or was their failure to come together a matter of various unfavourable circumstances, albeit of a long-lasting kind? In the light of a review of selected features of the history of sociology in its formative years in France, England, and Germany, I conclude that the latter explanation applies.

The 'absent synthesis' is to be explained essentially in terms of barriers to its emergence—in fact of an intellectual more than an institutional character—that were specific to the period and places in question, and of other yet more contingent difficulties.[23] Moreover, a pleasingly ironic *dénouement* unfolds. Of the intellectual barriers, by far the most serious turns out to be nothing other than the positivist conception of science as upheld by Comte and his followers, for the influence that this exerted on emerging sociology was inimical to probabilistic analysis and to the development of a theory of action in equal measure. The sociology of the future will, I suspect, still find more to learn from consideration of the problems created by the very real presence of this nineteenth-century positivism than from those arising from what increasingly appears as the *positivisme imaginaire* of the late twentieth.

[23] I hope that this essay may also in a small way support the efforts of those scholars—Anthony Oberschall, Martin Bulmer, and Jennifer Platt are obvious examples—who have reacted against the tendency to write the history of sociology as in effect the history of sociological theory and to leave the history of research largely out of account. This tendency has in fact lead to a great deal of distortion and misrepresentation, and not least in the context of debates over differing conceptions of sociology.

2

The Uses of History in Sociology:
Reflections on Some
Recent Tendencies

To TAKE up again the question of the uses of history in sociology may well appear regressive. For to do so implies, of course, making a distinction *between* history and sociology, which would now be widely regarded as untenable. Thus, for example, Philip Abrams, in his highly influential book, *Historical Sociology* (1980), has advanced the argument that, since 'history and sociology are and always have been the same thing', any discussion of the relationship of one to the other must be misguided; and Abrams in turn quotes Giddens (1979: 230) to the effect that 'there simply are no logical or even methodological distinctions between the social sciences and history—appropriately conceived'.

As Abrams is indeed aware, the position he adopts is in sharp contrast with that which would have been most common among sociologists two decades or so previously. At this earlier time, sociologists were for the most part anxious to differentiate their concerns from those of historians. For example, much use was made of the distinction between 'idiographic' and 'nomothetic' disciplines. History was idiographic: historians sought to *particularize* through the description of singular, unique phenomena. Sociology was nomothetic: sociologists sought to *generalize* through formulating theories that applied to categories of phenomena.[1] However, all this was in the period before the British sociological community lost its nerve over the idea of 'social science'—before, that is, the so-called reaction against positivism of the late 1960s and 1970s created a new mood in which political radicalism went together with intellectual conservatism.

This chapter is a revised version of the T. H. Marshall Memorial Lecture for 1989, given at the University of Southampton. It was first published in the *British Journal of Sociology*, 42 (1991). For helpful comments on various drafts, I am indebted to Klas Åmark, Robert Erikson, Stephen Mennell, Patrick O'Brien, and, especially, Gordon Marshall and Lucia Zedner.

[1] The distinction, like that between *Geisteswissenschaften* and *Naturwissenschaften*, originates in the nineteenth-century German debates on methodology that were referred to in the preceding chapter. For a brief discussion, see Collingwood (1946/1993: 165–83). An interesting example of the use of the distinction in the period referred to in the text, with the aim of differentiating, yet at the same time showing the complementarity of, history and sociology, is Bierstedt (1959).

My first contribution to the debate on 'history and sociology' (1962) dates back to this prelapsarian time, and was in fact a *critique of* the idiographic/nomothetic distinction. My remarks were not especially well received by either historians or sociologists, and this present contribution may, I fear, prove similarly uncongenial. For what I would now think important is that attempts, such as that of Abrams and Giddens, to present history and sociology as being one and indistinguishable should be strongly resisted.[2] To avoid, if possible, being misunderstood, let me stress that I do not seek here to re-establish the idiographic/nomothetic distinction, or at least not as one of principle. I do not believe, for example, that sociologists can ever hope to produce theories that are of an entirely transhistorical kind; nor that historians can ever hope to produce descriptions that are free of general ideas about social action, process, and structure. However, good grounds do still remain for refusing to accept the position that *any* distinction drawn between history and sociology must be meaningless.

To begin with, I would argue that the idiographic/nomothetic distinction is still pertinent if taken as one not of principle but of *emphasis*. Historians do—quite rightly—regard it as important that dates and places should be attached to the arguments they advance as precisely as possible; as Thompson (quoted in L. Stone 1987) has aptly remarked, 'the discipline of history is above all a discipline of context'. Sociologists—no less rightly—believe that they are achieving something if the time and space coordinates over which their arguments apply can be widened. And, from this, one use of history in sociology is immediately suggested. History may serve as, so to speak, a 're-sidual category' for sociology, marking the point at which sociologists, in invoking 'history', thereby curb their impulse to generalize or, in other words, to explain sociologically, and accept the role of the specific and of the contingent as framing—that is, as providing both the setting *and* the limits—of their own analyses.[3] However, it is not on such issues that I wish to concentrate here. My aim is rather to focus attention on another major difference between history and sociology that has, I believe, been much neglected but that carries far-reaching implications for sociological practice. This difference

[2] Clearly, my position has in important respects changed since the time of my earlier paper, as a result, I would like to think, of my having had much more experience, whether first- or second-hand, of research into societies both past and present. However, both history and sociology, and the typical orientations of their practitioners, have also changed. Today, inter-disciplinary, or rather adisciplinary, enthusiasm would seem to me to have gone too far, at least on the sociological side. And I find it of interest that a similar view has also been taken from the side of history by a distinguished practitioner who is by no means unsympathetic to sociology: see L. Stone (1987).

[3] This use of history is that with which I have in fact been most concerned in my own work on comparative social mobility (Erikson and Goldthorpe 1992a; and see further Chapter 3 below). The classic programme for a comparative macrosociology is that set by Przeworski and Teune (1970), which has as its ideal objective 'the replacement of the names of nations with the names of variables'. In so far as, in explaining cross-national variation in social structure or process (e.g. in mobility rates and patterns), the sociologist is forced into invoking institutional or cultural features, or indeed events, as specific features of national histories, then *pro tanto* the Przeworski–Teune programme must fall short of realization.

concerns the nature of the evidence that the two disciplines use or, more precisely, the way in which this evidence comes into being.[4]

Evidence in History and Sociology

As a trainee historian at University College London in the 1950s, I underwent a standard catechism on method, which began with the question: what is a historical fact? The answer that had to be given was: a historical fact is an inference from the relics. This answer struck me then, and still strikes me, as the best that can be given and as one of considerable significance. What the answer underlines is the obvious, but still highly consequential, point that we can know the past only on the basis of what has physically survived from the past: that is, on the basis of the relics—or of what may be alternatively described as the residues, deposits, or traces—of the past.[5] These relics are of very different kinds. They may, for example, be simply natural remains, such as bones or excrement; or again artefacts, such as tools, weapons, buildings, or works of art. But of most general importance are what one might call 'objectified communications': that is, communications in some written form and, especially, 'documents' of all kinds. Whatever their nature, it is these relics, and only these relics, that are the source of our knowledge about the past. Statements about the past—historical 'facts'—are inferences from the relics, and can have no other basis. In short: no relics, no history.

So far as the practice of history is concerned, there are two points about relics that it seems important to recognize: first, they are *finite* and, secondly, they are *incomplete*. The relics that exist are just a limited selection of all that could have survived, a sample, so to speak, of a total universe of relics, where, however, the properties neither of the universe nor of the sample are, or can be, known (cf. Murphey 1973; Clubb 1980). The relics of a given period may diminish, by being physically destroyed, but they cannot increase.

It is true, of course, that not all the relics that exist at any one time are known about. Historians always have the possibility of discovering 'new' relics, of adding to the known stock: and it is indeed an important part of their *métier* to do so. It is also true that from any set of relics, the inferences that can be made are *infinite*. The 'facts' that the relics yield will tend to increase with the questions that historians put to them and, in turn, with the range of the problems they address and with the development of their techniques of enquiry. However, none of this alters the situation that the relics themselves, in a physical sense—what is there to be discovered and interrogated—are finite and are, to repeat, a selection, and probably only a quite small

---

[4] For pertinent but brief comments by previous authors, see T. H. Marshall (1963: 38) and Bell and Newby (1981).

[5] I was myself put through the catechism by G. J. Renier, a remarkable teacher, whose work on historiography (1950) was our main text and is now unduly neglected. Also influential was Collingwood (1946/1993), especially the Epilegomena.

and unrepresentative selection, of all that could have survived. It must, therefore, be the case that limitations on the possibilities of historical knowledge
exist simply because it is knowledge of the past—because it is knowledge
dependent on relics. There are things about the past that never can be known
simply because the relics that would have been essential to knowing them
did not in fact survive.

Historians, we may then say, are concerned with *finding* their evidence from
among a stock of relics. In contrast, and this is the difference I want to stress,
sociologists have open to them a possibility that is largely denied to historians. While sociologists can, and often do, draw on relics as evidence in just
the same way as historians, they can, in addition, *generate* evidence. This is,
of course, what they are doing when they engage in 'fieldwork'. They are producing, as a basis for inferences, materials *that did not exist before.*[6] And it is,
I would argue, such generated evidence, rather than evidence in the form of
relics—in other words, evidence that is 'invented' rather than evidence that
is discovered—that constitutes the main empirical foundations of modern
sociology.

The immediate reason for this difference in the way in which historical and
sociological evidence comes into being is obvious: historians work 'in the
past', while sociologists *can also* work 'in the present'. However, behind this
immediate reason lies the difference of emphasis that I earlier referred to: sociologists do not seek to tie their arguments to specific time and space coordinates so much as to test the extent of their generality. Thus, if a sociologist
develops a theory intended to apply, say, to all industrial societies, it will be
only sensible at all events to *begin* the examination of this theory through
research conducted in contemporary rather than in past industrial societies;
and hence through research that permits the generation of evidence rather
than imposing a reliance upon relics.

If, then, there is here, as I would wish to maintain, a major difference
between history and sociology as forms of disciplined enquiry, what follows
from it for the uses of history in sociology? The main implication is, I believe,
clear enough. Because sociologists have the possibility of producing their own
evidence, over and above that of exploiting relics, they *are in a position of
advantage that should not be disregarded or lightly thrown away.* In other words,
sociologists should not readily and unthinkingly turn to history: they should
do so, rather, only with good reasons and in full awareness of the limitations
that they will thereby face. Here again I am, I suspect, in some danger of being
misunderstood. Let me therefore at once add that I do not in any way seek
to suggest that sociology is in some sense a 'superior' discipline to history:
rather, I am concerned to bring out just how difficult history is—since, as will
later emerge, I believe that some sociologists have clearly failed to appreciate
this. Nor do I suppose that generated evidence, in contrast to that in the form

---

[6] The one instance of which I am aware in which historians likewise generate their evidence is when they engage in 'oral' history. Here too, though, it may be noted that problems
of survival, and in turn of representativeness, are of large importance.

of relics, is unproblematic. I am well aware that it too must always be critically viewed as regards its completeness as well as its reliability and validity,
and indeed that in these latter respects special problems result precisely from
the processes of generation. However, what I do wish to emphasize are the
very real advantages that are gained where the nature and extent of available
evidence is not restricted by the mere accidents of physical survival; where,
moreover, the collection of evidence can be 'designed' so as to meet the specific requirements of the enquiry in hand; and where questions of the quality
of evidence can always be addressed, as they arise, by generating yet further
evidence through which to check and test the original.[7]

Some Illustrations of the Argument

To develop these arguments, I now turn to particular cases. To begin with, it
may be helpful if I give an example of what I would regard as a mistaken—
one might say, perverse—recourse to history on the part of a sociologist. I
take here Kai Erikson's book *Wayward Puritans* (1966), which is a study of
social deviance within the seventeenth-century Puritan community of
Massachussets Bay.

In his Preface, Erikson states his aims clearly. He begins with certain
hypotheses about social deviance drawn from a Durkheimian position, and
he aims to examine two hypotheses in particular: first, that some amount of
deviance is functional for a community in helping it to define its moral and
social boundaries, and thus in preserving its stability; and, secondly, that,
because of this functionality, deviance within any community will tend to
be at a fairly constant level over time. Erikson then proposes to take Massachussets Bay as a case study. 'The purpose of the following study', he writes
(1966: pp. vii–viii), 'is to use the Puritan community as a setting in which to
examine several ideas about deviant behavior. In this sense the subject matter
of the book is primarily sociological, even though the data found in most of
its pages are historical.' And, he goes on, 'The data presented here have *not*
been gathered in order to throw new light on the Puritan community in New
England but to add something to our understanding of deviant behavior in
general, and thus the Puritan experience in America has been treated in these
pages as an example of human life everywhere.' Judged in the light of this
statement, *Wayward Puritans* is, I would argue, a failure—and indeed a nec-

---

[7] Another way of putting much of this is to say, as does Clubb (1980: 20), that 'the source
materials upon which historians must rely are virtually by definition "process produced"'
and that they are, moreover, 'the residual process-produced data that have survived the
ravages of time'. Clubb notes that historians occasionally have at their disposal data that
were collected for social-scientific purposes, and that this is likely to be a more common situation for future historians. However, he then rightly comments that 'we can also imagine
that historians in the future will regard these data as no less process-produced, in this case
by the process of social research as archaically practised in the mid-twentieth century—and
will bemoan the fact that the wrong data were collected, the wrong questions asked, and
that the underlying assumptions and methods were not better documented'.

essary failure—because of its reliance on historical materials. The hypotheses that Erikson starts from are not seriously examined, and could not be, simply because Erikson does not have the evidence needed for this among the relics at his disposal.

Thus, as regards the first hypothesis, on the functionality of deviance, Erikson draws largely on court records, indicating the response of the authorities to antinomianism, Quakerism, and alleged witchcraft. But he has little evidence of how *the community at large*, as distinct from the authorities, reacted to such deviance or, for that matter, to its treatment by the authorities. In other words, he has no adequate basis on which to determine whether, in consequence of the deviance he refers to, there was, or was not, a stronger definition of the moral and social boundaries of the community. So far as popular perceptions and evaluations are concerned, he is without means of access. Likewise, in treating the second hypothesis, on the constant level of deviance, Erikson has to rely on official crime statistics, which, for well-known reasons, give only a very uncertain indication of the actual level of social deviance, and are influenced in their trend by a variety of other factors. However, unlike the sociologist of deviance working in contemporary society, Erikson cannot investigate in any detail the processes through which the official statistics were constituted, nor can he collect data of his own that could provide alternative estimates—as, say, through some form of 'victim survey'.

To be sure, the hypotheses that Erikson addresses are not ones that would be easily tested under any circumstances. But, given that they derive from a theory that pretends to a very high level of generality, there is all the more reason to ask why Erikson should impose upon himself the limitations that must follow from choosing a historical case. Why should he deny himself the possibility of being able to generate his own evidence, to his own design, and under conditions in which problems of reliability and validity could best be grappled with? Any sociologist, I would maintain, who is concerned with a theory that *can* be tested in the present should so test it, in the first place; for it is, in all probability, in this way that it can be tested most rigorously.[8]

I would now like to move on to consider cases where the recourse of sociologists to history *would* appear to have the good reasons that, I earlier maintained, should always be present. Here my aim is to illustrate what such reasons might be, but also—when they are acted upon—the difficulties that may be expected.

Sociologists, one might think, will most obviously need to turn to history when their interests lie in social change. However, it should be kept in mind that a recourse to the past—or, that is, to the relics thereof—is not the only means through which such interests may be pursued: repeated surveys and

---

[8] Skocpol (1984: 364) treats Erikson's intentions as being 'characteristic of historical sociologists who apply general models to history'. There can, of course, be little value in such a procedure unless there are *independent* grounds for believing that the models have some validity. But it should be noted that Erikson himself is clear that his concern is (see text) 'to examine several ideas about deviant behaviour' for which he does not appear to claim any prior validity.

life-course and panel studies, for example, are all ways of studying social change on the basis of evidence that is, or has been, collected in the present. Sociologists, I would argue, are compelled into historical research only when their concern is with social change that is in fact historically defined: that is, with change not over some analytically specified length of time—such as, say, 'the life cycle' or 'two generations'—but with change over a period of past time that has dates (even if not very precise ones) and that is related to a particular place. Sociologists have a legitimate, and necessary, concern with such historically defined social change because, as I have earlier suggested, they wish to know how widely over time and space their theories and hypotheses might apply.[9]

One illustration of what I have in mind here is provided by Michael Anderson's book *Family Structure in Nineteenth Century Lancashire* (1971). Anderson is concerned with the hypothesis that, in the process of industrialization, pre-existing forms of extended family and kinship relations are disrupted. Specifically, he is interested in whether or not this hypothesis holds good in the British case, that of the 'first industrial nation'. Thus, to pursue this issue, Anderson aims to examine just what was happening to kinship relations in Britain at the time when, and in the place where, the 'take-off' into industrialism is classically located. In contrast, then, with Erikson, Anderson has a quite clear rationale for turning to historical research. A second illustration is provided by Gordon Marshall's book *Presbyteries and Profits* (1980). Marshall is concerned with the 'Weber thesis' that a connection exists between the secular ethic of ascetic Protestantism and 'the spirit of capitalism'. In the long-standing debate on this thesis, the case of Scotland has several times been suggested as a critical one, in that, in the early modern period, Scotland had a great deal of ascetic Protestantism—that is, Calvinism—yet showed little in the way of capitalist development. Marshall's aim is then to re-examine the Scottish case for the period from around 1560 down to the Act of Union of 1707. Marshall points out that Weber himself always emphasized that his argument on the role of the Protestant ethic in the emergence of modern capitalism was intended to apply *only to the early stages* of this process: once a predominantly capitalist economy was established, its own exigencies, in the workplace and market, would themselves compel behaviour generally consistent with the 'spirit of capitalism' without need of help from religion. Again, then, Marshall, like Anderson, has obviously good grounds for his recourse to history.

---

[9] It may also be argued that sociologists have a legitimate recourse to history when their concern is with phenomena such as revolutions, major economic crises, mass panics, or crazes, etc., that not only happen rather infrequently but are in any event more amenable to investigation in retrospect than as they occur. I am not fully convinced by this argument (on the difficulty of a sociology of rarely occurring phenomena, see further Chapter 3), but for present purposes it is not necessary to contest it. Nor do I take up here a concern displayed with history by some sociologists that I would most certainly regard as illegitimate: that is, a concern with 'theorizing' history so as, it is hoped, to secure a cognitive grasp on its 'movement' or 'logic'. I have written critically elsewhere (Goldthorpe 1971, 1979) on the persistence of such historicism.

Now before proceeding further, I should make it clear that I have the highest regard for the two studies to which I have just referred. Both make signal contributions to the questions they address; and, for me, they stand as leading examples of how in fact historical sociology should be conceived and conducted. I say this because I want now to go on to emphasize the severe limitations to which the analyses of both authors are subject: *not* because of their deficiencies as sociologists, but simply because of the fact that they were forced into using historical evidence—forced into a reliance on relics—rather than being able to generate their own evidence within a contemporary society.

The relics on which Anderson chiefly relies are the original enumerators' books for the censuses of 1841, 1851, and 1861. On this basis, he can reconstruct household composition according to age, sex, and kinship relations, and he can also to some extent examine the residential propinquity of kin. But this still leaves him a long way short of adequate evidence on the part actually played by kinship in the lives of the people he is studying and on the meanings of kinship for them. He attempts to fill out the essentially demographic data that he has from the enumerators' books with material from contemporary accounts. But these would, I fear, have at best to be categorized as 'casual empiricism' and at worst as local gossip or travellers' tales. Titles such as *Walks in South Lancashire and on its Borders*, *A Visit to Lancashire in December 1862*, and *Lancashire Sketches* give the flavour. Anderson is in fact entirely frank about the problem he faces. 'It must of course be stressed', he writes (1971: 62), 'that just because interaction with kin occurred it is no necessary indication that kinship was important. The real test, which is quite impossible in any precise way in historical work, would be to examine the extent to which kinship was given preference over other relational contacts (and the reasons for this preference), and the extent to which contacts with kin fulfilled functions which were not adequately met if kin did not provide them'.

The point I want to make here would perhaps best be brought out if one were to compare Anderson's study of kinship with one carried out in contemporary society—let us say, for example, Fischer's study (1982) of kinship and of other 'primary' relations in present-day San Francisco. The only conclusion could be that the latter is greatly superior in the range and quality of data on which it draws, and in turn in the rigour and refinement of the analyses it can offer. And the point is, of course, not that Fischer is a better sociologist than Anderson but that he has an enormous advantage over Anderson in being able to generate his own data rather than having to rely on whatever relics might happen to be extant.

Turning to Marshall, one finds that he has problems essentially the same as those of Anderson. One of Marshall's main concerns is that Weber's position should be correctly understood, following the vulgarizations of Robertson, Tawney, Samuelson, and other critics; and in this respect Marshall makes two main points. First, Weber was not so much concerned with official Calvinist doctrine on economic activity as with the consequences of *being* a believing Calvinist for the individual's conduct of everyday life—consequences that the individual might not even fully realize. In other words, Weber's thesis was ultimately not about theology but subculture and psychology. Secondly, Weber's argument was that the Protestant ethic was a necessary, but not a sufficient, cause of the emergence of modern capitalism; there were necessary 'material' factors also, such as access to physical resources and to markets, the availability of capital and credit, and so on. Thus, Marshall argues, in evaluating the Weber thesis, it is not enough to look simply for some overt association between theology, on the one hand, and the development of capitalist enterprise, on the other. What is required is more subtle. It is evidence that believing Calvinists, on account of their acceptance of a Calvinist world view, were distinctively oriented to work in a regular, disciplined way, to pursue economic gain rationally, and to accumulate rather than to consume extravagantly—so that, *if* other conditions were *also* met, capitalist enterprise would then flourish.

Marshall's position here is, I believe, entirely sound. But it leads him to problems of evidence that he can in fact never satisfactorily overcome, despite his diligence in searching out new sources and his ingenuity is using known ones. And the basic difficulty is that relics from which inferences can systematically be made about the orientations to work and to money of early modern Scots are very few and far between. In other words, what is crucially lacking—just as it was lacking for Anderson and indeed for Erikson—is material from which inferences might be made, with some assurance of representativeness, about the *patterns of social action* that are of interest within particular collectivities. As Clubb (1980: 20) has observed, the data from which historians work only rarely allow access to the subjective orientations of actors *en masse*, and inferences made in this respect from actual behaviour tend always to be question-begging. And Marshall, it should be said, like Anderson, sees the difficulty clearly enough. He acknowledges (G. Marshall 1980: 35) that it may well be that 'the kind of data required in order to establish the ethos in which seventeenth-century Scottish business enterprises were run simply does not exist'—or, at least, not in sufficient quantity to allow one to test empirically whether Calvinism did indeed have the effect on mundane conduct that Weber ascribed to it.

The Problem of 'Grand Historical Sociology'

Let me at this point recapitulate. I have argued that history and sociology differ perhaps most consequentially in the nature of the evidence on which they rely, and that this difference has major implications for the use of history in sociology. I have presented a case of what, from this standpoint, must be seen as a perverse recourse to history on the part of a sociologist; and I have now discussed two further cases where, in contrast, such a recourse was justifiable, indeed necessary, given the issues addressed, but where, none the less, serious difficulties arise because of the inadequacy of the relics as a basis for treating these issues. To end with, however, I would like to move on from these instances of sociologists resorting to history in the pursuit of quite specific problems to consider, with my initial argument still in mind, a whole genre of sociology that is in fact *dependent upon history in its very conception*. I refer here to a kind of historical sociology clearly different from that represented by the work of Anderson or Marshall, and which has two main distinguishing features. First, it resorts to history because it addresses very large themes, which typically involve the tracing-out of long-term 'developmental' processes or patterns or the making of comparisons across a wide range of historical societies or even civilizations. And, secondly, it is based largely or entirely not on inferences from relics but rather on 'history' in the sense of what historians have written—or, in other words, not on primary but on secondary, or yet more derivative, sources.

The idea that sociologists might proceed by taking the results of historical research as their main empirical resource in developing wide-ranging generalizations and theories is not, of course, a new one. It was in fact a nineteenth-century commonplace. Its plainest expression was perhaps provided by Herbert Spencer when he wrote (1904: ii. 185; see also 1861/1911: 29) that, for him, sociology stood to works of history 'much as a vast building stands related to the heaps of stones and bricks around it', and further that 'the highest office which the historian can discharge is that of so narrating the lives of nations, as to furnish materials for a Comparative Sociology'. From the end of the nineteenth century, this understanding of the relationship between history and sociology met with severe criticism and rather rapidly lost support. Historians had indeed never taken kindly to the idea that they should serve as some kind of intellectual under-labourers; and sociologists became increasingly interested in developing their own methods of data collection.[10] However, in more recent times, a notable revival of what might be called 'grand historical sociology' has occurred. This was led by the appearance of Barrington Moore's *The Social Origins of Dictatorship and Democracy* (1966) and was then consolidated in the USA by the subsequent work of Wallerstein (1974–89) and Skocpol (1979) and in Britain by that of Perry Anderson (1974*a*, *b*), with other authors such as Hall (1985) and Mann (1986) following in their wake.[11] What I would now wish to argue is that the

---

[10] An early but cogent and, I suspect, highly influential, attack on Spencer by a pre-eminent historian was Maitland (1911). Note also Collingwood's critique (1946/1993: 263 6) of the last phase of 'scissors-and-paste' historiography, that of the 'pigeon-holers', whose approach was: 'Very well: let us put together all the facts that are known to historians, look for patterns in them, and then extrapolate these patterns into a theory of universal history.' On the sociological side, the late nineteenth century saw of course the beginnings in Britain of sample survey methods (see further Chapter 4) and a growing interest in other means of data collection.

[11] It might be argued that this 'new wave' of grand historical sociology was in fact led by Eisenstadt's *The Political Systems of Empires* (1963). But Eisenstadt's influence would seem to have been clearly less than that of Moore—chiefly, I suspect, because his highly academic

practice of these authors does in fact raise again all the difficulties inherent in Spencer's programme, and that the use of history in sociology as exemplified in their work is problematic in a far more fundamental way than in any of the studies earlier considered.

The authors in question would certainly not wish to represent their position in terms similar to those of Spencer. They would rather incline to the idea that history and sociology are one and indivisible; and, instead of viewing historians *de haut en bas*, they would surely wish to include them in the joint enterprise as equal partners.[12] None the less, the fact remains that grand historical sociology in its twentieth-century form, just as in its nineteenth, takes secondary historical sources as its evidential basis, and must therefore encounter the methodological difficulties that are entailed, even though its exponents have thus far shown little readiness to address, or even acknowledge, them. The root of their predicament is richly ironical. The revival of grand historical sociology can be seen as one expression of the 'reaction against positivism' within the sociological community to which I referred at the start (and see further Chapter 1); and yet its practitioners' own *modus operandi*—the use they seek to make of secondary sources—must depend upon what is an essentially positivistic conception of *historiography*, to which they would, I suspect, be reluctant to give any explicit support.

The catechism that I was put through as an undergraduate had a clear objective. It was to prompt a rejection of the view that the past—or at least certain well-documented aspects of the past, such as 'high' politics—could in principle be reconstructed, fact by fact, so that the distinction between history in the sense of what actually happened in the past and history in the sense of what is written about the past might be elided. Against this 'positivist' conception of historiography—as it was indeed labelled (see e.g. Collingwood 1946: 126–33)[13]—it was urged upon us that historical facts could not be cognitively established as a collection of well-defined items or entities, each independent of the rest, which, when taken together, would then dictate a specific and definitive version of the past. Rather, historical facts should be recognized as no more than 'inferences from the relics'; and inferences that had always to be weighted, so to speak, according to the security of their grounding, which were often interdependent—that is, stood or fell together—and which were of course at all times open to restatement, whether radically or through the most subtle changes of nuance.

Now, to repeat, I very much doubt if grand historical sociologists would wish to take up the defence of positivist historiography as against this latter

---

structural-functionalism accorded far less well with the prevailing mood of the later 1960s than did the *marxisant* tone and explicitly 'radical' commitment of Moore's work.

[12] Thus, for example, in a collection of essays edited by Skocpol (1984), consideration is given to the work of historians such as Marc Bloch, Charles Tilly, and E. P. Thompson alongside that of authors such as Eisenstadt, Moore, Wallerstein, and Anderson. Admirers of Bloch, in particular, might well be led to ask 'Que diable allait-il faire dans cette galère?'

[13] Then, as apparently later (cf. Carr 1961: ch. 1), the classic expositors of such positivism in historiography were taken to be von Ranke and, in Britain, Lord Acton.

view. But it is difficult to see how, *in practice*, they can avoid *assuming* an essentially positivist position. For, even if the procedures they follow in producing their sociology do not actually require the elision of the two senses of history, they still cannot afford to recognize a too indeterminate relation between them. Grand historical sociologists have to treat the facts, or indeed concatenations of facts or entire 'accounts', that they find in secondary sources *as if they were* relatively discrete and stable entities that can be 'excerpted' and then brought together in order that some larger design may be realized. In anti-positivist vein, Care Becker (1955) has expressly warned that historical facts should *not* be thought of as possessing 'solidity', 'definite shape', or 'clear persistent outline', and that it is therefore especially inapt to liken them to building materials of any kind. But the very procedures of grand historical sociologists push them back, willy-nilly, to Spencer's idea of using the stones and bricks of history to construct the great sociological edifice, and constructional metaphors do indeed reappear. Thus, for example, one finds Skocpol (1979: p. xiv) remarking that 'primary research'—which the comparativist 'has neither the time nor [all of] the appropriate skills to do'— 'necessarily constitutes, in large amounts, the foundation upon which comparative studies are built'. However, I would then wish to respond that the constructions that result are likely to be dangerously unsound. In particular, I would argue that in grand historical sociology the links that are claimed, or supposed, between evidence and argument tend to be both *tenuous* and *arbitrary* to a quite unacceptable degree.

As regards the first charge, it is, I would suggest, instructive to consider some fairly specific argument advanced by a grand historical sociologist, and to note the 'authorities' that are invoked as providing its factual basis; then, to work back from these citations—through perhaps other intermediate sources that are involved—until one comes to direct references to relics of some kind. What, I believe, one will typically find is that the trail is longer and harder to follow than one might have expected, and that, not infrequently, it reaches no very satisfactory end. For example, in *The Social Origins of Dictatorship and Democracy*, Moore spends several pages reviewing aspects of English economic history over the late medieval and early modern periods, and then concludes as follows (1966: 14): 'In the light of this general background there would seem to be little reason to question the thesis that commercially minded elements among the landed upper classes, and to a lesser extent among the yeomen, were among the main forces opposing the King and royal attempts to preserve the old order, and therefore an important cause, though not the only one, that produced the Civil War.'

However, if one actually examines the sources that Moore cites, both before and after this passage, the grounding of his argument is very far from apparent. Indeed, it is quite unclear just what is the evidence, at the level of relics, in the light of which there would be 'little reason to question' the thesis that Moore advances. In the authorities referred to—the main ones are Tawney (1912, 1941/1954) and Mildred Campbell (1942)—there is in fact remarkably little 'evidence' bearing in any direct way on the crucial link that Moore seeks to establish between economic position and political action. And such as there is cannot be regarded as evidence in the sense that relics themselves are evidence or, for that matter, the data of a social survey are evidence. Rather, what one has are series of inferences, often complex and indeed often quite speculative, which are drawn from relics that are manifestly incomplete, almost certainly unrepresentative, and in various other ways problematic—as the authors in question are very well aware. In other words, such 'facts' as are here available cannot be understood as separate, well-defined 'modules', easily carried off for sociological construction purposes, but would be better regarded simply as strands in heavily tangled, yet still often rather weak skeins of interpretation.

In effect, then, what grand historical sociologists seem to me to be generally doing is not developing an argument on the basis of evidence, in the manner of 'primary' historians or again of sociologists working on their 'own' research data, but rather, engaging in interpretation that is of, at least, a second-order kind: that is, in interpretation of interpretations of, perhaps, interpretations. And in consequence, I would maintain, the connection between the claims they make about the past and relics that could conceivably serve as warrant for these claims is often, as in the passage from Moore that I have quoted, quite impossibly loose. Following the practices that are here illustrated, history must indeed become, in Froude's words (1884: i. 21) 'a child's box of letters with which we can spell any word we please'.

As regards my second charge, that of arbitrariness, the idea of historiography as a matter of inferences from relics that are finite and incomplete is again directly relevant. It follows from this that historians working on the same topic, and indeed on the same relics, may quite reasonably come to quite different conclusions, as of course they may for other reasons too. But it further follows that there may be little or no possibility of their differences ever being resolved because the relics that would be necessary to settle the disputed issues simply do not exist. For grand historical sociologists, this then raises a major problem: where historians disagree, and may perhaps have to remain in disagreement, *which* secondary account should be accepted? By what criteria should the grand historical sociologist opt for one of two, or more, conflicting interpretations? Thus, to return to Moore and his treatment of the economic and social origins of the English Civil War, the question one may ask is: why, on this notoriously controversial matter, and one plagued by a lack of relevant evidence, does Moore choose largely to follow what has come to be thought of (not altogether fairly) as the 'Tawney' interpretation rather than any of its rivals? By the time Moore was writing, it should be said, the idea that the 'rising', commercially oriented gentry were key actors in the parliamentary opposition to the King and his defeat in the Civil War was in fact fast losing ground among English historians, both to interpretations that gave the leading role to other socio-economic groupings and, more importantly, to ones that questioned whether political allegiance in the Civil

War period had any close association at all with economic position and interest.[14]

The answer to the question I have posed is, I believe, as obvious as it is unsatisfactory. Moore favours the interpretation that fits best with his overall thesis of the 'three routes to modernity'; in other words, that which allows the English Civil War to be seen as an instance of a successful 'bourgeois revolution'. However, he still fails to present any serious case for this choice. Supportive sources simply receive accolades, such as 'excellent analysis' or 'unsurpassed account', while less congenial ones are disparaged as 'conservative historiography' (see e.g. Moore 1966: 6, 14, and the appendix).[15] This clearly will not do. But if mere tendentiousness is not the solution, what is? In the end, of course, any rational way of evaluating a secondary source must involve some judgement on the inferences made from the primary sources— that is, from the relics. But, once this is recognized, the methodological bind in which grand historical sociologists find themselves becomes only more apparent. Their large designs mean, they tell us, that they cannot themselves be expected to work directly from the relics but must rely on the studies of specialist authorities. However, they are then either forced into positivistic

---

[14] An essay important for its catalytic effect was Hexter (1958/1961). For a more recent critique of 'social change explanations' of the English Civil War, but certainly not one that could be dismissed as sociologically unsophisticated, see J. C. D. Clark (1986).

[15] In the Appendix, 'A Note on Statistics and Conservative Historiography', Moore takes up the difficulties posed for his interpretation of the Civil War by Brunton and Pennington's study (1954) of the members of the Long Parliament, which, as Moore notes, led Tawney himself to acknowledge that the division between Royalists and Parliamentarians 'had little connection with diversities of economic interest and social class'. Moore then tries to rework Brunton and Pennington's statistics to save what he takes to be Tawney's thesis against Tawney's own abandonment of it—but succeeds only in providing a nice example of the ecological fallacy.

It might be added here that the treatment of the English Civil War by both Wallerstein and Anderson is no more satisfactory. Wallerstein, who claims (1974–89: i. 8) that 'contrapuntal controversial work' is a positive advantage for his enterprise, reviews a wider range of literature than Moore but by an eirenical *tour de force* still ends up where he wants to be: i.e. able to claim that the English Civil War, though not a direct struggle between classes, none the less resulted from the formation of an agricultural capitalist class that the old aristocracy was forced to accommodate and in part to merge with, thus leading to the early creation in England of a 'national bourgeoisie' (see 1974–89: i, esp. 256, 269, 282, 297). It must, however, be pointed out that, of the 'authorities' whom Wallerstein cites, at least as many would reject this conclusion as would accept it. Perry Anderson, in contrast, refers to only a very limited number of secondary (or tertiary) sources and then, effectively disregarding all controversy, blandly asserts (1974b: 142): 'English absolutism was brought to a crisis by aristocratic particularism and clannic desperation on its periphery: forces that lay historically behind it. But it was felled at the centre by a commercialized gentry, a capitalist city, a commoner artisanate and yeomanry: forces pushing beyond it. Before it could reach the age of maturity, English Absolutism was cut off by a bourgeois revolution.' Once more it must be emphasized that it is essentially the interpretation of the English Civil War as a 'bourgeois revolution' that has been challenged by 'revisionist' historians over the last two decades or more.

My own judgement would be that the revisionists have indeed succeeded in undermining the supposed evidence for such an interpretation. But, further, I would doubt that, even if there *were* a valid 'social change explanation' of the English Civil War, adequate relics could be found to allow its validity to be demonstrated. What Hexter remarked (1958/1961: 149) apropos the initial Tawney *versus* Trevor Roper debate is likely to remain the last word: 'And what such masters of the materials of seventeenth-century history and of historical forensics cannot prove when they set their minds to it, is not likely ever to be proved.'

assumptions concerning the 'hardness' and 'solidity'—and also the 'transportability'—of the evidence that these works can yield; or, if they accept that what these sources provide is no more than rival complexes of inference and interpretation, then they must explain how they propose to choose among them *without knowledge of* the primary sources. Where historians themselves draw on secondary sources, it may be added, as, say, in situating their own primary research or in writing 'surveys' of a field, issues of the availability, quality, and so on of sources are typically discussed. Moreover, in the case of survey articles, and likewise in the writing of textbooks, authors are not under pressure to defend a particular interpretation but can present a review of different positions. Grand historical sociologists, in contrast, usually cannot afford such even-handedness; they need to use—that is, to choose among—secondary sources as evidence for or against a particular thesis.[16]

Since, then, I have been so critical of the methodological basis of grand historical sociology, I should, before finishing, consider what its exponents have themselves had to say on the matter. In fact, as I have already implied, they have said remarkably little. Methodological issues tend to be raised, if at all, in the early pages of their books, but then only to be dealt with in a quite perfunctory and unconvincing manner (see e.g. Moore 1966: pp. x–xi; Anderson 1974a: p. 8; Skocpol 1979: pp. xiv–xv; Mann 1986: pp. vii–viii, 3–4, 31–2). However, there is one statement by Skocpol, from the concluding chapter of a collection that she edited on the subject of method in historical sociology, that is of interest in several respects. Skocpol writes as follows (1984: 382):

Because wide-ranging comparisons are so often crucial for analytic historical sociologists, they are more likely to use secondary sources of evidence than those who apply models to, or develop interpretations of, single cases . . . From the point of view of historical sociology . . . a dogmatic insistence on redoing primary research for every investigation would be disastrous; it would rule out most comparative-historical research. If a topic is too big for purely primary research—and if excellent studies by specialists are already available in some profusion—secondary sources are appropriate as the basic source of evidence for a given study. Using them is not different from survey analysts reworking the results of previous surveys rather than asking all questions anew.

I would note, first of all, about this passage how clearly it shows the pressure that bears on grand historical sociologists to move towards the positivistic, Spencerian programme—'excellent' historical studies by specialists can be 'the basic source of evidence' for the wide-ranging sociologist. And also revealing is the reference to 'redoing the primary research', as if it were apparent that the same result as before would necessarily emerge. Secondly, I would point out that Skocpol is quite mistaken in the analogy she seeks to draw with survey-based research. The 'secondary analysis' of survey data to

---

[16] Furthermore, the central theses that are argued for by authors such as Moore, Wallerstein, and Anderson are ones which they themselves clearly see as being politically highly consequential, so that questions of how far their use of secondary sources is politically influenced and of what checks on political bias *they* would believe appropriate, inevitably arise.

which she refers is different from the grand historical sociologist's use of secondary sources, precisely because it *does* entail going back to the 'relics': that is, at least to the original data tapes and perhaps also to the original questionnaires or interview schedules. And it is then these materials that serve the secondary analyst as evidence, not the interpretations of the original analyst that may be, and indeed often are, disputed. Thus, a closer parallel would be between the secondary analyst of surveys and the historian who again works through and reinterprets a body of source materials discovered and initially analysed by a predecessor. Thirdly, I would remark that, by way of providing a rationale for the methodology of grand historical sociology, Skocpol has little at all to offer. Apart from her mistaken *tu quoque* argument directed at survey researchers, all she in fact says is that it would be 'disastrous' for grand historical sociologists if they were to be forced back to primary sources— which is scarcely a way of convincing sceptics.

What is actually of greatest interest is what Skocpol goes on to acknowledge in the paragraph that immediately follows the one from which I quoted: namely, that 'it remains true that comparative historical sociologists have not so far worked out clear, consensual rules and procedures for the valid use of secondary sources as evidence' and further that in this respect 'varying historiographical interpretations' are one obvious problem to be addressed. 'Certain principles', Skocpol believes, 'are likely to emerge as such rules are developed'. But, one must observe, so far at least, grand historical sociology is *not* significantly rule governed; its practitioners enjoy a delightful freedom to play 'pick and mix' in history's sweet shop.[17]

To sum up, then, I have argued that the view that history and sociology 'are and always have been the same thing' is mistaken and—dangerously— misleading. Sociology must, it is true, always be a historical discipline; sociologists can never 'escape' from history. It is, therefore, highly desirable that they should be historically aware—by which I mean, aware of the historical settings and limits that their analyses will necessarily possess, even if these

---

[17] Unlike Skocpol, the other authors earlier cited do not even appear to recognize the need for a methodology. Their main justification for grand historical sociology would seem to be simply that it gives 'the broad view' and is thus a necessary complement to 'specialists' history'. Thus, Moore writes (1966: p. xi): 'That comparative analysis is no substitute for detailed investigation of specific cases is obvious.' But, he goes on: 'Generalizations that are sound resemble a large-scale [*sic*] map of an extended terrain, such as an airplane pilot might use in crossing a continent. Such maps are essential for certain purposes just as more detailed maps are necessary for others.' Moore's cartography inspires no more confidence than his historiography. Assuming that in the above he means 'small scale' not 'large scale', a small-scale map, useful for an 'extended terrain', is dependent for its accuracy on the detailed surveying from which it is built up. And likewise, as a 'cliometric' and a 'conventional' historian have written together (Fogel and Elton 1983: 125), 'the quality of an historical interpretation is critically dependent on the quality of the details out of which it is spun. Time and again the interpretation of major historical events, sometimes of whole areas, has been transformed by the correction of apparently trivial details.' It should also be said that the methodology of grand historical sociology has attracted little attention from writers concerned with the methodology of the social sciences in general. One essay by Galtung (1979) may be noted, though its contribution to practice does not seem large.

settings and limits may never be precisely determined. But history and soci-ology can, and should, still be regarded as significantly different intellectual enterprises. A crucial source of the difference, I have sought to show, lies in the nature of the evidence that the two disciplines use: in the fact that his-torians have for the most part to rely on evidence that they can discover in the relics of the past, while sociologists have the considerable privilege of being able to generate evidence in the present.

As regards, then, the use of history in sociology, what I have sought to stress is that sociologists should not underestimate, or readily give up, the advan-tages that they can gain from having evidence that is 'tailor made', whereas historians have usually to 'cut their coats according to their cloth'. Where sociologists are compelled into historical research, by the very logic of their enquiries, then, I have suggested, they must be ready for a harder life—for research typically conducted, as one historian has put it, 'below the data poverty line' (Clubb 1980: 20). They must not only learn new techniques but also to accept new frustrations; in particular, those that come from realizing that issues of crucial interest are, and will probably remain, beyond their cog-nitive reach. Historical sociologists such as Anderson and Marshall have learnt well; and much of what they can in turn teach us stems from their sensitiv-ity to just what manner of inferences the relics available to them can, and cannot, sustain. In contrast, grand historical sociologists seem to me to have, so far at least, shied away from the major intellectual challenges that his-toriography poses, and to have traded implicitly on a conception of it that I doubt if they would wish openly to defend. Until, then, they do meet the challenges before them, and provide a coherent methodology for their work, the question must remain of how far this does possess a real basis in the relics of the past or merely an illusory one in a scattering of footnotes.

3

Current Issues in Comparative Macrosociology

ISEEK in this chapter to intervene in what is in fact a rather long-standing debate within comparative macrosociology, but one which appears of late to have acquired new vigour. The contending parties in this debate are now usually characterized as exponents of quantitative, 'variable-oriented' methodologies, on the one hand, and of qualitative, 'case-oriented' methodologies, on the other (see e.g. Ragin 1987; Rueschemeyer 1991; Janoski and Hicks 1994). I shall, however, argue that, while the issues caught up in the protracted and complex exchanges that have occurred do include ones of major importance, the form that the debate has taken has not been especially helpful in highlighting just what these issues are, nor yet in pointing to ways in which they might be more effectively addressed.

I shall develop my position as follows. To begin with, I give a brief account of the contrast, or opposition, that has been set up between variable-oriented and case-oriented approaches. I then pursue my central argument by considering three rather well-known methodological problems that are encountered in the practice of comparative macrosociology. These problems are ones that have in fact been chiefly discussed in connection with variable-oriented research. But, I aim to show, they are present to no less a degree in case-oriented studies and, contrary to what several prominent authors have maintained or implied, the latter can claim no special advantages in dealing with them. Largely on account of misconceptions in this regard, I conclude, much recent discussion has tended to obscure, and divert attention away from, questions of method that comparative macrosociology does now need to engage with more actively—in whatever style it may be carried out.[1]

This chapter is a revised and extended version of the Vilhelm Aubert Memorial Lecture for 1993, given at the University of Oslo. It was first published in *Comparative Social Research*, 16 (1997). For information, advice, and critical observations on previous drafts, I am indebted to Anne Gauthier, Andrew Hurrell, Olli Kangas, Philip Kreager, John Stephens, Laurence Whitehead, and Timothy Wickham-Crowley.

[1] This discussion, it should be said, has often ended on an eirenic note, the complementary nature of quantitative and qualitative work and the need to 'build bridges' between them being emphasized. Thus, the present chapter may appear disobliging and contrary to the prevailing spirit of methodological pluralism. But it seems to me, for reasons that will become clear, that often, behind the rhetoric of pluralism, a collaborative alliance is being proposed on terms that are in fact unduly skewed in favour of the case-oriented approach.

Variable-Oriented versus Case-Oriented Approaches

The variable-oriented approach to comparative macrosociology stems from a now famous proposal made by Przeworski and Teune (1970: ch. 1; cf. Zelditch: 1971: 269–73): that is, that the ultimate aim of work in this field should be to replace the proper names of nations (or of states or cultures) with the names of variables. Przeworski and Teune first illustrate the logic they would recommend by examples such as the following. Rates of heart attack are lower in Japan than in the USA. But, in seeking an explanation for this, we do not get far by treating the differing rates as simply 'Japanese' or 'American' phenomena. Rather, we have to drop proper names—or adjectives—and introduce generally applicable variables: that is, variables on which each nation can be given a comparable value. Thus, in the case in point, one such variable might be 'per capita consumption of polysaturated fat'.

Przeworski and Teune then of course go on to provide further illustrations of their position drawn from the social sciences; and, by the present day, one could in fact add to these entire research programmes in sociology—and political science—that essentially follow the approach that they advocate. As a paradigm case here, one might take research that is aimed at explaining cross-national differences in the size and institutional form of welfare states (for reviews, see Quadagno 1987; O'Connor and Brym 1988). In such research, the names of nations are typically 'replaced' by such variables as 'GNP per capita', 'proportion of population over age 65', 'degree of trade-union centralization', 'share of left-wing parties in government', and so on. That is to say, these are the independent variables, by reference to which the dependent variables—cross-nationally differing aspects of welfare provision—are to be 'accounted for'. The relationships that actually prevail between independent and dependent variables are then investigated statistically, through various techniques of multivariate analysis.

It is, for present purposes, important to recognize what Przeworski and Teune were defining their position *against*. Most importantly, they sought to challenge the 'historicist' claim that any attempt to make macrosociological comparisons must fail in principle because different national societies are *sui generis*: that is, are entities uniquely formed by their history and culture, which can be studied only, so to speak, in their own right and on their own terms.[2] In opposition to this, Przeworski and Teune point out that comparability and non-comparability are not inherent properties of things: whether meaningful comparison is possible or not is entirely a matter of the analytic concepts that we have at our disposal. Thus, apples and oranges may appear to be non-comparable—but only until we have the concept of 'fruit' (cf. Sartori 1994). At the same time, though, Przeworski and Teune do insist that, *if* the historicist position is accepted, then it must

---

[2] 'Historicist' is thus being used here in what one might describe as the sense of Meinecke rather than the sense of Popper.

indeed follow that a comparative macrosociology is ruled out. If nations can be studied only as entities in themselves that will not allow of any kind of analytic decomposition—if, in other words, nations can only be studied 'holistically'—then comparisons *cannot* be undertaken. Considered as wholes, nations *are* unique, and 'holistic comparison' is thus an impossibility. As Zelditch (1971: 278) later put the point: 'There is nothing else on earth quite like the United States (or the Navaho, or the Eskimo . . .) taken as a whole. Therefore the rule of holism [in comparative work] yields a clear and straightforward contradiction: only incomparables are comparable.'

However, if the variable-oriented approach thus developed out of a critique of holism, the case-oriented approach is usually taken to represent a revival of holism, and indeed one directed against the kind of analytic reductionism that Przeworski and Teune would favour. Thus, for example, Ragin (1991: 1–2) would regard it as being the very *raison d'être* of case studies that they allow a return to holism in comparative research: that is, they allow nations, or other macrosocial units, to be considered as 'meaningful wholes' rather than serving simply as the basis on which 'to place boundaries around the measurement of variables'.

It must, though, be noted that the holism that Ragin and others thus set against multivariate analysis is not as radical as might at first appear. Case studies are indeed regarded as the only way in which macrosocial entities can be treated in their distinctive historical contexts, in their proper detail and as each constituting, as Skocpol and Somers (1980: 178) put it, 'a complex and unique sociohistorical configuration'. But this, it turns out, does not imply a historicism of a quite thoroughgoing kind, which would deny the validity of any concepts that are formed in order to transcend particular cases (cf. Skocpol 1994: 328–9). It is still seen as permissible to 'abstract' from different cases certain of their 'features' or 'attributes', which can then be compared for theoretical purposes. In other words, variables *are* identified, even if sometimes behind a verbal smokescreen. Where holism enters in is with the insistence that, in any comparison, the unity of the particular cases involved should always be preserved. What is required is that, in the process of comparison, cases should always remain identifiable as such, rather than being decomposed into variables that are then interpreted only in the course of the simultaneous analysis of the entire sample of cases under investigation.

In actually pursuing holistic comparisons in this sense, exponents of the case-oriented approach appear to have found their chief methodological inspiration in the logic of John Stuart Mill (1843/1973–4): specifically, in Mill's 'canons', or rules, of experimental induction—the 'Method of Agreement', the 'Method of Difference', etc. (see e.g. Skocpol 1979: 36–7; 1984: 378–81; Skocpol and Somers 1980: 183–4; Ragin 1987: 36–42). Following Mill, it is believed, each case included in a comparative enquiry can be taken as representing the presence or absence of a given phenomenon of interest—each case, that is, can be taken as a 'naturally occurring' experiment relating to this phenomenon. Inferences regarding the causation of the phenomenon can then be drawn by considering which *other* features are *concomitantly* present or absent, and by in turn applying Mill's logical rules to the resulting set of comparisons. Thus, Skocpol, in her well-known study of social revolutions (1979) seeks to explain their outcomes by comparing national cases, on the one hand, in terms of whether or not revolutionary attempts succeeded and, on the other hand, in terms of the presence or absence of what she takes as likely determining factors: that is, various features of the agrarian economy and class structure, international pressures, internal political crises, and so on.[3]

It might seem that in both multivariate and logical comparisons alike the aim is in effect to 'control variation' in the making of causal inferences—so that the two approaches are not, after all, so very far apart. And, indeed, the application of Mill's methods in the comparison of cases has not infrequently been represented as itself a form of multivariate analysis (e.g. Smelser 1976: ch. 7; Skocpol and Somers 1980: 182–3; Dogan 1994: 35). However, as other commentators have pointed out (e.g. Lieberson 1992, 1994), there is one quite fundamental difference. The various forms of multivariate analysis used in quantitative work are statistical techniques, and the propositions to which they give rise are therefore *probabilistic*: they are based on associations or correlations that need not be perfect. In contrast, the methods proposed by Mill, being logical in character, entail propositions of a *deterministic* kind: they entail relationships that are entirely invariant. As will be seen later, this is a difference that matters, and indeed to overlook it is to neglect a major development in the history of sociological analysis: that which, in the course of the nineteenth and earlier twentieth centuries, saw sociology become part of 'the probabilistic revolution' (see Krüger *et al.* 1987*a*; Krüger *et al.* 1987*b*; and Chapter 12 below).

The distinction between variable-oriented and case-oriented approaches is not then a meaningless one. It captures an important divergence in preferred styles of comparative macrosociological research and further, one may suspect, in basic assumptions about the character of social phenomena. But, I would argue, focusing on this distinction will not in itself provide the key to an understanding of the more taxing methodological problems that arise in the conduct of such research; nor are attempts at combining or synthesizing the two approaches likely to make the main contribution to overcoming these problems, since they are in fact ones that confront both approaches alike. This argument I now seek to sustain with reference to what may be labelled as (i) the small N problem; (ii) the Galton problem; and (iii) the black-box problem.

---

[3] Whether or not Skocpol does in practice apply Mill's canons appropriately is a matter of some dispute. See e.g., Nichols (1986), Skocpol (1986), Ragin (1987: 38–42), Burawoy (1989), and Lieberson (1992). However, as will later emerge, I would see this as an issue that is over-shadowed by far more serious ones."

The Small *N* Problem

The small *N* problem arises in that, if nations or other macrosocial entities are taken as units of analysis, the number available for study is likely to be quite limited. Where individuals are the units, populations can be sampled so as to give *N*s of several hundreds or thousands; but where nations are the units, *N* cannot rise much above one hundred even if all available cases are taken, and is often far less. In applying techniques of multivariate analysis, serious difficulties tend therefore to be encountered in that *N* is not much greater than the total number of variables involved. Statistically, this means that there are too few degrees of freedom, that models become 'overdetermined', that intercorrelations among independent variables cannot be adequately dealt with, and that results may not be robust. Substantively, it means that *competing* explanations of the dependent variable may not be open to any decisive evaluation. Thus, it has recently been claimed (Huber *et al.* 1993) that, for just these reasons, the research programme on the determinants of state welfare provision—in which analyses based on a maximum of about twenty nations have been typical—has by now reached a virtual impasse. Theories privileging different sets of determinants can claim similar degrees of statistical support.[4]

The small *N* problem is then a real and troubling one. However, what I would wish to question are suggestions to the effect that it is a problem *specific to* the variable-oriented approach to comparative macrosociology, and that the case-oriented approach in some way or other allows it to be solved or circumvented. Most explicitly, Skocpol (1979: 36; cf. Rueschemeyer 1991: 27–8, 32–4) has maintained that application of the methods 'laid out' by Mill 'is distinctively appropriate for developing explanations of macro-historical phenomena' when the small *N* problem arises; that is, 'when there are too many variables and not enough cases'.[5]

This claim calls for comment in several respects. To begin with, it is unclear whether Skocpol realizes that Mill himself (1843/1973–4: esp. bk. VII, ch. 7) went to some lengths to explain that his rules of induction, being developed for use in the experimental sciences, were *not* appropriate to the study of social phenomena and that, if used, would be likely to prove inconclusive if

---

[4] Without seeking to deny the force of the general point being made here, one could question whether the illustration suggested is in fact the most apt. A good deal of the apparent conflict in results from welfare state research would appear to be resolved once differing understandings of the dependent variable are recognized: i.e. whether this is taken as the amount of social welfare *expenditure* or as the extent and quality of social *rights* to welfare (cf. Korpi 1989).

[5] It may be noted that, while Skocpol invokes Mill directly, Rueschemeyer refers rather to Mill at one remove: that is, via Znaniecki's notion (1934) of 'analytic induction', which, however, Rueschemeyer would wish to see developed beyond its reliance on the Method of Agreement alone (1991: 36 n. 12). In the present context it is of particular interest that Znaniecki contrasts analytic induction with 'enumerative induction', based on probability theory, and asserts that, since the former is capable of providing *exhaustive* knowledge of the situation under study, the latter is rendered superfluous.

not actually misleading. At all events, Skocpol fails to take sufficient account of certain assumptions on which Mill's methods depend but which, as various critics have followed Mill in observing (e.g. Nichols 1986; Lieberson 1992), are assumptions rarely, if at all, defensible in social research. For example, Mill's logic presupposes that, in any analysis, *all* potential causal factors can be identified and included—that is, that there are no 'unmeasured variables'; and further that there is no multiple (or 'plural') causation, nor again any interaction among causal factors.[6]

At the same time, though, Skocpol *is* well enough aware that Mill's canons are designed to lead to causal propositions of a deterministic kind—and does not appear much disturbed by this fact (see also Skocpol 1984: 378). What, therefore, her argument would appear to come down to is this: that, in circumstances where there are too few cases for the satisfactory evaluation of probabilistic theories, deterministic ones may none the less be established. However, to accept this position, it should be noted, one must be ready to believe not just that the social world is indeed subject to deterministic theory rather than being inherently probabilistic. One must *further* believe that socio-historical *data* can be obtained that are of such a quality and completeness, that are so error-free, that a probabilistic approach is not even required for the purposes of relating these data to (deterministic) theory (cf. Lieberson 1992: 106–7; King *et al.* 1994: 59–60). This latter implication at least is one that, I suspect, would be found by most sociologists, on due reflection, to be far more daunting than the small *N* problem itself.[7]

Various attempts have been made to develop the logical analysis of relatively small numbers of cases so as to overcome some of the more obvious limitations of Mill's methods in the context of social research. Most notable in this connection is perhaps the technique of 'qualitative comparative analy-

[6] Mill presented his canons in book III of *A System of Logic*, which is entitled 'Of Induction'. They are first formulated in ch. viii, 'Of the Four Methods of Experimental Inquiry'. His treatment of the 'moral'—i.e. social—sciences is quite separate, coming in book VI, 'On the Logic of the Moral Sciences'. His views on the unsuitability in this context of methods of experimental induction are found chiefly in ch. vii. For illuminating commentary, see Ryan (1970). Skocpol's discussion of the problems of applying Mill's methods is very brief (1979: 36–40) and her dismissive response (1994: 338) to Lieberson (1992) indicates only that she has failed to grasp the force of his argument. Rueschemeyer gives no recognition to the powerful critiques that have been made of Znaniecki's analytic induction—classically, by W. S. Robinson (1951).

[7] It may be found surprising that such strong 'positivistic' commitments are taken up within the qualitative camp. However, I have in the preceding chapter made the point that Skocpol and other 'grand historical sociologists' are in effect compelled by their dependence on secondary works as their main empirical resource to adopt a distinctively positivistic attitude towards historiography and, specifically, the nature of historical 'facts'. Further, Burawoy has acutely observed that Skocpol's reliance on inductive logic likewise puts limits on the doubts that she can allow herself about just what the historical facts are. For Skocpol, he remarks (Burawoy 1989: 773), 'the facts have a certain obviousness that they don't for historians', and she pays little attention to the controversies that rage over them: 'She is forced into this blindness in order to get her induction machine off the ground.' It may be observed that a similar penchant for inductive and deterministic accounts is to be found among exponents of case studies at a microsociological level—or at all events among those following in the 'Chicago' or 'symbolic interactionist' tradition. See e.g. the very explicit statements made in this regard by H. S. Becker (1992: 212) and also the discussion later in this chapter.

sis' (QCA) proposed by Ragin (1987), which is based on Boolean algebra. This technique aims to alleviate the small N problem by allowing inferences to be drawn from the maximum number of comparisons that can be made, in terms of the presence or absence of attributes of interest, across the cases under analysis. And, at the same time, it does permit—indeed is primarily directed towards—the analysis of multiple causation and interaction effects. Thus, Ragin (1994b: 328) maintains that, while a regression exercise with, say, seven independent variables and only eighteen cases would be generally regarded as untrustworthy, QCA would make possible the examination of all 128 (i.e. 2^7) different combinations of the causal conditions involved: that is, would in fact enable the analyst to address a degree of causal complexity far beyond the reach of regression.

Given the nature of QCA, Ragin would then further argue, it allows the macrosociologist to combine analysis with holism in that the distinctive features of particular cases need never be lost sight of. However, while this may be so, it is still somewhat misleading for Ragin to represent QCA as being a *synthesis* of the case- and variable-oriented approaches, since, as he indeed recognizes (1994b: 305–6), QCA remains, no less than Mill's methods, entirely logical and non-statistical in character. And it does, therefore, still share with the latter the major disadvantages of being unable to make any allowance either for 'missing variables' or for error in the data used.

Moreover, with QCA these disadvantages combine with two other evident weaknesses of the technique: its requirement that all variables should be treated as merely two valued; and its high degree of sensitivity to the way in which each case is coded on each variable. Thus, where essentially continuous variables are involved, such as 'GNP per capita' or 'proportion of population over 65', these must be reduced (with, of course, much loss of information) to more or less arbitrary dichotomies; and all subsequent results will then be strongly dependent on the way in which particular cases are allocated. If, on account of error in the original data, or in its treatment, even a single case happens to be placed on the 'wrong' side of a dichotomy, the analysis could well have a quite different outcome to that which would have been reached in the absence of such error. In an application of QCA, it should be noted, the independent variables are simply shown to be causally relevant—or not; no assessment of the *relative strengths* of different effects or combinations of effects is, or can be, made.[8]

---

[8] As an illustration of the critical point here made, one may take the application of QCA reported by Kangas (1994) in the context of a comparative study of the quality of health insurance provision. Through reanalysis of the data given in table 14.2 of his paper, it is possible to show that the result Kangas achieves—that high-quality provision (as of 1950) is associated with strong Christian Democracy in combination with a unified bloc of bourgeois political parties, but not with the level of working-class mobilization—turns crucially on the coding on the dependent variable in a single, borderline case, that of Switzerland, and on the particular solutions that are adopted to problems of contradictory cases and of missing combinations of explanatory variables that regularly arise with QCA. With these problems being treated in a somewhat different but equally defensible way and Switzerland taken as having high-rather than low-quality provision, which would certainly seem arguable (see also

In sum, the fact that QCA remains a logical technique means that its results are far more exposed to major distortion, both by difficulties in the selection of independent variables (cf. Amenta and Poulsen 1994) and by the occurrence of error in data, than are results derived from statistical techniques. And whether, then, QCA does actually mark any significant advance in the treatment of the small N problem, as, for example, Skocpol has recently claimed (1994: 309), must remain open to very serious doubt.[9]

What, I would argue, it is above all else necessary to recognize here is that *au fond* the small N problem is not one of method at all but rather of data: more specifically, it is a problem of *insufficient information* relative to the complexity of the macrosociological questions that we seek to address. Thus, in so far as exponents of the case-oriented approach in effect choose to restrict themselves to small Ns, they are unlikely ever to avoid the difficulties of 'too many variables and not enough cases' or, as King, Keohane, and Verba (1994: 119) put it, 'more inferences than implications observed'—no matter what resorts to Millian logic, Boolean algebra, or other technical devices they may attempt. Conversely, what is vital to overcoming the small N problem is in principle easy to state, albeit in practice toilsome, even where possible, to achieve: that is, simply to increase the information that we have available for analysis.

One way in which this can sometimes be achieved is by exploiting more fully the experience of those nations (or other macrosocial units) for which we do have good data sources. Thus, in comparative welfare state research various investigators (e.g. O'Connor and Brym 1988; Korpi 1989; Pampel and Williamson 1989; Huber *et al.* 1993; O'Connell 1994) have by now taken up the lead given by econometricians and demographers and have 'pooled' data for the same set of nations for several different time points. Observations— and degrees of freedom—are in this way increased, and appropriate checks and corrections can be introduced into analyses in order to allow for the fact that the successive 'waves' of information thus acquired are not, of course, entirely new and independent (see e.g. Stimson 1985; Hicks 1994). Such a

---

Kangas 1991), then the result of the entire analysis changes very significantly. Now, in fact, all that matters is the strength of Christian Democracy, and the unity or fragmentation of bourgeois parties joins the level of working-class mobilization as a quite irrelevant factor. Kangas, I should make clear, is not unaware of the problem of QCA here demonstrated; the main purpose of his paper is to compare the results he obtains from QCA with those deriving from different analytical approaches to the same problem and data.

[9] Skocpol chiefly bases her claim on the work of Wickham-Crowley (1992). However, this author's applications of QCA reveal exactly the same difficulties as those found in the instance discussed in the previous note. Thus, his analysis of causal factors in peasant support for guerrilla movements in Latin America turns crucially on certain codings that, as he himself recognizes, are highly doubtful on account of data problems. Readers who enjoy Boolean algebra can work out for themselves what would happen to Wickham-Crowley's conclusions if (accepting his way of handling problems of contradictory cases and missing combinations of explanatory variables) just a few of these problematic codings were changed: if, say (see his table 12.1 (1992: 306)) positive rather than negative codes were given to Cuba (Las Villas) on factor B (agrarian disruption) and to Guatamala (Zacapa) on factor D (peasant linkage); or—yet more dramatically—if, in addition, positive codings on factor D were also given to Nicaragua (north-central rural and north-west towns).

pooling strategy can then be reckoned as a valuable resource for macrosociologists following a variable-oriented approach; and King, Keohane, and Verba (1994: 221–3) have recently suggested various analogous procedures that might profitably be followed in qualitative studies.

More important, though, for the variable- and case-oriented approaches alike, is to increase the number of units to which comparisons extend; and further (cf. Przeworski 1987) to widen their geographical and sociocultural range, so that the greater variation thus obtained in supposed causal factors can improve the chances of deciding between competing theories. This will often mean bringing Third World nations into the analysis, and problems of data quality, which must always be of central concern in comparative work, may on this account be accentuated (cf. Dogan 1994: 40–1). However, the challenge thus posed should not be shirked. Bradshaw and Wallace (1991: 166) have argued for the particular appropriateness of case studies in the Third World, since, they maintain, calls for rigorous quantitative research must be biased against poor nations that lack adequate data or even computers. While this view is clearly well intentioned, I would still regard it as quite wrong-headed. Either the assumption is being made that case studies are, in some mysterious way, immune to problems of the reliability and validity of data with which quantitative researchers have to struggle or else case studies are being recommended for Third World use as some kind of 'inferior good'. It would surely be, from all points of view, a better strategy for First World social scientists to seek to help their Third World colleagues to collect *whatever* kinds of data, and to undertake *whatever* kinds of analysis, are in fact demanded by the nature of the substantive problems that they wish to pursue.[10]

The 'Galton' Problem

The 'Galton' problem is named after the nineteenth-century British polymath, Francis Galton. In 1889 Galton famously criticized a pioneering comparative analysis by the anthropologist Edward Tylor. Tylor (1889) claimed to show complex correlations among economic and familial institutions across

---

[10] Lack of data quality, and especially in regard to cross-national comparability, does of course still often impose serious limitations on macrosociological studies, whatever the technical resources they may command. However, it can be said that this problem does now attract growing critical attention among those engaging in quantitative research. See, for example, in the case of research in social stratification and mobility, the issues taken up in Treiman (1975), Goldthorpe (1985), Ganzeboom, Luijkx, and Treiman (1989), Erikson and Goldthorpe (1992a: ch. 2; 1992b). In some contrast, advocates of historical case studies especially would appear to resort to double standards. Thus, one finds Rueschemeyer, Stephens, and Stephens (1992: 26) commenting, with good reason, on the problem of 'not always reliable information' in quantitative studies of capitalist development and democracy—but just one page after an encomium on the 'towering achievement' of Moore (1966). Why, one wonders, do they not consider in an equally critical way the question of the reliability, or even the very existence, of the evidence to which Moore appeals in support of his central thesis—for instance (see Chapter 1 above) as regards the social sources of the English Civil War?

a wide range of societies, past and present. These correlations he then sought to explain from what we would now think of as a functionalist standpoint. Galton (1889*b*), however, questioned the extent to which Tylor's observations were *independent* ones, and pointed out that 'institutional' correlations might arise not only under the pressure of functional exigencies, or through other processes operating *within* societies; they might also be the result of processes of cultural diffusion *among* societies.

The problem of distinguishing between processes of these two kinds has subsequently plagued cross-cultural anthropology (Naroll 1970; Hammel 1980), and it obviously arises in comparative macrosociology to no less a degree. Thus, to revert to the investigation of welfare state development, it would be rather implausible to suppose that this development has proceeded quite autonomously in each national case, and free of such external influence as might have been exerted by the examples of, say, Bismarckian social policy in the nineteenth century, or the Beveridge Plan for post-war Britain, or, more recently, the 'Scandinavian Model' (cf. Therborn 1993).

Moreover, the Galton problem could be regarded as potentially more damaging at the present time than ever before. Claims that the treatment of nations as independent units of analysis has been untenable ever since the emergence of a 'world system' in the seventeenth century (Hopkins 1987; Hopkins and Wallerstein 1981) or that there now exists 'a highly institutionalized world polity' (Meyer 1987: 42) might well be thought exaggerated. But it could hardly be denied that, by the late twentieth century, the independence of 'national' observations is likely to be compromised, and not merely by the acceleration and intensification of cultural diffusion but further through the quite purposive actions of a whole range of international or multinational political and economic organizations. In this way, as Przeworski (1987) has recognized, the threat is created that the small N and Galton problems run together, as we do indeed enter into a world in which $N = 1$.

Lack of independence in observations, as well as limits on their number, do then undoubtedly create serious difficulties for cross-national research. However, just as with the small N problem, what I would wish first of all to stress is that, while the difficulties in question may be most *apparent* with the variable-oriented approach, they are by no means restricted to it; the case-oriented approach enjoys no special immunity.

Thus, the assumption that nations can be treated as units of analysis, unrelated to each other in time and space, is one required by the logical methods of comparison that are favoured in case-oriented research no less than by statistical methods. And indeed where historical cases are involved, the Galton problem is then likely to be encountered in a particularly troublesome form. The scarcely disputable fact that situations and events occurring at one time tend to have been influenced by situations and events occurring earlier clearly breaches the assumption of the independence of cases—as built into Mill's or any other logical method—and in a way that is not easily remedied. Thus, for example, one finds that Skocpol, in her study of revolutions (1979: 23–4, 39), has obviously to recognize that the course of the Chinese revolution up to 1949 was in various ways influenced by events in Russia in 1917 and subsequently. But this recognition has then to be kept quite apart from her logical analyses of the factors that determine revolutionary success, which it threatens to compromise (cf. Burawoy 1989). In other words, the use of Mill's canons and of narrative accounts that crucially rely on temporality cannot be integrated, but have to be left to play separate, and ultimately incompatible, explanatory roles (see further Kiser and Hechter 1991: 12–13; Griffin 1992: 412–13; also Skocpol 1994: 338).

Despite this, the Galton problem has in fact met with only a rather limited appreciation—and response—among exponents of case-oriented research. McMichael (1990) has proposed a solution through what he calls 'incorporated comparisons', which is apparently intended to take over the insights, while avoiding the 'rigidity', of a world-system perspective. But, since he presents his approach as an 'interpretative' one that can proceed 'without recourse to formal methodological procedures or a formal theory' (1990: 388), it is not easy to evaluate (nor, I would have to say, to understand). Another reaction is that of Sztompka (1988), which, however, is less an attempt to grapple with the Galton problem than a capitulation to it, and one that might be seen as somewhat opportunistic. The severity of the problem in the modern world, Sztompka maintains, is such that the whole agenda of comparative macrosociology needs to be changed—towards in fact a concentration on case studies! 'Globalization' has, in Sztompka's view, already made societal homogeneity and uniformity the norm. Thus, the central aim should no longer be to establish cross-national similarities or regularities of variation, using 'hard', quantitative techniques; rather, comparative work should now focus on the description and interpretation of 'enclaves of uniqueness'—that is, those deviant cases that stand out against globalization—and, for this purpose, should follow a 'soft', qualitative approach. Sztompka does not tell us just how such enclaves of uniqueness are to be identified in the absence of systematic comparison. But, in any event, in arguing as he does, as if an extreme version of the 'convergence thesis' had in fact been realized, he takes up a position that is well beyond the empirical evidence.

In addressing the Galton problem more pertinently, there are, I would suggest, two main points that need to be recognized. First, it is not so pervasive a problem as Sztompka and others (e.g. Scheuch 1989; Allardt 1990) would have us suppose. It is perhaps most regularly encountered in the comparative study of *public policy*, and especially of economic and social policy, for the pressures directly exerted by both international organizations and internationalized economies may alone bring about a high degree of uniformity of policy among nation states, quite apart from any diffusion of values and beliefs (Schmitter 1991). At the same time, though, it is not difficult to point to other areas of comparative research in which the Galton problem is far less apparent.

Consider, for example, recent research into class inequalities in educational attainment. This has revealed that in most modern societies such inequalities display a rather remarkable persistence over time (Shavit and Blossfeld 1993); but also that variation in the detailed pattern of inequality from society to society stems largely from differences in national educational institutions, which would seem endowed with substantial autonomy. Thus, even though governments—prompted, say, by international economic competition or 'world-system ideology' (cf. Ramirez and Boli 1987)—may have engaged in essentially similar programmes of educational expansion and reform, the processes of social selection that are distinctive to their indigenous institutions have proved hard to eradicate (see esp. Müller and Karle 1993; Ishida *et al.* 1995; Shavit and Müller 1998). Here, then, evidence of 'globalization' or convergence is, to say the least, not conspicuous.[11]

Secondly, it should be understood that, even where clearly present, the Galton problem does not necessarily preclude comparative analysis of a systematic kind. If, in a comparative study, national observations are known not to be independent, for whatever reason, it may still be possible to proceed by incorporating the processes that create this situation as an element in the analysis. That is, in the language of the variable-oriented approach, one can seek to 'model' interdependence itself, as in fact demographers and statistically minded geographers have been doing for some time (see e.g. Berry 1970; cf. Przeworski 1987). In the context of welfare state research, a notable pioneering contribution in this regard is that of Usui (1994). In a study of state-sponsored social insurance policies in a sample of sixty nations, Usui applies techniques of event history analysis in order to investigate how the development of these policies was influenced not only by 'domestic' factors but further by the establishment of the International Labor Office in 1919, and by its subsequent worldwide activities.

The further large potential of attempts at thus modelling interdependence may be brought out by reference to the recent work of Castles and others (Castles 1993*b*), who have introduced into comparative policy research the idea of 'families of nations'. Instead of attention centring on nations as 'unattached singles', they argue, more account should be taken of the affinities that exist among groupings of nations, as a result of shared histories and cultural traditions. Castles has in fact suggested (1993*a*: pp. xv–xvi) that recognition of such affinities may indicate the 'outer limits' of the Przeworski–Teune programme of replacing the proper names of nations with

[11] Even in public policy research the importance of diffusion and also of international economic or political pressure can be exaggerated. As regards the development of welfare state institutions, see, for example, Flora and Alber (1981), Garrett and Lange (1991), and Huber, Ragin, and Stephens (1993). For an insightful review of the recurrent problems of diffusionist theory itself, and in an area of prime application—fertility studies—see Kreager (1993). Sociological fashion as well as real world developments would seem to play a large part in current writing on 'globalization'. It is not long since the emphasis was rather on the 'non-exportability' of institutions—for example, of those of the 'Westminster model' to the new nations of the former British Empire or of Soviet institutions to the satellite nations of the USSR. Recall discussion of Stalin's comments about 'saddling cows'.

the names of variables, for policy similarities and differences among nations 'may be attributable as much to history and culture and their transmission and diffusion amongst nations as to the immediate impact of the economic, political and social variables that figure almost exclusively in the contemporary public policy literature'. And, Castles believes, the former kinds of effect are difficult to accommodate within the 'prevailing intellectual paradigm', as represented by the variable-oriented approach.

Now, as regards his substantive point on the importance of historically formed cultural patterns that transcend national boundaries, Castles may well be right. And, as will be apparent later, I share his concern with determining just where the theoretical limits of macrosociology, in whatever style it may be conducted, must in the end be drawn. But I do not see why the variables that replace the names of nations in quantitative analyses of comparative public policy need be *only* variables thought likely to have an 'immediate impact'; nor why one cannot, in principle at least, also include variables that do indeed seek to capture nations' historical affinities and the longer-term influences that derive from them. Indeed, I would argue that to attempt to do precisely this is the obvious way to explore further the idea of families of nations. In other words, there seems no reason why the insights provided by Castles and his associates should not serve as the starting point for appropriate quantitative analyses that would enable us to form more reliable judgements on what is, after all, crucially at issue: that is, the *relative importance*, in regard to policy developments and repertoires, of inter- as opposed to intra-societal, and of 'historical' as opposed to 'contemporary' effects.[12]

In sum, we should not be led into believing that claims regarding globalization or the existence of a world system or of families of nations necessitate some quite radical transformation of cross-national comparative macrosociology, and least of all one that would entail its restriction to case studies. In dealing with the Galton problem—where there are good grounds for supposing that it does indeed exist—the variable-oriented approach at all events has resources that are in fact only beginning to be exploited.

The Black-Box Problem

The black-box problem, even more than the small N or Galton problems, has been linked with the variable-oriented approach (see e.g. Rueschemeyer 1991: 26; Abbott 1992a: 54–62). A quantitative analysis may be undertaken which is successful in 'accounting for' a significant part of the variation in the phenomenon of interest—let us say, the sizes of welfare states. But such an analysis, it can be objected, still tells us rather little about just what is going on at

---

[12] Several contributors to the collection edited by Castles do in fact make at least implicit moves in the direction suggested. See in particular Busch (1993) on differences in anti-inflation policies and Schmidt (1993) on differences in male and female workforce participation rates and their determinants.

the level of the social processes and action that underlie, as it were, the inter-play of the variables that have been distinguished. We know the 'inputs' to the analysis and we know the 'outputs' from it; but we do not know much about why it should be that, within the black box of the statistical model that is applied, the one is transformed into the other. The problem is, of course, mitigated if 'intervening' variables are also included in the analysis, so as to give it a more finely grained character; and further, if both independent and intervening variables are chosen on theoretical grounds, so that certain causal processes may at least be implied. None the less, it can still be maintained that the black-box problem is seriously addressed only to the extent that such processes are spelt out quite explicitly, so as to provide a 'causally adequate' account of the actual *generation* of the regularities that are empirically demon-strated (see further Chapters 5 and 7 below).

The black-box problem, thus understood, has been seized upon by expo-nents of case studies in order to make the claim that the results of quantita-tive analyses must in effect be *dependent upon* case studies for their interpretation. Thus, Huber, Ragin, and Stephens (1993) have argued that the problem of conflicting explanations of the growth of welfare states can be solved only through a 'dialogue' between variable- and case-oriented research, and that it is case studies that must play the crucial part in identifying 'actual historical causal forces'. Likewise, Rueschemeyer (1991: 28; see also Rueschemeyer *et al.* 1992: ch. 2) has maintained, with reference to compara-tive research into capitalist development and democracy, that in this area the tradition of historical case studies is 'far richer in theoretical argument and analysis' than is that of quantitative work. Rueschemeyer accepts that quan-titative studies have established a clear positive association between capital-ist development and democracy; but, he is convinced, the 'key to the black box' that mediates this association will be found only in theory inspired by case studies and, especially, in 'explanatory ideas grappling with historical sequences'.

Again, however, I would wish to call into question the privileged status that is thus accorded to the case-oriented approach. To begin with, it should be recognized that while, just as with the small N and Galton problems, the black-box problem may be most apparent in quantitative work, it does in fact arise equally with the case-oriented approach where logical methods of com-parison are applied. Contrary to what Rueschemeyer suggests (1991: 32–3), logical methods too can establish only empirical regularities that may, at most, point to causal relations: they do not, in themselves, provide an account of the actual *processes* involved (cf. Burawoy 1989). And if, to this end, 'analytical induction' is accompanied by some narrative of historical sequences, then this, for reasons earlier noted, cannot be part of the logical method itself but only in fact a rather awkward appendage to it.

I would, furthermore, argue that the *theoretical* achievement of case studies is, in any event, a good deal less impressive than the authors cited above attempt to make out. Where the unity of cases is preserved—where cases are studied holistically, rather than being decomposed into variables—it is indeed possible, at least in principle, to provide detailed descriptions of 'what happened' in each case, and with due regard for the specific contextual features involved. But to have a narrative account of a sequence of historical events is *not* the same thing as having a theoretical account, even if one accepts—as I would be ready to do—that a historical narrative can itself constitute a form of explanation.[13] Most crucially, perhaps, such a narrative need not extend beyond the particular instance to which it is applied, or comparative narratives beyond the set of cases compared (cf. Skocpol and Somers 1980: 195). In contrast, a theoretical account must have *some* claim to generality. The explanation it provides of what is going on within the black box of a statistical or of a logical analysis is not one that is simply 'extracted' from the actual events involved in the instances covered by the analysis, but one that is, rather, derived from a theory that could, indeed should, apply to *other* instances falling within its intended scope or domain.

It might, of course, be suggested, and I would find it unexceptionable, that specific narratives may serve as a valuable resource for theory development: that is, by prompting attempts to conceive of some more general ideas that would allow the accounts given in different cases to be fitted into a deductive structure of argument. In other words, detailed case studies could play a *heuristic* role in the 'context of discovery', prior to the testing of any resulting theory against further, independent cases in the 'context of validation'. However, the distinction here involved is one that proponents of the case-oriented approach appear to find uncongenial, and that Rueschemeyer, for example (1991: 32–3; see also Rueschemeyer *et al*. 1992: 36; Skocpol 1994: 330), flatly rejects. The view that seems rather to be favoured is that the process of theory development should be advanced by successive inductions from particular cases—so that it becomes in effect essentially *merged with* the process of theory testing. The matching of developing theory against new inductions and its modification where it is found not to hold go on as one, seamless activity.

It is, however, in just this regard that the case for case studies becomes least convincing. The crucial point is that, if a theory is formed in such an essentially inductive way—without, so to speak, any deductive backbone—then it is hard to see how it can be genuinely tested at all. As it stands, such a theory does no more than recapitulate observations; and it is, moreover, difficult to know exactly how it would be properly extended beyond the particular circumstances from which it has been obtained so that an independent test might be attempted. Or, to put the matter the other way around, if a theory amounts to no more than an assemblage of inductions, the possibilities for

---

[13] I have in mind here the various arguments that have been advanced on the possibility of historical explanation being achieved without reference to general theories through the use of narratives that show how specific events form part of 'continuous series' (Oakeshott 1933), have 'followability' (W. B. Gallie 1964), are 'colligated' within a 'continuing process' (Walsh 1974), or are otherwise 'internally' rather than 'externally' connected. For a valuable brief review, see Dray (1993).

'saving' or 'patching' it in the face of contrary evidence are virtually unlimited. Generality can be claimed for so long as such a theory appears to fit the cases to which it is applied; but when it fails to fit, it can then be maintained that 'causal homogeneity' no longer holds, and that a somewhat different theory is required; and, in all of this, analysts can congratulate themselves on their 'sensitivity to context'![14]

However, the arbitrary delimitation of the scope of a theory—that is, a delimitation that the theory does not itself provide for—is an evident weakness. Thus, in the context of welfare state research, Korpi (1989: 324) has critically remarked that theories of 'state autonomy', as advanced by Skocpol and others (e.g. Orloff and Skocpol 1984; Weir and Skocpol 1985) on the basis of qualitative case studies, 'leave ample room for flexible *ad hoc* explanation', and has urged the need for such theories to be formulated in a way that would expose them to more stringent empirical critique. And yet more prominently, the charge of arbitrariness has been levelled against Skocpol's treatment of the Iranian revolution (1982), when taken in relation to her previous analyses (1979) of the French, Russian, and Chinese revolutions (Nichols 1986; Burawoy 1989; Kiser and Hechter 1991), since in the Iranian case a significant, yet seemingly quite *ad hoc*, theoretical shift is introduced: that is, popular urban demonstrations become a 'functional substitute' for peasant revolts and guerrilla activity (cf. Skocpol 1994: 313–14).

Finally in this connection, I would also question whether the account offered by Rueschemeyer, Stephens, and Stephens (1992) of the association between capitalist development and democracy does in fact bear out their contention that case studies afford a privileged ground for the development of theory capable of overcoming the black-box problem. Their account fails in this respect, I would suggest, precisely because of the degree to which the analysis of their cases leads them to hedge about their central argument on power struggles among social classes with exceptions and qualifications— relating to cross-national differences in the social construction of class interests, in the possibilities for class alliances, in the form of civil society, in the role of the state, in the impact of transnational relations, and so on (1992: esp. 269–81). Not only does the ratio of explaining to 'explaining away' thus seem rather low, but, further, it is notable that, when these authors come to address the key issue of the 'generalizability' of their theory beyond the cases they have examined (1992: 285)—to, say, east Asian or east-central European nations of the present day—what they have to offer is not a series of derived

---

[14] Again a close parallel can be noted with case studies oriented towards microsociological issues. Even a sympathetic commentator (Hammersley 1989: chs. 7, 8) is forced to acknowledge that problems of theory testing are acute with both 'analytic induction' and with the no less inductive 'grounded theory' (Glaser and Strauss 1967) to which it seems more common for case analysts working at a micro-level to appeal (see further Chapter 4). It is of interest that in a recent work Ragin (1994a: 94) should acknowledge that 'analytic induction'—of which his own QCA is in effect a systematization—is to be seen as primarily concerned with 'the degree to which the image of the research subject has been refined, sharpened, and elaborated in response to both confirming and disconfirming evidence'; or, that is, with no more than *conceptualization.*

hypotheses that would be testable against such new cases but yet more discussion of additional factors to be considered.[15] Now it may be that the awareness that Rueschemeyer and his colleagues here display of complexity and causal heterogeneity is empirically warranted. But, if so, what they have provided is a demonstration of the inherent difficulty of forming a theory of the relationship between capitalist development and democracy, and not that theory itself.

For macrosociologists seeking to treat black-box problems more effectively, I would then argue, case studies, whether historical or otherwise, have no distinctive value, and an absorption in their specificities may indeed divert attention away from what is in fact crucially required: that is, theory that is as general as it is possible to make it. As Kiser and Hechter (1991) have maintained, in a strong critique of the quality of theory in comparative historical sociology, to illuminate the black boxes represented by mere empirical regularities, we need more than just a redescription of the latter within a theoretical (sc. conceptual) framework that appears indefinitely modifiable as our database expands. Rather, theory must be sought that is general in that it permits the specification of causal processes that, if operative, would be capable of producing the regularities in question *and* would have a range of *further* implications of at least a potentially observable kind (see further Chapter 7). To the extent that theory is general in this sense, it can then claim both greater explanatory power, which theory must always seek, and greater openness to empirical test, which it must never evade.[16]

I would, moreover, add that such a concern with generality in theory might help macrosociologists to see the relevance of history to their enterprise in a different, and, I believe, more appropriate, way to that which appears currently in mode among exponents of the case-oriented approach. Instead of a recourse to history being regarded as essential to the development of theory, it might be better understood as marking the *limits of* theory: that is, the point at which what is causally important in regard to certain empirical findings is recognized not in recurrent social situations and processes that might be the subject of theory but rather in contingencies, distinctive conjunctures of events or other singularities that theory cannot comprehend.

---

[15] I would, as it happens, entirely agree with the *substantive* criticisms that Rueschemeyer and his colleagues make of earlier efforts at explaining the association between capitalism and democracy—that is, via 'modernization' theory. But I would totally disagree that it should be seen as a fault of this, or of any other theory, that it is insufficiently grounded in prior research or is indeed 'pure conjecture' (Rueschemeyer *et al.* 1992: 29; cf. Goldthorpe 1992*b*). Theories must be judged not by their empirical origins but by their empirical implications. And what better epitaph could a theory possibly hope for than that it was bold enough to provoke research and clear enough to be proved wrong by it?

[16] The responses to Kiser and Hechter of which I am aware are those of Quadagno and Knapp (1992), Skocpol (1994), and Somers (1998). The two former seem to me to concede far more than they effectively contest. That is, their authors show themselves ready to accept a much less demanding idea of theory than that of Kiser and Hechter and, in turn, the implication that comparative historical sociologists are not interested in testing theories in the way Kiser and Hechter would require. On Somers's paper, see my comment in Chapter 1 n. 13 above.

Since the foregoing is put somewhat abstractly, I may try to illustrate with reference to the primarily quantitative work that I have undertaken with Robert Erikson on comparative social mobility (Erikson and Goldthorpe 1992*a*). Perhaps the most notable finding of this work was that when inter-generational class mobility was considered net of all structural influences—or, that is, as 'social fluidity'—rates and patterns showed high stability over time within nations and, further, a large measure of similarity across nations. Such a degree of *in*variance clearly underlines the need for general theory. For hypotheses on the causal processes capable of producing temporal constancy and cross-national commonality of the kind that our quantitative analyses revealed will have to be derived from a theory of considerable scope: that is, from a theory which is precisely *not* 'sensitive to context'—unlike the theories of national 'exceptionalism' in regard to mobility that our results called into doubt—but applicable to societal contexts widely separated over both time and space. And in this respect, I should say, Erikson and I were able to make only a very modest beginning (on which, however, I attempt to build in Chapter 11 below).[17]

We also found, though, that, in so far as variation in social fluidity *did* occur cross-nationally, we could not account for it, to any large extent, in terms of other generalizable attributes of societies, in the way that the Przeworski–Teune programme would require. Our analyses pointed here to the far greater importance of historically formed cultural or institutional features or political circumstances that could not be expressed as variable values except in a quite artificial way. For example, *levels* of social fluidity were not highly responsive to the overall degree of educational inequality within nations, but *patterns* of fluidity did often reflect the distinctive, institutionally shaped character of such inequality in particular nations, such as Germany or Japan. Or again, fluidity was affected less by the presence of a state socialist regime *per se* than by the significantly differing policies actually pursued by the Polish, Hungarian, or Czechoslovak regimes on such matters as the collectivization of agriculture or the recruitment of the intelligentsia. In such instances, then, it seemed to us that the retention of proper names and adjectives in our explanatory accounts was as unavoidable as it was desirable, and that little was to be gained in seeking to bring such historically specific effects within the scope of theory of any kind.

In sum, black-box problems—essentially problems of 'making sense' of empirical findings—are unlikely to be alleviated by comparative macrosoci-

[17] While it is surely disappointing, it should not be thought a disgrace for sociologists to admit that they have not been able to develop a theory that will adequately account for their empirical findings. This is so because one cannot expect effective theory, in the sense I intend, to be produced at will, nor by following specified procedures or guidelines—as would appear the case with 'grounded theory'. I do not find it accidental that it is in case-oriented, qualitative sociology that the rather absurd use of 'theorize' as a *transitive* verb has become most common: i.e. it can, apparently, be demanded that a topic be 'theorized' in the same way as it can be demanded that the kitchen be cleaned or the shopping brought home. This confirms me in my belief that, typically, no more than (re)conceptualization is in fact involved.

ologists striving in effect to transcend the distinction between theory and history, for such attempts tend to lead merely to a weakening of our understanding of theory and of historicity alike, and in turn to a blurring of crucial differences in the nature of theoretical and historical explanations. A strategy of greater long-term promise would be to continue to pursue sociological theory that amounts to more than just the elaboration of concepts and aspires to generality in the sense indicated above, but at the same time to show due modesty in accepting that, for any kind of macrosociology, and no matter how theoretically accomplished it may eventually become, 'history' will always remain as a necessary residual category.[18] It may, furthermore, be a consequence of such a strategy that certain phenomena that macrosociologists have sought to study, and including, perhaps, revolutions or other kinds of 'regime transition', turn out to be ones on which theory can give relatively little cognitive grasp at all. That is to say, while it may be of interest to write the comparative history of these phenomena—their history as viewed within a common conceptual framework—they appear just too few, too interdependent, and too causally heterogeneous for anything of much use to be said in theoretical terms. In instances where the indications accumulate that this is indeed the case, then the course of wisdom must surely be to accept the situation with good grace. Macrosociologists will still be left with a very great deal to do, and there have not, after all, ever been any guarantees that a sociology of everything should be possible.

I have argued that, while a divergence can certainly be observed between variable-oriented and case-oriented approaches to comparative macrosociology, to concentrate attention on this divergence, or even on ways of overcoming it, does not provide the best focus for understanding and addressing major methodological issues that are encountered in this field. As King, Keohane, and Verba have emphasized (1994: ch. 1), we may distinguish between quantitative and qualitative *styles* of research in the social sciences, but each must still strive to meet the exigencies of the same underlying 'logic of inference' and contend with the problems to which this common requirement gives rise. Through an examination of three such problems, recurrent

[18] In other words (cf. Chapter 2), I would still see force in the nomothetic/idiographic distinction as applied to sociology and history—if, that is, it is understood as referring essentially to the direction of intellectual effort (and without any implication either that sociological theory must be entirely 'universal' or that historiography must avoid all general concepts). Claims that comparative historical studies applying some form of 'analytic induction' are capable of overcoming this distinction (e.g. Zaret 1978: 118; Skocpol 1979: 33–7) seem to me, for reasons given above, not to be borne out on the evidence of these studies themselves. And I would take leave to doubt that the further attempt now apparently being made via 'sociological narrativism' (see e.g. Griffin 1992; Quadagno and Knapp 1992) is any more likely to succeed. While I would certainly sympathize with efforts such as those of Abbott (1992a,b) to establish analogues between narrative accounts and causal explanations, there are still basic differences to be recognized among the kinds of narrative that may be deployed. For example, one may understand rational choice theory in terms of narratives (see further Chapter 6)—but ones which, in contrast to historical narratives, are generalized rather than specific, set in analytic rather than real time, and implicative rather than conjunctive in their structure.

within comparative macrosociology, I have tried to show how each can, and does, occur in the context of variable-oriented and case-oriented work alike. These problems are not in fact ones on which alternatives in research styles have much bearing, but are of a more elementary, which is not to say easier, kind. Thus, the small N problem is essentially a problem of insufficient information on which to base analyses—or, that is, on which to draw in making inferences; and it can be resolved, or mitigated, only by more extensive data collection, aided by techniques for exploiting to the full the information that is at any time available. The Galton problem, where it arises, is one of observations lacking a property—independence—that we would like to assume in our analyses; and, to the extent that interdependence among our units of observation is simply a feature of the way the world is, we must deal with this situation by seeking to represent the interdependence (or, better, the processes creating it) within our analyses, so that we cannot only recognize its presence but also assess its importance. And, finally, the black-box problem is one of how we move from descriptive to causal inferences or, that is, go beyond our empirical findings and the regularities they allow us to establish to an understanding of how these regularities are generated. Here what is crucial is to construct theory in a way that maximizes both its explanatory power and its openness to test against further empirical research—and that also allows us to see as clearly as possible where the limits to theoretical explanation are reached.

In this chapter, criticism has been more often directed against case-oriented than against variable-oriented research. This is not an expression of hostility on my part to qualitative research as such, whether in macrosociology or more generally, and especially not to such research of a historical character. Rather, it reflects my view that it is proponents of the variable-oriented approach who have, at all events, better appreciated and responded to the problems I have considered, while proponents of the case-oriented approach have sometimes failed to recognize that they too need to address these problems or, as I suggested at the start, have made claims to the effect that they dispose of special and privileged means of bypassing or overcoming them. My critical comments have then been chiefly directed against such claims. I have sought to show that they do not, at least as so far presented, have any very secure basis, and that, if they are to be maintained, they will need to be demonstrated far more cogently than hitherto. I would doubt if this will prove possible, since I see no reason at all to believe in such special and privileged means. The small N, Galton, and black-box problems pertain to quite basic issues that are likely to arise in any instance of comparative macrosociological research, whatever the style in which it is conducted. Whether investigators choose to work quantitatively or qualitatively, with variables or with cases, the inherent logic of these issues remains the same, and so too, therefore, will that of any solutions that may be achieved.

4

Sociological Ethnography Today:
Problems and Possibilities

I START in this chapter from the rather curious state that has now been reached in the debate within sociology between proponents of ethnographic and of survey-based research—a debate that represents one expression of larger and yet more complex oppositions between qualitative and quantitative or 'case-oriented' and 'variable-oriented' styles of data collection and analysis.[1]

Sociologists favouring ethnographic research, whether as actual practitioners or on more general grounds, were prominent in the so-called reaction against positivism of the late 1960s and 1970s, when survey methodology and its supposed philosophical foundations became a prime focus of criticism. In the face of this attack, the response of sociologists engaging in survey research, or reliant on the secondary analysis of its results, could only be described as muted. Few, it seems, were able to raise sufficient motivation to offer any systematic reply. The effort made in this respect by Marsh (1982) is distinguished not just by its quality but also by its rarity. However, what is today striking is the degree to which, despite the rather one-sided nature of the debate, the continuing contributions from supporters of ethnography have changed in their tone. Although 'positivist' still tends to serve as an all-purpose pejorative qualifier, calls for the outright rejection of the survey method are far less frequently heard and more common are pleas—albeit

This chapter has not been published previously. For advice, information, and comments on an earlier draft, I am indebted to Richard Breen, Robert Erikson, Roger Goodman, Peter Hedström, Janne Jonsson, Jennifer Platt, Federico Varese, and, especially, Martyn Hammersley and Wout Ultee.

[1] Ethnographic research is essentially qualitative and almost all ethnographies could be counted as case studies, while survey research can scarcely avoid being quantitative and variable oriented in some degree. However, there are, of course, various other qualitative methods than ethnography, and case studies may be based on a variety of qualitative and quantitative methods. At the same time, quantitative methods can also be applied in research that is neither case oriented nor survey based, as, say, in that which utilizes official statistical data that are collected via censuses or other legally enforced recording or registration procedures. I should further make it clear that in this chapter, as its title indicates, the main focus of my attention is on ethnographic research *in the context of sociology* rather than social anthropology, following the lines of demarcation that have been conventionally, if somewhat arbitrarily, drawn between these disciplines: i.e. I concentrate on ethnographic research as conducted within relatively large-scale and technologically and economically advanced societies.

made on differing grounds—for ethnography to be accepted *as an essential complement to survey research* (see e.g. Orum *et al.* 1991; Hammersley 1992; Katz 1997; Burawoy 1998). Such arguments indeed often appear to be of an essentially defensive kind, being linked to complaints that in contemporary sociology ethnographic work is unduly neglected or undervalued on account of the dominance that survey research has come to exert. But in some instances too they go together with a recognition that it is the scientific credentials of ethnography that are now increasingly in question—even to the extent that a 'crisis' of ethnography exists (e.g. Hammersley 1991: 15; Snow and Morrill 1993; Vidich and Lyman 1994: 38–43).

How, then, has this situation come about? Why is it that even though proponents of survey-based research did not for the most part bother to respond to radical criticism of their methodology, the survey tradition remains strong, both within sociology and social research more generally, while it is at the present time among the ethnographers that methodological concerns and uncertainties are most apparent?

One explanation for the continuing importance of survey research that has been offered, and that has been underwritten by at least some supporters of ethnography, is of an entirely 'external' kind. Survey research, it is argued, owes its success to the fact that it is an instrument of power or must at all events collude with power: 'power is its precondition' (Burawoy 1998: 16). This is so not only because such research requires substantial resources of a kind likely to be available only to government, big business, or major foundations. In addition, knowledge deriving from survey methodology is knowledge that is formed—in the name of objectivity—from outside and above the 'lifeworld' of those studied, and that is in turn aimed essentially at *control*. Moreover, it is held, from the 'hegemonic' position that they thus enjoy, the proponents of survey research can seek to impose their standards on other sociologists, ethnographers in particular, and to subject the work of the latter to 'inappropriate criticism' (Burawoy 1998: 15; see also Stoecker 1991). Ethnography is thus disfavoured and threatened; none the less, it still serves as the basis of an alternative, but equally valid, paradigm of social enquiry to that represented by survey research. Since ethnographers usually operate individually, in a 'craft' rather than a 'bureaucratic' mode, they need only modest resources and can thus avoid becoming compromised by power. Moreover, by entering directly into the lifeworld of their subjects, they seek to produce knowledge for the purposes not of control but rather of empathetic understanding, and especially so in the case of marginal, stigmatized, dispossessed, or otherwise subordinate and powerless groups.[2]

Such an account may have an appealing rhetoric but it does not stand up to serious examination. It is, of course, true that governments and other powerful agencies do routinely use survey research in order to collect information

---

[2] Élite groups may also be studied, but in this case ethnography is then often directed to the purposes, as Katz (1997: 405) puts it, of 'debunking charisma' and 'deconstructing deference'.

in the course of forming, implementing, and monitoring their policies. This could indeed be taken as good evidence that survey research *works*—that it, is a cost-effective way of producing information of a sufficiently reliable and valid kind to allow useful analyses of social phenomena to be made. However, it is also the case that many sociologists, and of widely differing political commitments, from neo–Conservatives through to Marxists, undertake survey research on a quite independent basis; and, further, that many more reanalyse the data-sets of 'official' surveys for their own purposes, often very different from those for which the surveys were initially designed, and then present new results and interpretations that may be highly uncongenial to official positions. A less simplistic explanation both of the success of survey research and of the current difficulties of ethnography would therefore appear to be needed, and one that is able to give due attention to 'internal' as well as to 'external' factors.

The argument that I wish to advance begins with the claim that the methods of enquiry that are used across the natural and the social sciences alike are informed by what might loosely be called a common 'logic of inference'—a logic of relating evidence and argument. The application of this logic presupposes that a world exists independently of our ideas about it, and that, in engaging in scientific enquiry, we aim to obtain information, or data, about this world that we can then take as a basis for inferences that extend *beyond* the data to hand, whether in a descriptive or an explanatory mode. This logic of inference can never be definitively codified: it has, rather, to be adapted and elaborated specifically in relation to different methodologies that are appropriate to different subject-matter areas and their problems. This work has been achieved with greatest coherence and refinement in the case of experimental methods, especially in the natural sciences. But, since the end of the nineteenth century, significant advances have also been made, of importance to both the natural and the social sciences, in the methodology of the statistical analysis of observational data. And the possibility of further developments is of course entirely open.[3]

The logic of inference, it must be stressed, does not guarantee that the knowledge that we acquire with its aid is certain. All processes of inference are in fact inherently *un*certain, on account both of inadequacies in data and of human tendencies towards error and bias. Recognition of the logic of inference serves rather to ensure that, in the application of any particular method,

[3] This position, it may be added, is highly consistent with the frequently made argument that it is not the task of philosophers of science to prescribe methodology for practitioners but rather to reconstruct, and perhaps refine and elaborate, the logic that the latter in fact use. The idea of a single logic of inference informing all scientific methods and in turn the case for its application in qualitative, just as in quantitative, work in the social sciences are cogently set out in King, Keohane, and Verba (1994: esp. ch. 1), to which I am indebted. If underwriting the position that these authors adopt is to be regarded as the *differentia specifica* of a positivist, then I would be happy to be classified as one, and also pleased that this much-abused term had at last been given some clear meaning in sociological debate. It should, though, be noted that accepting the idea of a single logic of inference does *not* imply accepting the natural science 'experimental model' of scientific enquiry, *nor* the 'covering-law' model of scientific explanation, *nor* the possibility of a 'neutral observational language'—each of which tenets has been taken as the infallible mark of Cain.

as explicit an understanding as possible exists of the *grounds* on which inferences are made and conclusions reached and in turn, therefore, of the grounds
on which these inferences and conclusions *may be subject to rational criticism.*
It is, in other words, by reference to this logic that questions can be raised
and debated of just how scientific claims follow from the evidence that is presented in their support and of what further evidence, were it to be adduced,
would result in these claims coming to be seen as mistaken. In sum, one could
say, it is the logic of inference that provides the basic rules according to which
the 'friendly-hostile co-operation' that Popper (1945/1966: ch. 23; 1994: esp.
ch. 3) regards as essential to scientific activity is carried on, and that enables
this activity to assume a social and public rather than merely a personal and
private character.

In outline, my argument will then be that, while both survey research and
ethnography began with at least an implicit commitment to the logic in question, this commitment has not been similarly sustained. Where problems in
survey research have been encountered by its practitioners, or have been
pointed out by critics, an effort has been made to overcome these problems
essentially by methodological refinements or innovations consistent with this
logic; and this effort I would see as being a key factor in the achievements of
survey research. In contrast, the history of ethnography, and especially its
recent history, must from this point of view appear as far more chequered.
Sociological ethnographers have responded on widely divergent lines to the
problems of method with which they have been confronted. Some—though
so far relatively few—have indeed been ready to accept that the logic of inference in ethnography can be no different from that which applies in survey
research or in the case of any other kind of scientific method, and have sought
to advance ethnographic procedures accordingly. Others, under the influence
of intellectual upheavals in social anthropology (see especially Clifford and
Marcus 1986; Clifford 1988) and of related postmodernist and other irrationalist fashions, have taken up a radically different position that in fact
entails relinquishing all social-scientific claims in favour of an understanding
of ethnography as simply 'writing'. The ethnographer aims not to *represent*
some independently existing lifeworld or culture but rather to give a fictive
account of a self-exploratory 'experience of the other', and one to which the
critical standards of art rather than of science must apply (cf. Gellner 1992).
Further, though, many sociological ethnographers—perhaps a majority—have
sought a 'third way', by pursuing which they would be able to avoid the
equally unacceptable extremes of either a capitulation to 'positivism' or the
abandonment of their scientific credentials. The appealing idea is that some
kind of alternative, non-positivist, version of social science might be formulated—characterized as 'critical', 'humanistic', 'reflexive', or whatever—that
would be able to claim parity of esteem with its positivist counterpart, and
that the practice of ethnography would then exemplify.[4]

---

[4] At the present time, 'reflexive' seems to be the favourite word to conjure with. It has,
however, to be said that what would be the distinctive features of a 'reflexive' sociology, at

What, however, I seek ultimately to show is that no such third way will prove viable, or, at all events, *not in so far as* the rejection of or departure from 'positivism' also implies an abandonment of the idea of a single logic of inference and leads to efforts to devise 'special' methods of enquiry and analysis that are believed to be in some way exempt from this logic. It is obviously open to ethnographers to secede from social science altogether—although they must then be ready to accept the various consequences of so doing.[5] But, if they wish to retain a place within social science, this cannot be entirely on terms of their own choosing. Rules of the game do exist, and, while failure to comply fully with them may be regarded as endemic, it is none the less important that the obligation always to try in principle to do so should be accepted.

In substantiating the argument that I have sketched out, I begin, in the second section of the chapter, by recalling an early confrontation between ethnographic and survey research, in which the methodological problems that have most seriously troubled ethnography, at least as conducted in the context of modern industrial societies, were first made apparent: that is, what I label generically as *problems of variation*. In the third and fourth sections I elaborate on these problems, and question attempts to deal with them that would seem to suppose that ethnography can in some way or other claim a special and privileged status. I suggest, rather, that solutions must be sought following the same basic logic as is applied in survey research. In the fifth section I start by noting criticisms made of survey research from the side of ethnography, and, in particular, in regard to what I label as *problems of context*. By in fact following though the logic of inference, survey researchers, I seek

---

the level of research and analytical procedures, remains desperately obscure. Thus, while Burawoy (1998) acknowledges the 'vagueness' of the idea in previous work (e.g. Bourdieu and Wacquant 1992), his attempts at greater clarity and specificity are scarcely impressive. Do we gain much in understanding just what a reflexive sociology would entail by being told that it 'enunciates the idea of *structuration*, which implies a reciprocal but asymmetrical constitution of local processes and extralocal forces—forces that can be economic, political or cultural, and more or less systematic' (Burawoy 1998: 14)? Likewise, Hammersley and Atkinson introduce the most recent edition of their text on ethnography (1995) by saying that 'The central theme of the book remains the importance of a reflexive approach'. But the few pages they devote to the idea of reflexivity (1995: 16–21) do little to show how the key tenets of proponents of this approach would differentiate them from many 'non-reflexive' sociologists (the present writer included) who would, for example, have no difficulty whatever in accepting that 'the orientations of researchers will be shaped by their socio-historical locations', or that 'behaviour and attitudes are often not stable across contexts and . . . the researcher may influence the context', or that 'data should not be taken at face value but treated as a field of inferences'. Moreover, when Hammersley and Atkinson come to treat actual issues of data collection and analysis, the idea of reflexivity, rather than being 'the central theme', seems more or less to disappear.

[5] One such consequence would obviously be that of relinquishing all claims on public resources devoted to social science. Furthermore, if the secession also involves a rejection of the very idea of science, and of associated ideas of rationality and truth, there would seem no grounds for, or point in, trying to argue the matter with the seceders. One cannot argue rationally with principled irrationalists; and those who hold that truth is merely 'political' (see e.g. Denzin 1997: 12) can have no complaints if they meet with a political response. Cf. the courageous remarks by Huber (1995) and also, from within sociological ethnography, by Hammersley (1999: 581).

to show, have produced a more effective response to these problems than seems often to be appreciated and have thus set an example that ethnographers might follow. However, there is, I recognize, one respect in which the criticism still carries real force, and especially in its degree of convergence with that from other sources. This concerns the neglect in much survey-based sociology of the social processes, or 'mechanisms', through which regularities demonstrated at the level of relations among variables are actually generated and sustained, and the failure to see that causal explanations of these regularities cannot themselves be given through the analysis of variables but have rather to refer to the action and interaction of individuals. In developing, but above all in *testing*, such explanatory accounts, I then conclude, an opportunity arises for a—methodologically enhanced—ethnography to make good its claim to be a vital part of the modern sociological enterprise and to engage in potentially highly revealing competition with survey-based research.

Surveys Versus Ethnographies: The Historical Origins

From the early nineteenth century onwards, as other European nations followed Britain into rapid industrialization, questions of poverty, labour relations, and, more generally, 'the condition of the working classes' seized the attention of humanitarians and moralists, social reformers, and politicians of all persuasions. At the same time, such questions also became a leading concern of social investigators, often private individuals but, increasingly, representatives of the state or other public bodies or of various voluntary associations. In Britain, from the 1830s, Royal Commissions and other forms of official inquiry became important agencies of research, alongside local 'philosophical' and 'statistical' societies. In continental Europe, the traditions of German *Universitätsstatistik* and of the French *enquête*, which dated back to the eighteenth century, were adapted to new circumstances and requirements. The character of the research thus undertaken was diverse, but, from the standpoint of the present, much could in fact be regarded as prototypical survey work. Information on a set of issues or topics was collected, on some more or less standard pattern, for relatively large numbers of individuals, and was then subjected to analysis, possibly though not necessarily numerical, before presentation. However, from the mid-nineteenth century a new method of research was developed, in part as an extension of, but in part also as a reaction against, the survey approach. This was the 'monographic' method of Frédéric Le Play and his followers, which, in retrospect, may be seen as sociological ethnography in one of its earliest manifestations (Zonabend 1992).

Le Play was trained and had worked as a metallurgist and mining engineer before becoming preoccupied with social problems and acquiring a detailed knowledge of the statistics of his day. He had little regard for 'philosophical' sociology, such as that of Comte, and believed that all science was founded on the close and sustained observation of the phenomena of interest. From this position, he was led to question various practices that were common in enquiries into working-class occupations or family life. For example, Le Play objected to the extent to which such enquiries tended to rely on information obtained from persons regarded as 'local authorities', such as civil servants, clergy, or doctors, rather than on information that was collected at first hand by appropriately trained investigators, either through the observation of workers or from interviews with them. Further, he maintained, only through such direct—and prolonged—contact with workers and their families could an adequate range and quality of information be acquired. It was important to know not only about workers' physical conditions of life, economic resources, family budgets, and so on, but also about their life histories and aspirations and their moral beliefs and values; and, in order to gain this more intimate knowledge in a reliable way, it was essential, Le Play held, for investigators to secure the confidence of workers, to speak to them in their own language and idiom, and to 'enter into their minds' (Silver 1982: 41–75, 171–83).

In the first edition of his major work, *Les Ouvriers européens* (1855), Le Play presented thirty-six monographs on particular families, expanded in the second edition (1877–9) to fifty-seven, in relation to a two-way typology: type of worker by type of society. On this basis, he believed that he could generalize from the individual case studied to the category that it was taken to represent—and, in turn, elaborate an empirically grounded theory of the institutional differentiation of social systems as well as a normative theory of social order. This generalizing confidence shown by Le Play, and by others who supported him in the use of the monographic method, would appear to have owed much to the statistical sociology of Quetelet (see further Chapter 12 below). According to Quetelet (1835/1842), *l'homme type*, who could in fact be equated with *l'homme moyen*—the average individual within any category—was the proper focus of social-scientific attention. For in the characteristics of this individual could be seen displayed in their pure form the effects of all constant or systematically varying causes that were at work; whereas with other individuals the tendency of their characteristics to deviate from the average in accordance with the 'error law'—that is, the normal distribution—served to show that they resulted from a range of unconnected 'accidental' causes of no particular scientific interest. Even a single case, if truly typical in this statistical sense, could therefore be taken as carrying general significance (cf. Desrosières 1991; 1993. esp. ch. 7). However, when towards the end of the nineteenth century the monographic method became subject to increasingly frequent counter-attacks from proponents of survey research, it was on the issue of what might be called typological generalization that criticism focused.

By the time in question, Quetelet's 'statistics of the average' were being superseded by the 'statistics of variation' pioneered by Galton, for whom

averages were merely fictitious and variation the scientifically important
reality. And it was in turn problems of variation that increasingly concerned
survey researchers. This concern arose primarily out of their efforts to devise
ways of constructing 'representative samples' of populations, or, in effect, to
develop a logic of descriptive inference from part to whole, and thus to be
able to show that surveys, even if only 'partial investigations', could still
effectively substitute for complete censuses. At the same time, though, they
were led directly to challenge the adequacy in this respect of the typological
approach. Kiaer, the leading advocate of representative sampling, objected to
a reliance on typologies as a basis for social investigation essentially on the
grounds that they could not satisfactorily accommodate the variation in individual cases that was present in real life. Even if the rationale of the typologies that were formed was itself sound, Kiaer argued (1901), a reliable basis
for generalization still did not exist. This was because a concentration on
types neglected not only extreme cases that might fall altogether outside the
typologies used but further, and more seriously, all of the variation that
occurred *around* the types that were distinguished. Other, more detailed criticism of the work of Le Play and the Le Playistes then served to bring out that
problems of variation in fact arose *at two different levels*: that is, first, in regard
to the choice of the individual cases that were taken to represent a type and,
secondly, in regard to the generalizations that were made from a series of
instantiated types to the 'whole': that is, the national population or other collectivity of interest.

In choosing the actual subjects of their monographs, Le Play and his followers would appear to have had no very specific procedures. Le Play himself,
although objecting to the practice of using local authorities as sources of information, still largely depended upon them for advice on which families could
be seen as average and thus typical within one of his predefined categories.
Le Play regarded such authorities as embodying the accumulated knowledge
and wisdom of their communities; but there was little reason for sceptics to
accept this view. It was in fact argued against Le Play that his authorities could
well be biased, in particular in a conservative direction, and inclined to pick
out families accordingly: for example, ones whose members could be relied
on to express general acceptance of the *status quo* and emphasize solidarity
rather than conflict. Such criticisms gained support from the results of several
restudies that were made in localities and among groups of workers who had
been represented by one of Le Play's monographs. The restudies tended to
find less harmony in community and workplace relations and less satisfaction among workers than Le Play's accounts had indicated (Lazarsfeld 1961;
Goldfrank 1972; Silver 1982: 54–75). Finally, aside from the question of the
typicality or otherwise of the subjects of particular monographs, the issue
could also be raised, as it was for example by Halbwachs (1933), of whether
Le Play did not seriously underestimate the diversity in standards and styles
of living of workers associated with any one of his types, and to the point at
which their analytical value had to be called into doubt.

When seeking to generalize on the basis of their monographs, the Le Playistes then found that problems of variation were compounded. To begin with,
even supposing that their typological categories were well represented by their
monographs—that the latter did refer to 'average' cases—there was the
problem of estimating the numerical importance to be attached to each category. Le Play himself showed little interest in this matter. Some of his followers, however, believed that a solution could be found in the use of official
statistics, arguing that these could provide the essential information for
forming such categories—' les moyennes qui conduisent le monographe à son
type'[6]—while at the same time indicating their relative size. But the further
problem of the extent of variation around each type remained, so that it was
still unclear just how the monographic method could lead to what Kiaer
referred to as 'une vraie miniature de l'ensemble qu'on observe': that is, one
that would accurately reflect both types *and* the nature and extent of deviations from them. Moreover, if typological categories were in effect to be
determined on the basis of the categories of official statistics, then the question could be raised of why cases for study should not be chosen simply by
sampling within these categories or some combination of them.

This was in effect the strategy followed by the survey researchers in their
quest for representativeness. Thus, Kiaer's pioneering study carried out in
Norway in 1894 (in connection with retirement pension and sickness insurance reforms) had a two-stage design: a number of districts were chosen by
reference to census statistics so as to be representative of the country as a
whole and then households in which detailed interviews were to be conducted were selected within each district with the specific aim of capturing
the full range of variation that existed in economic and social conditions:
that is, through what was known as 'purposive sampling' (Kiaer 1895).[7]
Subsequently, however, in the light of work by Bowley (1906, 1926; cf.
also Bowley and Burnett-Hurst 1915) and various others, sampling methods
became increasingly informed by probability theory, as this was developed
by the successors of Galton. And then, with the decisive intervention of
Neyman (1934), all forms of purposive sampling were in fact called into
question as lacking a clear theoretical basis and as leaving open a serious
possibility of bias, and appear to have been rather rapidly abandoned. A
new approach developed in which the purposive element in survey design
was clearly separated from sampling procedures. This approach comprised,
first, the *a priori* 'stratification' of the population under study or, in other
words, its proportionate division in the light of already well-established
knowledge of certain aspects of its heterogeneity and of the purposes of

---

[6] Émile Cheysson, one of the most talented of the Le Playistes, writing in 1890 and quoted
in Desrosières (1993: 263).

[7] It might be added here that the 'poverty' surveys carried out by Booth and Rowntree in
Britain in the late nineteenth and early twentieth centuries, and often highlighted in English-
language accounts of the history of empirical social research, in fact contributed rather little
so far as the methodology of surveys was concerned. In contrast, the major contribution of
Kiaer (who wrote mainly in Norwegian or French) has been grossly neglected.

the survey; and then, secondly, the 'probability', or, that is, the *random*, sampling of units *within* strata (Seng 1951; Kruskal and Mosteller 1980; Hansen 1987).

With such 'stratified random' sampling, survey researchers in fact arrived at a broadly satisfactory solution to problems of variation, as they perceived them: that is, as problems of inferring characteristics of populations via estimates from samples with a relatively small and known degree of error. Ethnographers did not, however, make any comparable progress. As I seek to show in the next two sections, what might be called, on the one hand, *problems of variation within the locales of ethnography* and, on the other hand, *problems of variation across locales* have persisted, and, although they have been recurrently addressed, no agreement even on the general approach to be taken to them would seem so far to have emerged, let alone procedures that might become codified as standard practice.

Problems of Variation within Locales

There would seem to be broad agreement on at least three characteristics of sociological ethnography that set it in contrast with survey work. First, it is research undertaken in 'natural' situations, as opposed to ones specifically set up for research purposes, such as that of the formal interview (or laboratory experiment). Secondly, it is research conducted via the ethnographer's own observation, in some degree 'participant', within the situation or situations studied, supplemented by interviews with actors of an informal, unstructured kind—'interviews as conversations'. And, thirdly, it is research aimed at the elucidation of actors' own definitions of their situation and of the meanings that they give to their actions within it, rather than, or at least prior to, the imposition of the investigator's concepts, as must in some degree occur where formal interview schedules or questionnaires are used.[8] But, given these characteristics, the following issue then inevitably arises. When the ethnographer is 'in the field'—in the locale of the ethnography—what principles of selection should guide the observation and conversations in which he or she actually engages? Since anything approaching total coverage will rarely be feasible, just *who* should be observed and questioned and, in turn, have *their*

---

[8] Within the broad agreement thus characterized, there are, of course, some evident divisions. Most notable, perhaps, is that (cf. C. Campbell 1996) between, on the one hand, those ethnographers who believe that the meaning of action is constituted entirely intersubjectively in the course of the face-to-face interaction of individuals in particular situations, and who therefore concentrate on questions of how actors manage to interpret and understand what each other is doing rather than on the courses and patterns of action that they in fact follow; and, on the other hand, those who would believe that it is on actual courses and patterns of action that interpretative effort should focus and that the meaning of these to individuals, and likewise individuals' definitions of the situations in which they act, do not have to be, and indeed often are not, themselves situationally specific. The presence of this, and other, divisions does not, I think, have any great bearing on at least the critical part of my argument.

patterns of meaningful action and *their* understandings of the lifeworld of the locale recorded and, ultimately, analysed?

In ethnographic work in classical social anthropology, much reliance was in fact placed on 'local authorities', otherwise known as 'key informants'. It would seem to have been accepted that such individuals could be identified in a fairly unproblematic way and that, with some prompting and checking, they could provide the basis for adequate accounts of at least the major institutional and cultural features of the (mostly tribal) societies that were studied. As Anthony Cohen (1984: 223) has put it: 'The chief could tell us about politics and war and hunting; the priest or shaman or witchdoctor about religious, magical or mystical affairs' and so on. Moreover, as Cohen also notes, it tended to be assumed that the cultures in question were 'monolithic' and that actors were highly socialized into them. Thus, it was scarcely envisaged that a widening of the range of informants might lead to a significantly different picture of the society being formed.[9]

Whether such a degree of confidence in key informants' accounts was justified may well be doubted.[10] But, for present purposes, the more relevant point is that, in the case of ethnography undertaken in modern societies, the idea of such informants pronouncing authoritatively on monolithic cultures is not one that could be given any very serious consideration. Nor indeed is it. In textbooks on ethnographic methods for sociologists problems of variation within locales are generally recognized and so in turn are ones of selection—or, that is, of sampling—in the course of data collection (see e.g. Burgess 1984: 53–9, 61–75; Miles and Huberman 1984: 41–2; Johnson 1990; Hammersley and Atkinson 1995: 45–53; Fetterman 1998: 32–3). Correspondingly, a disregard for such problems is taken to constitute grounds for legitimate criticism. Thus, to take one notable example, Hammersley and Atkinson (1995: 111–12) point out that Willis (1977) bases an ethnography of working-class boys in a secondary school largely on conversations with one grouping, 'the lads', who represent a well-defined counter-school subculture, while more or less ignoring another grouping that he identifies, the 'ear-'oles', who accept school norms and values. Willis, they object, provides no good reasons for

---

[9] In Cambridge in the 1960s I often attended Meyer Fortes's seminar, at which papers by graduate students and others based on fieldwork in West Africa were the staple. I several times asked questions about how the choice of informants was made, how important to the findings reported this choice might be, and so on. After one such intervention Fortes was driven to expostulate: 'Dammit, if I want to learn French, I don't need a random sample of Frenchmen to teach me. One competent native speaker is enough!' But the issue then arises of just how far in this regard the analogy between a language and a culture or set of social institutions holds up. While some linguists at least would maintain that a native speaker cannot in fact make a mistake in his or her own language, there are few sociologists who would suppose that 'lay members' cannot hold mistaken, or at any rate radically divergent, beliefs about their own society. It should, however, be added that some social anthropologists have seriously engaged with problems of fieldwork sampling (see e.g. Honigman 1973).

[10] Certainly, in the—now rather many—instances in which attempted replications or re-examinations of older anthropological ethnographies have led to their being challenged, the possibility is almost always raised (cf. Bryman 1994) either of their authors having being misled by informants, whether deliberately or not, or of informants having in fact represented only particular subcultures or social groupings.

endorsing 'the lads' as being the genuine 'spokesmen for the working class', nor any explanation for why, having found evidence of significant subcultural variation, he then denies the 'ear-'oles', and possibly other groupings too, the right to a voice. Moreover, various other, less obvious possibilities of unaccommodated variation leading to bias in ethnographies have been commented on: as, say, where certain very 'helpful', but not necessarily representative, individuals or groups threaten to dominate the data-collection process or where influential 'gatekeepers' or 'sponsors', through whom access to a locale has been achieved, then seek to slant the direction of the research and the choice of interviewees in a particular way (cf. Hammersley and Atkinson 1995: 59–67, 133–4).[11]

However, recognizing problems is one thing, devising generally accepted solutions to them, another. And, in this latter regard, a reading of both textbooks and sociological ethnographies themselves would suggest that still almost everything remains to be done. The main difficulty, I would argue, is that, on account perhaps of the fraught intellectual climate within which they now operate, even those ethnographers who most clearly see the need for methodological development and codification around the idea of a logic of inference are wary of complying too readily with what might be labelled as 'positivist' requirements and at the same time are too indulgent towards supposed alternative approaches. Thus, so far as problems of variation within locales are concerned, a number of such alternatives are in fact entertained, each of which, though, can be shown to have rather basic shortcomings.

To begin with, the suggestion has been made (see e.g. Orum *et al.* 1991: 19–21; Fetterman 1998: 11–12) that resort to the kind of inference that is typically involved in survey work—that is, from sample to population—is not the only way in which the representativeness of an ethnography can be underpinned. The 'verisimilitude' of any such qualitative account, or its 'authenticity', 'plausibility', or 'undeniability', can also be communicated to its readers by its literary style—a means, it may further be held, that is less readily available in the case of quantitative analyses. However, the trouble here is, rather obviously, that the appreciation of style as creating an effect of verisimilitude, etc., is not at all the same thing as having evidence of representativeness, and is moreover a highly subjective matter. What strikes *me* as an ethnography that 'rings true' may strike *you* as quite unconvincing; and we could then only pursue the matter in a rational way by moving from style to substance: that is, to the strength of the grounds, of the linkage between evidence and argument, on which the claim of representativeness is made— or, in other words, back to the logic of inference.[12]

[11] For example, problems arising in this way are suggested in the case of two classic 'street' ethnographies: that is, via the undue influence of 'Doc' in Whyte's *Street Corner Society* (1943) and of 'Tally' in Liebow's *Tally's Corner* (1967).

[12] One of the first ethnographies I ever read, and by which I was totally persuaded, was Redfield's study (1930) of Tepoztlán. But I then discovered the restudy by Lewis (1951). Should I have been so convinced by Redfield—or were, perhaps, my first impressions right? In regard to this and other similarly disputed cases, Bryman (1988: 76) has aptly observed

Again, it has been maintained that, while sampling of some kind may be necessary in data collection within the locale of an ethnography, this need not be—perhaps should not be—the probabilistic sampling characteristic of survey work (see e.g. Johnson 1990: ch. 2; Stewart 1998: 35, 47). Thus, one alternative that has been proposed is what is called 'judgemental' or 'opportunistic' sampling. Ethnographers should be alert to whatever possibilities for observation or conversation may happen to come their way and should then decide on which to concentrate in the light of their judgement of which are most 'appropriate' (Fetterman 1998: 32–3) or most likely to prove rewarding (Burgess 1984: 54–5). However, just as where appeal is made to the stylistic effects of an ethnography, the difficulty arises of disputed cases. *You* may think that an ethnographer has shown sound judgement in his or her selection, but *I* may suspect, say, that data collection has been recurrently biased in favour of a particular theoretical or ideological position.[13] And again the only way to proceed would be to get down to an examination of the actual grounds on which 'judgement' was exercised.

A yet further variety of non-probabilistic sampling that has been seen as well suited to ethnography is then 'theoretical sampling', as advocated by Glaser and Strauss (1967: esp. ch. 3; cf. Strauss and Corbin 1990: ch. 11). This is evidently sampling that, rather than trading on happenstance, is of a highly 'purposive' kind. The central idea would appear to be that the process of data collection should be controlled by 'emerging' theory, with the aim of allowing the investigator to try out and elaborate new concepts and categories until 'saturation' is reached: that is, until no further elaboration is empirically warranted. As Bryman has pointedly observed (1988: 117), theoretical sampling seems to be far more often referred to than actually used; and it is, moreover, unclear whether Glaser and Strauss intended it as a solution to problems of within-locale variation. But, even if they did, it is still hard to see how it could in fact answer. The ethnographer could let emerging theory dictate the selection of observations and conversations up to whatever point without thereby gaining any assurance that the data resulting from such sampling would adequately reflect the range of variation to be contended with. Indeed, in so far as the theory being developed was mistaken from the outset, the path then followed in data collection might be systematically biased towards *un*representative instances.[14]

that 'Brief conversations, snippets from unstructured interviews, or examples of a particular activity are used to provide evidence for a particular contention. There are grounds for disquiet in that the representativeness or generality of these fragments is rarely addressed. Further, field notes or extended transcripts are rarely available.'

[13] For example, the laboratory ethnographies of Latour (1987; see also Latour and Woolgar 1979) have many admirers within the sociology science, but, for me, Latour's choice and presentation of material have always seemed highly slanted and tendentious (cf. Gross and Levitt 1994: 57–62; Cole 1996).

[14] 'Theoretical sampling' is a key component in Glaser and Strauss's more general programme for 'grounded theory', which is characterized by an extreme inductivism (as well as, I would argue, by a failure to make a sufficiently clear distinction between theory and concepts). Thus, there seems to be little to prevent a situation in which a theory that, as initially

In sum, two main points may be made. First, reliance on inadequate or in effect pseudo-solutions to problems of variation within the locales of ethnography can serve only to undermine what is claimed as one of ethnography's greatest strengths, especially in relation to survey-based research: that is, its capacity not only to 'tell what it's all about' but further to 'tell how it is' from the actors' point of view. For all too often, as things stand, it is left quite unclear just how critical readers of an ethnography might assess whether they are indeed being told about 'all', or only a part, of what is going on and are being given insight into the subjectivity of all, or only some, of the actors involved.[15]

Secondly, in search of more effective solutions, ethnographers have in fact no alternative but to go down the same road as did survey researchers: that is, to adopt procedures that are in some way or other based on the demonstrated advantages of probabilistic sampling. Some such procedures have indeed been proposed for ethnographic work and occasionally implemented, most often, perhaps, in the case of the observation of patterns of action over time (e.g. McClintock *et al.* 1983; cf. Burgess 1984: 64–71). But it would seem important that they should become quite standard both in this regard and in the selection of interviewees also. Apart from misplaced fears of an apparent surrender to the hegemony of 'positivist' methodology, the main obstacle to a movement in this direction would appear to be similarly misplaced doubts about practicalities.

It has, for example, been held (Burgess 1984: 75; Fetterman 1998: 8–9) that random sampling will often be inappropriate or at least insufficient in an ethnography because certain individuals or groups *have* to be covered—i.e. their selection could not be left to chance—on account of the particular positions, roles, or statuses that they occupy or of their crucial theoretical relevance. But, if such firm *a priori* knowledge or clear theoretical direction is indeed available, then some form of stratification could be adopted with, if need be, differential sampling ratios (including, perhaps, some of 100 per cent) within strata.[16] Again, it has been argued that, since the locale of an ethnography is usually not all that well defined, sampling frames would be

formulated, is quite unsound is not rejected outright but is rather 'developed' through a series of *ad hoc* adaptations made in the face of uncongenial empirical findings. This risk can, moreover, only be increased by Glaser and Strauss's preference for conceptual fission and elaboration—to the point of 'saturation'—rather than for conceptual parsimony. Another form of non-probabilistic sampling that could easily lead to systematically biased results is 'snowball' sampling: i.e. in cases where the snowballing is limited by the social networks existing within one particular grouping in the locale (see Burgess 1984: 57).

[15] My own awareness of this problem dates from my reading of the study of a Yorkshire mining village by Dennis, Henriques, and Slaughter (1956) that was fairly close to the village in which I grew up. In relation to my own village, the authors' ethnography appeared to me to apply well to just *one* subculture among several that were generally recognized and that had their own rather distinctive social bases. But what grounds had I for judging whether the authors had given only a very partial account of 'their' village or whether this was in fact much more homogeneous than mine, despite being a good deal larger?

[16] Where this particular objection to probabilistic sampling is made, it is notable that the emphasis tends to be placed—in a rather 'positivistic' way?—on the 'hard', factual information that only certain individuals can provide.

difficult to construct (Hammersley and Atkinson 1995: 136–7). But what is here overlooked is that quite similar situations arise in survey research, so that some amount of slippage has regularly to be acknowledged between the theoretical population of a study and that which is actually sampled. Moreover, ethnographers could well have some compensating advantages in regard to sampling. In survey work a major problem now emerging is that of increasing, and most likely increasingly biased, non-response. In the small-scale setting of an ethnography not only might relatively high response rates be expected but, in addition, a better knowledge of non-respondents, and in turn a better estimation of any resulting bias, should be possible.

In all of this, it is essential that the point made earlier should be kept in mind: that pursuing methods responsive to the logic of inference is desirable *not* because reliable and valid results are thus guaranteed (though the chances of such results may be enhanced), but rather because the processes through which results, of whatever quality, are produced are thus made *transparent* and shortcomings from ideal requirements, which are in some degree inevitable, are fully exposed. The adequacy of surveys in capturing variation in phenomena of interest within populations can be, and routinely is, evaluated by critical reference to such matters as sampling frames, sample design, response rates, response bias, and so on. The adequacy of ethnographies in capturing within-locale variation should be open to evaluation on a comparable basis.

Problems of Variation Across Locales

Ethnographies are a form of case study in which the unit of study is usually not the individual but rather a social entity of some kind—a group or network, a community, an organization—that is treated in a 'holistic' way. In consequence of this and of the emphasis on intensive and prolonged fieldwork, it is common for an ethnography to be confined to the study of a single unit or to no more than two or three. Only rarely, one could say, does the number covered amount to double figures. How the units that will constitute the locale or locales of an ethnography are to be chosen is then a question of evident importance. In the context of classical social anthropology the argument could be made that it was in fact of value to carry out ethnographic work among *any* people or in *any* region not hitherto studied, before truly indigenous cultural and institutional forms disappeared for ever. But such an argument is obviously of less help to the sociological ethnographer. For the latter, the fundamental difficulty is that any kind of unit in which he or she has an interest may be expected to show some common features from one locale to another within the larger society but also some non-negligible degree of variation, and that it is then unlikely to be apparent from the study of only a small number of units which findings provide a reliable basis for sociological generalization and which do not. If research is undertaken within, say, industrial work groups, or isolated villages, or inner-city schools, how is the ethnographer to know how much and what part of what he or she observes is indeed recurrent across work groups, villages, or schools of the kind in question or is limited only to the particular locales that happen to have been picked out, each of which will, of course, have its own distinctive articulation with the larger society?

It has sometimes been suggested that ethnographers can simply sidestep the issue of how far their findings can be generalized by viewing ethnographies as being entirely idiographic in intent: that is, as being concerned purely with the description of the cases studied in all their detailed uniqueness and for their own intrinsic interest. But, while this is in itself a defensible position, it is a difficult one to hold to, at all events for those who would wish to argue for the continuing importance of ethnography in sociological research; and in fact most ethnographers do seek to draw conclusions from their work of some degree of generality. 'Cases' are, after all, usually understood as being cases *of* something.[17] Moreover, problems that are in this regard created by variation across locales are no less regularly and openly acknowledged in textbooks on ethnographic research than are those arising from variation within locales (see e.g. Burgess 1984: 59–61; Miles and Huberman 1984: 36–41; Bryman 1988: 87–91; Hammersley 1991: 24–7, 102–3; Silverman 1993: 160–2; Hammersley and Atkinson 1995: 42–5; Stewart 1998: ch. 5). However, what has here to be said once more is that, although acknowledged, these problems have not so far been treated in ways that have been able to command general acceptance—nor indeed in ways that would deserve to do so; and, again, it would seem, largely on account of a misguided concern to find alternative approaches to ones that might be thought too tainted by positivistic methodology and, in particular, as this is taken to be applied in survey work.

Thus, just as it has been supposed that a solution to problems of within-locale variation can be achieved without any consideration of inference from sample to population—by appeal to 'verisimilitude', and so on—so too is it believed that, in regard to problems of variation across locales, the idea of 'statistical generalization' can be discarded in favour of that of 'naturalistic generalization'. The latter, one understands, is successfully achieved when the findings of an ethnographic case study prove to be 'epistemologically in harmony with the reader's experience and thus to that person a natural basis for generalization' (Stake 1978: 5; cf. Denzin 1989) or when the data 'resonate experientially and phenomenologically' with the reader (Snow and Anderson

---

[17] Thus, Hammersley (1992: 189; though cf. 1991: 28) argues that at least with some ethnographies 'the issue of generalisability does not arise', since the case studied represents 'a population of one' and he cites as an instance of this Fielding's study (1981) of the National Front. However, it is evident enough from a reading of this study that Fielding is in fact concerned with far more than idiographic description. He is interested in the National Front as an example of a right-wing extremist movement, as an expression of political deviance, and as a context in which to study the role of individual will in participation in such deviance. And, in all these respects, generalization from the case of the National Front is clearly involved (Fielding 1981: esp. chs. 1, 10).

1991: 165). In this case, there is in fact a more or less explicit acceptance that what to one reader is a valid generalization need not be so to another; and not on account of any issue that would be open to rational examination and debate but simply in consequence of their having led different lives (cf. Gomm *et al.* 1999). What resonates with me may well not resonate with you, and there, unfortunately, the matter has to rest.

Likewise, the proposal of 'judgemental' or 'opportunistic' sampling as an alternative to probabilistic sampling for within-locale observation is paralleled by the argument that ethnographers can equally well proceed on the basis of opportunism tempered by judgement in their selection of locales. Considerations of representativeness, it is suggested, are of less importance in this respect, at least initially, than are those of ease of access, prior knowledge of the locale, the availability of 'inside' contacts, or mere physical convenience (Spradley 1980; Burgess 1984: 59–61). If there is reason to believe that the choice of locales thus made may limit the extent to which generalization will be possible, this can then be taken into account—that is to say, the ethnographer can use his or her judgement as regards representativeness—when eventually drawing conclusions from the study. However, as with such an approach to sampling within locales, the difficulty that arises is that of knowing on just what grounds this crucial judgement is being exercised or, in turn, could be challenged by critics. It would seem to be supposed that, after the fact, the ethnographer somehow has information to hand on the nature and extent of the variation that exists across locales that was not available before sampling or was not deemed relevant to this task.

Finally, though, one further argument regarding the problem of variation across locales should be noted that does in fact recognize that *some* logic of inference is needed in order to underpin the process of generalization but maintains that this is not the *same* logic as that which is appropriate in survey work. The origins of this argument lie in the distinction made by Znaniecki (1934) between 'enumerative' and 'analytic' induction. Its most explicit exposition is, however, to be found in a much-cited paper by Mitchell (1983). For Mitchell, Znaniecki's distinction is in fact best interpreted as one between two kinds of inference rather than induction: that is, 'statistical' inference and 'causal' inference. Generalization in survey-based sociology depends on a form of statistical inference and in turn on a sample being representative of the population from which it is drawn. However, with an ethnography, or indeed any kind of case study, generalization must rely on causal inference, on the analysis establishing certain 'essential' causal linkages among social phenomena, which, if found in the locale under study, will then necessarily be found in all comparable locales: 'We infer that the features present in the case study will be related in a wider population not because the case is representative but because our analysis is unassailable.' There is thus no point in the ethnographer trying to find 'typical' locales; a concern with this issue simply reflects confusion over the two kinds of inference. In fact, the causal linkages that can be extrapolated from a single ethnography may well be most clearly revealed within idiosyncratic locales (Mitchell 1983: 200, 204).

The question that at once arises here is, of course, that of how the ethnographer is in fact able to identify 'essential' causal linkages within the body of empirical data that a particular locale provides. The answer Mitchell gives—and it is the only one conceivable—is: on the basis of theory. Pre-existing theory enables 'significant elements' to be identified in the data, and the extent to which generalization is possible depends on the 'adequacy' of the further theoretical developments that are achieved (Mitchell 1983: 202, 203). But what has then to be observed is the nature of the demands that are thus made on theory. To be viable, Mitchell's approach requires theory that, as well as allowing generalizable causal processes to be conceptually separated out from 'the unique circumstances' of the ethnography, is furthermore *both* deterministic in character, so that the analysis of just one case is enough, *and* entirely correct in substance, so that the analysis becomes 'unassailable'.

The understanding of theory implicit in Mitchell's position is then one that, ironically, might well be described as positivist in something close to the original, nineteenth-century sense: theory is seen as giving certain knowledge of necessary, lawlike relations.[18] Today, such an understanding would not find great philosophical support, within the social sciences at least; nor, more to the point, can sociology in fact claim to have produced theory of the kind in question. Consequently, compelling instances of its use in the way that Mitchell would envisage are difficult to cite. Individual ethnographies may, of course, serve as the basis for the development of theory; but this is theory that, far from being unassailable, must then be exposed to test, and not least in order to determine the range of applicability, from one context to another, of the causal processes that it postulates.[19]

---

[18] This is, though, less surprising than it might at first seem. Mitchell's position is in direct line of descent from that of Znaniecki, and the latter's proposals for analytic induction amount in fact to little more than a highly simplified version of the 'canons' of induction proposed by John Stuart Mill for theory construction in the experimental—though *not*, it should be stressed, in the social, or 'moral'—sciences. It would seem that most of the authors who have approvingly cited Mitchell's arguments on generalization from ethnographies have simply not appreciated the nature of the theory that these arguments entail. I might add here that, in clarifying my own position on these matters, I owe much to energetic but always good-natured and illuminating argument with Clyde Mitchell over many years up to his death.

[19] Yin (1994: 30–2, 48–50) and Stewart (1998: 47–9) present what are in effect weaker versions of Mitchell's argument, in claiming that, in ethnographic (or other case-study) work, generalization should be seen as being not from sample to population but rather from case to theory, hypothesis or 'insight', with, in Yin's view, instances where a theory is supported from one case to another (little is said about *dis*confirmation) being the equivalent of the replication of results in experimental research. This is, however, to neglect the obvious but crucial fact that in experiments contextual conditions are controlled either physically or by randomization in a way that they cannot be in research undertaken in natural settings. Burawoy (1998: 14) likewise argues in favour of generalization from case to theory with the aim, however, of theory reconstruction rather than confirmation, and maintains that 'Because we begin with theory, a single case is quite sufficient for a progressive reconstruction'. This may be so but it is certainly not enough for theory testing unless, again, theory of a quite deterministic character is supposed. Analytic induction itself would by now appear to have been effectively abandoned in ethnographic work, at all events as a method of causal

In sum, whether the aim is simply description *or* theoretical advance, the problem of variation across the locales of ethnographies cannot be avoided; and neither, I would then argue, can the conclusion that, just as with problems of within-locale variation, solutions must be sought on the basis of the same sampling procedures that have become standard in survey work. Moreover, here too, it would seem, many ethnographers have moved some way towards accepting this conclusion, even if only implicitly, and more would be likely to do so, and more openly, were it not for the influence of poorly examined inhibitions about 'positivist' methodology.

Thus, for example, ethnographies are quite often taken as a basis for descriptive generalization on the grounds that the case or cases studied *can* be regarded as 'typical' or 'representative' of some population within which they fall; or, again, ethnographies are held to have theoretical significance on the grounds that they relate to cases that offer strategic advantages for research because of their 'deviant', 'leading edge', or 'critical' character or because they minimize or maximize certain crucial contrasts (Platt 1988; Stewart 1998: 58–9). But to argue thus can, of course, mean only that the importance of variation across locales, and likewise of the positioning of particular locales within this variation, is recognized; and, further, that some knowledge in these respects is claimed or supposed. Indeed, one can readily find recommendations made (e.g. Orum *et al.* 1991: 15; Hammersley 1992: 189–90; Gomm *et al.* 1999), much on Le Playiste lines, that official or other statistics produced via survey research should be utilized in order to establish the degree of typicality, or the nature of the atypicality, of ethnographic locales— and even while, perhaps, the general inappropriateness of the sampling approach of survey work to the selection of such locales is at the same time maintained.

However, of yet greater significance in this regard is the fact that certain ethnographies can by now be cited in which just this approach is quite explicitly pursued. An example of particular note is here provided by Jankowski's study (1991) of American urban gangs. This is based on thirty-seven gangs, randomly selected from an ethnically stratified list of all gangs known to be active in three major cities with widely contrasting ecological features. From the standpoint of a survey research handbook, Jankowski's sampling is by no means perfect; he does not, in fact, claim that it is, and, given the practical difficulties attendant upon his choice of research topic, it is difficult to see how it could have been. None the less, problems of variation across locales are clearly confronted, and what must be stressed is that shortcomings in the procedures followed do not detract from the ultimate virtue that derives from them: that, once more, of transparency. We know the rationale according to which Jankowski came to work in certain locales rather than in others; and we have the essential information that we need in order to evaluate his sampling, to point to ways in which bias might have been introduced, and to

analysis in the way intended by Znaniecki. In so far as it is still defended, it is simply as an aid in theory development (cf. Manning 1982).

form judgements for ourselves of how far his findings are likely to be applicable to urban gangs in America at large. Work such as Jankowski's does then constitute a challenge to which other sociological ethnographers should show themselves ready to respond. If such a sampling approach to the problems of across-locale variation can be implemented, with the advantages indicated, in the study of urban gangs, then why not in what would in general be the more favourable circumstances of studies of workplaces, local communities, schools, and so on? Or, if there *are* better approaches to such problems, then their superiority should be demonstrated, with studies such as Jankowski's serving as benchmark.[20]

Problems of Context in Survey Research and Possibilities for Ethnography

In the foregoing, I have maintained that problems of variation, both within and across locales, that were raised in criticism of the earliest efforts at sociological ethnography still persist today, and that little agreement has emerged about how a solution to these problems might be achieved. I turn now to what can be seen as a corresponding range of problems that are associated with survey-based sociological research, and that have in fact been frequently pointed to by proponents of ethnography: that is, what may be called problems of context. I aim to show *en passant* that survey researchers have in certain respects responded to these problems in a manner that ethnographers could find instructive; but my main concern is with one problem that remains and that, moreover, provides new possibilities for ethnography to demonstrate its continuing importance to the sociological enterprise.

As suggested earlier, it is characteristic of ethnography that it is carried out in natural situations and relies on participant observation and 'interviews as conversations' in order to reach, at least as a primary goal, some understanding of the meanings that individuals give to these situations and to the patterns of social action in which they are involved. In contrast, it has then been claimed, survey-based research must, through its essential techniques, *abstract* individuals from their natural situations—that is, from their social contexts—and thus introduce into the research process a significant degree of artificiality. A sample of individuals is selected from within a population, usually a quite large one, and data are collected from the members of this sample via questionnaires or formal interviews following a prepared schedule. But, it is held, to ground sociological enquiry in the study of such 'atomized' individuals is likely to prove in various ways misleading. For example, the attitudes and beliefs that individuals express in interviews, in response to more or less standardized questions, may be largely products of the circum-

---

[20] What would seem an unacceptable away of evading this challenge is to seek to compartmentalize Jankowski's work by taking it, as does Burawoy (1998: 17), as simply representing the 'positive tradition' within ethnography.

stances of the interview itself rather than attitudes and beliefs that would actually guide the actions of the 'respondents' in the course of their every-day lives. In other words, one set of problems of context in survey research are in effect those of the reliability and validity of the data obtained. In addition, it has been contended that survey data, whatever their quality, must be subject to serious restriction in their scope. In relating to the attributes of individuals, or at all events to individuals' perceptions and reports, such data cannot provide any direct information pertaining to the supra-individual level of structured social relationships, which, as well as being of interest in itself, will also of course condition and influence the experience and action of individuals. A further problem of context in survey research is then that of how such 'contextual effects' are to be detected and their importance assessed.

Problems of the kind thus far indicated are, however, ones that survey researchers have for long recognized. They are, moreover, ones that in recent years they have addressed with greater success than hitherto, and essentially, it could be said, *by following through the basic logic of their established methods of data collection and analysis.* Thus, in regard to problems of the reliability and validity of data, and of 'subjective' data in particular, a variety of statistical techniques have been developed directed towards, on the one hand, determining the extent to which such problems exist and, on the other, enabling due allowance to be made for the 'error' present in data in the course of their analysis. At its most sophisticated, what this approach entails is the elaboration of probability models for survey response in which such response is taken to be a function *both* of the attributes of individual respondents *and* of the questions they are asked, the context in which they are answered, and so on (for a particularly instructive series of papers on the issue of 'non-attitudes', see Converse 1964, 1970; Duncan 1982; Brooks 1994a,b).

Likewise, the problem of contextual effects has been addressed by extending the data-collection process in survey research so as to include information not only on individuals but further on the social entities in which they are involved—groups, networks, communities, organizations, and so on—which can, of course, also be sampled, and by then applying to such hierarchically structured data sets various techniques of multilevel modelling. It thus becomes possible for estimates to be made of the actual degree to which variation at the individual level shows association with contextual factors—for example, variation in academic performance with features of schools or variation in voting with features of constituencies—independently of variation in the attributes of individuals themselves (here a relevant series of papers would be Lazarsfeld 1959; Blalock 1984; DiPrete and Forristal 1994).

Indeed, in consequence of such advances, survey researchers might well consider themselves now to be in a position to mount a strong counter-critique of ethnography. It could, for example, be pointed out that conducting interviews as conversations rather than more formally does not in some magical way simply make problems of the reliability and validity of data disappear; these problems demand serious attention from ethnographers also. Or, again, it could be remarked that, while in ethnographies contextual effects are often claimed or supposed, this is not to say that they are actually demonstrated through some method that is open to critical inspection.[21] However, I do not seek here to pursue such issues but rather to take up a further problem of context in survey-based research, underlined by ethnographers, that I would see as being of a different order from those considered above and with which sociologists reliant upon such research have yet to come to terms.

Ethnographers have often maintained that the ultimate concern of their research is with social processes: that is, with patterns of situated social action and interaction, continuing through time, that are integral to the lifeworlds that they explore. Their methods of enquiry, based on a long-term involvement in natural situations, are those most apt to the understanding of such processes, whereas in this regard survey research, with its focus on the atomized and in turn 'decontextualized' individual, is at a serious disadvantage. Such a position is, moreover, readily developed into the further argument that, because of the privileged access that it gives to social processes, ethnography must play a key role in the study of social causation (see e.g. Miles 1983: 117). Survey research is well suited to establishing associations among social phenomena, at all events at the level of statistical relations among variables; but ethnographic research comes into its own when it is a matter of explaining in terms of social processes why these relations are found. Thus, for instance, Fetterman (1998: 3) maintains that, while a survey approach would be more appropriate than ethnography in determining the distribution of different ethnic groups across a national occupational structure, ethnographies would be required in order to show how unequal ethnic representation in specific occupations is actually brought about—to show how this outcome is actually produced 'on the ground'.

For present purposes, this argument gains in significance in the degree to which it can be allied with forceful criticism from other quarters of the idea that social causation can be established directly via the statistical analysis of survey data (see further Chapters 5 and 7). On the one hand, it has been objected by theorists of social action that 'variable sociology' cannot itself provide causal explanations of the regularities it describes, since such explanations must ultimately refer to the action and interaction of individuals through which the demonstrated relations among variables are actually created. On the other hand, it has been pointed out by statisticians that infer-

---

[21] Two points might be added here. First, in regard to problems of the reliability and validity of data in ethnography, even the best discussions (e.g. Kirk and Miller 1986) would seem, just like discussions of problems of within- and across-locale variation, to be much stronger on diagnosis than on prescription. Secondly, in regard to contextual effects, results from the multi-level modelling of survey data would indicate that these effects are often far *less* important than ethnographers' claims or indeed much textbook sociology would lead one to expect.

ences that are thought to be derived from the 'causal' modelling of survey data cannot in fact come from such modelling alone, since this must itself rest on theoretical assumptions (whether recognized or not) about social processes, which are then quite crucial to the validity of the results obtained.

There would, therefore, appear to be an emerging consensus that, in attempts at explaining established social regularities, the elaboration of what might be called their underlying generative processes—or, alternatively, 'causal mechanisms' (cf. Hedström and Swedberg 1998c; also Blossfeld and Prein 1998)—is indeed essential. And in this way, I would then argue, an opportunity is opened up for sociological ethnography to establish its role as an essential complement to survey research on rather more specific and more secure grounds than those hitherto advanced. This opportunity would consist *not* in ethnography pursuing any special advantage as regards the actual construction of accounts of generative social processes, as, say, in the inductive style envisaged by Mitchell or again in that favoured by proponents of 'grounded theory', but rather in ethnography providing a distinctive medium through which such accounts, whatever their provenance, *could be exposed to empirical test*.[22]

If it is accepted that explanations of observed social regularities have in the end to be given 'micro-to-macro' rather than 'macro-to-micro'—that is, in terms of situated social action and of its intended and unintended consequences rather than by reference to the functional and structural exigencies of social systems—it would then seem to follow that such explanations, in the form of narratives of action, will be open to most direct test through precisely the kind of intensive, 'context-embedded' study in which ethnographers engage. That is to say, it is through this kind of enquiry that it should be possible to see hypothesized generative processes, or what has been called 'local causality' (Miles and Huberman 1984: 15), actually at work. Thus, to return to Fetterman's example of disparities among ethnic groups in their representation in different occupations, one could question his implied view that ethnographers are in some way in a privileged position to suggest generative processes; but one could at the same time recognize that, once such explanations for the established regularities have been proposed—as, say, in terms of adverse 'labelling' and discrimination by employers or of migration chains and ethnic social networks—then ethnographic research would appear an apt way of investigating whether processes of the kind invoked do in fact operate. It would certainly be difficult to retain belief in their efficacy if, in well-designed and sustained fieldwork in a series of appropriately selected locales, no indication of their presence could be found.

[22] As is recognized in the text, ethnographic research may indeed suggest theory; but, contrary to what is claimed by proponents of 'grounded theory', there is no reason for supposing that having inductive, rather than deductive, or indeed purely speculative, origins in itself contributes to the validity of a theory. Theories, like all ideas, are to be judged by their consequences—specifically, by whether they stand up to test—and not by their antecedents.

In so far, then, as sociological ethnography does have advantages over survey-based research in its capacity to study social action and interaction in context, it is, I would maintain, primarily through the testing of accounts of generative social processes that this advantage can, and should, be exploited. However, further in this regard, there are two qualifications that need to be made.

The first is that, if ethnography is to contribute effectively to sociological analysis in the way in question, it is essential that the problems of variation both within and across locales that were earlier reviewed should indeed be dealt with through ethnographers taking more seriously than hitherto the logic of sampling as this has been developed in survey research. On the one hand, it has to be recognized that, since the social regularities that are to be explained will themselves be probabilistic, the accounts of generative processes that are suggested will need to be ones that are directed towards capturing 'central tendencies' in social action and its consequences. There is no requirement, nor any warrant (see further Chapter 5), for deterministic explanations, such as those to which 'analytic induction' supposedly leads, and in which *every* 'seemingly anomalous' case (cf. H. S. Becker 1992: 210–12) is covered. In testing hypothesized accounts, it will, therefore, be vital that fieldwork procedures should enable within-locale variation to be appropriately handled and, in turn, make it possible for a fairly reliable understanding to be reached of what patterns of action (if any) can be regarded as representing central tendencies in a given locale and of the nature and extent of the variation that occurs around them. For example, in the case of the under- or over-representation of ethnic groups in different occupations, individual instances illustrative of almost *any* conceivable causal process *might* be encountered in the course of fieldwork. But the sociologically important issue is that of deciding just which of the processes that have been proposed are sufficiently dominant in the locale studied to be capable of generating, as an aggregate effect, the regularities in the pattern of association between ethnicity and occupation that are generally observed.[23]

On the other hand, it would seem no less vital that ethnographic research should be so designed that problems of across-locale variation are also adequately treated: that is to say, so that some rationally defensible basis exists for generalization from the findings that particular ethnographies yield. Even if social processes that have been suggested as generating a given outcome are clearly in evidence within a given locale, or set of locales, the question will still remain of whether these processes could be expected to operate similarly in other locales. There is, of course, no reason why a particular outcome should not be produced in several different ways and, perhaps, ones of widely

---

[23] A consequence of the failure, earlier noted, of Willis (1977) to deal adequately with problems of within-locale variation in his study of working-class boys is that the processes of alienation from school on which he concentrates are not in fact adequate to account for the rates and patterns of educational participation or of subsequent social mobility on the part of such children that are demonstrated at a macro-level by survey research. Willis appears to be remarkably ill-informed about such rates and patterns (see further Chapter 8).

differing prevalence from one context to another. Thus, ethnic disparities in occupational attainment could be found, say, in one locale to be brought about primarily through direct discrimination by employers but, in another, more through the timing of waves of immigration and their social organization. The empirical testing of hypothesized generative processes, whether via ethnography or otherwise, should then be such that this issue of 'causal heterogeneity' can be seriously addressed, rather than being invoked, as it often tends to be in 'grounded theorizing', merely as an excuse for adhoccery (see Chapter 3). Moreover, a more secure handling of problems of across-locale variation in this regard would also be important in helping theory construction that does have a stronger deductive component to go beyond simply the accumulation of what Coleman (1964: 516) aptly calls 'sometimes-true' theories and Elster (1990: 247–8) merely 'causal models', as distinct from theories. Testing whether *possible* causal processes are actually realized in locales that can be reliably positioned within a range of variation is of obvious relevance to what must be the further ambition of explicitly spelling out 'domains of application': that is, of developing theories that comprise coherent accounts of which of the causal processes that they specify will in fact be most likely to operate in which kinds of context.[24]

The second qualification that should be made to the idea of ethnography playing a distinctive role in the testing of explanations given in terms of causal social processes can be simply stated. It is that, while ethnography's role may here be distinctive, this is not to say that it will be unchallenged. A quite different, and in fact largely contrasting, approach can be identified, and one, moreover, that could be implemented essentially within the survey research tradition.

This approach starts from the position that, while 'micro-to-macro' accounts of generative processes of action are indeed crucial to sociological explanation, the study of these processes in themselves is highly problematic. This position may be given a philosophical justification on broadly Humean lines: causation itself cannot be directly observed but must always be in some way or other a matter of inference from observations. But, more relevantly, perhaps, for present purposes, the pragmatic argument is also advanced that a convincing research methodology for determining patterns of social action and interaction has yet to be developed and, in particular, as regards the understanding of actors' subjectivity. The capacity of social scientists to gain access to actors' values, beliefs, attitudes, goals, or preferences, let alone to their more complex mental constructions, such as 'definitions of the situation', is viewed with a radical scepticism—and regardless of whether this

---

[24] For good illustration of this issue, see Gomm, Foster, and Hammersley (1999). In this regard, hypothesis testing via ethnography is still likely to be troubled by the small N problem (cf. Chapter 3). One potentially valuable way in which this problem could be addressed is through the use of 'meta-analysis'. But here again developments in the context of ethnography would seem so far to lag well behind those in other, more quantitatively oriented fields. Compare e.g. Glass, McGaw, and Smith (1981) with Wolf (1986).

access is sought via observation or interviews, participant rather than
non-participant observation, or informal rather than formal interviewing
techniques.

From this position, then, it is maintained that, in seeking to test explanations of established social regularities in terms of causal processes of action,
the most viable strategy will be to focus not on immediate but rather on more
indirect implications. That is to say, instead of attempting to observe the
hypothesized processes actually in operation 'on the ground', within particular locales, it will be better to proceed by asking: if these processes are indeed
generating the regularities in question, then what *other* regularities, similarly
open to reasonably secure empirical demonstration, are implied and ought to
be discovered? Thus, in seeking to test the claim that it is the discriminatory
practices of employers that create a skewed occupational distribution of
certain ethnic groups, it will be less effective to try to observe such discrimination as it actually takes place within firms or communities—what exactly
would this entail?—than to spell out what other consequences should be
expected if discrimination is indeed in operation and then to see whether
evidence of these can be found, as, say, from extensive survey research. The
case of discrimination in employment (whether by ethnicity, gender, or otherwise) is in fact a particularly apt one to take here, since, precisely on account
of the difficulty of proving its occurrence directly, much attention has been
given, for policy and legal as well as academic reasons, to specifying what
could be regarded as indirect indicators of discrimination at work: for
example, differing relationships across groups in the relation between qualifications and experience, on the one hand, and levels of pay or rates of promotion, on the other.

It is not my purpose here to come to any final judgement on the merits of
hypothesis testing via what might be called the direct or indirect approaches.
Although I would regard the issue as being one of the most important and
difficult that arises in contemporary sociology, and indeed in social science
more widely,[25] it will, I believe, be decided only in the light of long-term experience of relative performance. Moreover, while the two approaches might
appear to diverge sharply on basic principles, there would in practice seem to
be no difficulty and some evident advantage in, for the time being at least,
pursuing them together. In the present context, the main conclusion to be
drawn from the foregoing discussion is then that, if in this regard sociological ethnography is to compete effectively, the need is yet further underlined
for renewed attention to be given to its methodological basis: that is, both in
relation to problems of within- and across-locale variation, which, as I have
sought to show, are a specific historical legacy, and at the same time in relation to problems of the reliability and validity of data, and of 'subjective' data

---

[25] See e.g., within economics, the interesting reflections of a heterodox institutionalist such
as Piore (1983) and of an orthodox econometrician such as Manski (1993).

in particular, which are problems that ethnography does not escape but shares with the survey tradition.[26]

In this chapter I have examined the idea that ethnography might represent a radical alternative to 'positivist' sociology of the kind that finds its main empirical resource in survey-based research. I have maintained that, while sociologists can, of course, apply a variety of different research methods, all must in some way or other be conformable to the same underlying logic of inference through which a basis is provided for the rational construction and criticism of scientific arguments. If, then, an ethnography that rejects 'positivism' is an ethnography that rejects this logic, such an ethnography must place itself outside social science—which is indeed, according to some currently influential irrationalist authors, its only conceivable location. I would regard these authors as totally misguided; but their position is, in this respect at least, a consistent one. Correspondingly, I have argued, those ethnographers who wish to retain their social-scientific credentials must in principle accept a commitment to research methods that do acknowledge the logic of inference, and must therefore in practice aim either to show just how the methods characteristic of ethnography are in fact informed by this logic or to modify and develop them appropriately. What I have chiefly aimed to criticize are claims to the effect that there is some 'third way' available: one that will allow ethnographers to continue to work honourably within the social-scientific community but under, as it were, a different aegis to its other members and with the benefit of some special and privileged methodological licence.

I have pursued detailed criticism on these lines with reference to a set of problems that appear quite crucial in sociological ethnography and that were apparent from its very origins: that is, problems of variation both within and across the locales of ethnography. While these problems have been readily recognized by ethnographers, they still remain without any generally accepted solution. Basically the same problems—in effect those of making inferences from part to whole—were encountered by survey researchers and, for their purposes, were rendered tractable through the development of sampling methods. However, on account, it would seem, of inhibitions over the apparent acceptance of a 'positivist' approach, ethnographers have made no concerted effort to adapt the logic of sampling to the circumstances of their own style of research, and have instead shown a predilection for

---

[26] It might be added that in this respect major benefits are to be expected from the increasing use of computers in ethnographic work: not so much from what is thus to be gained analytically, at least with existing ethnographic software (cf. Hammersley and Atkinson 1995: 193–204), but simply from the requirement thereby imposed upon ethnographers to constitute the results of their research as a data set with accompanying documentation that is fully open to examination and criticism in the public domain. The improvement in standards of survey research consequent upon the establishment of survey data archives and the requirement for publicly accessible documentation was immense.

various alternative, 'third-way' solutions. On examination, these prove rather obviously inadequate, and most commonly, one could say, because they are not of a kind that involve objective, transparent procedures nor therefore that are able to allow for any critical assessment of their application in particular cases.

In regard, then, to problems of context, which have been endemic in survey-based sociology on account of its focus on the 'decontextualized' individual and which have afforded ethnographers evident possibilities for critique, I have noted that survey researchers have in certain respects responded in promising fashion, essentially by extending the logic of their standard techniques. None the less, any sociology that remains entirely at the level of relationships among variables is still vulnerable to the charge, which others have of late joined ethnographers in pressing, that it cannot adequately address issues of social causation; or, more specifically, that it cannot itself penetrate to the processes of situated social action and interaction that alone can be the source of the empirical regularities that it describes. Ethnography, with its focus precisely on such processes, would thus seem here to have a clear advantage. But this advantage, I have then argued, should be understood as lying not in the distinctive capacity of ethnography to produce causal accounts of established social regularities, as, say, through inductive procedures, but rather in ethnography constituting a style of research with an evident appropriateness to the empirical testing of such accounts, however they may be derived. Any form of 'local causality' that is hypothesized in the form of generative social processes should, it may be held, be open to demonstration through appropriately sited and conducted ethnographic research, if it does indeed operate.

It is then on this basis that sociological ethnography may most convincingly be represented as, at all events, an essential complement to survey-based research. However, what I have further maintained is that an ethnography capable of sustaining such a claim, in what for the foreseeable future will be a difficult and contested area, will not be one that appeals to some ill-conceived and unconvincing 'third-way' methodology. To the contrary, in order to rise to the competitive challenges that it will surely face, ethnography must cease, as one author (Katz 1997: 410–11) has put it, to 'beg off' the kinds of methodological issue with which survey research has for long grappled, and instead aim to make its own contribution in this regard.

Finally, I should no doubt acknowledge that for a sociologist who is not an ethnographer to write an essay in this vein could well be regarded as something of an impertinence, if not worse. There are, however, two points that I would put forward in mitigation. First, as I noted at the outset, sociological ethnography would now seem to be widely regarded, among its practitioners as well as outsiders, to be in a state of disarray, if not crisis. There is little agreement about the way ahead and methodology appears to be the main source of contention. Secondly, as I would read the situation, those who wish to see ethnography as accepting the same underlying 'rules of the game' as survey-based, and indeed other, methods of sociological research are not at the present time in the ascendancy. Intellectual fashion is against them and would appear, rather, to encourage increasingly *avant-garde* ethnographies such as, say, would culminate in 'the sixth moment' envisaged and celebrated by Denzin (1997).[27] If this judgement is anywhere close to the mark, then no apology at all for intervention from without is required: ethnography is obviously far too important to be left to ethnographers.

[27] As support for this view, I would cite the recent *Handbook of Qualitative Research*, edited by Denzin and Lincoln (1994), which, for a volume that was presumably supposed to give a balanced review of the field, reveals a strong postmodernist bias in both the choice of contributors and the slant of their contributions.

5

The Quantitative Analysis of Large-scale Data Sets and Rational Action Theory: For a Sociological Alliance

IN SOCIOLOGY today, the quantitative analysis of large-scale data sets (QAD) and the deployment of rational action theory (RAT) are not closely related activities. In this chapter, however, it is my aim to show that they could with advantage become highly complementary features of the sociological enterprise; and, further, that the desirability of creating stronger ties between QAD and RAT is in fact well brought out by an examination of the main lines of criticism that each presently encounters.

For the purposes of my argument, I define both QAD and RAT in rather broad terms. QAD is taken to cover any analysis of extensive social data—though typically data collected via survey research—that involves the statistical investigation of relationships existing among variables. RAT refers to any theoretical approach that seeks to explain social phenomena as the outcome of individual action that is construed as rational, given individuals' goals and conditions of action, and is in this way made intelligible (*verständlich*).[1] Throughout the chapter, I illustrate methodological points that arise by reference to substantive work. For the most part, such illustrations are drawn from research in social stratification, not just because this is my own field of special interest but also because it is that from which examples have in fact been most often taken in previous discussion of several issues that are of central concern.

This chapter was first published in the *European Sociological Review*, 12 (1996). Earlier drafts benefited greatly from comments made by Peter Abell, Hans-Peter Blossfeld, David Cox, Nan Dirk De Graaf, Dudley Duncan, Ray Fitzpatrick, Martin Hollis, Colin Mills, Garry Runciman, Ian Shapiro, and Wout Ultee.

[1] I recognize (see further Chapter 6) that there exists an entire 'family' of rational action theories, and that, as well as family resemblances, significant differences are also to be observed. Indeed, I opt for the designation of rational action theory rather than the more common 'rational choice theory', since the latter tends to be used in a narrower sense than would suit my purposes. In particular, while rational action does entail choice in that one course of action rather than another is taken, such action need not, as I would wish to understand it, always follow from the implementation of a formal and explicit decision-making procedure (cf. Collins 1996). The varieties of RAT are not in fact all that consequential for the argument of the present Chapter, but in writing it I have had chiefly in mind those that I believe (again see Chapter 6) will prove to be of greatest value in sociology.

To account for the lack thus far of any 'special relationship' between QAD and RAT would require an essay in the history of sociology (see Chapter 12). Here, it must suffice to say that, in so far as sociologists engaging in QAD have sought to relate their work to theoretical issues, they have shown no particular interest in RAT—as opposed, say, to structural-functionalism or Marxism—while advocates of RAT have been concerned to emphasize its generality and in turn its applicability in *all* styles of empirical enquiry. Thus, Friedman and Hechter (1988: 212) represent the 'agnosticism' of RAT in regard to different types of data and techniques of analysis as being one of its main attractions; and Boudon (1987) has gone further in maintaining that the 'individual paradigm' in sociology, by which he intends a version of RAT, differs from the 'nomological paradigm', in which the quest is for evolutionary or functional laws, in being just as apt to the explanation of historical *singularities* as of macrosocial regularities of the kind that QAD is able to display.

In some contrast with these prevailing attitudes and arguments, the position I here maintain is that exponents of QAD and of RAT could now derive particular advantage through paying more attention to each others' work, recognizing the potential complementarities that exist, and in effect entering into a collaborative alliance. While I would not wish to suggest that such an alliance should be of an exclusive kind, I do believe, and will seek to show, that there are at the present time rather specific reasons why QAD needs RAT and RAT needs QAD; and, further, that the particular emphases and modifications that an alliance would encourage, if not necessitate, on either side would be ones likely to be beneficial to the future development of QAD and RAT alike.

The Need of QAD for RAT

In recent years it has become a standard criticism of QAD that, although typically based on 'individual data', such as that collected from respondents to surveys, it tends to be conducted without systematic reference to the idea— let alone to a theory—of *individual action*. For instance, Abbott (1992a) has undertaken a detailed textual examination of what he takes to be a representative case of QAD (Halaby and Weakliem 1989, a study of the influence of worker control on the employment relationship), and has argued that, in general, the analyses offered are couched in terms of variables and their effects rather than of individuals and the courses of action that they follow. It is, in other words, variables rather than individuals that 'do the acting'. Individuals are seen not as acting themselves but merely as being 'the locale for the variables doing their thing' (Abbott 1992a: 55–6). It may be possible, Abbott recognizes, to trace a narrative of the action underlying the analysis—that is, a narrative that entails the relationships empirically established among variables—which is of an *implicit* kind; but it tends to be only where unexpected and problematic results are thrown up that such 'interpretation' is attempted in any more explicit way. These exceptional instances are, however, highly revealing: they bring out the fact that practitioners of QAD do in the end accept, even if only covertly, that causality in social processes cannot be established from quantitative analyses in themselves but is rather 'logically dependent' upon action narratives (Abbott 1992a: 57).

Abbott's critique forms part of a more general consideration of the practices of 'standard-positivist' sociology, which he evidently sees as being in need of more or less radical reconstruction. However, it has to be noted that his animadversions on QAD are scarcely novel; and what is in the present context of particular interest is that among those who have previously advanced essentially similar arguments are indeed well-known exponents of RAT who would not normally be counted within the 'anti-positivist' camp.

Thus, Coleman (1986a: 1314–15) was one of the first to observe the seeming paradox that sociologists engaged in 'empirical, statistical survey research' are largely reliant on individual data but analyse such data with little apparent concern for questions of individuals' purposes or intentions. Supposedly causal explanations of individuals' *behaviour* are given in terms either of their social characteristics or of characteristics of their environment, and without reference to any 'intervening action orientation'. The success of this approach tends then to be gauged simply by the amount of variation in behaviour that is 'accounted for', and no need for explanations to be systematically related to a theory of action is recognized. Likewise, Boudon (1987: 61–2), taking the particular example of quantitative studies of social mobility and status attainment, has maintained that in these studies 'the units of analysis are not individuals but variables'. The influence of one variable on another—for example, of education on occupational status—is presented in some quantified form and then, typically, findings of this kind 'will be considered final results'. In other words, no effort is made to show how the statistical relations between variables derive from their 'real causes', that is, the actions of individuals.[2]

Practitioners of QAD might well reply that critical comment on these lines is somewhat disingenuous. They are not, they would say, *quite* so naïve as simply to identify association among variables with patterns of social action and interaction, nor thus to suppose, for example, that a man's education 'causes' his occupation in the same way that, say, a sprained ankle would cause him to limp. And, they might go on, the reason why action narratives are often only implicit in their analyses is that they are typically concerned with testing substantive hypotheses, the theoretical derivation of which is already provided elsewhere. For example, they are concerned to investigate whether or not the association between education and occupational status is strengthening over time because such a tendency is a direct implication of a

---

[2] See further in this connection the fascinating exchange between Hauser (1976) and Boudon (1976), in which, it might be said, Hauser wins most of the battles but Boudon wins the war.

well-known theory of changing social selection under advanced industrial-ism: that is, a theory that holds that such selection becomes increasingly 'mer-itocratic' as criteria of 'achievement' replace those of 'ascription' (see further Chapter 11). In turn, this emphasis on hypothesis testing also explains why fuller interpretations tend to be given of problematic results: where empir-ical findings do not conform with the theory under examination, the provi-sion of some alternative understanding of their generation at the level of social action is obviously called for.

However, even if such a response is justified, it is of course still one that accepts rather than disputes the central claim of the authors previously cited: namely, that QAD in itself is incomplete and that its contribution to soci-ology will be seriously limited unless it is allied in some way or other to accounts of social action. And, once this claim is accepted, it is then difficult to deny the desirability of such accounts being in all instances as explicit and detailed as it is possible to make them. For, apart from anything else, how far QAD can serve as an effective means of testing theories of macrosocial processes will often be heavily dependent on the degree of their elaboration at the micro-level. Thus, simply to show a strengthening association over time between education and occupational status is in itself of rather little help in evaluating the theory of an increasing meritocratic emphasis in social selec-tion. As several commentators have observed, such a finding is equally con-sistent with a rival theory that sees the dominant tendency as being not so much towards meritocracy as 'credentialism': that is, an increasing use of formal qualifications in selection, promoted by interested occupational asso-ciations and educational bodies, and in which managements connive more for reasons of convenience than demonstrated efficiency. In other words, the two theories differ crucially in the action narratives, or 'storylines', by which they account for the *same* empirically observed tendency. And a requirement for any useful adjudication between them must therefore be that this differ-ence is fully spelled out so that the alternative narratives can themselves be exposed to further empirical test.

The need for QAD to become more theoretically informed has, moreover, of late been forcefully underlined as a result of criticism emanating from a quite different quarter from that so far considered: that is, criticism not from theorists who might feel unduly neglected, but rather from statisticians who have become increasingly sceptical of some of the more ambitious versions of QAD that have been attempted within sociology and other non-experimental social sciences.

In this regard, several papers by Freedman (1985, 1991, 1992a,b) on the uses—or abuses—of 'structural equation', and in particular causal path, models have perhaps been of greatest impact (see also Holland 1988). Although these interventions have provoked some lively debates, the main outcome would appear to be a widening acceptance, and even on the part of those using such models, of their limitations and dangers. In the late 1960s practitioners of QAD were offered the attractive possibility that structural equation modelling might serve in sociology as a substitute for experimental methods; and, by the 1980s, this approach had in fact become firmly established in many areas of empirical work. As Berk has observed (1988: 155), 'few ... questioned the fundamentals; causal inferences followed automatically from structural equation models'. Today, however, a clearly different situation prevails.

At a technical level, the criticisms advanced by Freedman and others of causal path modelling in sociology focus on the dubious validity of the stochastic assumptions that need to be made about the distributions, individual and joint, of the variables involved.[3] In turn, much of the debate that has ensued has been concerned with just how far such assumptions are in fact breached, how much this matters, and how far any shortcomings that do occur can be made good by various technical 'fixes'. For present purposes, though, what is of greater interest is the degree of consensus that appears to have emerged on a number of more fundamental matters concerning the relationship of modelling to theory.

First of all, it would by now seem to be widely accepted that it is *not* in fact possible to derive causal inferences 'automatically' from the results of statistical modelling, whether deemed structural or otherwise; nor indeed, some would wish to add, from *any* kind of investigative methodology, even an experimental one. As Hope has put it (1992: 32), in a response to Freedman, few present-day epistemologists would expect to find, in either the social *or* the natural sciences, 'a Baconian organum for grinding theories out of observations'. And, from this position, causality is then more readily understood as a theoretical claim than as a directly accessible feature of the world itself.[4]

Secondly, it is in turn generally agreed that, far from theory being output from causal path and suchlike analyses, it is, rather, necessary input to them. Thus, in a causal path diagram, the ordering of variables, at the very least, must be given by theory, and what the analysis then provides is quantitative estimates of the various effects that are taken to be operating upon the dependent variable. It follows that, if the theory is wrong, that is, *inconsistent with the social processes actually generating the data*, the statistical calculations will be vitiated. Freedman argues (1992a) that a model seriously intended as a structural one should be sufficiently well grounded theoretically to enable predictions to be made of the results of *interventions* in the system of variables it represents—but that there is little reason to believe that the quality of theory informing causal path models in sociology is sufficient to give them

---

[3] While Freedman's major published contribution (1992a) is ostensibly directed against an instance of causal path modelling in Hope (1984), its real target, as Duncan (1992) has recognized, should be taken as Blau and Duncan's *The American Occupational Structure* (1967)— the *locus classicus* of causal path modelling in sociology (though see n. 5 below). This latter work was in fact the subject of an earlier critique by Freedman (1983) that remained unpublished.

[4] Thus, Holland (1986a, 1988) argues that what statistics can contribute to causal inference (even when allied to experimental designs) lies not in the *identification of the causes* of known effects, which is the task of theory, but rather in the *measurement of the effects* of the causes that theory postulates. For further discussion of Holland's position, see Chapter 7 below.

this capacity. And Hope (1992: 34) concurs: for the most part, he accepts, such modelling 'does *not* license counterfactual claims'.[5]

Thirdly, there appears also to be consensus, albeit with differences of emphasis, that in sociology causal path and other models that have been represented as 'structural' would for the most part be better regarded as having simply *descriptive* functions: that is, as serving to show only patterns of association, not causation. Thus, Hope suggests (1992: 34–6) that causal path analysis should be understood as attempting not to model microsocial processes *per se* but rather to provide a summary of their overall, macrosocial *outcomes*. In status attainment research, for example, causal path models do not tell us about the ways in which individuals actually get qualifications, are offered jobs, take up jobs, and so on, but about the patterns that ultimately emerge 'from a manifold of decisions: personal, institutional and political' and 'when all social forces have exerted their effects'. Correspondingly, Freedman would himself acknowledge (e.g. 1992*a,b*) that, at this descriptive level, some intriguing and consequential facts about social stratification have been produced by causal path analyses, even though he might wish also to argue that simpler statistical techniques could have served just as well and with less risk of their results being misinterpreted.

The common ground that would seem to have been established within the debate on statistical modelling might therefore be summed up as follows. Even in its most advanced forms, QAD cannot serve as a source of explanations in itself. It would, rather, be better regarded as, in the first instance at least, a source of *explananda*—a means of establishing evidence of regularities that *call for* theoretical understanding. Moreover, the contribution that QAD may in turn make towards reaching such understanding will not be through the demonstration of causal processes directly. It may, perhaps, be so devised as to help investigators form ideas about such processes (see e.g. Cox and Wermuth 1993), but, even so, its primary importance must again lie in the provision of evidence: in this case, evidence that, as Freedman puts it (1992*b*: 111), can 'serve as a link in a chain of reasoning about causes' where, however, 'the causal inference rides on the argument, not on the magic of least squares'. In other words, the argument itself must be not statistical but substantive: it must be concerned not with relations among variables but with the ways in which the data constituting the *explanandum* are actually brought into being.

The distinction here taken up between descriptive and structural models is one that is in fact echoed and developed in a wider context in recent contributions by several other commentators: for example, by Cox (1990) in sepa-

---

[5] It should in this connection be noted that over twenty years ago, in an introductory text on structural equation modelling, Duncan (1975: esp. 151–2) not only elaborated the technical problems involved but warned of the dangers of regarding such modelling as being in itself a way of conducting sociological analysis and emphasized the essential role of theory. More recent contributions that likewise serve to bring out the full extent of the theoretical demands of causal modelling in sociology include Lieberson (1985) and Blossfeld and Rohwer (1995*a*: esp. ch. 1).

rating 'empirical' from 'substantive' models or by Rogosa (1992) in contrasting 'statistical models' *per se* with 'scientific models' as expressed in statistical form. What is, evidently, the shared concern is to bring out the difference (though without supposing it to be absolute) between applying statistical techniques, on the one hand, in what might be called a 'pre-theoretical' mode in order, as Merton (1987) has put it, to 'establish the phenomena' and, on the other hand, in order to model the processes through which—from some theoretical standpoint—the phenomena are seen as being produced.[6]

Once, then, such a discrimination in the uses of QAD is made—instead of QAD being taken as providing, as it were, *explanandum* and explanation simultaneously—the need for an independent theoretical input becomes apparent. And, I would add, the development of QAD itself may at the same time be expected to benefit: that is, through further encouragement being given to tendencies already apparent for its practitioners to break free from a preoccupation with statistical methods constructed around the idea of normal and continuous distributions in the interests of treating their data with greater descriptive fidelity. The growing attraction to sociologists in recent years of alternative techniques such as loglinear modelling or event history analysis can, I believe, be largely understood from this point of view.[7] It is not difficult to show—and status attainment research using path analysis would serve well to illustrate the point—that problems are likely to arise if the descriptive work necessary to establish the specific explanatory tasks that theory must address is not adequately accomplished *before* the modelling of causal processes is attempted.[8]

If, then, it is accepted that in sociology the uses of QAD, far from being a substitute for theory, can be properly understood *only in their relation to theory*, the question that in the present context remains is, of course, that of why such theory should be RAT. Proponents of RAT might wish simply to say that,

---

[6] To make such a distinction is not to suppose that the phenomena to be explained can be established without recourse to *concepts*, which may then in turn reflect some theoretical stance. But even where data are constituted in terms of a conceptual approach that is theoretically well derived, it does not follow that the explanation of any regularities that are revealed will, for this reason, be at once apparent. As Popper has emphasized (e.g. 1976*b*: 18–31), the same problem or *explanandum* may well be arrived at through quite different conceptual approaches; and, if an explanation is then to be provided, further theoretical advance will obviously be required.

[7] It is of interest that, as Clogg (1992) has documented, loglinear modelling and event history analysis are alike instances of statistical techniques that have to a significant extent advanced *via* their sociological applications, in contrast to those on which sociology tended previously to rely which were mostly imports from biometrics, psychometrics, or econometrics. And further of interest is the growing readiness to reject the idea, deriving from Stevens's (1946) theory of scale types, that using categorical or discrete data entails an inferior form of measurement (see esp. Duncan 1984: ch. 4).

[8] Thus, for example, from the loglinear modelling of intergenerational social mobility tables that also incorporate an educational variable (see e.g. Ishida *et al.* 1995), it has become apparent that the part played by education cannot be realistically treated as being uniform across all origin-to-destination transitions alike, as causal path models usually suppose. Or again, event history analyses (cf. Blossfeld and Rohwer 1995*a*) have indicated that it is inadequate in such models simply to suppose a temporal ordering of variables (e.g. education comes before 'first job'), without also considering the 'temporal shapes' of the dependencies that are taken to be involved.

following on the intellectual collapse of structural-functionalism in both its liberal and Marxist versions, RAT represents the only theoretical approach now on offer that has serious explanatory potential, at least at a macrosocial level (cf. Kiser and Hechter 1991) or, perhaps, to make out a general case for RAT's 'paradigmatic privilege' (cf. Abell 1992). However, two further arguments may be advanced to suggest the *special* suitability of RAT as theory to be utilized in conjunction with QAD.

First, as earlier noted, QAD is usually undertaken with data sets that result from survey work or other extensive data-collection exercises. In such investigations, the amount of information that can be obtained about the characteristics of particular individuals, or about events or decisions in which they have been involved, is subject to obvious constraints, and has moreover to be elicited in a fairly standardized form via questionnaires or interview schedules. It is, therefore, scarcely feasible to build up information of the highly differentiated kind that might result from more intensive research, carried out, say, within a limited social milieu by means of repeated interviewing, observational methods, and so on. However, it is a feature of RAT that it does not require accounts of individual actors or action that are based on 'thick' description. Neither the psychology nor the phenomenology of human action is a focus of analytic attention: no attempt is made to capture the full diversity of the cognitive or motivational aspects of action nor of the nuances of its subjective meanings. The primary analytic concern of RAT, at least as typically deployed in sociology, is with elucidating the micro-to-macro link: that is, with showing the ways in which a number, and often a very large number, of individual actions come together so as to generate macrosocial phenomena of interest. And no more descriptive detail or theoretical understanding is sought at the individual level than is called for by efforts to this end (cf. Abell 1992; Coleman and Fararo 1992).[9] Thus, what are often seen as the characteristic limitations of survey-type data are not in fact ones likely to create major difficulties in the use of RAT, of the kind that clearly could arise where attempts are made to treat individual action through either psychological or phenomenological approaches that, as Lindenberg (1992: 7) has put it, 'are greedy with regard to information about each individual'.[10]

[9] This, I would emphasize, should not be thought of as a shortcoming. As Stinchcombe (1993: 27) has aptly observed, it is scarcely desirable, from an explanatory point of view, that the mechanisms invoked to account for regularities observed at a higher—i.e. more macro—level should then entail 'complex investigations' at a lower level: 'There is no beauty in understanding pressure, temperature and volume of gases by the behavior of molecules if the molecules have to be a lot more complex than the behavior of the gases being explained, if all their quarks and colors have to enter into the statistical mechanics.' For a much earlier statement of essentially the same position as that taken up by Coleman and Fararo and by Abell, see Popper (1945/1966: ch. 14).

[10] See further in this connection Lindenberg's (1985, 1990) useful distinction between the concepts of individual₁, appropriate to psychology, where both analytic *and* explanatory primacies lie at the individual level, and individual₂, appropriate to RAT as applied in sociology (or economics), where explanatory primacy remains at the individual level, via the principle of methodological individualism, but analytic primacy is shifted to the aggregate level. See also the insightful reflections on this issue of Boudon (1990: 42–3), inspired by passages from

Secondly, though, it is not just that the type of data usually subjected to quantitative analysis may be unable to support elaborated accounts of individual action: it is also the case that the action narratives that are typically required in order to complement QAD *should not be* ones that aim at either descriptive or explanatory completeness. Consider the kind of narratives advocated, for example, by Howard Becker (1992), with illustrations drawn from case-study research in the tradition of Lindesmith (1948) or Cressey (1953). The aim here is, Becker tells us, to give, step by step, 'the story of how something *inevitably* got to be the way it is'. Narrative analysts in this tradition 'are not happy unless they have a *completely deterministic* result'—and, indeed, to the extent that 'Every negative case becomes an opportunity to refine the result, to rework the explanation so that it includes the seemingly anomalous case' (H. S. Becker 1992: 210, 212; emphasis added).[11] Now one might wish to question whether deterministic accounts of action can in fact be a serious goal for sociologists (or adhoccery a serious methodological principle): there are good grounds for viewing the social world, or at all events the basis of its study, as being necessarily probabilistic in character (cf. Duncan 1984: ch. 8; Lieberson 1992; King *et al.* 1994: ch. 2). But, for present purposes, the important point is that storytelling in the manner favoured by Becker *is simply not consistent with the kinds of result that QAD produces*. As Becker himself points out, the regularities that are established by QAD *are* of a probabilistic kind, and it must then follow that 'completely deterministic' accounts of the underlying action would lead to such regularities being *over*-explained. Or, to put the matter another way, if deterministic theory were indeed appropriate for understanding the ways in which macrosocial regularities are generated at the level of individual action, one would expect the probabilities shown up by QAD to be much closer to 1—and 'variation explained' to be much closer to 100 per cent—than is in fact the case.[12]

So far as the analysts to whom Becker refers do come anywhere near to demonstrating 'inevitable' outcomes, it is, one may suggest, only because their accounts rely less on theory that has any claim to generality than on the invocation of conditions highly specific to the milieux within which their case studies are conducted. However, the regularities that emerge from QAD tend to be of greatest interest, considered, that is, as *explananda*, where, though only probabilistic, they none the less hold *across* different milieux, set apart in time and space, and in turn, perhaps, in their institutional and

Simmel. From the position here taken, criticisms both of RAT and of survey data of the kind advanced by Scheff (1992) become strictly irrelevant.

[11] As I argue in Chapter 3 above, an analogous determinism is supposed at the macro-level in the work of sociologists such as Skocpol and Ragin, in so far as they eschew quantitative and probabilistic, in favour of qualitative and logical, analyses that are inspired more or less directly by the methodology of John Stuart Mill.

[12] And, as Duncan has aptly commented (1975: 166–7), having argued that a complex social system could hardly operate other than to some degree stochastically, 'The sociologist who despairs of his low R^2s would do well to ask himself if he would want it otherwise—would he care to live in the society so structured that his particular collection of variables accounts for 90% instead of 32% of the variance in Y?'

cultural contexts. Thus, in stratification research, examples of such regularities would be the persistence over decades of class inequalities in educational attainment and mobility chances, or the extent of similarities in patterns of social fluidity, both across subpopulations within national societies and among such societies themselves (see e.g. Erikson and Goldthorpe 1992*a*; Shavit and Blossfeld 1993; Ishida *et al.* 1995). If, therefore, a better understanding of regularities of this kind is to be obtained, theoretical accounts with priorities just the reverse of those implied by Becker are what is required. It is generality, not determinacy, that must be sought.

In this respect, then, RAT has obvious attractions. The action narratives to which it gives rise do not, or at least need not, relate to specific actors or to specific courses or conditions of action at given times or places, but can rather be treated as narratives of a highly generalized character. Their aim is not to 'tell the whole story' in any particular case, even supposing this were possible, but to capture *common* elements or, in other words, patterns of action that recur in many cases. This they seek to do through having a structure that is implicative rather than conjunctive: that is to say, the 'steps' that RAT narratives comprise are linked together in the form of 'practical syllogisms' (cf. von Wright 1971) rather than just temporally. The purpose of these narratives is not to demonstrate how something 'inevitably got to be the way it is' as, so to speak, a piece of natural history, but rather to bring out what in the Popperian version of RAT would be called the 'logic' of a certain *type* of situation (Popper 1945/1966: ch. 14; 1957: ch. 29; 1994; and see further Chapter 6 below). Given that certain goals are pursued under certain conditions, the idea is to show which courses of action the various actors involved would then be expected to follow according to some criterion of rationality and, of course, with what consequences. These actions and consequences will not necessarily be observed. What is common to a certain set of situations—the underlying logic that the RAT narrative seeks to capture—need not be what actually generates action in any *particular* instance: the whole story is *not* being told. But, on the other hand, RAT would in this way appear apt, in principle at least, to the explanation of the probabilistic, yet often wide-ranging, regularities in social action and its outcomes that QAD has the ability to reveal.

The Need of RAT for QAD

If it is by now a standard criticism of QAD that it neglects the actors and the processes of action that generate the regularities it displays, it is a yet more routine criticism of RAT that it derives from a conception of the actor and of the nature of action that is of a quite unrealistic kind (see e.g. Etzioni 1988; Frank 1990; Smelser 1992). Put at its most simple, the objection to RAT is that human beings frequently do not, and perhaps *cannot*, act in a rational manner, and therefore that a theory of rational action, however rigorously it may be developed from its initial assumptions, will in its actual application to most areas of social life have at best only a limited explanatory power.[13]

In more detail, it may be argued that any coherent idea of rational action must imply a certain relationship between actors' goals, beliefs, the evidence for these beliefs, and the actions that then follow. Actors act rationally when, in the light of well-grounded beliefs, they choose those courses of action that are best calculated to realize their goals (cf. Elster 1989b: ch. 4). Such a schema, however, makes apparent just how rationality could at several different points be threatened and, perhaps, defeated. Individuals may not know just what their goals (or desires or preferences) really are: they may be uncertain, confused, ambivalent or inconsistent. Again, the beliefs that guide their actions may not be well grounded but, rather, ill informed, uncritically held, muddled, or just plain wrong. Further, in moving from beliefs to action, individuals may not succeed in finding that course of action that, given their goals, would be optimal for them: they may fail to consider all the possibilities, miscalculate probabilities, or indeed not calculate at all but simply act in habitual or impulsive ways. And, finally, even where individuals do have well-defined goals, well-grounded beliefs, and are capable of determining the best way to proceed to their goals, they may still then lack the *will* to act as they know that they should.[14]

Moreover, it is not just that such deviations from the requirements of rational action can plausibly be suggested: their quite regular and widespread *occurrence* would seem beyond serious doubt. Apart from the experience of everyday life, there is by now an impressive array of research findings in the psychological literature (for a review, see Sutherland 1992), to show that individuals do display strong propensities to fall into irrational, or at all events non-rational, thought and action in a great variety of ways.

It is, then, perhaps not surprising that advocates of RAT, in responding to the charge that their approach lacks realism, have sought in the main to argue on heuristic and methodological rather than on empirical grounds. Thus, what they have most usually contended (see e.g. Elster 1979: pt. iii; Abell 1992) is that it is necessary at least to *begin* with an idea of rational action, since it seems only by reference to this that other kinds of action can be usefully identified; and, further, that it is when action is treated as in some sense rational that it becomes most readily intelligible or, in other words, can most obviously be treated as something other than mere behaviour.

[13] A further standard objection raised against RAT is that it offers no systematic account of how the goals, desires, or preferences towards which rational action is directed are themselves formed. Proponents of RAT have readily acknowledged the correctness of this objection but have at the same time observed—appropriately, I would believe—that neither has any other theoretical approach contributed much to an understanding of how the ultimate ends of action are determined, and that current attempts at addressing this problem from a RAT standpoint are at least as promising as those made from rival positions (cf. e.g. Friedman and Hechter 1988; Abell 1992; Hechter 1994).

[14] Such potential failures of rationality and their implications have been exhaustively analysed at a theoretical level in the work of Elster (see esp. 1979, 1983b, 1989a,c).

Such replies have force (as I shall argue further in the following essay). None the less, they might be thought in themselves a not entirely adequate basis for a major programme of theory development. The importance is thus highlighted of a first way in which RAT could benefit from an alliance with QAD. What I would suggest is that, in so far as RAT is used together with QAD—that is, in order to account for regularities in action and in the outcomes of action as demonstrated by QAD—it is possible to provide a stronger and more positive reply to those who would question the foundations of RAT in the way that has been indicated.

The gist of the argument to be made is captured by Hernes's observation (1992: 427) that aggregates may be regarded as more rational than their individual members, and its underlying mathematics have been well set out by Stinchcombe (1968: 67–8 n. 8)—albeit in a somewhat different context from the present.[15] The crucial analytical point may be put as follows. Suppose that in their actions in some respect the members of an aggregate or collectivity are subject, on the one hand, to an influence that bears on all alike and, on the other hand, to a variety of influences not deviating *systematically* from the common influence and bearing only on particular individuals or small groups. It can then be shown that, even if the 'common' influence is clearly weaker than the 'idiosyncratic' influences taken together, knowledge of the former is still likely to allow a large part of the variation in the behaviour of the aggregate to be accounted for. This result comes about—and will, other things being equal, emerge the more strongly the larger the aggregate—essentially because the effects of the idiosyncratic influences tend to 'cancel out' and thus leave the effects of the common influence, even if relatively weak, as still the decisive ones at the aggregate level. When, therefore, RAT is used to provide an explanation for probabilistic regularities revealed by QAD, it is no longer necessary to suppose that all actors concerned at all times act in an entirely rational manner: *only* that the tendency to act rationally, in the circumstances that prevail, is the common factor at work, while deviations from rationality are brought about in a variety of ways and with a variety of consequences.

Consider, for example, the following finding reported on the basis of quantitative studies (e.g. Handl, n.d.; Portocarero 1987; Erikson and Goldthorpe 1992a: ch. 7) carried out in several different modern societies. In these societies a marked degree of class homogamy prevails, and, further, the level and pattern of the association that exists between the class origins of women and the class positions of their husbands is with only small—though cross-nationally recurrent—exceptions essentially the same as that existing between men's class origins and the class positions they

---

[15] Stinchcombe's more general concern is with the way in which 'proportionality factors' of any kind within a population can remain close to constant over time, despite rapidly changing individual characteristics. The basic mathematical idea involved can be traced back to Penrose (1946) if not indeed to Quetelet. Hechter (1987: 31–3) also takes up Stinchcombe's argument in a RAT context, but for the more limited purpose of defending the assumption of actors' similar preference orderings over a given set of choices.

eventually obtain through their employment. In other words, if it is known how men of a given class origin have become distributed within the class structure in the course of their employment, it can be predicted, with no great inaccuracy, how their 'sisters' will have been distributed by marriage.

Now, the decision to marry and the choice of a marriage partner have in fact been singled out by critics of RAT (see e.g. Scheff 1992: 102) as instances of action where the non-rational may be expected to loom large; and, for the purposes of the argument at least, let this be acknowledged. However, it does *not* then follow that the possibility is precluded of giving an explanation of the above finding in terms of RAT: an explanation, that is, that would seek to show how the regularity revealed, and also the recurrent exceptions to it, are generated by men and women pursuing similar goals in marriage and labour markets alike, and thus exploiting class-linked resources and responding to class-linked constraints to the best of their abilities. All that needs to be supposed to make a RAT explanation viable in principle is that some, even if quite small, element of rationality is the *shared* feature among the actors involved. As March puts it (1978: 588), 'Even a small signal stands out in a noisy message'; or, as Hernes concludes (1992: 428), 'a gleam of rationality in minds that are otherwise obscure and cloudy goes a long way in explaining what happens in aggregate. We do not always need strong assumptions of rationality in order to benefit from rational actor models.'[16]

In order to bring out more clearly the force of the argument here being advanced, it may be helpful also to refer to a contrasting case: that is, one in which a RAT approach is taken to the explanation not of a probabilistic regularity in social action but rather of a unique event—Boudon's (1987) 'historical singularity'. What has in this regard become almost a paradigm case, in discussion among philosophers at least, is the great British naval disaster that occurred off the coast of Tripoli in 1893 when in the course of a complicated manœuvre attempted by the British Mediterranean Fleet two battleships collided and over 350 men, including the Commander-in Chief, Vice Admiral Tryon, lost their lives.

This event was first taken up by Watkins (1963, 1970; see also Jarvie 1972: ch. 1; Runciman 1983: 203–7) in order to illustrate an argument that explanation in terms of 'the rationality principle' or 'the logic of the situation' has a general validity: that is, need not be restricted to instances where actors succeed in attaining their goals as intended but is just as applicable to those

---

[16] The possibility does, of course, remain that there may be other common—i.e. non-idiosyncratic—influences bearing on the collectivity of actors apart from that of rationality. The most obvious alternatives are shared beliefs that cannot be understood as rational, even in the given conditions; or shared commitments to values and related social norms that cannot be understood in rational—i.e. instrumental—terms. It is then in no way accidental that the most engrossing and consequential of current debates in modern sociological theory should centre on issues raised in this connection (see e.g. Boudon 1994; Elster 1989*a*: esp. ch. 3; Coleman 1990: esp. chs. 10, 11; Hechter 1994); and it is, moreover, encouraging that these appear also to be debates to which, as I later suggest, empirically based interventions can contribute significantly.

particular cases where they fail to do so and indeed where their actions 'seem more or less irrational or even downright crazy' (Watkins 1970: 167). Watkins seeks to show that one can go beyond what he calls 'non-rational pseudo-explanations' for Admiral Tryon attempting the 'impossible' manœuvre that led to the collision—that is, explanations suggesting that he was drunk, suffering from fever, or otherwise deprived of his senses. One can instead provide a rational reconstruction of the incident in which Tryon and all others involved are seen as acting in ways that, given their objectives and the prevailing circumstances, are quite intelligible. The disaster is explicable as the outcome of misunderstandings of an entirely understandable kind.

However, the difficulty here is that Watkins's reconstruction relates essentially to what happened *after* Tryon had thought up the fateful manœuvre. It does not explain just why Tryon wished to undertake such a manœuvre, nor, more seriously, why he gave orders for it in such an elliptical and indeed perplexing form that, as Watkins's own account recognizes, Tryon's subordinates were themselves required to engage in 'rational reconstruction' in order to make any sense of his intentions—a task in which, understandably, they failed. Moreover, what also remains exogenous is the fact that Tryon quite frequently gave orders that appeared designed to challenge his officers to query or defy them. One may, therefore, accept Watkins's account as plausible and in fact illuminating so far as it goes, but still maintain that in explaining the disaster major weight must rest with idiosyncratic aspects of Tryon's conduct, on which a clinical psychologist might best be qualified to throw light. Considered as a rational actor, Tryon would seem to fall at the very first hurdle: that is, to have been uncertain or ambivalent as to what his objective was—to have the manœuvre efficiently carried out, to give his subordinates a combined intelligence and initiative test, or to assert his right to their unquestioning obedience.[17]

For present purposes, the point to be emphasized is then that, *pace* Boudon, using RAT in order to understand regularities in action established in respect of situations recurring within a relatively large aggregate or collectivity *is* a quite different proposition from using RAT to 'make sense' of a historical singularity (cf. Popper 1994: ch. 8)—and a more readily defensible one. In the former case, a strong argument exists to show how, in principle, rationality in action, even if no more than a 'gleam', could none the less be the decisive influence in generating what is empirically observed; in the latter case, no such argument can be made. Indeed, in any particular situation and sequence of action it is entirely possible—as Watkins's account of the Tryon disaster could be taken to show—that, even though most of the actors involved do act rationally for most of the time, what chiefly determines the outcome is still just one expression of unreason.

The charge of an undue lack of realism in its basic assumptions is that which has been most often levelled against RAT. However, over recent years, as

---

[17] There are several accounts of the disaster by naval historians. Watkins draws primarily on Hough (1959).

publications expounding and elaborating RAT in one form or another have become more numerous, a further, though related, line of criticism has emerged: namely, that, while much effort has indeed gone into theory development, too little has gone into theory *application*, so that the explanatory pay-off of RAT in regard, at all events, to the classic problems of sociological analysis has remained disappointingly small. Thus, for instance, Ultee (1991: 47), in evaluating the work of Dutch exponents of RAT (e.g. Lindenberg and Wippler 1978; Lindenberg 1982, 1983), has concluded that, although their 'meta-analytical schemes' illustrate how central issues of macrosociology, such as those of solidarity and inequality, *might* be addressed on the basis of RAT, 'since their approach has not been linked to specific substantive questions, high yields are not to be expected in the near future'. And it is of further interest to note that Green and Shapiro (1994) have taken up an essentially similar position in launching a forceful critique of the 'pathologies' of RAT within American political science. Devotees of RAT, Green and Shapiro argue, are more concerned with its elaboration than with its empirical testing; they can claim rather few instances in which RAT has demonstrated real explanatory power in regard to major political-science questions; and it is suspicious that their efforts at application tend to show to best advantage in fields that are 'evidence poor'.

While such judgements might be thought unduly negative—at all events if the achievements and potential of RAT are evaluated in relation to those of other theoretical approaches—it could scarcely be denied that the style in which RAT has thus far been typically presented is such as to attract critical comment of the kind illustrated. The crucial distinction that here arises is well expressed by Hechter when he writes (1987: 55–6) that there are two possible grounds for advancing new theory: first, in order to explain, or to explain better than before, a particular set of findings and, second, in order to resolve a theoretical problem *per se*. In his study of group solidarity, Hechter makes it clear that his grounds are the latter; and it would be true to say that, in the work of most other leading proponents of RAT, a similar emphasis is to be found. Furthermore, a tendency is now apparent to go significantly further than Hechter down the road of, so to speak, 'autonomous' theory development—and in just the way that Ultee and Green and Shapiro would regret.

Thus, while Hechter (1987: 168) does focus his attention on a specific social phenomenon, group solidarity, and aims to develop a general theory of it, Elster, for example, appears to have come to the view that the quest for theory in this sense should be abandoned, and that social scientists should concentrate simply on formulating causal models or what he prefers to call 'mechanisms': that is, 'small and medium sized descriptions of ways in which things happen' or 'a little causal story, recognizable from one context to another' (1990: 247–8; cf. Hedström and Swedberg 1998*a*). As identified and collected, such mechanisms could come to serve as a 'toolbox' of explanatory devices to which social analysts could resort as and when might seem appropriate

(Elster 1989*b*: ch. 1). Likewise, Hernes suggests (1992: 425–6; see also 1989) that what RAT permits is the accumulation of models that are of a 'sometimes-true' character (cf. Coleman 1964: 516–19): that is to say, they are capable of providing the 'inside story' or 'sociologic' of real-life action *in so far as they happen to 'match' it*. However, if a particular model does not give a good match, then another must be taken from the 'depository' of such models or a new one devised.

Such arguments have a disarming modesty. But, as well as sitting ill with claims for the paradigmatic privilege of RAT in sociology,[18] they can scarcely allay fears of theory development becoming increasingly detached from central substantive concerns. For, as Hernes (1992: 427) well recognizes, abstract models can be constructed to which 'there never has corresponded any real phenomena and never will—they are, so to speak "never-true" theories. But to make them up and play with them may nevertheless provide deep pleasure—as any journal in theoretical economics evinces.' Further, the reference here to economics may perhaps be yet more apposite than Hernes intended. For it is in economics that it has become most apparent that the position that he and Elster adopt creates a serious difficulty regarding the relationship between theory and research. As several recent writers on the methodology of economics have observed (see esp. Blaug 1991; 1992: chs. 3, 4, 16; Hutchison 1988), if theory is formulated in such a way that its 'domain of application' remains unspecified, it becomes immune to falsification through empirical findings: every apparent refutation can be countered by the argument that the theory was being applied to the 'wrong' kind of case, and the theory may then be returned, unscathed, to the depository. But the question in turn arises: if research cannot be designed in order to test theory and if the validity or otherwise of a particular line of theoretical development cannot be judged by reference to research, how are either theorists or researchers to gain any indication of what the most profitable direction and focus of their efforts might be? The crucial activities of setting research against theory, or theory against research, lose all creative tension; it is, in Blaug's apt phrase, 'like playing tennis with the net down'.[19]

---

[18] There is, I should make clear, no reason to suppose that authors such as Elster and Hernes would themselves wish to be associated with such claims. Elster at least would clearly expect his toolbox to contain more than just RAT-based models.

[19] It is of interest that even a philosopher of science such as Hausman (1992), who upholds the importance of models (as distinct from theories) in economics as means of conceptual elaboration and who emphasizes the problems of a 'falsificationist' methodology, should still believe that economists need to give more serious attention to theory appraisal via data collection and analysis, and that this might in turn lead to a sharper recognition of the point at which the 'qualification' of a theory is less appropriate than its radical modification or indeed abandonment. I should add that, although Elster does not address the problem of the relation of theory and research that I here raise, he is entirely clear about the crucial distinction from which it stems: that is, between theory in a restricted sense—or what he would prefer to call the specification, or model, of a causal mechanism—and what he would regard as theory proper. Theory in this latter sense must *include* a statement of its domain of application: 'it is supposed to tell you which mechanisms operate in which situations' (Elster 1990: 247).

If, therefore, as indeed seems the case, a real danger exists of the connection between RAT and the research process becoming increasingly tenuous and problematic, a second way may be identified in which RAT could benefit from closer ties with QAD: that is—to revert to Hechter's distinction—by its proponents concentrating more on the application of RAT to specific explanatory tasks, rather than on theory development for its own sake, *and taking QAD as their preferred source of explananda*. Authors of expository works may be justified in presenting merely illustrative applications of RAT and, perhaps, ones chosen to demonstrate its power in a particularly striking way. But if, at all events, the case for paradigmatic privilege is to be furthered, then sceptics will need to be persuaded of the explanatory value of RAT across a range of issues that are less evidently hand-picked and of widely acknowledged substantive importance. And they will also need to be shown how, in the light of research, RAT can in fact be evaluated against rival approaches—as well as one RAT-based explanation against another. From this standpoint, then, the empirical regularities revealed by QAD would appear to provide an especially appropriate opportunity for RAT to establish its claims: *hic Rhodus, hic salta!* These are regularities of a macrosocial character, emergent from the actions of large numbers of individuals, often over lengthy periods of time, and thus ones in regard to which RAT, with its primary analytic focus on the micro-to-macro link, should be able to show off its potential to good effect. And, as already argued, they are *explananda* in regard to which RAT can operate without the necessity for any very strong—that is, obviously unrealistic—assumptions of individuals acting always and entirely in a rational manner. In addition, though, two other grounds can be set out in favour of RAT combining with QAD in the way I would propose.

First, the empirical regularities that are demonstrated by QAD, while more extensive in space and time than those likely to emerge from ethnographies or other kinds of case study, tend also to be both more reliable and more refined than those that may be built up on the basis of, say, historical sources or official statistics or by applying 'cut-and-paste' methods to existing monographic literature. In other words, resorting to QAD should generally facilitate the process of 'establishing the phenomena': that is, of ascertaining, before one proceeds to explanation, that there is, in Merton's words (1987: 2–6), 'enough of a regularity to require and allow explanation'. This should be a matter of particular importance for proponents of RAT, since seriousness in establishing the phenomena would seem the best way of countering suspicions that they are inclined to elaborate theory for its own sake rather than to serve specific explanatory purposes, or to set up problems in just such a way that favoured theories can be shown to be apposite—for example, by postulating certain 'stylized facts' that, on examination, may turn out not to be facts at all (cf. Green and Shapiro 1994: 35).[20]

---

[20] A cautionary tale in this regard is provided by the ingenious attempt made by Boudon (1974; see also 1982: ch. 2) to explain, from a RAT standpoint, what he took as a puzzling conjunction in modern societies of increasing educational provision, declining class differ-

Secondly, and yet more importantly, where regularities revealed by QAD are taken as *explananda*, greater possibilities would appear to exist than with regularities based on other forms of data and analysis for the testing of rival hypotheses. Within the context of QAD, these hypotheses can be set against the same or similar data sets and their performance directly compared. Proponents of RAT, I would then suggest, may in this way gain advantage from the standpoint of, so to speak, both offensive and defensive strategy.

On the one hand, opportunity is thus provided of meeting the charge that the strength of RAT explanations is often not compared with that of explanations of differing theoretical provenance (cf. Green and Shapiro 1994: 36–8) and, further, of demonstrating the superiority of the former in a compelling fashion. As an apt illustration here one may take studies of the *consequences* of social mobility—for reproductive behaviour, patterns of sociability, political partisanship, and so on. That mobility does indeed have consequences in these respects is indicated by a substantial body of research findings: the phenomena are established well enough. However, quite different explanations have been suggested of how the observed regularities are produced. A broad contrast might in fact be made between explanations in terms of changing economic interests, resources, and constraints that are implicitly if not explicitly RAT-based, and explanations in terms of status striving, frustration, or anxiety that are of a more 'psychologistic' nature. It is usually not possible to judge between such rival explanations just by inspecting the data as presented in the form of percentage distributions or through other relatively simple descriptive statistics. But advances in modelling technique, culminating in 'diagonal-reference' models, a form of non-linear logistic regression (Sobel 1981, 1985; De Graaf and Heath 1992; Clifford and Heath 1993), have steadily improved the chances of making effective evaluations. And such evaluations have then proved mainly to go in favour of hypotheses more consonant with a RAT approach.[21]

On the other hand, hypothesis testing in the context of QAD would appear to offer a rewarding approach to a crucial problem of RAT itself that has

entials in educational attainment, but more or less constant rates of intergenerational social mobility. While, in its spirit, this attempt is entirely in accord with what is here being advocated, it is now apparent, in the light of better data and more appropriate analyses than were available to Boudon, that his problem is non-existent. A decline in class differentials in educational attainment is *not* a general feature of modern societies or, at all events, not in the sense of a declining influence of class origins on children's 'transition probabilities' at different branching points in their educational careers—with which Boudon was crucially concerned (see Shavit and Blossfeld 1993). Thus, the lack of trend in intergenerational mobility rates need, on this account at least, occasion little surprise (see further Chapters 8, 9, and 11 below).

[21] The most detailed analyses have concerned the effects of mobility on voting (see e.g. De Graaf and Ultee 1990; Clifford and Heath 1993; De Graaf *et al.* 1995; Cautrès 1995). With reference to the argument of the preceding section, it is of interest to note that Cox (1990: 169–70), in a general review of the differing roles that models may play in statistics, takes diagonal reference models as a social-science example of the bridging of 'empirical' and more 'substantive' concerns; or, that is, of a movement towards models that 'aim to explain what is observed in terms of processes (mechanisms), usually via quantities that are not directly observed, and some theoretical notions as to how the system under study "works"'.

preoccupied its more thoughtful supporters no less than critics: namely, that of just where the boundaries of its explanatory range should be taken to lie. As Elster (1989b: 36) has remarked, 'The first task of a theory of rational choice is to be clear about its own limits.' So far, the tendency has been to treat this task in a rather introverted way as essentially a theoretical or indeed philosophical one, and empirical materials have been drawn on, if at all, for only illustrative purposes.[22] However, several instances can by now be cited of a more systematic empirical approach being taken—that is, an approach through QAD; and the stage may well have been reached at which, from a sociological standpoint at least, such endeavours will prove more fruitful than further resort to data-free *lucubrations de chambre*.

For example, to return again to the study of class inequalities in educational attainment, Gambetta (1987) has specifically investigated the extent to which a RAT approach would appear capable of accounting for the differing careers that are typically followed by working- and middle-class children within the Italian educational system. Applying logit modelling to survey data, he produces results that are in large part consistent with the hypothesis that these children, and their parents, are in fact engaged in the rational pursuit of life plans, although ones differentially 'filtered' both by class-linked constraints and by expectations of success in more ambitious educational options. Such a hypothesis would, at all events, appear better supported than alternatives that would see educational choices as in effect spurious, because essentially predetermined by either class-structural or class-cultural forces. However, Gambetta does recognize that there is *some* evidence of 'sub-intentional' influences also being present. Both working-class and middle-class children display 'inertial' tendencies that would seem to reflect a degree of *over*-adaptation to their objective situations: that is, the former tend to be too pessimistic about their chances of educational success, while the latter are too optimistic. To this extent, then, it could be supposed that not just random, but socially structured, restrictions on rationality operate in a 'behind-the-back' way, which must in its nature lie beyond the reach of RAT (though see further Chapters 8 and 9 below).

Similarly, Weakliem and Heath (1994) have examined—also using logit modelling techniques, though of a more advanced kind—how far RAT-based hypotheses can account for the persisting association in British electoral politics between vote and class. The result is that RAT again emerges with a good deal of credit: the class–vote association *can* to a substantial extent be explained in terms either of individuals' policy preferences or of their retrospective assessments of parties' records that are consistent with their perceived class interests. But, again too, a qualification appears to be required. Some part of the class-vote association still remains that is *not* explicable in these terms and that Weakliem and Heath cannot in fact show to be mediated by any set of attitudes or beliefs, but that *is* related to measures of individuals'

---

[22] This is, in fact, true of my own attempt at clarification in the chapter that follows.

exposure to class-linked 'social influence'. In other words, the suggestion is once more that a behind-the-back process, and one, therefore, that RAT cannot accommodate, is at work.

In sum, through recourse to QAD as the basis of hypothesis testing, the explanatory value of RAT, relative to that of other theoretical approaches, can be brought out, and at the same time knowledge, which one may hope will be cumulative, can be gained of the circumstances and of the ways in which the limits of RAT in sociological explanation are most likely to be encountered. And it might in this latter respect be added that the recognition of such limits does then lay down a fair challenge to theorists of different orientation to spell out just how they would wish to understand the nature of the influences that have to be invoked when the explanatory resources of RAT are exhausted, rather than these being left as merely 'residual' effects.[23]

The starting point of this Chapter was a recognition of the fact that in present-day sociology rational action theory and the quantitative analysis of large-scale data sets are concerns pursued largely in isolation from each other. Certainly, no special relationship between them is recognized or actively sought. In so far as QAD has been directed towards theoretical issues, no tendency is apparent for these to be ones particularly associated with RAT rather than with other theoretical approaches; and, while proponents of RAT have been among the sharpest critics of QAD for its failure to spell out the theory of action that it typically presupposes, they have at the same time wished to emphasize the equal appropriateness of RAT as a basis for all styles of sociological enquiry, regardless of the differing kinds of problem, data, or analytical method involved.

My main purpose has, however, been to show that, especially when the nature of current criticism of both QAD and RAT is examined, it is apparent that a closer *rapport* between them would in fact be to their mutual benefit. QAD clearly does need to be informed by some explicit theory of action, at all events where it is used with more than purely descriptive ambitions; and RAT, in view especially of its claims to generality rather than determinacy, would appear distinctively suited to providing accounts of the generation of the probabilistic regularities, often extensive in time and space, that QAD has the capacity to reveal. Conversely, proponents of RAT should find in the results of QAD empirical materials that offer particularly attractive opportun-

---

[23] Two further features of the work of Gambetta and of Weakliem and Heath alike should in this connection be noted. First, the models they fit are mostly ones inspired by RAT-based hypotheses, and the extent to which these fail to account for their data is then assessed in effect by reference to the residuals (in the statistical sense) under these models. This could, however, be unfair to RAT in so far as the models are misspecified (which is a particular worry with the relatively crude ones applied by Gambetta). Secondly, these authors themselves acknowledge difficulties in suggesting, let alone demonstrating, plausible explanations of how the residual effects, assuming them to be real, are actually generated. Gambetta (1987: esp. 93–9) considers, among other possibilities, that of distorted cognitive or judgemental processes, while Weakliem and Heath speculate about 'subconscious conformity' with class opinion.

ities for demonstrations of RAT's capacity to elucidate the micro-to-macro link: that is, ones that relate to issues of major substantive interest and that at the same time allow extreme assumptions of rationality in social life to be relaxed in the direction of greater realism. Furthermore, in so far as QAD is thus taken as a preferred source of *explananda*, significant advantages would also seem likely to follow, both in making out the case for the superior explanatory power of RAT relative to that of other theoretical approaches and in addressing the question of the boundaries to its explanatory range that RAT must still ultimately accept.

6

Rational Action Theory
for Sociology

IN PAPERS that have appeared over the last decade or so, a number of sociologists have sought to persuade their colleagues to become more familiar
with rational choice, or—as I would prefer to call it—rational action theory
(RAT), and to make greater use of it in their substantive work (see e.g.
Coleman 1986a; Friedman and Hechter 1988; Lindenberg 1990; Abell 1992;
Hedström 1996). I am in general sympathy with the arguments that these
authors have advanced; and it may be useful here to say that I also share in

(i) their commitment to methodological (as distinct from ontological)
individualism or, that is, to the *explanatory* primacy of individual
action in relation to social phenomena;
(ii) their belief that a theory of action must therefore be central to the sociological enterprise; and
(iii) their further belief that, while in the choice of such a theory, its aptness
to problems of the macro-to-micro link is an obvious consideration,
yet more important is the fact that *analytic* primacy in sociology lies
with the consequences (intended or unintended) of individual action
or, that is, with the converse, micro-to-macro link (see esp. Coleman
1990: ch. 1).

However, the present chapter does not aim to make out once again the general
case for RAT. Its concerns differ from those of papers of the kind noted above
in the following way. I start from a more explicit recognition than has perhaps
previously been made that RAT is not a highly unified intellectual entity.
Rather, there is a whole family of RATs and, as well as 'family resemblances',
significant differences have also to be observed. In the preceding chapter, I
sought to show that distinctive advantages might follow from a collaborative
alliance between sociologists favouring RAT and those engaged in the quantitative analysis of large-scale data sets; and, for this purpose, I believed it sufficient to understand RAT in a broad and largely undifferentiated fashion.

This chapter was first published in the *British Journal of Sociology*, 49 (1998). I am particularly
indebted to Adam Swift for a lengthy critique of an earlier draft, and also, for further helpful
comments and advice, to Raymond Boudon, Richard Breen, Cecilia Garcia-Peñalosa, Michael
Hechter, Rolf Höijer, Martin Hollis, David Lockwood, Federico Varese, and an anonymous *BJS*
reviewer.

Here, in contrast, my main concern is to analyse the varieties of RAT according to several criteria that I shall set out, and then to address the question of where, within the variation displayed, sociologists might best look for the particular kind of RAT that would hold out greatest promise for them. Thus, while the authors previously cited were chiefly engaged in comparing RAT in rather general terms with other major theoretical approaches pursued by sociologists and in setting out its strengths and defending its alleged weaknesses, my attention will centre on comparisons made *within* the RAT family and on the advantages and disadvantages for sociologists of RAT in its differing versions.

It might, therefore, be supposed that this chapter will be chiefly of interest to sociologists who are already in some degree convinced of the merits of a RAT approach. I would, however, hope that, at least among more open-minded sceptics and critics, it could lead to a better appreciation of RAT—if only in countering the view, still prevalent among sociologists (see e.g. Hirsch *et al.* 1987), that RAT is no more than a dubious import from economics, and in showing that, when considered in its full diversity, RAT can be seen to have deep roots within the classic sociological tradition.

One other preliminary remark should be made. Consistently with the position indicated in points (i) to (iii) above, I take it that the phenomena with which sociologists are concerned are social regularities of some kind that can be established, on a probabilistic basis, within collectivities ranging from national populations, through variously defined subpopulations, down to the level of local communities, associations, or households.[1] The typical explanatory task is then to show how these regularities are created and sustained or, perhaps, modified or disrupted, through the action and interaction of individuals. As argued in the previous chapter, the model of the actor to be used in this task does not have to be one that is capable of capturing all the particular features—all the idiosyncrasies—of the actions of the flesh-and-blood individuals involved, but only the 'central tendencies' in their action that are seen as relevant to the explanation that is being sought. Thus, if a RAT approach is adopted, it need not be claimed that all actors at all times act in an entirely rational way: only that the tendency to act rationally (however this may be construed) is the most important common—that is, non-idiosyncratic—factor at work. The 'law of large numbers' will then ensure that it is the rational tendency that dominates. An analogous point could, of course, be made with respect to rival theoretical approaches, such as, say, those that would see patterns of action as being primarily shaped by individuals' responsiveness to shared cultural values or social norms. It is, therefore, on the basis of such an understanding that any empirical evaluation of different approaches must in the end be made. As Sen has argued

---

[1] Reference is often made here to 'social systems'. However, I see no point in committing oneself to this concept unless it is going to be put to explanatory use—as, typically, in conjunction with that of 'equilibrium'. While RAT can, of course, operate as an element within such an explanatory strategy—as, most obviously, in mainstream economics—it is not dependent on it; and whether a sociological 'generalization' of the equilibrium theory of economics (see e.g. Coleman 1990) will prove of much value remains, in my view, highly debatable.

(1986: 11; and see also 1987), while there is little doubt 'that getting at actuality via rationality' will entail distortion, the important questions are those of how much distortion and of what kind (for example, systematic or non-systematic), and of whether differing assumptions about the motivation of individual action would do better or worse: 'Ultimately, the relative advantages of . . . alternative approaches have to be judged in terms of their results.'

The Varieties of RAT

How the varieties of RAT are understood will, of course, depend on the criteria of differentiation that are applied. Here, I will adopt three such criteria, which seem to me those most relevant to the task in hand. I will aim to distinguish different kinds of RAT according to whether they

   (i) have strong rather than weak rationality requirements;

   (ii) focus on situational rather than procedural rationality; and

   (iii) claim to provide a general rather a special theory of action.[2]

How far, and in what ways, these criteria are interconnected will, I hope, emerge as the discussion proceeds.

Strong versus weak rationality requirements

Rational action may be understood as action of an 'outcome-oriented' kind in which certain requirements are met regarding the nature of, and the relations among: actors' goals, their beliefs relevant to the pursuit of these goals, and the course of action that, in given circumstances, they then follow.[3] However, from one version of RAT to another, these requirements appear as stronger or weaker.

Rationality requirements may be seen as at their strongest where they extend to actors' goals in themselves, as well as to their beliefs and the action they take towards their goals on the basis of their beliefs. It has, however, to be said that no version of RAT has gained wide acceptance in which the

---

   [2] Among distinctions that I do not consider, perhaps the most notable is that between RAT as based on 'parametric' rationality, where a passive environment is supposed, and RAT as based on 'strategic' rationality, where the rational action of one actor depends on that of all others involved—i.e. game theory (cf. Elster 1983b: ch. 1). Since both approaches have been shown to have important sociological applications, the distinction is not of great consequence for my present purposes.

   [3] Some further comments on terminology may be helpful here. I follow Elster (1983a: ch. 3) and various other authors in distinguishing action from behaviour (or, alternatively, treating action as a special kind of behaviour) in that action is *intentional*, in contrast with behaviour that can be understood only as 'externally' caused. However, as will later be seen, I differ from Elster in wishing to subdivide intentional action so that non-rational, as well as rational and irrational, action is specifically recognized. Finally, on grounds indicated in the preceding chapter, but which are in fact far more relevant here, I prefer to speak of rational action theory rather than rational choice theory.

requirement of rationality of goals—or of associated desires or preferences—has been understood in a *substantive* sense. This reflects the difficulties that have been encountered in attempts to specify criteria for such substantive rationality. All those that have at various times been formulated, and including those embodied in 'critical sociology' in the sense of the Frankfurt School, have proved highly contestable (cf. Elster 1983*b*: 35–42; 1989*c*: 5–7). Rather ironically, what might be called the Humean view of reason as applying *wholly to means*, and not to ends, has in this way been reinforced.

Most commonly in RAT the nature of actors' goals is then regarded as being exogenous to the theory and thus unrestricted. Actors' goals are to be determined empirically, and may be 'ideal' as well as 'material', altruistic as well as egoistic.[4] In so far as rationality requirements do here arise, they are ones of only a *formal* kind relating to consistency or lack of contradiction. Thus, in the version of RAT expressed in mainstream economics, consistency in preferences is required in the sense of transitivity: if an actor prefers *a* to *b* and *b* to *c*, then *a* must also be preferred to *c*. It should, though, be noted that the further requirements that are in this case imposed—that preferences should display what are technically known as 'completeness' and 'continuity'—are *not* ones of rationality, but simply of the mathematical techniques through which economists seek to represent preferences by a 'utility function' (Farmer 1982: 185–7). In other words, 'economic man' here takes on peculiarities that need not be attributed to 'rational man' *per se* (see further Elster 1983*b*: 8–10; 1989*c*: 9–10; Hausman 1992: ch. 1).

It is when one turns to the treatment of beliefs within RAT, and of the relation of beliefs to action, that variation in rationality requirements of a more significant kind becomes apparent. Economics undoubtedly provides the instances in which requirements in these respects are strongest. Thus, in RAT as applied in much neoclassical economics questions of the rationality of beliefs and of the grounding of action in beliefs are simply dealt with by the *assumption* that actors have 'perfect knowledge' and use this in the best way possible to achieve their goals—that is, to maximize their utility (or, in the case of entrepreneurs, their profit). Moreover, even where limits on actors' information are recognized, in situations of risk or uncertainty, it is still supposed that they have as much information and can calculate as accurately as such situations will allow in order to maximize their 'expected', or 'subjectively expected', utility. What is involved here remains formidable. As Simon has put it (1983: 13–14), it is assumed that the actor

---

[4] Some proponents of RAT (e.g. Harsanyi 1969; Hechter 1994) have sought to identify the goals towards which rational action is *in general* directed: for example, economic gain, social acceptance, power. But it is not clear whether this entails more than providing a series of heads under which any more specific goals can, in some way or other, be catalogued. The fact that RAT does not seek to endogenize actors' goals is frequently referred to as a major limitation. But, given the lack of success of theories of action that have attempted this move, from that of Talcott Parsons onwards, the strategy of proceeding empirically might appear to have something to commend it.

contemplates, in one comprehensive view, everything that lies before him. He understands the range of alternative choices open to him, not only at the moment but over the whole panorama of the future. He understands the consequences of each of the available choice strategies, at least up to the point of being able to assign a joint probability distribution to future states of the world. He has reconciled all his conflicting partial values and synthesized them into a single utility function that orders, by his preference for them, all these future states of the world.

Thus, whether the complications of risk and uncertainty are acknowledged or not, the issue of 'realism' would seem bound to arise: that is, the issue of whether actors do in fact make choices according to the rationality requirements that utility theory entails. And, since it has been possible to show empirically that, very commonly, they do not (see e.g. Schoemaker 1982; Hogarth and Reder 1986; Appleby and Starmer 1987), those theorists who would set a relatively high premium on realism in basic assumptions have sought to develop other versions of RAT in which such requirements are clearly weaker. The key idea that has been exploited in this connection is that of *subjective*, as opposed to *objective*, rationality: that is, the idea that actors may hold beliefs, and in turn pursue courses of action, for which they have 'good reasons' in the circumstances in which they find themselves, even though they may fall short of the standard of rationality that utility theory would presuppose.

Within economics, and administrative science, the best-known example of RAT modified in this way is the theory of 'bounded rationality' that has been elaborated by Simon and his associates (see esp. Simon 1982: ii; 1983). Proponents of this theory argue that, even where actors have complete information, the sheer complexity of situations may be such—as, say, in chess—that to maximize is not feasible, and it becomes rational, from the actor's point of view, to 'satisfice' instead: that is, to act so as to meet certain criteria that, in the actor's judgement, indicate that a course of action is 'good enough'. And it is then further held that where, as is usually the case, actors have *in*complete information, satisficing is unavoidable. For the question arises of how far it would be rational to try to obtain *more* information, and it is doubtful if any 'optimality' criteria can in this respect be specified (cf. Elster 1983b: ch. 1; 1989c: 15–17). At some point, a decision must be taken, on subjective grounds, to act on the information that is already to hand.

A further version of RAT based on the idea of subjective rationality but oriented towards more sociological concerns is that developed by Boudon (1989, 1994) and, in his most recent work, labelled as the 'cognitivist model' (1996, 1998). Boudon is primarily interested in how individuals may, with good reason, hold, and in turn act upon, beliefs that are objectively mistaken. A key source of inspiration for his work is the neo-Kantianism of Max Weber and Simmel and, in particular, the latter's argument (1900/1978, 1905/1977) that reasoning that is perfectly valid in itself may lead to false beliefs because it is carried out in the context of certain implicit, unexamined propositions (*a priori*) that are inappropriate—though perhaps far from evidently so. What Boudon then maintains is that, where individuals appear to act in a way that falls short of rationality because of their mistaken beliefs, it should not be automatically supposed that these beliefs are in some way 'externally' caused: for example, that they are, in the jargon of cognitive psychology, beliefs formed 'hot' under affective influences, such as desires, fears, or frustrations. They may well be beliefs formed 'cold' through inferential processes that, while they happen to be misleading in the particular context of their use, are in themselves sound enough. And Boudon would indeed argue that sociologists should seek to go as far as they can in explaining mistaken beliefs on just these lines. For in so doing they can treat true and false beliefs as being reached by essentially similar processes, rather than as calling for quite different kinds of explanation; and at the same time they can make adherence to mistaken beliefs intelligible in a way that it could not be if externally caused.

Finally here one other example of RAT should be noted in which the requirements of—subjective—rationality are at their weakest: that is, that embodied in the 'analysis of situational logic' as proposed by Popper (see esp. 1957; 1972: ch. 4; 1994) and developed by various of his followers (e.g. Jarvie 1964, 1972; Watkins 1970; Agassi 1975). In this case, the aim is to understand action as rational simply in the sense of being 'appropriate' or 'adequate', given actors' goals and given their situation of action *which is taken to include their beliefs*. In effect, then, not only actors' goals but their beliefs also are exempted from rationality requirements. What is important is not the differentiation of beliefs in terms of the degree of rationality with which they are held—Popper would deny that it is possible to justify beliefs rationally (cf. Caldwell 1991: 22–3)—but rather the fact *that* they are held and their specific content. Indeed, proponents of this approach would argue that it can, and should, be applied to instances where actors hold, and act upon, seemingly quite irrational, even crazy, beliefs—as, for example, in Jarvie's (1964) study of Melanesian cargo cults. If a view is taken of the actors' situation that is larger than, and indeed encompasses, their own, then, it is supposed, some underlying 'logic' to their action will be discovered. In other words, just as in neoclassical economics, rationality is assumed *ab initio*, even if in a much more attenuated sense. It has, though, further to be recognized that no claim is made that the assumption that individuals do act appropriately or adequately to the situations in which they find themselves—'the rationality principle', as Popper calls it—is *true*. Indeed, Popper acknowledges (1994) that, taken as a universal principle, it is certainly false. None the less, its retention is warranted on methodological grounds in that it is essential to the formulation of specific explanations of action of a kind that do stand or fall by empirical tests. This last point has given rise to a good deal of puzzlement and discussion (see e.g. Hands 1985; Caldwell 1991; Blaug 1992: 231–3). It is, however, one that should become clearer when Popper's position is again considered in the following section.

Situational versus procedural rationality

Within the family of RAT, variation in the strength of rationality requirements relates in a rather complex way to the further variation that occurs in the emphasis that is given to rationality in action as situationally rather than as procedurally—or, one might say, psychologically—determined.

To revert to mainstream economics, it is clear that in this case rationality in action is understood essentially as a response or *re*action to the situation— that is, a market situation of some kind—that actors face. Given their preferences, the way for them to act rationally, as it is assumed that they will act, is situationally constrained to an extreme degree (cf. Latsis 1976). Thus, as several authors have noted, the paradox arises that the theory of 'rational choice' *par excellence* turns out to imply that little real choice in fact exists: for, typically, the actor's situation is characterized as a 'single-exit' one. Economic man becomes, in Hollis's words (1994: 185–6) 'a mere throughput' between his preferences, which he need only arrange in order, and the 'automatically computed' choice that ensures that his utility is maximized. Indeed, for some economists (e.g. M. Friedman 1953; G. Becker 1976), such a pattern of choice is *so* automatic that it need not even be supposed that actors are conscious of following it or could therefore explain just what they had done.[5]

In most obvious contrast to this position is that taken by Simon and his followers. Their project of constructing a weaker but more realistic version of RAT around the idea of subjective rationality goes together with a concern to shift the analytic focus of RAT away from the situation of action to the acting individual. If one begins with the idea of objective rationality, Simon argues (1982: esp. pt. viii), then all conditions of interest are located 'outside the skin' of the actor; but with the idea of subjective rationality, which implies satisficing rather than maximizing behaviour, attention has to centre on conditions existing 'inside the skin' of the actor and in particular on human computational—that is, information-processing—capacities and the constraints that *they* impose. Thus, exponents of the 'behavioural' economics and administrative science that have been inspired by Simon's work start from the evidence, already referred to, that the requirements of objective rationality are rarely attained in real-world decision-making, and aim to model the processes of thinking and choosing involved in such action in ways more consistent with the findings of modern experimental psychology. In so far as rational action is invoked, they would maintain, its nature and its limits have in this way to be given a defensible empirical grounding.

---

[5] An addendum made to this argument by some economists is that the prevalence of such subconscious rationality is guaranteed by 'natural selection' exerted through market forces. Thus, for example, firms led by entrepreneurs or managers who are not profit-maximizers will simply be eliminated. For pertinent critical comment, see Langlois (1986: 243–7), Sen (1987), and Blaug (1992: 99–105).

Other social scientists, with somewhat wider substantive interests, have accepted this basic position, but have then sought to develop further versions of RAT sensitive to *both* procedural and situational influences and to their interaction. For example, in several contributions Lindenberg and Frey (e.g. Lindenberg 1989, 1990; Frey 1992; Lindenberg and Frey 1993) have tried to provide more secure psychological foundations for the idea of subjective rationality stemming from the actor's own 'definition of the situation' by drawing on 'prospect' or 'framing' theory (see Kahneman and Tversky 1979). And a complementary perspective is represented by Boudon, who, as earlier noted, is likewise concerned with the formation of subjectively rational, even if objectively mistaken, beliefs, but for whom it is also important that the psychological processes here involved should be better understood as regards their *social* determination. Boudon would thus wish to see the cognitive psychology that informs RAT being grounded in a new 'cognitive sociology' or what he alternatively describes as 'a new sociology of knowledge'. It would be the task of the latter 'to try to identify and clarify typical situations where the mental processes characteristic of subjective rationality lead to false beliefs' (1994: 247).

Finally, though, it is important to note that acceptance of the idea of subjective rather than objective rationality can still go together with a quite undiluted, and principled, commitment to situational determinism. This is demonstrated by the position taken up by Popper and the analysts of situational logic.

For Popper it is vital to establish that a commitment to methodological individualism in no sense entails a commitment to 'psychologism': that is, to the view that any social science must ultimately be based upon, and reducible to, the operation of 'psychological laws of "human nature"' (see esp. 1945/1966: ch. 14, 'The Autonomy of Sociology'; also 1976a: 101–4; 1994; cf. Agassi 1975). To the contrary, the model of the individual actor employed in the social sciences should, so far as 'internal' characteristics are concerned, be a minimal one, and the rationality that is taken to characterize this actor calls for little, if any, psychological elaboration. From this standpoint, then, no great interest need attach to the computational issues on which Simon focuses, nor indeed to any other aspects of the psychological functioning of individuals. What is important is not actors' mental states or processes but the nature of the beliefs or, as Popper would rather have it, of the (objective) *knowledge* that is situationally available to them and in which their (subjective) understanding is anchored (see esp. 1972, 1976a). The rationality principle, the principle that actors do act appropriately or adequately in the situations in which they find themselves, then simply serves—and is indeed sufficient—to 'animate' the analysis (Popper 1994: 169): that is, to enable it to be seen why the action taken does indeed follow from what the analysis has revealed about actors' goals and about the constraints and possibilities of their situation, relevant knowledge *y compris* (cf. Langlois 1986: 229–31). Or, to adopt the idiom favoured by von Wright (1971, 1972), one could say that the rationality principle ensures that a 'practical syllogism' is in fact carried through.[6]

It should, therefore, be now more apparent why Popper does not seek to defend the rationality principle empirically but rather on methodological grounds (cf. Farr 1985). Its methodological significance is that, in being substantively 'almost empty', it requires that it is the situation of action that becomes the focus of attention: 'that we should pack or cram our whole theoretical effort, our whole explanatory theory, into an analysis of the situation' (Popper 1994: 169–71). And it is, then, to what follows from this effort, rather than to the rationality principle that directs it, that empirical tests are applicable and that should 'take the strain' if these tests are unfavourable (see also Farmer 1992).

A general versus a special theory

The two criteria so far considered thus generate wide differentiation within the family of RAT, and they would, moreover, appear to be directly cross-cut by the third criterion still to be introduced: that is, that of the extent to which versions of RAT aim to provide a general rather than a special theory of action.

Limits to the explanatory scope of RAT are reached, by definition, wherever the concept of action itself appears as inappropriate and gives way to that of behaviour that must be externally explained: that is, in psychological or biological terms that do not entail reference to intentionality in any sense. But the further issue of relevance here is that of how far different forms of RAT recognize yet narrower limits resulting from the existence of types or domains *of action* in regard to which, however, the concept of rationality offers little explanatory purchase. It is again convenient to begin with RAT as found within economics: not, though, in this respect as representing an extreme case but rather as illustrating in itself more or less the full range of possibilities.

Numerous examples could be cited from the history of economics of attempts to define the scope of RAT, as expressed in economic analysis, by reference to certain domains of action as characterized in terms either of motivation or of institutional context. Thus, economic analysis is said to apply to action that is directed towards the pursuit of wealth or to the satisfaction of material needs and wants, or again to action that occurs within systems of exchange based on money and markets. In all these instances, then, economics is treated as, in Hausman's (1992) phrase, 'a separate science', and RAT in turn as a special theory.

---

[6] The essential similarity between the positions reached by Popper and von Wright—independently, it would seem—has attracted remarkably little comment, even where it might have been expected (see e.g. Koertge 1975, 1979). It is, however, of interest that Watkins (1970: 209), in a discussion of the rationality principle, remarks that this principle 'effects a two-way connection . . . It says that a man who has a decision-scheme issuing in a practical conclusion will try to act in accordance with that conclusion . . . It also says that, given that a man was not drugged, hypnotized, sleep-walking, etc. but *acting*, then his action was the acting out of the practical conclusion of a decision-scheme.'

However, the development of more ambitious claims can be traced back at least to Robbins (1932/1949: esp. ch. 1), who explicitly rejects a 'classificatory' approach to the delimitation of economic analysis. Such analysis, he argues, should be seen as applying not to particular domains of action but rather to particular *aspects* of action *in general*. It applies, in his view, wherever questions arise of the relation of means to ends or, more exactly, of 'the disposal of scarce means' which have 'alternative uses'—that is, which could be used in order to satisfy competing ends. In other words, RAT, as deployed by the economist, is the appropriate theory of action in all circumstances in which such 'economizing' is entailed; it has no restriction to action occurring within economic relations or institutions as conventionally understood.

The tendency here apparent towards 'economic imperialism' can then be seen as reaching its culmination in the work of Gary Becker (see esp. 1976). For Becker, RAT—and indeed RAT in the form of utility theory—is capable of serving as a quite general theory of social action, which is just as applicable to the explanation of, say, crime, church attendance, or suicide as of consumption patterns or share dealings. *All* social action can be viewed from the standpoint of individuals maximizing their utility from a stable set of preferences and accumulating optimal amounts of information and other inputs to the multiple markets, monetized or not, in which they are involved. Where action appears to deviate from the expectations of utility theory, little is gained, Becker would argue, from resorting to explanations in terms of irrationality, cultural tradition, value commitment, value shifts, and so on—just as might seem convenient. For such explanations are essentially *ad hoc* and indeed often contradictory. In contrast to those that derive from a theory of rational action, they lack a coherent basis, and the question is left unanswered of just why human action should be sometimes rational but sometimes not. Where seemingly 'anomalous' findings arise, therefore, the better strategy is simply to reanalyse the situation on the assumption that some feature of it was initially misunderstood.

Other versions of RAT may be identified that also seek to provide a generalization of economics but that appear somewhat less 'imperialistic' in that they are to a greater degree influenced by behavioural economics of the kind pioneered by Simon. For example, Frey (1992) has sought to show that such economics, as informed by cognitive psychology and also by social-psychological theories of perception and learning, can be developed into a 'science of human behaviour' of a quite comprehensive kind (see also Hirshleifer 1985; Lindenberg 1990). However, perhaps the position that can in this respect be most interestingly set alongside Becker's is that of Popper and the Popperians.

For Popper, the analysis of situational logic is certainly an approach to be followed in all the social sciences—and in the humanities, too, in so far as the explanation of action is involved. At one point Popper does in fact state that his aim is that of generalizing utility theory (1976a: 117–18). None the less, it is clear that he would at the same time wish to trace back the origins of his approach to the hermeneutic tradition of textual scholarship and historiography (1972: ch. 4; cf. Farr 1983, 1985), and such origins are strongly indicated in the way in which generality is sought—in particular, the accommodation of action that is not, at first blush, readily understood as rational. The weakening, or 'emptying', of the concept of rationality in the way that was earlier noted can be seen as a direct application of the 'principle of charity' in interpretation that characterizes the hermeneutic tradition. That is to say, observed action is as far as ever possible to be 'reconstructed' *as* rational, in the situation in which it occurs, so that it may in turn be rendered intelligible—that is, *verständlich*—rather than being left to explanation of a merely external kind.

Finally, though, while all efforts made to apply RAT across the social sciences, and beyond, reflect the evident appeal of moving towards a more unified theory of action, it has also to be noted that, of late, a greater awareness would seem to have emerged among its proponents of the need to recognize its explanatory limits: that is, not only in regard to (sub-intentional) behaviour but, further, in regard to (intentional) action that still cannot usefully be brought under the rubric of rationality. Thus, Boudon, who represents his 'cognitivist model' as an extended form of RAT (1996, 1998), would still acknowledge that 'hot'—that is, emotionally charged—processes as well as 'cold' ones can and do lead to mistaken beliefs and action based thereon. And again Coleman, who grounds his major theoretical work (1990) in RAT and, implicitly, draws on its varieties in a quite eclectic fashion, does none the less at various points give an important place to modes of action that lie beyond its explanatory range, in particular in the formation of trust relations and of 'social capital' more generally.

In other words, although these authors are much concerned to show that RAT *can* provide compelling accounts of many social phenomena not usually thought of as exhibiting rationality in action—for example, magic and ideologies, panics, mob violence and revolutions, or indeed the formation of the normative structures to which other theories of action appeal—they would still in the end accept that RAT can be no more than a special theory. Thus, rather than striving in the manner of the followers of Becker or Popper *always* to find *some* way of 'saving' action as rational, they would in effect take up a position that has been somewhat more openly expressed by Elster (1989c, 1993; see also Fararo 1996): that is, that RAT should be viewed not as itself constituting a general theory of action but rather as being that currently available (special) theory around which the effort to achieve greater generality could best be organized.

Which RAT for Sociology?

The outcome of the foregoing analysis of the varieties of RAT can be graphically, if somewhat crudely, represented as in Fig. 6.1. I turn now to the question of where, within the 'space' of the variation thus displayed, the interest of sociologists could best focus, and in this regard I assume two *desiderata*.

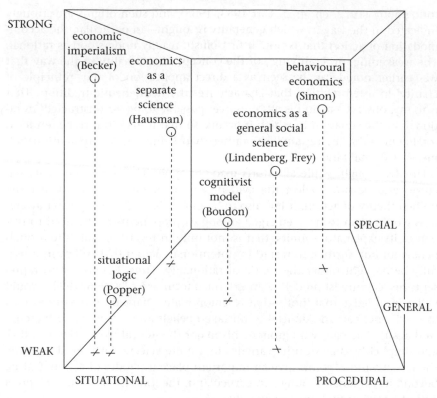

STRONG

economic
imperialism
(Becker)   economics
   ○   as a
                    separate   behavioural
                    science   economics
                    (Hausman)   (Simon)
                       ○   ○
                                    economics as a
                                    general social
                                       science
                                    (Lindenberg, Frey)
                                         ○
                          cognitivist
                            model
                           (Boudon)   SPECIAL
                              ○

            situational
               logic
             (Popper)   GENERAL
                ○

WEAK

        SITUATIONAL   PROCEDURAL

FIG. 6.1. Varieties of RAT

Sociologists should be looking for the kind of RAT that (*a*) can offer greatest
explanatory power in regard to action generating social regularities via the
micro-to-macro link but that (*b*) will be most likely, where its explanatory
power fails, to promote further research through 'progressive problem shifts'
rather than merely defensive 'immunization stratagems' (cf. Lakatos 1970). I
will proceed by reference to the same three criteria of differentiation as previously used, although, as will become apparent, evaluations made from one
to another are not always independent.

Strong versus weak rationality requirements

Versions of RAT that impose the strong requirements of objective rationality
are attractive in that they allow clear predictions to be made about how actors
will—indeed *should*—act in given situations. Economists appear irrevocably
committed to such strong forms of RAT in which the positive and the normative are in effect combined. As Hausman has remarked (1992: 278), the
methodological distinctiveness of their discipline would appear to be depen-

dent upon such theory. However, from a sociological standpoint, two major disadvantages arise. First, and as previously noted, the assumptions involved appear unrealistic and indeed in various respects empirically untenable. Secondly, where these versions of RAT fail, problem-shifts are not typically recognized of a kind that would seem likely to guide sociological research onto promising lines.

For example, in the face of action that evidently does not conform to the criteria of rationality that are imposed, one response is simply that of postulating hitherto unrecognized features of the situation—unobservable 'psychic' income or costs seem a favourite option (e.g. G. Becker 1976: 7, 11)—which, once taken into account, render the action rational after all. Thus, rather than the theory stimulating further research of any kind, it is in effect 'closed' and would appear to degenerate into little more than a set of tautologies.[7]

Alternatively, if action is accepted as truly anomalous, it has then to be accounted for in terms of 'residual categories', the inadequacies of which, at least for purposes of sociological analysis, were classically exposed by Parsons (1937: esp. ch. 2). Only two possibilities appear to exist. One is for the action in question to be treated as *irrational*—that is, as action that has *failed to be* rational as a result of 'ignorance or error' (themselves left unexplained). In effect, the emphasis is here shifted to the normative character of the theory, and it is the actor, not the theory, that is deemed to be 'wrong'. The other possibility is for the action to be reconstrued simply as behaviour that is then to be explained externally by reference to non-social aspects of the situation, notably 'heredity and environment'. But in this way the scope for a *verstehende* sociology is severely, though arbitrarily, reduced. No conceptual space is allowed for action of a non-rational kind nor yet for action that, while not rational by the criteria imposed, could still be open to interpretation—i.e. could be made intelligible—as rational in the circumstances in which it occurred.

There would, therefore, seem little doubt that sociologists will be best served by some version of RAT that is weaker than that of mainstream economics in requiring only subjective rationality: that is, a version that treats as rational both holding beliefs and acting on these beliefs where actors have 'good reasons' for so doing. However, the crucial question that then of course arises

---

[7] Gary Becker (1976: 7) argues that the important question is whether or not the theory is closed in a 'useful' way—i.e. one that allows testable propositions to be formulated. But, even supposing that this is the case, what then matters is how theorists respond to empirical evidence indicating that such propositions are false (Schoemaker 1982: esp. 539–41, 554). Are they ready to consider that the theory might be misconceived, and perhaps radically so, or do they draw on the possibilities for immunizing stratagems that its closure offers? Becker rarely, if ever, indicates what kind of evidence he himself would regard as being inconsistent with the theories he advances, but, for a review—by sociologists—of empirical findings that stand in apparent contradiction to a range of his theoretically grounded claims, see Baron and Hannan (1994). Of late, it should be recognized, more economists have shown themselves ready to criticize Becker's position (see e.g. Blaug 1992: ch. 14) and at the same time to work with conceptions of 'bounded' rationality. Of particular sociological interest in this regard are the 'transaction-cost' economics of Williamson (1985, 1996) and others (see further Chapter 10 below).

is that of how, once the standard of objective rationality is dropped, 'good reasons' are to be understood. RAT in its stronger forms may unduly limit the possibilities for *verstehen*; but problems can also be created if, in the attempt to make action intelligible as subjectively rational, the principle of charity in interpretation is stretched too far. Thus, with Popperian analyses of situational logic and the abandonment of any concern with the rationality of beliefs, the threat of a lapse into tautology again looms all too clearly (Gibson 1976). And even where empirical tests of such analyses can be specified, it may still often be difficult to know (cf. Hollis 1987: 187–8) just how far the rationality in action that is 'reconstructed' does indeed reflect reasons that were actually operative—or merely the ingenuity of the analyst.

One may, then, agree with Boudon (1994: 254–5) that the most appropriate basis for RAT in sociology will be a conception of the—subjective—rationality of actions and of related beliefs that has requirements of an 'intermediate' strength. But what must of course in this case be further provided is some means of defining the bounds of this conception: that is, not merely via a formal typology of action but via criteria that can be applied so as to determine just which of empirically ascertained modes of action are and are not comprised.

This is a crucial but far from easy task, and one that I do not claim here to accomplish in any definitive way; much will in any event depend on how well proposed solutions fare in actual research practice. However, as a starting point, I would suggest that one should hold onto the idea of rational action as being outcome-oriented or 'consequentialist' (cf. Elster 1991), in the sense that it derives from some kind of cost-benefit evaluation made by actors of the different courses of action that are available to them relative to their goals (whatever the nature of these might be). Such evaluation need not be conducted entirely explicitly or continuously, let alone correctly from an objective point of view; but it should at all events be sufficient to ensure that actors have a capacity to respond appropriately, as they would see it, to their situation of action and to changes therein, and to the trade-offs that arise between one possible course of action and another. In turn, then, non-rational action may be identified in that its evaluation in these terms either does not occur or is overridden by other kinds of motivation.

For example, with the purely typological distinction between rational and 'traditional' action, a problem arises if patterns of action that are grounded in cultural tradition appear at the same time to possess a clear underlying rationality. For example, in studies of peasant societies traditional agricultural practices have often been represented as providing effective solutions to problems of economic organization or family cohesion. However, what could in such cases be taken as the key consideration is whether or not these patterns of action are adaptable to situational change. If in the face of change that erodes their former effectiveness they are none the less maintained simply because this is what 'tradition' itself demands—because 'this is what has always been done'—and regardless of the fact that the achievement of recognized goals is thus frustrated, then attempts at rational reconstruction would appear misguided. The degree of charity required becomes self-defeating.[8]

Likewise, the distinction between rational action and action that expresses adherence to a social norm may prove difficult to implement in that action of the latter kind could itself be rational: that is, where it follows from an assessment of the sanctions, positive and negative, associated with a norm. But here too the decisive issue could be seen as that of how far the action in question is in fact open to modification in the light of its probable consequences and of those of other courses of action that are available, or that become available as the situation of action changes. If the degree of actors' commitment to a norm, or underlying value, unconditionally dominates what would otherwise have been their choice of action on the basis of comparative cost-benefit evaluations, so that they comply with the norm to their recognized (net) cost, then it would again seem best to acknowledge that the limits of the applicability of RAT are reached. Attempts at saving such action as rational—that is, at making it appear outcome oriented—could no doubt be envisaged: for example, by interpreting it as having the ultimate goal of maintaining actors' integrity, identity, or 'self-image'. But to resort thus to an understanding of rationality in terms of what Coleman (1990: ch. 19) has called the individual's 'internal action system', or of 'multiple selves', while of evident fascination for philosophers, would seem likely to create far more problems than it solves so far as RAT in sociology is concerned, and especially if it is kept in mind that the *explananda* here are typically regularities evident in or deriving from action on the part of large numbers of individuals.[9]

What the instances considered above have in common is, then, that they relate to modes of action that are not usefully treated as rational in that actors in effect accept ideational constraints on their ability to respond to their situation in ways that they could appreciate as being to their advantage. While intentionality has clearly to be recognized, the determination of such action comes into conflict with the idea of rationality in so far as, to adapt an argument from Sen (1977; see also 1986), a wedge is driven between actors' per-

[8] That is to say, if traditional action is rendered rational by dint of supposing the maintenance of tradition to be itself the goal. A similar approach to that outlined in the text could be taken in regard to the distinction between rational and habitual action. It has been advanced as a critique of RAT that a man does not decide anew each morning how to shave his face but just acts 'out of habit'. This could, however, be entirely rational. If one believes that one has worked out the best way to shave, why constantly return to the problem? What would be irrational would be not to adapt to change—i.e. to reconsider the matter if information became available to suggest that by using other equipment, a different technique, etc., one could achieve a worthwhile improvement

[9] As Sen has put it (1977: 327), 'One way of defining commitment is in terms of a person choosing an act that he believes will yield a lower level of personal welfare to him than an alternative that is also available to him.' The view here taken of the scope of RAT thus implies significantly more restriction than that of Boudon (1996, 1998), who, in advancing his 'cognitivist model', argues that the 'good reasons' that actors may have for their actions need *not* be limited to 'the cost-benefit comparison type': for example, rational action can be 'axiological', rather than outcome-oriented, in following consistently from a value. Although Boudon here appeals to Weber's notion of *Wertrationalität*, it should be noted that Weber himself recognized (Max Weber 1922/1968: 26) that, from the standpoint of *Zweckrationalität*, action of a *wertrational* kind must always be judged *irrational*.

sonal *choices* and their personal *welfare* (and even if the latter is allowed to entail more than simple self-interest).

An approach on the lines indicated is clearly open to both refinement and extension. But, by pursuing it, sociologists have the possibility of developing a version of RAT, based on 'intermediate' rationality requirements, that can claim ample explanatory scope while at the same time being protected against the damaging consequences of either tautological closure or a resort to residual categories of a too capacious kind.[10]

Situational versus procedural rationality

In regard to the strength of rationality requirements, a strategy of the *via media* can then be advocated. However, when one turns next to the issue of whether, in the sociological application of RAT, attention should focus on situational or on procedural rationality, such a strategy appears a good deal less appropriate. Here, in contrast, the strong case, I would believe, is that in favour of sociologists taking up a rather extreme position: that is, one well towards the 'situational' end of the range of variation that was earlier described.

The more negative side of this case has in fact already been made by various authors, drawing on the basic insight of Popper—or indeed of Weber—that sociological explanation, even when grounded, as it should be, in individual action, does not have to depend on any elaborated psychology of the acting individual.[11] Lindenberg (1985, 1990) has usefully distinguished between the concepts of individual$_1$, appropriate to psychology where both analytic and explanatory primacies lie at the individual level, and individual$_2$, appropriate to sociology (or economics) where explanatory primacy is again at the individual level—via the principle of methodological individualism—but analytic primacy shifts to the aggregate, or macro, level. And others have then gone perhaps further than would Lindenberg himself in maintaining, on essentially Popperian lines, that in the context of RAT individual$_2$ should remain 'psychologically anonymous'. That is to say, the model of the rational actor should be endowed with no more than the minimum 'inside-the-skin' attributes necessary for the explanatory purposes in hand, and, if possible, ones that do not imply a commitment to any particular brand of psychological

---

[10] A further distinction that would obviously call for attention is that between rational and expressive action. Action pursued 'for its own sake' could be regarded as rational where, for example, actors set its intrinsic rewards against the costs involved; but instances of 'enthusiasm', 'rapture', 'fervour', etc., must be recognized where action clearly does not derive from any kind of cost-benefit considerations.

[11] Weber's most extended discussion of the issue is to be found in a neglected paper (Max Weber 1908/1975) in which he forcefully criticizes an attempt by Lujo Brentano to provide marginal utility theory with a foundation in experimental psychology—specifically, in the Weber-Fechner law that the strength of a stimulus must increase in geometric ratio if the perceived strength of sensation is to increase in arithmetic ratio. (The co-proposer of the law was Ernst Heinrich Weber—no relation of Max.) Though I know of no direct evidence that Popper was influenced by this paper, there are frequent references in his work to Weber's *Gesammelte Aufsätze zur Wissenschaftslehre*, in which it was reprinted.

theory. Little explanatory advantage is to be gained if lower-level processes invoked in order to account for higher-level regularities are themselves of a yet more complex character (cf. Coleman and Fararo 1992; Stinchcombe 1993; and Chapter 5 above).

More positively, however, it could also be argued that a version of RAT with a situational rather than a procedural emphasis is particularly appropriate for sociology—at all events once the requirement of objective rationality is abandoned. The question that then arises is that of just how action may fall short of the objective standard, but in such a way that it is still open to understanding as subjectively rational. For Simon, given his 'inside-the-skin' preoccupations, it is above all the limitations of human information-processing capacities that preclude objective rationality, and actors are thus subjectively rational when they do the best they can in the face of these limitations: that is, by aiming to satisfice rather than to maximize. For Popper, in contrast, objective rationality is primarily constrained by deficiencies in information—or knowledge—*per se*, and actors are subjectively rational when they do the best they can in the light of beliefs derived from the knowledge that is situationally available to them.

Thus, while Simon's procedural concerns direct research attention to aspects of individual psychology, Popper's situational concerns lead to clearly more sociological questions. The former approach may well be apt to the study of relatively formal decision-making as, say, by business or administrative leaders—to which Simon and those influenced by him have indeed chiefly devoted their efforts. But the latter approach would appear that better suited to understanding central tendencies in the kinds of decision that are made, usually of course in a far less formal and explicit way, by individuals in the course of their everyday lives, and that sociologists pursuing RAT are in turn likely to invoke as the basis of their explanations of emergent macrosocial regularities: for example, such decisions as whether to leave school or to stay on, to get married and to whom, to have children and how many, to vote for this party rather than that, to participate in a voluntary association or social movement, to engage in a criminal activity, and so on.

Boudon, as earlier noted, urges the need for an understanding of subjective rationality that is supported by both cognitive psychology and a new cognitive sociology. It may, however, be further remarked that, of the many illustrations that Boudon (1994, 1996) gives of his argument, it is those where objective rationality can be seen to be restricted by situational limits on knowledge, rather than by failures purely in information-processing, that appear to carry the larger sociological significance. This is so, I would suggest, because inferential errors of the latter kind, at least as they arise in everyday life, will tend to be more readily corrected, simply by processes of social learning, than will those of the former kind, which have a structural basis (cf. Elster 1983*b*: 144–8).[12]

---

[12] Consider a trickster attempting to exploit the tendency discussed by Boudon (1994: 235–6) for individuals to miscalculate how best to bet on the toss of a coin known to be

In short, I would believe that Abell (1992: 198; cf. Friedman and Hechter 1988) is right in maintaining that, for sociologists wishing to comprehend subjective rationality, the modelling of actors' 'information environments' must be of primary concern: that is, unlike (most) economists, sociologists should aim to treat the information available to actors as a product of the social relations in which they are involved. Abell's position, it may be added, is thoroughly Popperian, not just in his effective underwriting of Popper's methodological injunction to 'pack or cram' as much explanatory effort as possible into the analysis of the situation of action but again in his recognition that the social structuring of knowledge is a no less important aspect of that situation than the structuring of other resources of, say, a material kind.[13] And, where such comprehensive situational analysis is achieved, it could well be that the Popperian conclusion will in turn be found to hold good: that the need for sociologists to address questions of procedural rationality at the level of individual psychology is rather slight.

Finally, the point should here be made that, while explanations of action in terms of situational rationality take the form of reconstructions *ex post actu*, rather than entailing predictions, this in no way precludes their testing or indeed their refutation. To the contrary, it may be seen as a further advantage of a focus on situational rather than procedural rationality that it leads to explanations that are pre-eminently open to criticism on grounds of fact and of logic alike. On the one hand, the analysis of situations of action depends, as Koertge (1975: 445) has put it, on 'independent evidence for each component', with special importance attaching to the empirical grounds for any 'unorthodox utilities' that may be attributed to actors; and claims thus made would seem more readily challenged than 'psychological hypotheses' about actors (Latsis 1976: 22; Tsebelis 1990: 40), especially where large numbers are involved. On the other hand, the attribution of rationality to actors that 'animates' situational analyses can, as earlier noted, be regarded as the completion of a practical syllogism that may in turn be questioned, and again without reference to mental states. A critic could accept the description provided of the situation of action but still seek to show that the actors involved could, just as rationally, have acted in some other way to that observed—that is, that the situation was not a 'single-exit' one and that the explanation offered is at all events incomplete; or, more radically, that the

---

heavily biased. The trickster might make some money initially, but knowledge of how to win (even if not of the underlying mathematics) would soon spread among the public. In contrast, the tendency that Boudon further considers (1994: 247–8) of many teachers to believe, in a context of educational expansion, that standards of educational achievement are falling, even if this is not in fact so, is likely to have much greater social persistence. The source of the error here is not the inability of the individuals concerned to calculate correctly but the situationally restricted, and thus partial and misleading, nature of the relevant knowledge that is most immediately available to them.

[13] This does not, of course, imply or warrant any neglect of material resources and constraints in the situation of action. RAT, at least in the version I would favour, is very readily allied with class analysis. Chapters 8–11 represent an attempt to put the present preaching into practice—and also to correct the bizarre misunderstanding on the part of some sociologists that RAT is unduly 'voluntaristic'.

syllogism advanced is in some respect flawed, so that no adequate basis is in fact provided on which the observed action can be comprehended as rational—that is, that a new analysis must be essayed.[14]

A general versus a special theory

The foregoing does then in some large part predetermine the view that I take on the question of whether RAT should be considered as a general or a special theory of action. If one argues, as I have done, that sociologists should opt for a version of RAT that refers to action that can be treated as subjectively rational, but with full recognition then being made of the need to delimit what shall count as such action and to focus enquiry on its situational understanding, it obviously follows that RAT in such a version will be a special theory. Certain modes of action (as well as externally caused behaviour) must be seen as lying outside its scope. There is, however, one important challenge that can be raised against this position that I should address, and one important qualification to it that I would myself wish to make.

As earlier noted, accepting RAT as a special theory of action avoids the difficulties encountered by versions that claim generality when forced by anomalous findings into either tautology or a reliance on dubious residual categories. But, as was also noted, if RAT is viewed as only a special theory, then the question can be seriously pressed, as, for example, it is by Gary Becker (1976: 14), of just why action should be 'compartmentalized' so that it is sometimes viewed as rational but sometimes not.

The most promising approach to a solution is, I believe, for exponents of RAT to seek to avoid merely *ad hoc* appeals to varieties of non-rational action by developing the capacity of their theory actually to explain under what conditions such action is likely to occur in sociologically significant ways. A valuable lead in this regard is given in a recent paper by Hechter (1994). Action that follows from an unconditional commitment to 'immanent' as opposed to 'instrumental' values is, Hechter argues, most likely to cut across patterns of rational action where immanent values are neither universal (for example, biologically determined) nor merely idiosyncratic but, rather, distributed non-randomly among populations—as, say, in relation to class, ethnicity, or gender. Research should then focus on the processes of action—which may themselves be open to interpretation as rational—through which heterogeneous values come to be thus distributed and in turn, perhaps, institutionalized into normative structures.

---

[14] If sociologists have available respondents' own accounts of their action, as, say, through interviews, the rationality that is reconstructed in situational analyses can be subjected to a further check, which is likely to be especially relevant where 'unorthodox utilities' are postulated. As P. C. Cohen (1976: 149) has remarked, it is easier for historians and ethnographers to make the conduct studied by them appear rational in that 'dead men can never answer back and ethnographers' informants used not to be able to do so'. At the same time, though, actors' accounts need not be regarded as entirely privileged, but rather as being open to criticism, on grounds of fact and logic, in just the same way as sociologists'. This latter point is an important one in considering the issue of the place of attitudinal and other 'subjective' data in the development and evaluation of RAT-based explanations (cf. Opp 1998).

It is of particular interest that the way in which Hechter would thus treat what he refers to as the 'interference' of value-commitments in rational action runs essentially parallel to that in which Boudon would treat the 'deviation' of subjectively rational action from objective standards. That is, instead of seemingly anomalous action being accommodated *ad hoc*, the aim is to 'endogenize' it through a genuine theoretical development. And, as Hechter implies (1994: 320), in so far as this can be achieved, the challenge can then be thrown back to critics such as Becker likewise to endogenize the manipulation of 'utility functions' to which they *in extremis* are inclined to resort.

Hechter's paper can also serve to introduce the qualification that I would make to the idea of RAT as a special theory of action. Although RAT should be thus regarded, it can at the same time, I would argue, claim to be a *privileged* theory: that is, not just one theory of action among others but rather *the* theory with which attempts at explaining social action should start and with which they should remain for as long as possible (cf. Abell 1992; Boudon 1994). Thus, it is from this standpoint entirely appropriate that Hechter should pose his problem as being that of the 'interference' that in certain social contexts value-committed action creates.

In fact, most proponents of RAT, in whatever version, would implicitly or explicitly share in this view, even if not always on the same grounds. And it is then in this respect that they are brought together in sharpest conflict with proponents of other theories of action who are led to maintain a more or less contrary position: that is, that it is non-rational action—for example, action guided by values and social norms or prompted by emotions—on which explanatory effort should in the first instance focus, with rational action then being treated as itself a derivative of certain normative and affective conditions (see esp. Etzioni 1988: 90–2, 152; also Denzin 1990; Scheff 1992). As stated at the outset, it is not my intention in this chapter to become involved in the general debate over RAT. So, although I regard this latter line of argument as quite uncompelling, I shall here respond to it only indirectly in seeking to restate the case for the privilege of RAT in the version that I would see as having greatest attraction for sociologists. This case comprises three different though connected points.

First, it may be held that the very idea of rational action is *prior to* that not only of irrational but also of non-rational action. Rational action is action of a kind in which certain requirements are met regarding the nature of, and the relations among, actors' goals, their beliefs, and the courses of action that they in fact follow. Just as, then, stronger and weaker conceptions of rationality are defined as these requirements are made more or less demanding, so are departures from particular conceptions of rationality to be defined in terms of certain associated requirements not being met. In other words, we need some idea of rationality in action as setting a pattern that may or may not be followed before we can talk about irrational or non-rational action: the latter 'make sense', as Elster has put it (1979: 154; cf. 1989c: 28–30), only 'against a background of rationality' (see also Davidson 1976, 1980). How we might proceed the other way around is difficult to envisage, and it can thus be claimed that other theories of action in effect derive their conceptual basis from RAT.

Secondly, this conceptual privilege is linked to what might be called hermeneutic privilege. Here the argument is that, whether as social scientists or as social actors ourselves, we can best say that we understand the action of others—that it becomes intelligible to us—when we can construe this action as rational. Thus, as Hollis has expressed it (1987: 6–9), it is through the category of rationality, rather than through the vaguer one of 'meaning', that the problem of 'other minds' and, in turn, that of 'other cultures' can be most effectively approached. It is rationality 'which lets us make most object- ive yet interpretive sense of social life'. Any *verstehende* sociology must then be crucially reliant upon RAT, and especially on a version that invokes sub- jective rather than objective, and situational rather than procedural rational- ity. Where observed social regularities can ultimately be accounted for in terms of actors pursuing their goals as best they know how in the situations in which they find themselves, we can claim that the action and interaction involved is intelligible to us in a fuller sense than if, say, we are forced in the end (as we may be) to appeal to actors' unreflective conformity to tradition or to their unyielding value-commitments. For in these latter cases—at all events if we are not ourselves under the sway of the traditions or values in question—problems of interpretative understanding still obviously remain (cf. Max Weber 1922/1968: 6–7; Tsebelis 1990: 44–5).

Thirdly, the hermeneutic privilege of RAT can be connected with a further claim of explanatory privilege: that is, a claim as regards *Erklären* as well as *Verstehen*. If it is the case that a satisfactory explanation is one that serves to resolve intellectual tension, then it would seem an especially appropriate *ter- minus ad quem* for sociological analysis that it can show as rational the action generating the social regularities that it addresses. In Coleman's words (1986*b*: 1), the rational action of individuals has 'a unique attractiveness' as the basis of sociological theory, since 'the very concept of rational action' is one of '"understandable" action that we need ask no more questions about'; or, as Hollis (1977: 21) succinctly puts it, 'rational action is its own explanation'. Conversely, it is when RAT fails, when there is no way of denying the preval- ence of systematic irrational or non-rational action, that 'black boxes' remain and there is clearly more explanatory work to be done (cf. Boudon 1998).

I have sought to distinguish versions of RAT according to whether they have strong or weak rationality requirements, focus on situational or procedural rationality, and purport to be general or only special theories of action. Soci- ologists, I have then maintained, will tend to be best served by a form of RAT that has rationality requirements of intermediate strength, that has a prim- arily situational emphasis, and that aims to be a theory of a special, although at the same time a privileged, kind. To revert to the space delineated in Fig. 6.1, the area I would recommend for sociological colonization thus lies at a middling height, far to the left and closer to the back than the front, with, say, the position allocated to Boudon marking its lower-right-front corner. The arguments I have advanced do, I would like to think, have a degree of coherence that a summary on the following lines may serve to bring out.

If a subjective conception of rationality such as the one I have advocated is adopted, serious efforts must be made to complement this conception in two different respects. First, it is important to analyse the conditions under which actors come to act—systematically rather than just idiosyncratically— in a way that is rational from their point of view, even if deviating from the course of action that would be objectively rational. Secondly, criteria must be developed by reference to which action that is open to understanding as sub-jectively rational can be demarcated from action that is not, and analyses in turn undertaken of the conditions under which such non-rational action— again of a systematic kind—is most likely to occur. Progress in both these directions then requires that sociologists should concentrate their explana-tory efforts on the situation of action rather than on the psychology of the acting individual. While still adhering to a RAT approach, they may aim to show how social structural and procedural features of this situation may subvert objective, though not subjective, rationality (as in Boudon's new soci-ology of knowledge); or, further, lead to subjectively rational action being cross-cut by action with clearly different motives and meanings (as in Hechter's proposed sociology of immanent values).

Even in such an extended version, RAT would claim to be only a special theory of action. Its exponents might, indeed should, be expected to push the theory to its furthest limits—to seek in effect to 'reduce' accounts of social regularities in terms of cultural traditions, values, and norms as far as poss-ible to ones given in terms of rational action—because of the distinctive hermeneutic and explanatory advantages that could thus be gained. But such reductionism would always require empirical justification, while appeals that might still be made to non-rationality, rather than being *ad hoc*, would be provided with their own sociological grounding.[15]

---

[15] It is also by proceeding on these lines, I would believe, that sociologists can best address the central 'macro-to-micro' issue that arises with RAT: i.e. that of whether RAT differs in its potential across different kinds of society and culture. For example, the appropriateness of RAT to the understanding of individual action has been represented, in a developmental per-spective, as depending on the extent to which societies have themselves become 'rational-ized'; or again, from the standpoint of a radical relativism, on the degree of cultural dominance of one particular—Western—conception of rationality. In contrast, underlying the claims that I have made, at all events for the privilege of RAT, is the assumption of what Popper (see esp. 1945/1966: chs. 23, 24), echoing Kant, has called 'the intellectual unity of mankind', to which the idea of rationality provides the *passe partout*. There would by now seem clear indications (e.g. Goody 1996: esp. chs. 1, 2) that attempts to address this issue at the level of abstract societal or cultural typologies are of limited value, and that it is far more illuminating to investigate empirically, across societies and cultures, those more particular structures and processes—at the level of social networks, group affiliations, and institutions— by which patterns of action are guided into conformity with specified standards of rational-ity or are deflected from them.

7

Causation, Statistics, and Sociology

IN A PAPER of great insight, though sadly posthumous, Bernert (1983) noted a long-standing uncertainty among sociologists in regard to the concept of causation and its use in their work. 'Uncritical adulation' in the later nineteenth century gave way to 'complete rejection' in the early twentieth, followed in turn, in the years after the Second World War, by 'pragmatic utilization'—a position that, one might add, has itself been subject to rising criticism in the period since Bernert's review. These vicissitudes in the 'career of a concept' have to be understood, as Bernert shows, in the context not only of the development of sociology itself but of larger scientific and philosophical debates.[1] In this chapter I seek, much in the spirit of Bernert's contribution, to draw attention to some results of statisticians being increasingly involved in such debates, and further to consider the reception in, and potential for, sociology of the new understandings of causation that have thus emerged.

The founders of modern statistics might be regarded as representatives of the era in which the concept of causation was viewed with scepticism. At least for Pearson (1892), it was a mere 'fetish', carried over from metaphysical, pre-scientific thinking, which was to be abandoned and replaced by that of correlation, at once both more general and more precise. However, an opportunity for statisticians to make a more constructive contribution came at a later point with the introduction by philosophers, in the 1940s and 1950s, of the idea of 'probabilistic', as opposed to 'deterministic', causation: that is, the idea, roughly, that, rather than causes being seen as necessitating their effects, they might be regarded simply as raising the probability of their occurrence (for reviews and more recent developments, see Salmon 1980; Eells 1991). A probabilistic view of causation might be associated with the argument that the world itself is non-deterministic; but such a view could also be

· This chapter is a revised and extended version of the twenty-ninth Geary Lecture given at the Economic and Social Research Institute, Dublin, in 1998 and first published by the ESRI in 1999. For helpful comments on earlier drafts I am indebted to Hans-Peter Blossfeld, Richard Breen, Pat Clancy, Tom Cook, David Collier, David Cox, Robert Erikson, David Freedman, Michael Gähler, Janne Jonsson, Máire Ní Bhrolcháin, Donald Rubin, and Wout Ultee.

[1] Bernert's paper concentrates on the concept of causation in American sociology but is in fact of quite general relevance.

favoured simply on the grounds that, whether the world is deterministic or not, it is too complicated, and our knowledge of it too error-prone, to permit anything other than probabilistic accounts to be provided. The latter position, at least, is one that would seem likely to commend itself to most sociologists—despite some recent attempts to uphold both the desirability and the possibility of causal explanations in sociology that are of an entirely deterministic kind (see e.g. Ragin 1987; H. S. Becker 1992; and, for critical comment, Lieberson 1992, 1994; Sobel 1995; and Chapter 3 above).

In what follows, I take up three different understandings of causation that have been importantly shaped by contributions from statisticians. These I label as

  (i) causation as robust dependence;
 (ii) causation as consequential manipulation; and
(iii) causation as generative process.

I sketch out these positions in a deliberately broad and non-technical way. My concern is not with different individual formulations of each position and their internal coherence from a philosophical or a statistical point of view. I am interested, rather, in differences among these positions considered generically and with the question of what each might have to offer to 'working' sociologists who wish to engage in causal analysis of some kind.[2] I treat the three ideas of causation in the above order, and then, drawing especially on the last, outline a further position that, it seems to me, could be—and indeed to some extent already is—both viable and valuable in sociology.

Causation as Robust Dependence

The starting point here is with the proposition, widely recognized in both philosophy and statistics, that, while correlation—or, more generally, association—does not imply causation, causation must in some way or other imply association. The key problem that has then to be addressed is that of how to establish whether, or how far, the observed degree of association of variable X with variable Y, where X is temporally prior to Y, can be equated with the degree to which X is *causally significant* for Y.[3] It may indeed be that the probability of Y, given X, is greater than the probability of Y given not-X; but this is not in itself sufficient to demonstrate that X is a cause of Y. For example, it could be that a third variable (or set of variables), Z, is the cause

---

[2] Other reviews of issues of causality from a statistical point of view, from which I have greatly benefited, are Holland (1986a), Berk (1988), Cox (1992), and Sobel (1995).

[3] I am aware of some special cases in which it might be argued that causation is present in the absence of association: e.g. where X does have an effect on Y, which, however, happens to be *exactly* cancelled out by a further and opposing effect that X exerts on Y via a third variable, Z. For present purposes, I believe that such cases can be safely disregarded. I might also add that here, as throughout, I assume that effects cannot precede causes and further that plural or 'multifactorial' causation may operate.

of both X and Y, so that, if one conditions on Z, the association between X and Y disappears: that is, Y becomes statistically independent of X and any supposed causal link between X and Y is revealed as spurious. It could, though, also be that conditioning on Z does not entirely remove the association between X and Y but merely weakens it. In this case, the implication is not that X is a spurious cause of Y, but only that there is *some part* of the observed association between them that does not reflect the causal significance that X has for Y. A solution to the problem of moving from association to causation has then generally been pursued through an argument to the effect that X is a 'genuine' cause of Y in so far as the dependence of Y on X can be shown to be robust: that is to say, cannot be eliminated through one or more other variables being introduced into the analysis and then in some way 'controlled' (see esp. Simon 1954; Suppes 1970).

One particularly influential version of the attempt to understand causation in this way is that proposed by Granger (1969) in the context of the analysis of econometric time series, which has the further, more distinctive, feature of treating causation explicitly in terms of predictive power. A variable, X, 'Granger causes' Y if, after taking into account all information apart from values of X, these values still add to one's ability to predict future values of Y. In principle, 'all information' here refers to all information that has been accumulated in the universe up to the point at which the prediction of Y is made. In practice, however, Z has to refer to some particular information set, and what counts as a Granger cause would seem to be any non-zero partial correlation that improves the analyst's forecasting ability. Thus, as Holland (1986a) has argued, Granger causation is established essentially through the detection and elimination of spurious causal significance, or of what Granger himself calls 'non-causality': X is *not* a Granger cause of Y, relative to the information in Z, to the extent that the correlation between X and Y disappears, given Z. That is to say, the idea of robust dependence is crucial.

This same idea is also to be found, though again with a particular slant, in methodological programmes developed within sociology—most obviously, perhaps, in Lazarsfeld's proposals for 'elaboration' in the analysis of survey data (see e.g. Kendall and Lazarsfeld 1950; Lazarsfeld and Rosenberg 1955; Lazarsfeld *et al.*, 1972). Lazarsfeld is, like Granger, concerned with detecting spurious causation, but in the interests less of prediction than of explanation. Thus, a further and seemingly more positive strategy that Lazarsfeld advocates is to begin with a correlation between X and Y that is of substantive interest—say, a correlation between area of residence and vote; but then, rather than supposing any direct causal link, to seek an explanation *of the correlation itself* by finding one or more prior variables, Z—say, social class or ethnicity—that, when brought into the analysis, will reduce the partial correlation of X and Y to as close to zero as possible. To the extent that this is achieved, Z can be viewed as the cause of both X and Y—or, at all events, until such time as further 'elaboration' might bring the robustness of their dependence on Z itself into question.

The regression techniques taken over from econometrics and biometrics, including causal-path analysis, that became familiar in quantitative sociology from the 1970s onwards marked important advances on Lazarsfeldian 'elaboration' in both their refinement and scope. But, as Davis (1985) has shown (see also Clogg and Haritou 1997), so far as the basic understanding of causation is concerned—causation as robust dependence—a clear continuity can be traced. It is in fact the methodological tradition thus represented that has served as the main vehicle for the 'pragmatic utilization' of the concept of causation by sociologists that Bernert sees as characteristic of the post-war years. However, as I suggested at the start, growing dissatisfaction with this position has of late been apparent, and among sociologists whose primary interest is in empirical research as well as among theorists and methodologists.

At the source of this dissatisfaction is a problem with the idea of causation as robust dependence to which attention has been drawn from various quarters. If causation is viewed in this way, then, it would appear, establishing causation becomes *entirely* a matter of statistical inference, into which no wider considerations need enter. Causation can be derived directly from the analysis of empirical regularities, following principles that are equally applicable across all different fields of enquiry, and without the requirement for any 'subject-matter' input in the form of background knowledge or, more crucially, theory. This implication might not appear too disturbing if, as with Granger, the essential criterion of causation is taken to be increased predictive power. But most philosophers of science would find this a too limited view, and would wish to regard causation as entailing something more than (if not other than) predictability—on the lines, say, of 'predictability *in accordance with theory*' (cf. Feigl 1953; Bunge 1979). Moreover, among economists, and even among econometricians (e.g. Geweke 1984; Basmann 1988; Zellner 1988), there are many who would maintain that, while 'Granger causation' may be an idea of great practical utility for the purposes of forecasting, it can lead to *causal explanation* only when the demonstrated statistical relationships are provided with some rationale in theory and, moreover, in theory ultimately at the micro-economic level. In a discussion of prediction in economics, Sen (1986: 14) observes that the magnitudes of concern to the forecaster are all social magnitudes, and that variables such as prices, investment, consumption, and money supply 'do not, naturally, move on their own, untouched by human volition'. Thus, while 'mindless macroeconomics' may serve as a basis for predictions—or, at all events, for 'simple and immediate' ones—any 'deep explanation' of the movement of the magnitudes involved can, in the end, be gained only through theory, and of a kind that makes reference to the 'objectives, knowledge, reasoning and decisions' of individuals acting in society.

In sociology itself forecasting is a far less prominent activity than in economics, and it is then scarcely surprising to find that the treatment of causation in terms of predictability has been still more sharply rejected, and that arguments analogous to that of Sen on the need to go beyond the analysis of variables have been very widely expressed. Especially from the standpoint of methodological individualism, sociologists have strongly criticized the supposition that statistical techniques can in themselves provide adequate causal explanations of social phenomena. Such techniques can show only relations among variables, and not how these relations are actually produced—as they can indeed only be produced—through the action and interaction of individuals (see Boudon 1976, 1987; Coleman 1986a; Abbott 1992a; also Lindenberg and Frey 1993; Esser 1996; Hedström and Swedberg 1998a,b).

For example, if, in a causal-path analysis, a path is shown as leading from educational attainment to level of occupation or of income, it does not make much sense to talk, on this basis, of education *causing* occupation or income. Individuals get jobs because other individuals or employing organizations offer them jobs or because they make a place for themselves, as self-employed workers, in some market for goods or services. And likewise they get income because employers pay them or because they secure fees or make profits. Thus, even if it is clear from statistical analysis that how well individuals fare as regards jobs and income is dependent in some part on their educational attainment—and that this dependence is indeed robust—the question remains of just how this dependence comes about. It could be that education provides saleable knowledge and skills; but it could also be that education is used by employers chiefly as an indicator of job-seekers' psychological or social characteristics; or, again, that education allows individuals to pass 'credentialist' filters chiefly set up to suit employers' convenience or to restrict the supply of labour to particular kinds of employment. To establish a causal link between education and occupation or income would then require, in the first instance, situating the variable of 'educational attainment' within some generalized narrative of action that would represent one or other such process that is of a 'causally adequate' kind. And, in the interests of clarity, consistency, and subsequent empirical testing, it would then be further desirable that any narrative thus advanced should be not merely *ad hoc* but rather one informed by a reasonably well-developed theory of social action.

It should, moreover, be noted that such questioning of the capacity of 'variable sociology' to produce causal explanations has received strong reinforcement from objections raised by statisticians to the way in which techniques such as causal-path analysis have actually been applied in sociology. Most notably, Freedman (esp. 1992a,b, 1997; also 1983, 1985, 1991; and cf. Clogg and Haritou 1997) has built up a cogent critique around three main points: first, that such modelling itself requires a theoretical input to determine the variables to be included, their causal ordering and the functional form of relationships between them, secondly, that, in so far as the theory is mistaken—that is, is inconsistent with the social processes that actually generate the data used—the results of the analysis will be vitiated; and, thirdly, that available sociological theory may just not be strong enough to help produce models that can be treated as genuinely 'structural'—that is, so parameterized that their coefficients are sufficiently invariant and autonomous to sustain claims about the consequences of changes in the variables deemed to be 'exogenous'. For instance, a model might purport to show, on the basis of past observations, the degree to which inequalities in income among classes or ethnic groups are dependent on differences in their educational attainment; but if, as a result, say, of policy intervention, educational differentials were to be reduced, it could be seriously doubted whether reductions in income inequalities would then follow in the manner expected under the model.

In sum, an understanding of causation simply as robust dependence would seem best regarded more as a feature of sociology's past than of its future—of the period in which it was widely, although for the most part unreflectingly, believed that the making of causal inferences would be facilitated *pari passu* with the advance of statistical methodology. To conclude thus is not, I would stress, to imply that no such advance was achieved, nor that techniques such as causal-path analysis have proved of no value in sociology. Rather, it is to suggest, and the point will in due course be developed further, that the potential of such techniques for sociology has been misjudged—though less, it should be said, by the real pioneers than by their epigoni[4]—and now stands in need of serious re-evaluation.

Causation as Consequential Manipulation

Among statisticians, the idea of causation as consequential manipulation would appear to have emerged in reaction to that of causation as robust dependence from a relatively early stage. Cook and Campbell (1979: 26) claim to be expressing a long-standing view when they contend that this latter idea, or what they themselves call the 'partialling approach', does not adequately accord with the understanding of causation in 'practical science'—which they would, apparently, see as best exemplified by medical or agricultural science. Here, attention centres specifically on 'the consequences of performing particular acts' or, in other words, on establishing causation through experimental methods; and this, they urge, is the paradigm for causal analysis that should in general be followed. Subsequently, a number of statisticians (see

---

[4] Lazarsfeld, for example, always urged that elaboration should go together with 'interpretation', which involved specifying intervening variables in the supposed causal connection and the provision of some appropriate narrative or 'storyline'. Again, Duncan's standard work (1975) could scarcely be more explicit on the problems that sociologists must face, and overcome, if they are to produce valid causal-path models. It is of particular interest to read one of his main cautionary passages in conjunction with Freedman's critique, outlined in the text above: 'A strong possibility in any area of research at a given time is that there are *no* structural relations among the variables currently recognized and measured in that area. Hence, whatever its mathematical properties, no model describing covariation of those variables will be a structural model. What is needed under the circumstances is a theory that invents the proper variables . . . There were no structural equation models for the epidemiology of malaria until the true agent and vector of the disease were identified, although there were plenty of correlations between prevalence of the disease and environmental conditions' (Duncan 1975: 152).

esp. Rubin 1974, 1977, 1990; Holland 1986*a,b*) have developed and refined this position in a technically impressive way.

In outline, the argument is as follows. Causes can be only those factors that could, conceptually at least, serve as 'treatments' in experiments: that is, causes must in some sense be manipulable. In turn, the indication of genuine causation is that if a causal factor, X, is manipulated, then, given appropriate controls, a systematic effect is produced on the response variable, Y. Understood in this way, causation is always relative. It is, in principle, determined by *comparing* what would have happened to a 'unit' in regard to Y if this unit had been exposed to X (treatment) with what would have happened if it had not been exposed to X (control). This formulation gives rise to what Holland (1986*a*) has called the 'Fundamental Problem of Causal Inference': that is, it is not possible in the same experiment for a unit to be both exposed and not exposed to the treatment. But the problem has a statistical solution. One can take the whole population of units involved and compare the *average* response for exposed units with the average response for control units, with the difference between the two being then regarded as the average causal effect.[5] For this solution to be viable, however, it is essential that various conditions are met. Units must be assigned to the treatment or control subsets entirely at random; and the response of a unit must be unaffected either by the process of assignment itself or by the treatment (or absence of treatment) of other units. In sum, the conditions required are, ideally, those of randomized experimental design, as elaborated in statistical work from Fisher's (1935) classic study onwards.

There would seem to be wide agreement that the idea of causation as consequential manipulation is stronger or 'deeper' than that of causation as robust dependence (cf. Holland 1986*a*; Cox 1992; Sobel 1995, 1996). With the latter, it is observed, a variable X can never be regarded as having causal significance for Y in anything more than a provisional sense, for it is impossible to be sure that all other relevant variables have in fact been controlled. At any point, further information might be produced that would show that the dependence of Y on X is not robust after all, or, in other words, that the apparent causal force of X is, at least to some extent, spurious. In contrast, in so far as causation is inferred from the results of appropriately designed experiments, the issue of spuriousness is avoided: the random assignment of units to exposure or non-exposure to the treatment variable replaces the attempt—the success of which must always be uncertain—to identify and statistically control all other variables that might be of causal significance.

Such an argument carries force. None the less, it is at the same time important to recognize that, in moving from the one understanding of causation to the other, a far from negligible redefinition appears to occur of the actual

---

[5] Holland (1986*a*: 947) distinguishes this 'statistical' solution from the 'scientific' solution typically pursued in laboratory experiments, which rests on various assumptions concerning the homogeneity of units and the invariance of measurements made of their properties.

problem being addressed. To put the matter briefly, while exponents of causation as robust dependence are concerned with establishing *the causes of effects*, exponents of causation as consequential manipulation are concerned—and more narrowly, it might be thought—with establishing *the effects of causes*. Holland (1986a: 959) indeed acknowledges this. Although 'looking for the causes of effects is a worthwhile scientific endeavour', he argues, 'it is not the proper perspective in a theoretical analysis of causation'. It is more to the point to take causes simply as 'given' or 'known', and to concentrate on the question of how their effects can most securely be measured. The main justification offered for this stance would seem to be (see esp. Holland 1986b: 970; also 1988) that, while statements in the form 'X is a cause of Y' are always likely to be proved wrong as knowledge advances, statements in the form 'Y is an effect of X', *once they have been experimentally verified*, do not subsequently become false: 'Old, replicable experiments never die, they just get reinterpreted.'

In assessing how appropriate to sociology the idea of causation as consequential manipulation might be, this shift in focus must not be lost sight of, and I shall indeed return to it. But a more immediate issue is the extent to which the idea can be applied at all, given that most sociological research is not—and, for both practical and ethical reasons, cannot be—experimental in character.

What would in this regard be recommended by those subscribing to the principle of 'no causation without manipulation' is that in their empirical work sociologists should seek as far as possible to mimic experimental designs and, in particular, through what have been called, in a rather special sense, 'observational studies'. Such studies are those in which a treatment or, in a social context, a political or administrative 'intervention' of some kind actually takes place; or, at very least, in which it is possible to understand the situation studied *as if* some treatment or intervention had occurred (cf. Rosenbaum 1995: 1). The problem of approximating the requirements of randomized experimental design, it is argued, can then be addressed by making the process of unit assignment, whether actual or supposed, itself a prime concern of the enquiry. Specifically, researchers should attempt to identify, and then to represent through covariates in their data analyses, all influences on the response variable that could conceivably be involved in, or follow from, this process. Thus, in a study of, say, the effects of a vocational education and training scheme on workers' future earnings, it would be necessary to investigate any possible selection biases in recruitment to the scheme (that is, in the assignment of individuals to the treatment rather than the control subset), any unintended effects of recruitment or non-recruitment (for example, on workers' motivation), any links fortuitously established with labour markets during the scheme, and so on, so that all such factors might be appropriately taken into account in the ultimate attempt to determine the effect on earnings of the treatment *per se*: that is, the education and training actually provided.

A difficulty at once apparent here is that of how it can be known if the set of covariates that is eventually established does indeed warrant the assumption that, given this set, treatment assignment and unit response *are* independent of each other. Have *all* relevant influences been represented and adequately measured and controlled? A whole battery of statistical techniques has in fact been developed to help answer such questions (see e.g. Rosenbaum 1995). However, valuable though these techniques are, it is still difficult to avoid the conclusion that, in non-experimental social research, attempts to determine the effects of causes will lead not to results that 'never die' but only to ones that have differing degrees of plausibility. And since this plausibility will in part depend on the existing subject-matter knowledge and theory that, presumably, guide the selection of covariates, such results will have to be provisional in just the same way and for just the same reasons as those of attempts to determine the causes of effects via the 'partialling approach'.

Furthermore, it is still difficult to see how observational studies in the sense in question could have anything other than a quite marginal role in sociology. While they could well be taken to represent the preferred design in evaluation research, it would appear no more than a statement of fact to say that, in most other forms of enquiry in which sociologists presently engage, they could have little application—and even if this statement might then invite the conclusion that sociological research is not in general of a kind adequate to sustain causal analysis.

In this regard, the crux of the matter is, of course, the insistence of Rubin, Holland, and others that causes must be manipulable, and their consequent unwillingness to allow causal significance to be accorded to variables that are not manipulable, at least in principle. In this latter category are those variables that are 'intrinsic' to units—that is, part of their very constitution. Proponents of a manipulative view of causation would argue that an intrinsic variable may be considered as an *attribute* of a unit and shown to be associated with other variables, but that it cannot meaningfully be said to have 'effects' on them, since in the case of such a variable it does not make any sense to envisage a unit as taking a different value from the one that it actually has. The only way for an intrinsic variable to change its value would be for the unit itself to change in some way—so that it would no longer be the same unit. Thus, to give a sociological example, one could discuss the association that exists between sex (or again, say, race), on the one hand, and educational attainment, on the other. But it would be no more meaningful to speak of sex as being a cause of such attainment than it would be to make statements about what level of education Ms *M* would have achieved had she been a man or Mr *N* had he been a woman.

It is in fact this restriction imposed on variables that can be treated as causes that has led to most objections from sociologists and other social scientists, and also from philosophers, to the principle of 'no causation without manipulation' (see e.g. Geweke 1984; Glymour 1986; Granger 1986; Berk 1988). However, what I wish further to suggest here is that, from a sociological standpoint at least, this restriction is worrying not just because of the difficulties that arise over the causal significance of attributes, on which discussion has in fact so far centred, but also, and indeed more so, because of those that arise in another, quite different respect: that is, over the causal significance of *action*. This argument can be developed on the basis of a simple but illuminating example from Holland (1986*a*).

Holland considers the three following statements, each of which could be taken to suggest causation in some sense.

(*A*) She did well in the exam because she is a woman.
(*B*) She did well in the exam because she studied for it.
(*C*) She did well in the exam because she was coached by her teacher.

To begin with (*C*), this refers to an intervention—that is, coaching by the teacher—and thus the idea of causation as consequential manipulation, which Holland supports, is clearly applicable. In apparent contrast, the reference in (*A*) is to an attribute—sex—and in this case the suggestion of causation would, from Holland's position, be mistaken. However, as Berk (1988: 167) has observed, in a sociological context, what may seem *prima facie* to be a reference to an attribute, such as sex or race, often turns out to be a reference, rather, to a social construct built up around an attribute (see also Rubin 1986). Thus, (*A*) could be quite plausibly taken as claiming that women do well not because of their (biologically fixed) sex but because of their (in principle, alterable) gender; and a 'manipulative' causal interpretation would then be possible, with the implication that, if the social construction or perception of gender were to be changed in some way, women would do less well.

It is, I would believe, statement (*B*) that, from Holland's point of view, creates the really serious problems. Here there is reference neither to an intervention in regard to a manipulable factor nor to an attribute. The obvious elaboration of (*B*) would be as follows: she had the goal of doing well in the exam; she believed that studying for the exam was the best way of achieving this goal; therefore she chose to study; therefore, her belief being correct, she did well. It may be noted that the form of this narrative is of the general kind that, as earlier seen, has been proposed by both economists and sociologists in order that adequate recognition may be made of the human action that must underlie all statistically demonstrated social regularities: that is, a narrative given, to use Sen's words again, in terms of individuals' 'objectives, knowledge, reasoning and decisions'. And most sociologists would, I believe, wish to regard this kind of explanatory narrative as being causal in character: the woman's doing well was caused by her taking appropriate means to this end. But, as Holland (1986*a*: 955) indeed appreciates, such accounts cannot in any very convincing way be reconciled with the idea of causation as consequential manipulation, and primarily because of 'the voluntary aspect of the supposed cause'.[6] Thus, either a limit to the applicability of this idea has

---

[6] The difficulty for Holland here is that of reconciling purposive or 'outcome-oriented' and rational action on the part of an individual with the idea of 'caused' action in the sense he

here to be accepted or else sociologists must be required to reform, in at least one rather crucial respect, the language of causation that they are accustomed to using. This problem of agency, as it might be called, is one reason, Holland concedes, why the argument over what constitutes proper causal inference has to be left, and is likely to remain, 'without any definitive resolution'.

It has, moreover, to be noted that a version of the problem may well arise in 'observational' studies in sociology, in the special sense noted above: that is, studies that seek to determine the effects of some kind of intervention and that would thus appear to offer the best possibility for implementing a manipulative approach to causation. In such studies, it cannot be supposed that the response of the units involved—that is, ultimately of the individuals affected or potentially affected by the intervention—will be of the same nature as that of the units in an experiment in some applied natural science. These individuals are likely to know that the intervention is taking place, to have beliefs about what its aims are and what might follow from it, and then to relate their understanding of the situation to their own interests and goals and to act accordingly—which could in fact mean acting so as actually to counter or subvert the intervention. In the case, say, of the introduction of some kind of positive discrimination in education, with the aim of reducing class or ethnic differentials in attainment, it could be that members of those classes or ethnic groups whose children would not benefit and who might lose their competitive advantage in schools and labour markets could respond—that is, act—so as to preserve this advantage: as, for example, by devoting more of their own resources to their children's education or by trying to modify processes of educational or occupational selection so that their children would still be favoured. And such a response could indeed occur, in a pre-emptive way, even where the intervention was not made: that is, within educational administrations or geographical areas assigned to the 'control' rather than the 'treatment' subset.

In such circumstances, at least one of the crucial requirements of randomized experimental design would then clearly be breached: that is, that the response of a unit should not be influenced by whether other units are treated or not. And still more basic issues do in any event arise. For example, is an intervention to be regarded as causally consequential if it would have had an effect had it not at the same time caused an offsetting response? And would it make any sociological sense to try to control for such a response, even supposing that this were in some way possible?

would favour, which must take on the character of a response to an intervention. It might be noted that a somewhat related objection to treating the reasons for actions as their causes was advanced by chiefly neo-Wittgensteinian philosophers on the lines that causation must entail causes and effects that are logically independent, whereas the reasons for an action and the actual course it follows will, at least in the case of rational action, be logically connected (see e.g. MacIntyre 1962). However, the force of this objection has been increasingly questioned and the idea of reasons for action as representing at all events one kind of causation among others would appear by now to have gained rather wide philosophical acceptance (see e.g. Toulmin 1970; Mackie 1974: ch. 11; Davidson 1980: esp. chs. 1 and 14). On the application of this same idea in economics, see Helm (1984).

The very fact that such questions can be asked serves then to re-emphasize the difficulties of translating an approach to causation developed within applied natural science into a social-science context.[7] So far at least as sociology is concerned, the ultimate source of these difficulties might be specified as follows. The approach allows conceptual space for human action, and in particular for action of a purposive or 'outcome-oriented' kind, *only in* the roles of experimenter or 'intervener'. Once the experiment or intervention is made, all else has to follow in the manner simply of bacteria responding to a drug or plants to a fertilizer: that is, in ways to which considerations of individuals' 'objectives, knowledge, reasoning and decisions' have no further relevance. In turn, a rather paradoxical if not contradictory position is arrived at. It is maintained that only through purposive action taken in the role of experimenter or intervener can genuinely causal processes be set in motion— 'no causation without manipulation'; yet action taken by individuals in *other* roles, in the everyday pursuit of their goals by what they believe to be the best means (their response to interventions included) cannot be accorded causal significance and, in this case, precisely because of its 'voluntary aspect'.

The idea of causation as consequential manipulation does therefore face sociologists with something of a dilemma. There is wide agreement that one has here a more rigorously formulated, even if narrower, understanding of causation than that founded on the idea of robust dependence; yet it appears far less appropriate to, and applicable in, sociological analysis. Two main reactions on the part of sociologists have so far been apparent. One, which is perhaps best expressed by Sobel (1995, 1996), entails acceptance of the manipulative approach as that which, as it were, sets the standard for the making of causal inferences. Sociologists should, therefore, seek wherever possible to conduct research on an experimental or at least quasi-experimental basis and, if this is not possible, still to take this approach as providing the conceptual framework within which the validity of causal inferences should be judged—discomfiting though this may often be. The other, contrasting reaction is that to be found most fully argued in the work of Lieberson (1985). This entails a straight rejection of the attempt to impose the experimental model (or, at any rate, that adopted in medical or agricultural research) onto sociology, on the grounds that this represents an undue 'scientism'—that is, an undue regard for the form rather than the substance of scientific method— and with the implication, then, that sociologists have to find their own ways of thinking about causation, proper to the kinds of research that

---

[7] It might be thought that similar problems with experiments to those envisaged in the text could also arise in applied natural science. For example, the (perhaps apocryphal?) case is sometimes cited of an agricultural experiment in which the treatment of certain plots resulted in very heavy crops, which then, however, attracted large numbers of foraging birds, so that the eventual yield on these plots was less than on those not treated. But the birds just wanted to eat: they were not trying to stop the treatment working by countering its effects. Again, there are well-known problems of how to take into account patient non-compliance in clinical trials, which clearly involves action (or inaction) on the part of patients. But it would still not be generally supposed that patients have the objective of actually subverting trials.

they can realistically carry out and the problems that they can realistically address.

The position that I would myself wish to take up in this regard, while representing an appreciative response to those of both Sobel and Lieberson, is one that is more strongly influenced by the third understanding of causation that I initially identified, that of causation as generative process.

Causation as Generative Process

This idea of causation has been advanced by statisticians in several versions. It does not, though, to the same extent as the two understandings of causation already considered reflect specifically statistical thinking. It would appear to derive, rather, from an attempt to spell out what must be *added to* any statistical criteria before an argument for causation can convincingly be made. Thus, Cox (1992: 297) introduces the idea in noting a 'major limitation' of the manipulative approach to causation—and likewise, it would seem, of the approach via robust dependence (cf. Cox and Wermuth 1996: 220–1): namely, that 'no explicit notion of an underlying process' is introduced—no notion of a process 'at an observational level that is deeper than that involved in the data under immediate analysis'. Similarly, Simon and Iwasaki (1988) have maintained that, in moving from association to causation, more must be entailed than just time precedence or manipulation in establishing the necessary asymmetry: that is, that X has causal significance for Y rather than *vice versa*. The assumption must also be present that the association is created by some 'mechanism' operating 'at a more microscopic level' than that at which the association is established (Simon and Iwasaki 1988: 157). In other words, these authors would alike insist (and see also Freedman 1991, 1992*a,b*) on tying the concept of causation to some process existing in time and space, even if not perhaps directly observable, that actually generates the causal effect of X on Y and, in so doing, produces the statistical relationship that is empirically in evidence. At the same time, it should be said, they would also recognize that the accounts that are advanced of such causal processes, in order to illuminate the 'black boxes' left by purely statistical analysis, can never be taken as definitive. They must in all cases be ones that are open to empirical test; and, even where they appear to be supported, it has still to be accepted that finer-grained accounts, at some yet deeper level, will in principle always be possible.[8]

---

[8] As Suppes (1970: 91) has aptly observed, the accounts of causal processes or mechanisms given by one generation become themselves the 'black boxes' for the next. It may be added that it is essentially Holland's recognition of this point that leads him to wish to concentrate, as a statistician, on determining the effects of causes rather than the causes of effects—'on what can be done well rather than on what we might like to do, however poorly' (1988: 451). But it could be replied, first, that this is to be unduly discouraged by what is a quite general feature of the pursuit of scientific knowledge; and, secondly, that, at least in the case of sociology, what can be done well and less well by statistics appears less clear-cut than Holland might suppose (cf. Smith 1990).

Such an approach to causation is clearly seen by its proponents as being essentially that which prevails, even if only implicitly, in general scientific practice (cf. Simon and Iwasaki 1988: 149–51; Freedman 1991; Cox 1992: 297) and, presumably, in non-experimental as well as experimental fields. In fact, the subject-matter area in which this approach has perhaps been developed most explicitly is that of epidemiology (see e.g. Bradford Hill 1937/1991, 1965); and it is at all events this that provides the obvious paradigm case—that of smoking and lung cancer. Statistical analysis of observational data was able to show a strong association between smoking and lung cancer and, further, that this was robust to the introduction of a range of possible 'common' causal factors. But what was crucial to the claim for a causal link was the elaboration of an underlying, generative process on the basis of the isolation of known carcinogens in cigarette smoke, histopathological evidence from the bronchial epithelium of smokers, and so on. Freedman (1997: 129) emphasizes the diversity of sources from which the evidence that supports the proposed generative process derives, and notes that its force 'depends on the complex interplay among these various studies and the [statistical] data-sets'.

As I have said, those statisticians who have upheld the idea of causation as generative process have tended to represent it as a necessary augmentation of the two understandings of causation examined earlier. But whether the same relationship is in both cases involved might be questioned. In regard to causation as robust dependence, causation as generative process would indeed seem an obvious complement. It at once allows for the objection that causation cannot be established simply through general procedures of statistical inference, without need for subject-matter input. If some account is required of the processes that are believed to be creating the statistically demonstrated dependence, then this account will have to be given largely on the basis of subject-matter knowledge; and the more thoroughly the account is informed by prevailing theory, rather than being merely *ad hoc*, the more coherent—and testable—it will be (cf. Bradford Hill 1965; Cox and Wermuth 1996: 225–6).

However, in regard to causation as consequential manipulation, the idea of causation as generative process would appear not just as complement but also in certain respects as corrective. To begin with, a focus on just how causal effects are brought about serves to reduce the significance accorded to different kinds of independent variable. Thus, even if it is thought improper to speak of an attribute as being a true cause of, rather than merely associated with, a dependent variable, the key issue can still be seen as that of how the relationship, however labelled, is actually produced. For example, even if 'She did well in the exam because she is a woman' is taken to refer to the fixed attribute of sex (rather than to potentially changeable gender), what is important is the nature and validity of the account given of the process that underlies the association appealed to—as, say, an account on the lines that the hard-wiring of females' brains has evolved in ways that give them an advantage over men in the kind of examination in question. And at the same time, in a social-science context, the attaching of causal significance to action, far from being a source of difficulty, could rather be taken as the *standard* way of constructing an account of a causal process: 'She did well in the exam because she studied for it' is no longer in any way problematic.[9]

Furthermore, it is also important to recognize that an emphasis on causal processes serves to direct attention back to the question of the causes of effects as opposed to that of the effects of (assumed or, supposedly, known) causes (cf. Smith 1990). In turn, a shift is implied away from the strong 'verificationist' position, which would see the purpose of causal analysis as being to determine the effects of causes, via experimental methods, in a 'once-and-for-all' way, and which, as well as being open to some philosophical doubts, is in any event scarcely supportable in sociological practice. An understanding of causation in terms of generative processes consorts far better in fact with a 'falsificationist' position. Hypothetical but adequate accounts of such processes are advanced—that is, the processes envisaged would in principle be capable of generating the statistical relationships addressed—and further empirical enquiry is then undertaken to try to test whether it is these processes that are actually at work. This might well lead to a negative result, but even a positive one would remain no more than provisional, since, as earlier remarked, it is accepted that final accounts of causal processes will never be reached.

If, then, the idea of causation as generative process can be seen not only as augmenting the ideas of causation as robust dependence and of causation as consequential manipulation but also, in the latter case, as entailing some degree of modification and reorientation, a basis does, I believe, become discernible on which an alternative approach to causal analysis, appropriate to sociological enquiry, might be developed. That is, one that would enable sociologists to go beyond the merely 'pragmatic utilization' of the concept of causation as, say, through unreflective causal modelling, without, however, requiring them to take up an understanding of causation too restrictive to allow them to pursue their own legitimate purposes.

An Alternative for Sociology

The approach to causal analysis that is here proposed, in part drawing on and in part elaborating a position that I have already to some extent developed in the two preceding chapters, is presented in the form of a three-phase sequence:

(i) establishing the phenomena that form the *explananda*;
(ii) hypothesizing generative processes at the level of social action;
(iii) testing the hypotheses.

[9] Nor would be: 'They took measures to counter the policy intervention because they believed it was detrimental to their interests.'

It should, however, be stressed that such a presentation is intended primarily to ease exposition. In practice, the three phases are unlikely to be so readily separable in any particular piece of sociological work as this schematic treatment might suggest.

Establishing the phenomena

This phrase is taken from Merton (1987), who seeks to make the seemingly obvious but, as he shows, often neglected point that, before advancing explanations of social phenomena, sociologists would do well to have good evidence that these phenomena really exist and *that they express sufficient regularity to require and allow explanation*. Merton's emphasis on regularity has particular importance here. To begin with, it would seem necessary for sociologists to recognize that their explanatory concerns are in fact with regularities rather than singularities, such as, say, individual lives or unique historical events (cf. Chapters 3 and 5 above). And, further, the nature of the basic linkage between sociology and statistics is in this way clearly brought out. If sociologists' *explananda* consist of social regularities of one kind or another, then statistics is, if not the only, at all events the most reliable and versatile means of demonstrating that such regularities exist and of clarifying their nature; and especially so, it might be added, in the case of regularities that are not readily apparent to the 'lay members' of a society in the course of their everyday lives but are revealed only through the—perhaps rather sophisticated—analysis of data that have been collected extensively in time or space.

However, establishing the phenomena is an essentially descriptive exercise and in so far as it is achieved statistically it is statistics in descriptive mode that will be relevant. In this connection, it is of interest to note that various critics of current causal modelling methods in sociology (e.g. Lieberson 1985: esp. 213–19; Freedman 1992*a,b*; Abbott 1998) have regretted the way in which enthusiasm for such methods has led to the disparagement of overtly descriptive statistical work, and would in effect join with Merton in urging on sociologists the importance of using quantitative data to show, in Lieberson's words, 'what is happening' before they attempt to explain 'why it is happening'. What then may be suggested—as indeed the critics in question all in one way or another do—is that the whole statistical technology that has underpinned the sociological reception of the idea of causation as robust dependence, from Lazarsfeldian elaboration through to causal-path analysis, should be radically re-evaluated. That is to say, instead of being regarded as a means of inferring causation directly from data, its primary use should rather be seen *as* descriptive, involving the analysis of joint and conditional distributions in order to determine no more than patterns of association (or correlation). Or, at very most, representations of the data might serve to *suggest* causal accounts, which, however, will need always to be further developed theoretically and then tested as quite separate undertakings.[10] Moreover, once the independent role of description is in this way accepted, a range of statistical techniques other than those that have been aimed at causal analysis would seem capable of making a major contribution: for example, loglinear (and related) methods of analysing categorical data, where no distinction between independent and dependent variables need be entailed and attention centres specifically on structures of association and interaction; or again, as Abbott (1998) argues, various non-probabilistic techniques of scaling, clustering, and sequencing that are even more clearly dedicated to descriptive tasks.

What gives arguments for the importance of description their real force is not just that instances can readily be found in the sociological literature of the recent past of what might be regarded as 'premature' causal analysis—i.e. instances in which causal models were applied that later descriptive work showed to be based on mistaken suppositions (see further Chapter 5). In addition, and more positively, various cases can also be cited in which the chief statistical accomplishment has been to identify and characterize important social regularities that were hitherto unappreciated, or incorrectly understood, by in effect separating out these regularities from their particular contexts. For example, loglinear modelling has been applied to demonstrate how temporal constancy and a large degree of cross-national commonality in relative rates of social mobility—or patterns of social fluidity—can underlie historically and geographically specific and often widely fluctuating absolute rates (see Featherman et al., 1975; Hauser et al. 1975; Goldthorpe 1987; Erikson and Goldthorpe 1992a; and also chapter 12 below). Likewise, sequential logit modelling, as pioneered by Mare (1981), has been used in order to show up more or less constant class differentials in educational attainment during eras in which educational provision has steadily expanded and in which the 'effects' of class origins on educational attainment overall would thus appear to decline—that is, simply on account of increased rates of participation (see e.g. Shavit and Blossfeld 1993; and Chapter 8 below). Or again, event history analysis has enabled uniformities in the pattern of life-course events in relation to family formation or dissolution to be distinguished across periods and places characterized by widely differing political, economic, and social conditions (Blossfeld and Huinink 1991; Blossfeld and Rohwer 1995b). It is important that the use of rather advanced statistical techniques for these purposes of what might be called sophisticated description should be clearly distinguished from their use in attempts at deriving causal relations directly from data analysis.

[10] In this regard, the use of graph theoretical representations of structures of conditional independence and association among variables would seem to have potential value (cf. Cox and Wermuth 1996), although this method has not so far been widely applied in sociology. Computerized algorithms have also been developed to search for possible representations of this kind on the basis of correlation matrices from particular data sets. For a lively debate on what might or might not be thus contributed to the understanding of causation, see McKim and Turner (1997).

Hypothesizing generative processes

Social regularities, once relatively securely established by descriptive methods, are then to be regarded as the basic *explananda* of sociological analysis: sociological problems are ones that can all in one way or another be expressed in terms of social regularities—their formation, continuity, interrelation, change, disruption, and so on.[11] When, therefore, analysis becomes causal, social regularities represent the effects for which causes have to be discovered. And this task, contrary to what proponents of the idea of causation as robust dependence would seem to have supposed, cannot be a purely statistical one but requires a crucial subject-matter input.

From the position of methodological individualism that I would here adopt—and from which most of the critiques earlier noted of a purely 'variable sociology' explicitly or implicitly derive—this input has then to take the form of some account of the action and interaction of individuals. In effect, a narrative of action must be provided that purports to capture the central tendencies that arise within the diverse courses of action that are followed by particular actors in situations of a certain type: that is, situations that can be regarded as sharing essential similarities in so far as actors' goals and the nature of the opportunities and constraints that condition their action in pursuit of these goals are concerned. And, in turn, a case must be made to show how these central tendencies in action would, if operative, actually give rise, through their intended and unintended consequences, to the regularities that constitute the *explananda*.

The theory that underlies such hypothesized processes will then obviously be a theory of social action of some kind; and, in this respect, the two main alternatives that would appear available might for convenience be labelled as rational-action theory and norm-oriented action theory. On grounds I have earlier set out (see Chapters 5 and 6), I would regard the former as having conceptual, explanatory, and interpretative privilege over the latter, though quite possibly needing to be complemented by it. Rational action theory allows for the fuller expression of the idea of reasons as causes for action; and an appeal to the rationality of action, in the sense of its grounding in what for actors are good reasons for their actions, in terms of perceived costs and benefits, represents a uniquely attractive end point for any sociological explanation to reach. However, for present purposes, the important point is that, *whatever* theory of action is favoured, it should be used to enable as explicit and coherent a formulation as possible of the generative processes that are

---

[11] It is important to note that such problems do in fact arise not only, as it were, endogenously to the development of sociology but also exogenously to this development—most obviously, perhaps, from various kinds of applied, even purely 'administrative', social research. While I would then entirely agree with authors such as Hedström and Swedberg (1998*a*,*b*) in their insistence that the main requirement of theory is that it should explain, I believe that they place a too exclusive emphasis on the role of theory in the discovery of problems and, correspondingly, underestimate that of empirical research—and especially of large-scale survey research—with primarily descriptive goals (cf. R. Erikson 1998).

proposed and in this way facilitate their evaluation as regards both their causal adequacy and their empirical presence.[12]

In particular, it is at this stage that questions of what might be called causal form and causal hierarchy should be clarified. Thus, authors such as Lieberson (1985: esp. ch. 4) and Blossfeld and Rohwer (1995a: ch. 1) have stressed the need to specify whether causal processes are seen as symmetrical or, rather, one way and irreversible, and whether they entail lags, thresholds, or other distinctive temporal features in their effects. And Lieberson (1985: esp. ch. 7) has further emphasized the need to distinguish between 'basic' causal processes and ones of a more 'superficial' kind (the former often being less open to direct observation than the latter). Thus, to revert to an earlier example, if differentials in educational attainment are in fact treated as a basic cause of income inequalities among classes or ethnic groups, then action, such as some kind of political intervention, that brought about a reduction in these differentials would be expected to close income gaps also. But if educational differentials are seen as only a superficial cause of income inequalities, with the basic cause lying elsewhere—say, in processes grounded in more generalized social inequalities or in discrimination—then what would be expected to follow from their reduction would not be a corresponding decrease in income inequalities but simply changes *consequent upon the latter remaining unaltered*: for instance, a weakening of the association between education and income while, perhaps, that between other factors—say, family contacts—and entry into well-paid employment became stronger.

Testing the hypotheses

As indicated earlier, the first test of any causal explanation of a social regularity that is put forward must be that of its adequacy: would the generative process hypothesized, assuming it to be operative, in fact be capable of producing the regularity in question? It is here worth pointing out that, the fuller and more refined the description of the regularity, the stronger the explanatory demands that will be made and the more likely it is that certain candidate accounts can be eliminated at this stage.[13] However, it may be supposed

[12] A concern for the theoretical basis of hypothesized generative processes is also important to prevent purely *ad hoc* switching—as occurs, for example, where sociologists draw on rational action theory in explanations of regularities in the class–vote relationship but then on norm-oriented action theory in explanations of why individuals vote at all. Such switching *may* be appropriate, but the grounds for it have always to be spelled out: i.e. the attempt should be made to specify which kinds of process will operate under which conditions. As argued in Chapter 5, there are dangers in thinking that sociologists can simply accumulate a collection of models of causal processes or mechanisms of many different kinds, items from which can then be used (or discarded) just as seems convenient.

[13] For example (and this is argued in more detail in the chapter that follows), once it is recognized just what it is that needs to be explained about class differentials in education— i.e. why in most modern societies they have remained little changed in a context of generally increasing rates of educational participation—it at once becomes apparent that 'culturalist' accounts (e.g. Bourdieu 1973; Willis 1977) do not meet the initial requirement of causal adequacy. For if the main source of these differentials were indeed to lie in radically divergent class subcultures, with working-class families attaching a lower value to edu-

that more than one adequate account will be possible, and further testing is then required to try to determine which—if any—of the processes hypothesized is actually at work. In other words, the issue shifts from that of the adequacy in principle of an account of a causal process to that of its empirical validity.

In this connection, what crucially matters are the implications that follow from any account that is advanced: if the generative process suggested does in fact operate to produce, or help to produce, an established regularity, then what *else* should be empirically observable? It may be that the process, or at least some features of it, should be observable directly (cf. Chapter 4 above); but if the action and interaction of relatively large numbers of individuals are involved or interaction that is not of a localized, face-to-face kind, then this may scarcely be feasible.[14] The alternative is to devise more indirect tests by specifying other effects to which the process should give rise apart from those constituting the regularities it purports to explain, although likewise of an empirically ascertainable kind. Such direct or indirect tests may be made through whatever methods appear most appropriate; and it is indeed important that separate tests of particular implications should be undertaken, and repeated, on the basis of different data sets and analytical techniques (cf. Berk 1988).[15] Thus, while it might seem that, at this stage, attention does after all come to focus on the effects of—given—causes rather than on the causes of effects, this is within the context not of randomized experimental design but of (what should be) a theoretically informed account of a generative process that is subject to ongoing evaluation, and with the outcome being falsification or, if testing is withstood, simply corroboration, rather than the verification of effects of a 'once-and-for-all' kind.

To illustrate, one could take the case of the consequences for children of parents' marital break-up.[16] An association would appear to be established between break-up, on the one hand, and, on the other, children leaving school at the minimum age and experiencing various other seemingly adverse effects. But disagreement arises over whether, or how far, break-up can be

cation than families in more advantaged class positions and their children being thus systematically alienated from the educational system, then what one would have to expect in course of educational expansion would be *widening* differentials. But there is no evidence of this. Working-class children have in fact taken up expanding educational opportunities at much the same rate as children of other class origins, although they have not in most societies been able to exploit these opportunities to the extent necessary to close the attainment gap.

[14] A related issue that arises here is that of the part to be played in the testing of accounts of generative processes at the level of social action by 'subjective' data: i.e. data that relate directly to individuals' orientations towards, and definitions of, the situations in which they act. While there can be no objection to the use of such data in principle, legitimate doubts at the level of practice, and especially regarding data quality, do persist. For relevant discussion, see Opp (1998) and Robert Erikson (1998).

[15] It is, of course, quite likely that the data sets that are used to establish particular social regularities will not be those most suitable, from the point of view of the information they contain, for purposes of testing supposed generative processes. This points up the importance of recognizing the distinction between these phases of enquiry.

[16] What follows is much influenced by, and draws on, Ní Bhrolcháin (forthcoming).

given causal significance in these respects. For instance, it is not difficult to think of possible 'common' causes—say, personality factors or parental conflict—that could lie behind both marital instability *and* poor parenting and its consequences for children. The key issue may then be regarded as that of whether the children of those couples who *do* break up would have fared better if their parents had in fact stayed together, and in this way Holland's 'Fundamental Problem of Causal Inference' is directly encountered: the same couple cannot both break up and not break up. Moreover, a statistical solution via experimental design is here scarcely possible; and from the point of view of causation as consequential manipulation, the strategy to be pursued would then have to be that of viewing break-up as if it were an intervention, and attempting to overcome the 'assignment' problem by introducing a set of relevant covariates into the analysis: that is, so that a comparison could be made between the children of parents who did and who did not break up on the basis of, as it were, 'all else equal to the time of break-up'. However, as remarked earlier, it remains far from clear how the completeness of such a set could ever be determined and definitive results thus claimed, any more than they could be from the standpoint of causation as robust dependence. It would indeed appear that the more attention analysts have given to the problems of defining and including appropriate covariates, the more sceptical their conclusions have become (see esp. Ní Bhrolcháin *et al.* 1994).

The alternative strategy that is here proposed is that those who wish to investigate what, causally, underlies the association between marital break-up and adverse features of children's future lives should begin by spelling out as fully as they are able the way or ways in which they believe that the effects in question are produced—that is, by giving accounts of adequate generative processes; and that these accounts should then be empirically tested, by reference to their further implications, as extensively as possible. The more detailed the accounts are, the more likely it is that they will differ in their implications so as to allow critical comparisons to be made: as, say, between children who have lost a parent through marital dissolution and those who have lost a parent through death; between siblings who experience their parents' break-up at different ages; between children who remain with a single parent after break-up and those who acquire a step-parent; between children experiencing break-up in differing contexts, in terms of prevailing rates of break-up, the extent of social support for single parents, and so on.

In fact, one recent contribution can be taken as marking at least a first step in seeking to implement such a strategy. Jonsson and Gähler (1997), considering the possible effects of marital break-up on children's educational attainment in Sweden, first identify a number of 'plausible causal mechanisms' and then carry out analyses on a large-scale longitudinal data set in order to test for the presence of such mechanisms. Interestingly, the mechanism, or generative process, for which strongest corroboration was found was one that had received little previous attention in the debate: that is, a 'downward-mobility' process through which, when children are separated from the parent with the higher educational and/or occupational achievement, their own educational and occupational aspirations tend to fall (see also Gähler 1998). There are in fact quite close analogies here, via the 'structural' theory of aspirations (Keller and Zavalloni 1964), with processes that have been suggested, and have received some support, in explaining persistence and change in class and gender differentials in educational attainment more generally (cf. Boudon 1974; Gambetta 1987; and Chapters 8 and 9 below). None the less, it is important to note that what the authors claim is still only evidence for, and not definitive proof of, the operation of such a process, and they are careful to point out what might prove to be special features of the Swedish case.[17]

For the present, the—diversified and repeated—testing of suggested generative processes on the basis of particular implications derivable from them is, perhaps, the most that can be asked for. It should, though, finally be said that the logical conclusion to which the entire approach outlined would lead is that of testing on the basis of statistical models *of these processes themselves*. The important distinction in this regard is that made by Cox (1990) between 'empirical' and 'substantive' statistical models, or by Rogosa (1992) between statistical models *per se* and scientific models expressed in statistical form (see also Sørensen 1998). Models of the former kind are those that sociologists normally use and are concerned with relations among variables that may be determined through techniques of rather general applicability. Models of the latter kind, however, are intended to represent real processes that have causal force (whether or not directly observable). They are therefore crucially informed by subject-matter theory and can in turn serve as the vehicles through which such theory is exposed to test in a fairly comprehensive way. In particular, as Cox has observed, it should be possible for such models to be applied in simulation exercises: 'The essential idea is that if the investigator cannot use the model directly to simulate artificial data, how can "Nature" [or, one could add, "Society" (JHG)] have used anything like that method to generate real data?' (1990: 172). In sociology, accounts of processes capable of producing observed regularities are not yet for the most part expressed in sufficiently specific and theoretically informed ways to permit 'substantive' models to be developed—greater efforts at formalization might help in this respect—and, correspondingly, the simulation approach to hypothesis testing is not at a very advanced stage. None the less, there are by now at least indications that its potential in helping to integrate theoretical and quantitative empirical work is becoming more fully appreciated (see e.g. Halpin 1999).

---

[17] Another relevant study, though more psychological in orientation, is that reported by Rutter (1981; and see also 1994), who advances the hypothesis that, in explaining the association between marital break-up and children's disorderly behaviour, the 'mediating mechanism' is tension resulting from marital conflict rather than the break-up itself. Rutter is then able to show how this hypothesis can be tested, again on the basis of longitudinal data, through the comparison of cases of temporary separations arising from marital conflict and those arising for other reasons and also of cases where, following such a separation associated with conflict, a reduction or increase in conflict was subsequently recorded.

The general point that, I believe, emerges most clearly from the foregoing might be put as follows. If contributions made by statisticians to the understanding of causation are to be taken over with advantage in any specific field of enquiry, then what is crucial is that the right relationship should exist between statistical and subject-matter concerns.

Thus, it could be said that the idea of causation as robust dependence does have a certain appropriateness in so far as the main aim of research is prediction and, in particular, prediction in the real world rather than in the laboratory or, in other words, forecasting. The importance that this idea has had in economic forecasting is not, therefore, at all surprising. However, where the ultimate aim of research is not prediction *per se* but rather causal explanation, an idea of causation that is expressed in terms of predictive power—as, for example, 'Granger' causation—is likely to be found wanting. Causal explanations cannot be arrived at through statistical methodology alone: a subject-matter input is also required in the form of background knowledge and, crucially, theory. This is the upshot of the critiques made by sociological theorists and statisticians alike of the pragmatic or, one could say, atheoretical use of the concept of causation by quantitative sociologists on the basis of essentially 'partialling' procedures from Lazarsfeldian elaboration through to causal-path analysis.

Likewise, the idea of causation as consequential manipulation is apt for research that can be undertaken primarily through experimental methods and, especially, to revert to Cook and Campbell, to 'practical science', where the central concern is indeed with 'the consequences of performing particular acts'. The development of this idea in the context of medical and agricultural research is as understandable as the development of that of causation as robust dependence within applied econometrics. However, the extension of the manipulative approach into sociology would not appear promising, other than in rather special circumstances. It is not just that in sociological research practical and ethical barriers to experiments, or interventions, often arise: it can be accepted that statisticians have made major advances in the methodology of quasi-experimental studies, even if the latter can scarcely claim to provide 'once-and-for-all' results in the way that might be thought possible with true experiments. The more fundamental difficulty is that, under the—highly anthropocentric—principle of 'no causation without manipulation', the recognition that can be given to the action of individuals as having causal force is in fact peculiarly limited. That is, it extends only to those actually in the role of experimenter or intervener: otherwise, what Holland calls the 'voluntary aspect' of action, and including action taken in response to an intervention, creates major problems.

The idea of causation as generative process is not, in the same way as the two other ideas of causation that have been considered, linked to a particular body of statistical work. It does, none the less, appear to offer the best basis, as I have sought finally to show, on which statistical and substantive concerns can be related in causal analysis in sociology. First, it places the emphasis on the causes of effects: in other words, it implies that such analysis begins with the effects—the phenomena—for which a causal explanation is then sought. And in sociology it is in establishing the phenomena that statistics has a basic contribution to make, in an essentially descriptive mode. Secondly, the idea of a generative process specified at a 'deeper' or 'more microscopic' level than that of the data that constitute the *explananda* fits closely with the analytical approach of at least those sociologists adhering to the principle of methodological individualism, who would thus insist on the need for causal explanations of social phenomena to be grounded ultimately in accounts of the action and interaction of individuals, and who have criticized a purely 'variable sociology' from this point of view. Thirdly, the recognition that final, definitive accounts of generative processes will never be reached means that empirical evaluations of such accounts, in regard to whether the processes they suggest do in fact operate to produce the effects attributed to them, are not expected to achieve once-and-for-all verification but either falsification or, at best, what might be described as corroboration pending improvement. Statistics has then again an evident role to play in testing such accounts via their particular, empirically ascertainable implications on, for now, a 'catch-as-catch-can' basis. But this role will be enlarged in so far as sociologists are able to develop their accounts of generative processes to the point at which statistical methods can also be applied in creating 'substantive' models of these processes themselves.

8

Class Analysis and the Reorientation of Class Theory: The Case of Persisting Differentials in Educational Attainment

IN AN ESSAY published elsewhere, Gordon Marshall and I have set out the case for class analysis as a research programme. The aim of this programme could be summarized as that of enquiring into the interrelations that prevail among class structures, class mobility, class inequalities, and class formation (or decomposition). Viewed in this way, we argued, class analysis 'does not entail a commitment to any particular theory of class' but, rather, provides a context in which 'different and indeed rival theories' may be formulated and assessed (Goldthorpe and Marshall 1992: 382).[1]

It is specifically to such theoretical development and critique, within the research programme of class analysis, that I wish to turn in the present contribution. I take the development of theory to be a more ambitious and difficult enterprise than simply the elaboration of concepts. The key requirement of theory, as here understood, is that it should have *explanatory* force. A sociological theory is of value to the extent that it can provide an account of how established social regularities come to be as they are—and to the extent that, through the wider implications it carries, it remains open to further empirical test. Since, then, the prime purpose of theory is to explain, an exercise in theory development in any particular substantive area may appropriately start from a consideration of the relevant *explananda*: of just what it is that *calls for* explanation. In the present case, a historical perspective may perhaps best serve to clarify matters.

Looking back over the nineteenth and the twentieth centuries, two broad strands of class theory can be distinguished, the Marxist and the liberal, which are in fact addressed to obviously related yet significantly differing *explananda*. Marxist class theory, as Elster (1985: esp. ch. 6) has well brought

This chapter was first published in the *British Journal of Sociology*, 47 (1996), as part of a special number in honour of David Lockwood. I am grateful to Tony Atkinson, André Béteille, Richard Breen, Robert Erikson, Jean Floud, A. H. Halsey, Anthony Heath, Janne Jonsson, Walter Müller, and Adam Swift for helpful comments on earlier drafts.

[1] Remarkably, this statement has led to the supposition (Pahl 1993) that Marshall and I would conceive of class analysis as being entirely *a*theoretical!

out, is primarily concerned with class formation and, in particular, with explaining the incidence and forms of collective class action. Such action was, of course, of key importance in Marx's overarching theory of history: all history was 'the history of class struggle', and was periodized by the revolutionary outcomes of such struggle. But all history was also the history of the development of the forces of production and of the contradictions thus created with established relations of production. For Marx, and for his followers, therefore, a crucial problem was that of how exactly these two lines of argument should be integrated—and especially as they were applied to capitalist society (cf. Lockwood 1981; 1992: pts. 3, 4). The abiding theoretical task was to explain just what were the processes through which intensifying internal contradictions would actually generate the degree of class consciousness and of class conflict necessary for the working class to act out its historically appointed role as the 'gravedigger' of capitalism.

Liberal class theory emerged largely in reaction to its Marxist equivalent. Its starting point was the fading prospect of working-class revolution as the economic advance of capitalist societies proceeded without any sustained threat to their political stability. However, as elaborated in the context of a supposed 'logic' of industrialism, rather than of capitalism, it became in effect a theory of the general decline of class. What the liberal theory aims primarily to explain (Goldthorpe 1992a; Erikson and Goldthorpe 1992a: ch. 1) is how, in the course of development of industrial societies, class formation gives way to class decomposition as mobility between classes increases and as class-linked inequalities of opportunity are steadily reduced. These tendencies, it seeks to show, follow most importantly from the demand imposed by the logic of industrialism for an ever more efficient utilization of human resources—as reflected in the expansion of educational provision, the egalitarian reform of educational institutions, and the progressive replacement of criteria of ascription by criteria of achievement in all processes of social selection (see esp. Blau and Duncan 1967; Treiman 1970; see also Kerr et al. 1973; Kerr 1983). Thus, it may be understood how, within an increasingly 'open' and 'meritocratic' form of society, conditions are created that at a political level first of all facilitate the 'democratic translation of the class struggle'—the abandonment by national working classes of revolutionary for civic, electoral politics—and then further undermine the connection between class membership and political action even in the individualized form of voting behaviour (cf. Goldthorpe 1996a).

However, while the *explananda* of Marxist and of liberal class theory may in this way be contrasted, it is one feature they have in common that is here of main significance: namely, that of being essentially spurious. In both cases alike, major theoretical efforts have been made to elucidate the generative processes of something that has not in fact happened.

That this is so on the Marxist side is, of course, notorious. As Lockwood has bluntly put it (1992: 166), 'Nothing . . . has been more disconcerting to Marxist theory than the massively awkward fact that no advanced capitalist society has produced anything resembling a revolutionary proletariat since the upsurges in working-class protest after the First World War.' Marxist sociologists have then had to resort to a variety of means of coming to terms with this fact, including, especially of late, that of ceasing to be Marxists. Indeed, *if* class analysis is conceived of in a Marxist or *marxisant* fashion, so that its ultimate purpose can *only* be the understanding of class formation and collective class action as key dynamic factors in long-term social change, then a sceptical view of its future might well be taken, or, at very least, its radical reconstruction be thought necessary.[2] However, what chiefly serves to show that class analysis—in a quite different version from the Marxist—can still lay claim to a viable and important *problematik* is a further 'massively awkward fact': namely, that the general 'withering-away' of class, to the explanation of which the liberal theory is addressed, is also a historical outcome that, while often scheduled, has yet to be observed.

In the decades following the Second World War, and during which the liberal theory achieved its fullest expression, the economic development of industrial societies went ahead at a quite unprecedented rate. It would, therefore, seem reasonable to suppose that, over this period, any logic of industrialism with the potential to undermine the prevailing force of class within these societies should have initiated well-defined trends of change indicative of this potential. But such trends have proved remarkably hard to establish. Indeed, to have shown that, in a number of key respects, they have simply not occurred might be regarded as the main achievement to date of class analysis as a research programme.

Thus (as Marshall and I sought to document) the available evidence from investigations into both educational attainment and social mobility is scarcely supportive of the idea of a generalized, long-term movement towards greater equality of life chances for individuals of differing class origins. Rather, class inequalities in these respects appear typically to display marked temporal stability, extending over decades and including those of the 'long boom'. Further, studies that have purported to show a comprehensive 'decline in class politics' within the advanced democracies have of late been called into doubt by results from more sophisticated analyses that reveal that class–party linkages are of a more enduring kind than has been supposed, and that, in so far as changes are apparent, they are cross-nationally quite variable.

Research findings of the kind in question do then pose grave difficulties for the liberal theory. But this is not their only significance. For present purposes at least, the more important point is that such findings should themselves now be regarded as constituting the serious *explananda* to which class theory needs to be directed. Macrosocial regularities, expressing salient features of

---

[2] As would, for example, seem already under way in current work that takes seriously the general problem of collective action, in the light especially of Olson (1965), and is then concerned with the specificities of the historical conditions under which forms of class-based mobilization might occur. See e.g. various contributions in Hechter (1983), Goldthorpe (1984), Taylor (1988).

the class stratification of modern societies, have been empirically demonstrated. But, thus far, these regularities have been left opaque. The theoretical challenge that arises is, therefore, to develop some explanation of just
how they are created and sustained. A major reorientation of class theory is
here implied. Rather than such theory being, as in both its Marxist and liberal
forms, concerned ultimately with explaining the dynamics of class, in regard
either to class formation or decomposition, what would now appear of central
importance is to account for the stability of class or, at all events, for the very
powerful resistance to change that class relations and associated life chances
and patterns of social action would appear to display.

   In what follows, I will, first of all, outline what *kind* of theory appears to
me most appropriate and promising for the task in hand. I will then seek to
make a start in applying such theory by attempting an explanation of just
one of the regularities referred to above: that of the persistence of class differentials in educational attainment. As noted, the widening of educational
opportunity and its supposed effects in weakening the influence of class on
individual life chances plays a central role in the liberal theory; and an
attempt to explain why liberal expectations in regard to class and education
have not been met might in turn point the way to accounting for similarly
failed expectations in other respects (see further Chapter 11).

Rational Action Theory and Class Analysis

Both Marxist and liberal theories of class form part of larger theories of long-
term societal change that are of a functionalist and also a teleological or 'historicist' character. The inherent developmental logic of capitalism, on the one
hand, and of industrialism, on the other, are seen as impelling societies on a
particular course of change directed towards a particular end. However, the
source of the failure of these theories may in large part be traced back to the
fact that the functional exigencies they envisage have not proved to be sufficiently powerful over the course of history to make social actors 'follow the
script' that was written for them. Or, one could say, the supposition that
macrosocial change could be understood without serious analysis of the orientations, goals, and conditions of the action of individuals left both theories alike seriously lacking in 'micro' foundations.

   Here, I seek to avoid any such difficulty by starting from an acceptance of
methodological—though not ontological—individualism: that is, from the
position that all social phenomena can and should be explained as resulting
from the action and interaction of individuals. Thus, the theory that I shall
try to develop will be one that aims to show how the macrosocial regularities that I take as *explananda* are the outcome of such action and interaction,
whether in simple or complex, intended or unintended, desired or undesired
ways. In the course of providing such an account, I shall indeed make reference, without further elaboration, to institutions or other social structural

features that, for the purposes in hand, I simply take as given. None the less, the assumption remains that these features too are no more than the products of past action and its consequences and could, in principle, be shown to be such.

I shall, furthermore, opt for rational action theory (RAT). That is to say, I shall aim to give an account of how the *explananda* I treat derive from individual action that can itself be understood as rational. I take this option because I would see such an appeal to rationality as representing the most satisfactory terminus of any sociological analysis. As Coleman has put it (1986b: 1), rational action has 'a unique attractiveness' as a basis for theory in that it is a conception of action 'that we need ask no more questions about'; or, in Hollis's words (1977: 21), 'rational action is its own explanation'.

The version of RAT that I take up implies, however, a notion of rationality of only 'intermediate' strength (see further Chapter 6). I assume that actors have goals, usually have alternative means of pursuing these goals, and, in choosing their courses of action, tend in some degree to assess probable costs and benefits rather than, say, unthinkingly following social norms or giving unreflecting expression to cultural values. I also assume that actors are to a degree knowledgeable about their society and their situations within it—in particular, about opportunities and constraints relative to their goals—rather than, say, being quite uninformed or ideologically deluded. In sum, I take it that actors have both some possibility and some capacity for acting autonomously and for seeking their goals in ways that are more or less appropriate to the situations in which they find themselves.

At the same time, though, I would recognize that departures from the standard of 'perfect' rationality are very frequent. I make no assumption that actors are always entirely clear about their goals, are always aware of the optimal means of pursuing them, or in the end do always follow the course of action that they know to be rational. For present purposes at least, these latter assumptions are not in fact required in order to create the possibility of a viable RAT approach. Since the concern here is with explaining macrosocial regularities that result from the actions of large numbers of individuals, all that need be supposed is that the tendency of actors to act rationally in the circumstances that prevail is the *common* factor influencing them—even if relatively weak—while propensities to depart from rationality operate randomly in many different ways. The 'law of large numbers' will then ensure that it is the rational tendency that dominates (see further Chapter 5).

The focus of RAT is on how actors come to choose particular courses of action in pursuit of their goals, using the resources that they command and adapting to the opportunities and constraints that characterize their situation. If, then, RAT is to be applied in the context of class analysis in the way envisaged, it will be essential to show not only how actors' goals are intelligible in relation to the class positions they hold but, further, how their actions directed towards these goals are conditioned by the distribution of resources, opportunities, and constraints that the class structure as a whole entails.

In the following, class positions will be taken as defined by employment relations in labour markets and production units and, more specifically, by two main principles: first, that of employment status, which distinguishes between employer, self-employed, and employee positions; and, secondly, that of the regulation of employment, which distinguishes employee positions according to whether this regulation occurs via a 'labour contract' or a 'service relationship' (see further Erikson and Goldthorpe 1992a: ch. 2, and Chapter 10 below). Classes themselves will then be understood, in a minimal sense, as collectivities of individuals and families holding particular class positions over time. In elaborating the theoretical arguments that will be advanced, I shall concentrate, simply to keep the discussion within bounds, on the two employee classes that most clearly exemplify the second principle noted above: on the one hand, the 'service class', or salariat, of professional, administrative, and managerial employees (Goldthorpe 1982, 1995a), and, on the other hand, the working class of wage-earners in chiefly manual occupations. It should, however, be evident enough how the arguments in question might be appropriately extended.

As most class analysts have recognized, the differentiation of class positions in terms of the resources their incumbents command, the opportunities available to them, and the constraints imposed on them does not imply that classes can be consistently ordered on any single 'dimension'. This is so because the differences involved may be ones of 'kind' as well as 'level', as, say, in the case of those that would set apart the class positions of self-employed workers and of employees. None the less, broad contrasts can, of course, still be made between what might be described as 'more advantaged' and 'less advantaged' classes. Thus, by virtue of the employment relations in which they are involved, members of the service class are typically advantaged over members of the working class, not just in their current incomes, but further through their incremental salaries and career prospects, their more favourable chances of maintaining continuity of employment, and the greater security that they can expect in sickness or old age.

In trying to explain the persistence of class differentials in educational attainment, I shall invoke only such basic or 'constitutive' features of class—that is, those that derive directly from employment relations—rather than ones of a more contingent kind. In particular, I shall avoid reference to distinctive class values, norms, 'forms of consciousness', or other supposed aspects of class cultures or subcultures. For this would, of course, mean going beyond the minimal conception of classes earlier indicated: that is, it would be to imply that class formation was at a level at which a 'capacity for socialization' (Featherman and Spenner 1990) was present. And not only might such a claim, in some instances, prove difficult to justify empirically (cf. Erikson and Goldthorpe 1992a: 217–27), but, as will emerge, explanations that rely on the existence of such systematic cultural differences between classes do not in any event appear apt to the *explananda* in question.

Since I regard this chapter as only a first step in theory development, I shall set out my arguments in a quite informal way. An attempt at formalization is presented in the following chapter. I shall, however, seek to clarify my position by contrasting wherever possible the empirical claims and implications that follow from it with those deriving from apparent alternatives.

Class Differentials in Educational Attainment and Their Explanation

I take the degree of temporal stability of class differentials in educational attainment to be a genuine rather than a spurious problem for class theory; or, to follow Merton (1987: 6), I take it to be a phenomenon that is 'established' in the sense that we have 'enough of a regularity to require and allow explanation'. None the less, the nature of the regularity should still be spelled out rather more exactly.

With the expansion of educational provision in economically advanced societies, primary and then secondary education, in some form or other, became universal, compulsory, and free; and further, especially since the mid-twentieth century, growing numbers of young people have remained in education beyond the compulsory period and have also gone on into higher education, often being supported in this latter case by grants, soft loans, or other forms of subsidy. Within national populations, the average level of educational attainment has thus risen substantially. However, empirical research across a wide range of societies has recurrently led to the finding that, once all effects of expansion *per se* are properly allowed for, class differentials in educational attainment have changed very little across successive birth cohorts, from those of the early decades of the century onwards. More specifically, if one envisages educational careers as comprising a series of transitions, or 'branching points', then, as these successively arise, children of less advantaged class origins have remained, to much the same extent, more likely than children of more advantaged origins to leave the educational system rather than to continue in it; or, if they do continue, to follow courses that, through the kinds of qualification to which they lead, reduce their chances of continuing further. It is true that for certain national societies evidence of some reduction in such disparities has been produced. But this is then usually in contradiction with other results for these same cases and in any event points to shifts of only a rather slight or a specific kind—that is, to ones that are limited to particular transitions, cohorts, or classes. What, in other words, is *not* found is any clear and compelling evidence of a *generalized and sustained* reduction in class differentials in educational attainment of the kind that the liberal theory would lead one to expect.[3]

---

[3] The crucial advance in modelling in this respect was that made by Mare (1981) and the most extensive collection of research papers, following Mare's approach, is Shavit and Blossfeld (1993). See also Erikson and Jonsson (1996b).

Why, then, should this be so? The explanatory approach that has thus far been most favoured is one that starts from a supposed connection of some kind between class and culture. In its weaker forms, this approach simply takes over earlier theories of the *famille educogène* (see e.g. Halsey *et al.* 1961: pt. iv; Banks 1971: chs. 4, 5). The prevailing culture of more advantaged classes, it is held, leads to parents within these classes setting a higher value on education than parents in other classes and being better equipped to encourage and promote educational success on the part of their children. Such theories, one may accept, contribute significantly to the explanation of why class differentials in educational attainment should exist in some degree or other. However, they do not take one very far with the problem of their temporal stability. That is to say, they do not give any indication of why the cultural effects that they invoke should have maintained their differentiating force, virtually undiminished, over generations, and especially in the context of the social transformations engendered by advancing industrialism, including major educational expansion and reform. All that is offered in this regard seems to be an essentially circular argument: the fact that differentials have not been reduced is itself the evidence that the influence of class cultures persists.[4]

In stronger versions of the approach, an attempt is made to meet the difficulty in question in that theories explicitly of 'cultural reproduction' are advanced (e.g. Bourdieu and Passeron 1970; Bourdieu 1973; Bowles and Gintis 1976; Willis 1977). The educational system, as it functions within the totality of class relations, is seen not as a means of utilizing talent more effectively or of widening opportunities but rather as an agency of social control. Cultural reproduction, it is maintained, is necessary to social structural reproduction, and 'dominant' classes therefore use their power in order to ensure that schools operate in an essentially conservative way. This they do by imposing a pedagogy that requires of children an initial socialization into the 'dominant' culture as a condition of educational success. Class differentials in attainment are thus created via the unequal endowments of appropriate— though in large part arbitrarily defined—'cultural capital' that children bring with them into the educational system; and they are maintained because schools do not seek to offset, but rather to exploit, such inequalities, albeit in the name of recognizing merit. Moreover, being thus debarred from educational success, children of working-class origins in particular are led to collude in their own disadvantage, whether through a passive acceptance of their 'failure' or through involvement in counter-school subcultures that enable them to express resistance to the established order even though at the same time reinforcing their position of subordination within it.

---

[4] On the general difficulty in culturalist explanations of providing evidence of the independent variable that is sufficiently removed from that which constitutes the dependent one, see Barry (1970: ch. iv) and also the apt observations of Boudon (1990: 41) on the modish notion of *habitus*. I would also include under culturalist explanations—and the foregoing critique—those advanced from anti-egalitarian positions that emphasize differences among classes simply in their 'taste' for education (see e.g. Murphy 1981 and esp. 1990: 49–50).

However, while theories of cultural reproduction do in this way offer an account of why class differentials persist, this account again still founders on the very facts of educational expansion. It is simply not the case that children from less advantaged class backgrounds have been excluded from, or have themselves rejected, the educational system to anything like the extent that these theories would suggest. As Halsey, Heath, and Ridge (1980: esp. ch. 5) have argued specifically against Bourdieu, educational expansion—in many respects *demand-led*—implies not the reproduction of cultural capital but rather its very substantial growth. In Britain, as these authors show, and indeed elsewhere, the *majority* of children entering more selective and academic forms of secondary education during the post-war decades were 'first generation'; and, by now, the same thing could also be said of those entering higher education. In other words, proponents of theories of cultural reproduction would appear to be betrayed by their rather gross misunderstanding of the degree to which in modern societies opportunities for upward educational—and also class—mobility between generations have indeed been enlarged and exploited.[5]

Although, then, theories of a 'culturalist' inspiration, despite their currency, must be reckoned as for one reason or another unsatisfactory for the explanatory task in hand, the nature of the difficulties they encounter does at all events help clarify just what must be required of a theory of a more adequate kind. That is, it must be able to offer an explanation of why class differentials in educational attainment have persisted, *but* one that can at the same time accommodate the more or less continuous increase in the participation of young people in education and in their overall levels of attainment that has been the general experience of advanced societies.

To try to meet this requirement, I would suggest a theory that is in direct line of descent from that advanced by Boudon (1974). Although, as will be seen, I diverge from Boudon at a number of points—as well as in my definition of the problem to be addressed[6]—I follow him not only in his general RAT approach but further in two more specific respects: first, in starting from the 'structural' theory of aspirations of Keller and Zavalloni (1964) and, secondly, in regarding the processes that generate class differentials as operating in two different stages.

Keller and Zavalloni argue, in opposition chiefly to Hyman (1954), that, rather than class differences in levels of aspiration, educational or

---

[5] Thus, Bourdieu (1973) starts from the assumption that such mobility is 'controlled' and concerns only 'a limited category of individuals, carefully selected and modified by and for individual ascent'. Similarly, Willis (1977: 126–8) believes that opportunities for upward mobility created by economic growth exist for the working class in 'only in relatively small numbers' (compare the results reported in Goldthorpe 1987: tables 2.2 and 3.1), and follows Bourdieu and Passeron (1970) in supposing that educational qualifications do not really help working-class children to take up these opportunities.

[6] On the basis of the—very inadequate—evidence then available to him, Boudon was led to believe that inequalities of educational opportunity in advanced societies had in fact been in steady decline, and therefore took up the problem of why this had not apparently generated any increase in social mobility.

occupational, being interpreted culturally—that is, as reflecting differing class values—they may be alternatively, and more parsimoniously, understood in structural terms. The aspirations reported by individuals, Keller and Zavalloni propose, should be assessed not by an absolute standard but *relatively*: that is, relative to the class positions in which the individuals are presently located. From this standpoint, for example, aspirations to attend university on the part of children of working-class and of service-class origins would not be treated as being on the same level; rather, the former would be regarded as having the higher aspirations. In turn, then, it need not be supposed that the tendency of children from working-class families to pursue in general less ambitious educational careers than children from service-class families derives from a 'poverty' of aspiration: the patterns of choice made could be more or less equivalent ones. It is simpler to assume that there is no systematic variation in levels of aspiration, or related values, among classes, and that variation in the courses of action that are actually taken arises from the fact that, in pursuing any given goal from different class origins, different 'social distances' will have to be traversed—or, as Boudon (1974: 23) more usefully puts it, different opportunities and constraints, and thus the evaluation of different sets of probable costs and benefits, will be involved.[7]

Such an assumption has, moreover, not just the virtue of parsimony but further that of being consistent with the experience of educational expansion. As greater opportunities for secondary and higher education have been created, children from less advantaged class backgrounds *have* proved ready to take these up and indeed *to a similar degree to children from more advantaged backgrounds*. That is to say—and the point is an important one—although class differentials appear in general to have been little reduced, there is no evidence from any modern society that these differentials have appreciably *widened*, which is the consequence of expansion that theories invoking the reproduction of class cultural divergence would lead one to expect.

Boudon's acceptance of the positional theory of aspirations is then related to the distinction he proposes between the 'primary' and the 'secondary' effects that serve to stratify educational attainment. Primary effects are those that create class differentials in initial achievement and thus in 'demonstrated ability' in school. It is at this level that Boudon would acknowledge the importance of class cultural influences—that is, in regard to actual performance rather than aspirations; and he thus largely underwrites the idea of the *famille educogène*. However, it is on secondary effects that his attention is focused: that is, on those effects that come into play as children reach the various transitions or branching points comprised by the educational system and that condition the choices they make. Some choices may, of course, be

---

[7] There is, in fact, evidence to suggest that the educational and occupational aspirations actually expressed by children of different class backgrounds are now growing more similar (see e.g. Furlong 1992: ch. 7). In other words, rather than the problem for the working class being one of a 'poverty' of aspiration, it could, in the absence of change in differential attainment, become more one of aspirations frustrated.

formally denied to some children simply on grounds of insufficient ability. None the less, what is important to recognize is that most children do still have significant choices open to them: whether to leave school or to stay on, to take more vocational or more academic courses, to seek to enter higher education, and so on. And it is at this stage that considerations arising from the relationship between class origins and envisaged destinations—educational and in turn occupational—become crucial. That is to say, Boudon sees the choices in question as being determined via the evaluations that children and their parents make of the costs and benefits of, and the chances of success in, the different options they might pursue. Further 'stratification' of educational attainment, he then argues, will result through the evaluation of more ambitious options tending to be the less favourable, the less advantaged the class position from which they are viewed and the greater, therefore, the relative level of aspiration that they entail. Thus, even among children who, through the operation of primary effects, reach similar educational standards early in their school careers, secondary effects will still produce class differentials in attainment in so far as these children start from—and view their prospective careers from—differing class origins.

Following on this, Boudon's main concern is to establish that, as children's educational careers extend, it is the influence of secondary rather than of primary effects on attainment that becomes increasingly dominant—a claim that has in fact met with a good deal of opposition (see e.g. Halsey *et al.* 1980: 128–33; Erikson and Jonsson 1993). However, for my own purposes, I would wish to develop Boudon's theoretical approach towards a different end: that is, to show that it is on secondary rather than primary effects that attention must centre if the question of change, or rather absence of change, in class differentials under conditions of educational expansion is to be effectively addressed.

Primary effects can, in fact, be understood more broadly than by Boudon (cf. Halsey *et al.* 1980: 127) as comprising *all* those influences, whether cultural or psychological or genetic, that shape what is taken (arbitrarily or not) to be the distribution of ability in the earlier stages of schooling. These effects can be seen as establishing, together with the structure of the educational system, a *potential range* of educational outcomes overall and, likewise, of class differentials in these outcomes. However, it is then secondary effects, operating through the decisions actually made by children and their parents regarding particular educational options, that must determine just how these potentialities are realized. With educational expansion and reform, the constraints on choice that primary effects impose will tend to weaken (and even if these effects do persist throughout educational careers) in that the degree of selectivity in successive transitions, in terms both of ability and resources, will be reduced. More children, in total, will stay on in education beyond the compulsory period, take more academic courses, enter higher education, and so on. And greater scope is thus created, at the level of secondary effects, for less advantaged children to bring their 'take-up' rates of relatively ambitious educational options closer to those of more advantaged children. In other words, educational opportunity *is* increased in the sense that the objective structure of opportunities is made generally more favourable. But, for present purposes, the crucial question is, of course, that of the particular pattern on which these enlarged opportunities are in fact exploited.

It may at this point be instructive to refer to the case of *gender* differentials in educational attainment. What emerges from recent research (see esp. Shavit and Blossfeld 1993) is that in the course of the decades of expansion these differentials have shown a marked decline across virtually all advanced societies. Former disparities in favour of males have in many instances been largely eliminated—or even reversed—as, one might suggest, parents and their daughters have come to reach more positive cost-benefit evaluations of education for women in the light of changing gender relations and labour-market conditions. Thus, the problem that arises in the case of class differentials is thrown into sharp relief: why is it that a comparably general, even if less dramatic, process of equalization, such as would be predicted by liberal theory, has not been apparent?[8]

From the general position that I have taken, I would suggest an explanation that may be summed up in the following proposition. Class differentials in educational attainment have persisted because, even though, with educational expansion and reform, the *general* balance of costs and benefits associated with more ambitious options has steadily changed so as to encourage their take-up, little concurrent change has occurred in the relativities between *class-specific* balances: that is, between such cost-benefit balances as they are on average assessed from the standpoints represented by different classes of origin. What needs then further to be shown, or at all events hypothesized, is why, in this latter respect, such stability should have prevailed.

The RAT Explanation Developed

In the liberal theory one of the main bases of the expectation that class differentials in educational attainment will decline is the idea that costs will be a steadily waning influence on educational decision-making by parents and children. The direct costs of education, in the form of fees, maintenance, and the purchase of books and equipment, will be much reduced through growing public provision of free or subsidized education at all levels; and indirect costs, usually estimated in terms of earnings forgone by children who remain in education beyond the minimum school-leaving age, will tend to be discounted in a context of economic growth and generally rising family incomes.

---

[8] With gender differentials, in contrast to class differentials, there is, of course, little reason to expect that, in the absence of secondary effects, they will still be sustained in some significant degree by primary effects. This does not, however, detract from the point that the virtual collapse of gender differentials indicates that purely normative influences on educational choice will be rapidly modified as cost-benefit balances change.

Thus, there will be rather few children, of whatever class background, who do not continue in education simply because of a lack of the necessary economic resources. Here, as indeed in other respects, the liberal argument undoubtedly has force; but at the same time several important considerations are neglected.

To begin with, there is the obvious point that, even if family income no longer represents a constraint *stricto sensu* on children's educational careers, it may well still affect the *probability* of their taking one rather than another of the various options facing them. And it has then further to be recognized that, while generally rising affluence has indeed characterized industrial societies, it is far less clear that there has been any major reduction in class differentials in family income or, perhaps yet more relevantly, in the effects of class position—that is, of differing employment relations—on the stability of earnings or on the course that earnings typically follow in lifetime perspective.

On the one hand, there can be little doubt that fluctuations in earnings remain more pronounced among manual wage-workers than among salaried employees on account of piece- and time-rate payment systems, a greater reliance on pay for overtime or shift working, and greater exposure to loss of pay through sickness, accident, or unemployment. Thus, the consequences for family living standards of incurring a certain level of costs on children's education will be less easily calculable within the working class and, in turn, a greater degree of caution in this regard can be expected. On the other hand, differences have also persisted (Westergaard and Resler 1975: 81–2; Phelps Brown 1977: 263–9; and see also Fig. 10.3 below) in the tendency for earnings in professional, administrative, and managerial positions to show rising curves with age for clearly longer periods than in manual or routine non-manual employment; and it is, moreover, towards the end of the period of children's compulsory education, when crucial educational choices have to be made and when the question of opportunity costs first arises, that the earnings curves of parents in different classes are likely to be at their most divergent. In the course of their forties, the earnings curves of service-class parents will still tend to be moving upwards, while those of parents in less advantaged class positions will already have flattened out. Thus, for families in such differing class situations, absorbing the costs, direct and indirect, of children remaining in education is likely to have quite contrasting implications for the *trend* in their living standards (cf. Lane 1972, and Chapter 10 below).[9]

It should in this connection also be noted that public subsidies for education are not in the main 'targeted' on those families with the greatest need

---

[9] For a valuable reminder of the continuing importance that working-class children—perhaps more than their parents—attach to the opportunity costs of staying on at school beyond the minimum leaving age, see Micklewright *et al.* (1988) and Bynner (1991). If entry into higher education follows, the reduced material standard of living that they incur may of course extend up to their mid- or late twenties. With children from more advantaged families, this disadvantage is likely to be offset by parental support in various forms (cf. Erikson and Jonsson 1993, 1994*a*).

for them. To the extent that the principle of universal, compulsory, and free education applies, means-testing is precluded and, further, those eligible for subsidized higher education can only be those who have opted for it—and, previously, for the school courses that lead to the requisite qualifications. Thus, in so far as state support for education does not succeed in reducing class differentials at early branching points in the system, it will thereafter tend to help families in more advantaged classes to maintain their higher take-up of what is in fact the most expensive kind of educational provision (cf. Goodin and Le Grand 1987).

In sum, the declining influence of costs is surely part of the explanation of the growth in all modern societies in the total number of children remaining in education beyond the compulsory period. But it is not at all apparent—and the liberal theory throws no light on the matter—just what, so far as costs are concerned, might result in children of less advantaged class origins choosing to stay on in school and to pursue more extended educational careers *at a more rapidly increasing rate* than others. Rather, it may in this regard be suggested that the more or less unchanging class differentials in educational attainment that are observed do no more than reflect similarly unchanging relativities as between the costs of education and typical levels and dynamics of family income from class to class.

A further basis of liberal optimism regarding the reduction of class differentials is the assumption that, while the costs of education to the individual diminish, its perceived benefits will increase. As criteria of ascription give way to criteria of achievement in social selection, education becomes the key to economic success, and is generally recognized as such. Thus, the tendency will be for children of all class backgrounds alike to continue in education for as far as their abilities will take them. However, it is once more the case that, although the liberal argument is relevant to explaining the general rise in educational levels, it underestimates the self-maintaining character of class inequalities. It neglects the fact that educational decision-making remains conditioned by the class situations in which it takes place, and that this is likely to lead to differing evaluations of benefits, as well as of costs, so that change is again inhibited in the ways in which, from class to class, primary effects are modified by secondary effects in producing the pattern of ultimate educational outcomes.

For example, one may suppose that, in viewing education as an investment good, the chief concern of families in more advantaged class positions is that their children should obtain qualifications sufficient to preserve an intergenerational stability of class position or, at very least, to guard against any decisive downward mobility (see further Chapter 11). Thus, service-class parents will be more likely than others to encourage their children to go on from school into higher education of some kind. And, moreover, they may be expected to give such encouragement more frequently, and with an increasing commitment of resources, *as a consequence of* educational expansion itself. As Thurow has argued (1972), the development of a generally better-educated population means that more advantaged families are under constant pressure to make greater investments in their children's education as a form of 'defensive expenditure': that is, as one necessary just to maintain their advantage. Considered as an investment good, education is, to an important degree, 'positional' (F. Hirsch 1976): what counts, so far as returns in employment are concerned, is not the actual amount of education that individuals have but the amount relative to their competitors in the labour market. In the case of service-class families, it may then be expected that the importance that is attached to qualifications adequate to maintain class stability, together with parents' capacity to absorb the costs involved, will lead to children attempting to enter higher education even where their ability levels are such that, as regards the chances of a successful outcome, the investment is a rather high-risk one.

Boudon (1974: 30) has suggested that this tendency is accentuated as a result of higher education becoming a social norm that children are induced to follow through family or peer-group pressures. But while this argument may hold good for certain status groups or milieux *within* more advantaged classes, it is not one that I would myself wish to invoke in the explanation of regularities as extensive, temporally and spatially, as those here in question. A more important consideration might be that, with rising living standards, more service-class families are able to regard higher education for their children as, in the first instance, simply a desirable *consumption* good—although, of course, with resources still being available to create further opportunities, whether through additional education or otherwise, in the event either of failure or of the qualifications initially achieved not appearing to offer sufficiently attractive labour-market prospects.[10]

Turning now to families in less advantaged class positions, the theoretical expectation must be that they will view the possibility of higher education for their children in an altogether more guarded way. In their case, other, less ambitious—and less costly—educational options would be adequate to the goal of maintaining class stability, while also providing quite good chances of some eventual degree of upward movement. For working-class families, for example, the 'best buys' for their children, despite places in higher education becoming more widely available, could still appear to be vocational courses, linked perhaps to subsequent on-the-job training, which would reduce the chances of relegation into the ranks of the unskilled or unemployed (cf. Arum and Shavit 1995; Müller and Shavit 1998) while increasing those of relatively quick entry into skilled manual or technical or supervisory positions. It is, moreover, important to recognize that, in the case of working-class children, a *failed* attempt at obtaining higher-level academic qualifications is likely to be more serious in its consequences than for children from families enjoying superior resources. For as well as representing a loss in itself, it would also

[10] In the spirit of David Lockwood's famous Steinian comment (1960) on the supposed normative significance of working-class families buying washing machines in the 1950s, one might observe that 'three years at university is three years at university is three years at university'. In other words, one could question whether, net of economic considerations, a 'taste' for higher education should be any more class differentiated than that for standard consumer durables.

imply further opportunity costs if an alternative, say, vocational option were then to be taken up, and in some cases might actually preclude such an option or impose direct costs as a result of age limits on entry or on the provision of financial support.[11] Thus, among children of less advantaged origins, a prevailing tendency just the opposite of that among the children of the salariat may be anticipated: that is, for academic courses of the kind leading to higher education to be turned down even by some of those with ability levels that would favour a successful outcome.[12]

Boudon would here also wish to bring 'social' as well as 'economic' considerations into the analysis. Working-class children, he suggests, may be reluctant to pursue academic routes that would imply their eventual mobility away from their communities, as well as their class, of origin (Boudon 1974: 30). However, I would again not wish to follow him, if only because of scepticism about the 'social costs' that mobility entails (cf. Goldthorpe 1987: chs. 6, 7); and his suggestion does, in any event, seem of doubtful relevance to explaining the persistence of class differentials in educational attainment, since working-class communities of the solidaristic kind that it presupposes have in most modern societies been in steady decline.

What thus emerges from the foregoing are two, related, arguments that develop my initial explanatory proposition regarding the lack of convergence in class-specific evaluations in educational decision-making:

(i) that class differentials in the take-up of more ambitious educational options have been maintained because so too have conditions in which the perceived costs and benefits of these options lead to children in less advantaged families requiring, on average, a greater assurance of success than their more advantaged counterparts before such options are pursued;

(ii) that the persistence of these differing propensities over time can be seen to have a rational basis once the implications of the resources, opportunities, and constraints that continue to typify differing class situations are taken into account.

The first of these arguments is one that, I believe, can now be left to empirical assessment. The main implication is that a particular pattern of associa-

---

[11] It is with considerations such as this that the approach here followed most obviously diverges from the 'human-capital' approach taken by most economists of education. In their perspective, as Arum and Hout (1998: 471) have put it, education appears 'as a fungible linear accumulation, like a financial investment'; but in fact the actual institutional structures of modern educational systems 'offer an array of choices and constraints that defy the simple linear formulations' of the economists' models. For an interesting discussion from this point of view of the operation of the German apprenticeship system, see Jonsson et al. (1996).

[12] A further question of potentially large importance here is that of whether returns to education, and especially at higher levels, as measured in terms of either income or class destinations, are lower for children of less advantaged than of more advantaged class backgrounds. Unfortunately, studies thus far undertaken show little consistency in either their methods or results. See e.g. Hauser (1973), Petit (1975), Papanicolaou and Psacharopoulos (1979), Björklund and Kjellström (1994), and Jonsson (1995).

tion prevails between class origins, children's demonstrated academic ability, and the kinds of educational decision that they take. A number of studies, from different periods and places, have in fact already revealed a pattern of just the kind in question: that is, they have shown that, *even when ability level is held constant*, children are more likely to enter longer-term and more academic courses, the more advantaged the class origins from which they come (see e.g., for Britain, Micklewright 1989, Wadsworth 1991; for the USA, Sewell and Hauser 1976; for France, Duru-Bellat and Mingat 1989, Duru-Bellat *et al.* 1992; for Sweden, Erikson and Jonsson 1993). Such findings have sometimes been taken to indicate that children of less advantaged backgrounds face discrimination in their academic careers in the form of an 'ability handicap' that is imposed, consciously or otherwise, by teachers or academic administrators. But an alternative, or at all events additional, interpretation is here proposed in terms of the higher level of ability that less advantaged children will need to show before they, and their parents, are likely to regard more ambitious educational options as, on balance, the best ones for them to follow. The question to be further investigated is then, of course, that of whether there is also evidence that within particular nations this tendency has indeed remained, as would be hypothesized, rather little altered over time, and despite educational expansion and institutional reform.[13]

As regards the second argument, further clarification of just what is at issue empirically could still be thought desirable. An attempt to provide this may be made with reference to the work of Gambetta (1987). From his study of decision-making by parents and children within the Italian educational system, one of the leading conclusions Gambetta reaches is that working-class families are indeed far more sensitive to the chances of success than are middle-class families. He contrasts the way in which the latter 'light-heartedly' expose their children to failure in high school and beyond with the 'extreme caution' of the former (Gambetta 1987: 171–2). But Gambetta then raises the question of how far these differing orientations *can* be regarded as rationally grounded. Although he is in general sympathetic to the RAT approach to explaining class differentials, as pioneered by Boudon, it is here that he sees the main need to qualify it. His empirical results show that class still exerts an influence on educational choices *even when family income and parental education are controlled*: that is, middle-class families are still more ambitious, and working-class families less ambitious, in the choices they make relative to their children's ability. This finding he then takes as indicating that parents and children do not simply respond to the limits and possibilities that are typical of their class situations in a conscious manner but, subintentionally, *over*-adapt. They 'short-circuit' themselves by attempting,

---

[13] It is in fact for Britain that one has the clearest suggestion so far of such stability since the two papers cited in the text are based on longitudinal studies of children born in 1946 and in 1958. Unfortunately, while the pattern of results reported is the same, strict quantitative comparisons are not possible because of a lack of comparability in data and methods, but see Breen and Goldthorpe (forthcoming).

on the one hand, too much and, on the other hand, too little, as compared with what a rational appreciation of the probabilities of success and failure would indicate. In other words, parents and children are subject to the influence of 'behind-the-back' processes that, in their very nature, must lie beyond the scope of RAT (Gambetta 1987: esp. 86–100, 180–6).

Now I do not believe that Gambetta's analysis in this regard is all that secure, and it certainly calls for confirmation. He is engaged in the dangerous practice of providing an *ex-post* interpretation of a residual effect, which could well be no more than the result of misspecification in the model he applies. Furthermore, as he recognizes (1987: 93–9), the question of how the 'inertial forces' to which he appeals might actually operate has to be left with no very plausible answer. None the less, Gambetta's work does have the merit of bringing out the way in which, in relation to educational decision-making, the boundaries of the explanatory potential of RAT are in principle to be drawn and, in turn, the general form that would need to be taken by radically alternative accounts of how the differing propensities of more and less advantaged families are determined.

The key empirical issue that arises can be stated as follows. In explaining persisting class differentials in educational attainment, *do* 'inertial forces' of some kind or other need to be invoked that entail the over-adaptation of parents and children to the realities of their differing class situations? Or is it rather the case, as I have sought to argue, that persisting differentials are simply one expression of the way in which the unequal distributions of opportunities and constraints that characterize a class society contribute to their own perpetuation through the quite rational adaptive strategies that they induce on the part of those who must act under their influence? To produce evidence that would allow adjudication between these two possibilities will surely not be easy. It will mean entering into a closer examination of how educational decisions are actually made and in particular, I would believe, of what quantity and quality of *information* actors typically have available to them, or actively seek, and further of how they process this information (cf. Manski 1993). The methodological resources of sociologists in this area are a good deal less developed than those that have enabled them to analyse the pattern of the eventual outcomes of educational decisions across populations and subpopulations and over time. But the challenges that arise must be accepted if empirical research is to go beyond its descriptive task of 'establishing the phenomena' and become effectively allied with the development of theory that has real explanatory power.

Evidence from a Deviant Case

In the foregoing, the emphasis has been on the need to reorient class theory so that, instead of offering accounts of processes of class formation or class decomposition that have not in fact occurred, it addresses well-documented macrosocial regularities testifying to the resistance to change that prevailing class relations express. There is, however, no suggestion here that such regularities have the status of 'iron laws' that operate entirely without exception (or that must extend indefinitely into the future). Thus, in the case of educational attainment on which I have concentrated—just as with mobility chances or voting patterns—instances can be cited where, in one way or another, the effects of class have seemingly changed and indeed weakened. In conclusion of this chapter, therefore, it is pertinent to ask how promising the theoretical approach I have outlined would appear to be when it is a matter not of explaining the long-term persistence of class differentials in educational attainment but rather their diminution. The value in theory development of 'deviant-case analysis', or of the exception that 'proves' (*sc.* tests) the rule, has for long been recognized.

As earlier observed, where research findings have indicated declining class differentials in educational attainment in a particular national society, the trend shown up has usually been of a rather limited kind and its reality open to debate in the light of the results of other enquiries. However, there is at all events one case in which the evidence of declining differentials is clear-cut and has been quite consistently confirmed on the basis of several different data sets: that is, that of Sweden (see e.g. Jonsson 1988, 1993; Jonsson and Mills 1993; Erikson and Jonsson 1993, 1994*b*). In Sweden over the period 1930 to 1970, and possibly beyond, educational expansion was accompanied by a narrowing in the probabilities of children of different class backgrounds staying on in school rather than leaving after the compulsory period and, likewise, in the probabilities of their taking up more advanced secondary courses and entering higher education. In particular, children of working-class and also of farm families improved their levels of educational attainment as compared with those of children of the salariat.

If then, as I have argued, class differentials in general persist because little change occurs in the relativities of cost-benefit evaluations of educational options as these are—rationally—made in different class situations, what ought to be found in the exceptional Swedish case is evidence of change, that is, of *convergence*, both in these relativities and in the social realities they reflect. In other words, evidence should exist of the features of employment relations that differentiate class positions being modified or their effects in some way offset.

In fact, quite extensive research findings are already available to show that over the period in question economic inequality in Sweden was generally in decline. Personal incomes became more equally distributed (Spånt 1979), and to a rather extreme degree as viewed in comparative perspective (Smeeding *et al.* 1990; Fritzell 1993), while income differences between broad occupational groupings also fell, to the disadvantage especially of higher-level professional, administrative, and managerial employees (Åberg *et al.* 1987). It would in addition seem likely that in Sweden highly developed social policies, 'active' labour-market policies, and powerful trade unions together reduced to a greater degree than in most other advanced societies the differences in economic security that exist as between wage-workers and salaried staff (Esping Andersen 1985, 1990; Vogel 1987; Persson 1990; Hibbs 1991).

Further, though, as well as such circumstantial evidence, results are now to hand from a sophisticated time-series analysis undertaken by Erikson (1996), aimed at establishing more specific linkages between changing economic and social conditions in Sweden and the trend in educational differentials. Two points of main importance can be noted. First, there is little sign of economic growth, rising levels of consumption or educational expansion *per se* having any connection with greater educational equality. Secondly, though, the trend in this direction *is* in certain respects associated with educational reform—notably, the introduction of comprehensive schools, which eliminated early 'branching points'; *and*, more generally and more strongly, with what Erikson would interpret as increasing economic security, in particular for the working class, as indexed primarily by declining rates of unemployment.[14]

It would surely be premature to claim that increased equality in Sweden has, in fact, come about in a way that confirms my account of why, in general, class differentials in education remain little altered: again, the need for further, more detailed, evidence is apparent. None the less, what has emerged thus far from the analysis of Swedish 'exceptionalism' is at all events consistent with this account, and, it may be added, by the same token must tell clearly against the contentions of the liberal theory. As Erikson (1996) concludes, not just the deviant character of the Swedish case but what is further known of its dynamics, points to the fact that increasing equality in educational attainment is by no means the more or less automatic outcome of inherent features of advancing industrialism. At very least, other conditions must be present, and the strong indication is that 'one of these is political action'. Indeed, it could be that the egalitarian tendencies apparent in Sweden in this, as in various other, respects[15] will in the end have to be seen as quite specific to—and thus limited by—the period of a distinctive political conjuncture (cf. Castles 1978; Esping Andersen 1985; Tilton 1990) that has perhaps now reached its close.

Conclusion

It would then appear that a duly reoriented class theory should aim to break with what I earlier referred to as the functionalist and teleological character

[14] It has been argued, sometimes with apparently supporting evidence (e.g. Pissarides 1981), that by reducing opportunity costs unemployment encourages children to stay on in full-time education. But for a well-documented case to the contrary, indicating that rising unemployment leads more children who are able to get jobs to take them rather than investing in further education, see Micklewright *et al.* (1988).

[15] On further Swedish distinctiveness as regards the relative equality of class mobility chances, and the political context of this, see Erikson and Goldthorpe (1992*a*: 164–5, 177–80), and also Chapter 12 below.

of both its Marxist and liberal forerunners in two different ways. In present circumstances, its major task, I have argued, must be seen as that of accounting for the long-term stability of class relations and associated inequalities—for, in effect, their inherent self-maintaining properties. And here the prime need is for secure micro-foundations in the analysis of individual action, and of its intended and unintended consequences, where individuals are seen as acting as members of classes in the sense of being subject to the differing levels and forms of opportunities and constraints that their particular class situations imply. However, in so far as such theory is also called upon to explain processes of change, suggestive of a significant weakening—or, should the case arise, a strengthening—of the influence of class, it would seem likely that it will then have to turn to the analysis of action at a different level: that is, the action of political élites, and of the organizations they command, which is specifically directed to modifying relations in labour markets and production units that constitute the matrix of class. Strangely, or perhaps not so strangely, this last point is one that many years ago I argued, together with David Lockwood, in a very different context—in fact, in the last chapter of the last volume of the *Affluent Worker* series—but there, too, against the claims of Marxist or liberal immanentism and by way of asserting the importance of the 'degrees of freedom' that always remain to political creativity.

9

Explaining Educational
Differentials: Towards a Formal
Rational Action Theory
(with Richard Breen)

IN THE light of recent research in the sociology of education, which has involved extensive over-time and cross-national analyses (see esp. Shavit and Blossfeld 1993; Erikson and Jonsson 1996*b*), it would seem that the following empirical generalizations can reliably be made and constitute *explananda* that pose an evident theoretical challenge.

(i) Over the last half-century at least, all economically advanced societies have experienced a process of educational expansion. Increasing numbers of young people have stayed on in full-time education beyond the minimum school-leaving age, have taken up more academic secondary courses, and have entered into some form of tertiary education.

(ii) Over this same period, class differentials in educational attainment, considered net of all effects of expansion *per se*, have tended to display a high degree of stability: that is, while children of all class backgrounds have alike participated in the process of expansion, the association between class origins and the relative chances of children staying on in education, taking more academic courses, or entering higher education has, in most societies, been rather little altered. Children of less advantaged class origins have not brought their take-up rates of more ambitious educational options closer to those of their more advantaged counterparts.

(iii) It has, though, to be recognized that this latter generalization is not entirely without exception. In one national case at least, that of Sweden, there can be little doubt that class differentials in educational attainment have indeed declined over several decades (Erikson and

This chapter was first published in *Rationality and Society*, 9 (1997). I am grateful to my co-author, Richard Breen, for allowing me to include it in this collection. Helpful comments on earlier drafts of the paper were provided by David Cox, Robert Erikson, Ineke Maas, Cecelia Garcia-Peñalosa, Brendan Halpin, Aage Sørensen, Tony Tam, and two anonymous referees.

Jonsson 1993); and, while some conflict of evidence remains, a similar decline has been claimed for the Netherlands (De Graaf and Ganzeboom 1993) and for Germany (Müller and Haun 1994; Jonsson *et al.* 1996). Thus, any theory that is put forward in order to explain the more typical persistence of class differentials should be one that can at the same time be applied *mutatis mutandis* to such 'deviant' cases.

It would in addition be desirable that such a theory should be capable of yet further extension in order to account for a third regularity that has emerged from the research referred to.

(iv) Over a relatively short period—in effect, from the 1970s onwards— *gender* differentials in levels of educational attainment, favouring males over females, have in nearly all advanced societies declined sharply and, in some instances, have been virtually eliminated or even reversed. In other words, while the process of educational expansion has not in the main led to children from less advantaged family backgrounds catching up those from more advantaged backgrounds in their average levels of attainment, in families across the class structures of contemporary societies daughters have tended rather rapidly to catch up with sons.

In the preceding chapter, an explanation of persisting differentials in educational attainment, sensitive to the further requirements indicated above, was developed from the standpoint of rational action theory. Here, our aim is to refine this theoretical account and to express it in a formal model. In this way we would hope to clarify its central arguments and in turn the wider implications that it carries. Since such attempts at the formalization of theory are still not very common in sociology, the chapter may also serve to stimulate discussion of the merits or demerits of this kind of endeavour. In the remainder of this introductory section we set out certain background assumptions of our subsequent exposition that will not be further discussed. The more specific assumptions on which our model rests will be introduced, and their significance considered, as the chapter proceeds.

We assume, to begin with, that class differentials in educational attainment come about through the operation of two different kinds of effect, which, following Boudon (1974), we label as 'primary' and 'secondary'. Primary effects are all those that are expressed in the association that exists between children's class origins and their average levels of demonstrated academic ability. Children of more advantaged backgrounds are in fact known to perform better, on average, than children of less advantaged backgrounds in standard tests, examinations, and so on. Primary effects, as will be seen, enter into our model but, fortunately, in such a way that we need not take up the vexed and complex question of the extent to which they are genetic, psychological, or cultural in character. It is, rather, secondary effects that for us play the crucial role. These are effects that are expressed in the actual choices that children, together perhaps with their parents,[1] make in the course of their careers within the educational system—including the choice of exit. Some educational choices may of course be precluded to some children through the operation of primary effects: that is, because these children lack the required level of demonstrated ability. But, typically, a set of other choices remains, and it is known that the overall patterns of choice that are made are in themselves—over and above primary effects—an important source of class differentials in attainment.

We then further assume that, *in their central tendencies*, these patterns of educational choice reflect action on the part of children and their parents that can be understood as rational: that is, they reflect evaluations made of the costs and benefits of possible alternatives—for example, to leave school or to stay on, to take a more academic or a more vocational course—and of the probabilities of different outcomes such as educational success or failure. These evaluations, we suppose, will in turn be conditioned by differences in the typical constraints and opportunities that actors in different class positions face, including the levels of resources that they command. However, what we seek to dispense with is any assumption that these actors will also be subject to systematic influences of a (sub) cultural kind, whether operating through class differences in values, norms, or beliefs regarding education or through more obscure 'subintentional' processes. Not only do we thus gain in theoretical parsimony, but we would in any event regard the 'culturalist' accounts of class differentials in educational attainment that have so far been advanced as in various ways unsatisfactory (cf. Chapter 8).

Finally, two other assumptions, regarding the structural context of action, should also be spelled out. On the one hand, we suppose the existence of a class structure: that is, a structure of positions defined by relations in labour markets and production units. And, in addition, we need to assume that within this structure classes are in some degree hierarchically ordered in terms of the resources associated with, and the general desirability of, the positions they comprise.[2] On the other hand, we suppose an educational system—a set of educational institutions that serve to define the various options that are open to individuals at successive stages in their educational careers. And here, too, we have a more specific requirement: that is, that this system should possess a diversified structure that provides options not just for more or less education but also for education of differing kinds, and that in turn entails individuals making choices at certain 'branching points' that they may not be able later to modify, or at least not in a costless way. It might be thought that this latter requirement will tend to limit the applicability of our model to educational systems of the more traditional European, rather than, say, the

---

[1] We do, in fact, treat children and their parents as a single decision-making entity, but there is nothing in the model that we shall go on to propose that need preclude the possibility of intra-familial disagreements, bargaining, compromises, etc.

[2] We need not, for present purposes, be committed to any particular theory of how different levels or kinds of resources derive from different class positions (but cf. Chapters 10 and 11).

American variety: that is, to ones where the type of school attended is likely to be more consequential than the total number of years spent in education. However, we would argue that, on examination, educational systems such as that of the USA turn out to be more diversified than is often supposed, so that children do in fact face educational choices that involve considerations that go beyond simply 'more' or 'less': for example, in the American case, with the choice at secondary level between academic and vocational tracks.[3] It is further of interest to note how two American authors have specified in this regard the divergence between assumptions that we and they would share and those of most economists working within the human capital paradigm. While for the latter education appears as a 'fungible linear accumulation, like a financial investment', a more realistic view would be that educational systems, the American included, 'offer an array of choices and constraints that defy . . . simple linear formulations' (Arum and Hout 1998: 1).

A Model of Educational Decisions

The model we present is intended to be generic: that is, one applicable in principle to the entire range of decisions that young people may be required to make over the course of their educational careers as regards leaving or staying on or as regards which educational option to pursue. However, in the interests of simplicity, we will here set out the model as it would apply just to the choice of leaving or continuing in education. The salient elements of the exposition are shown in Fig. 9.1 by means of a decision tree. Here we assume that pupils must choose whether to continue in education—that is, follow the 'stay' branch of the tree—to the completion of a further level (as, say, in the decision in the British case of whether or not to continue to A level after GCSE) or to leave and enter the labour market—that is, follow the 'leave' branch. Continuing in education has two possible outcomes, which we take to be success or failure. Because remaining at school often leads to an examination, we equate success with passing such an examination. This is indicated by the node labelled P in Fig. 9.1, while failing the examination is indicated by the node labelled F. Leaving is then the third educational outcome in our model—that is, in addition to those of staying in education and passing and staying and failing—and is indicated by node L.

In deciding whether to continue in education or leave, parents and their children, we suppose, take into account three factors. The first of these is the cost of remaining at school. Continuing in full-time education will impose costs on a family that they would not have to meet were their child to leave

---

[3] Arum and Shavit (1995) show that, while opting for a vocational rather than an academic track in secondary education does reduce American students' chances of continuing into higher education, it also serves as an important 'safety net' for those who do not in fact continue. In particular, for 'non-college-bound' students, vocational education improves labour-market prospects relative to those associated with other tracks by raising the chances for males of entering skilled manual work and for females of entering routine nonmanual work as against less favourable outcomes, notably unemployment.

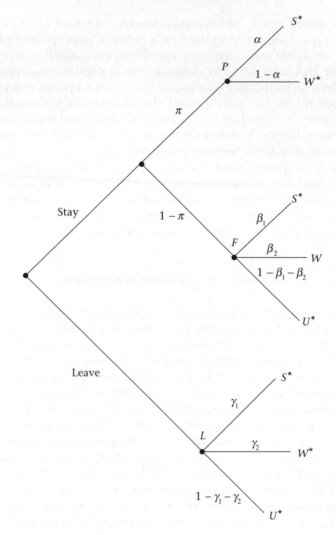

FIG. 9.1. A single decision tree

school: these include the direct costs of education and also earnings forgone. We can therefore express these costs relative to the costs of leaving by setting the latter to be zero and the former as $c > 0$. The second factor is the likelihood of success if a pupil continues in education. Since we distinguish only between success and failure, subjective beliefs about the chances of success at the next stage of education can be captured in our model by a single parameter, which we label π. This parameter measures the subjective conditional probability of passing the relevant examination given continuation. The third factor is then the value or utility that children and their families attach to the three educational outcomes represented by P, F, and L in Fig. 9.1. In our model this factor is expressed in terms of beliefs about the chances of access that each outcome affords to three possible destination classes.

For the purposes of our exposition, we take these classes as being the service class or salariat of professionals, administrators, and managers (S^* in Figure 1), the working class (W^*), and the underclass (U^*)—the class, say, of those with only a precarious place in the labour market and in only the lowest grades of employment if not unemployed. However, it should be emphasized that nothing of significance attaches to this choice of classes, except that, as earlier noted, we need to have a hierarchical ordering. Thus, the service class is regarded as comprising the most advantaged and most desirable positions and the underclass the least advantaged and least desirable, with the working class falling in-between. This ranking of classes is, moreover, assumed to be universally recognized or, at all events, not to vary across the population in any socially structured way.[4]

As we have said, each of the three possible educational outcomes in our model has attached to it subjective probabilities of access to each of the three possible destination classes. So, as Fig. 9.1 shows, for pupils who remain at school and pass their examination, node P, the probability of access to the service class is given by α. There is no path linking this educational outcome to the underclass. This means that anyone who reaches this particular outcome is believed to be certain to avoid this class. It follows, therefore, that the probability of entering the working class, conditional on having been educationally successful, is given by $1 - \alpha$. At the other two outcome nodes, F and L, there is a positive probability of entering all three destination classes. So, for the outcome F (remaining at school and failing) the probability of access to the service class is given by β_1, the probability of access to the working class by β_2, and the probability of access to the underclass by $1 - \beta_1 - \beta_2$. For the L outcome the corresponding probabilities are then given by the γ parameters.

We repeat that these are all subjective probabilities. Just as with π, the values for our various α, β, and γ parameters reflect people's beliefs: in this case, about the returns to various educational outcomes conceptualized in terms of access to more or less desirable locations in the class structure. In principle, therefore, these parameters could vary widely across individuals and families. Again, though, we assume a societal consensus in regard to a set of beliefs that then serve as conditions on the parameters in question and that may be stated as follows.

(i) $\alpha > \beta_1$, and $\alpha > \gamma_1$. It is generally believed that remaining at school and succeeding affords a better chance of access to the service class than does remaining at school and failing or leaving school. Our model does not require that we make any assumptions about the relative magni-

---

[4] Empirical support for the idea of such a consensus on the general desirability of different kinds of occupation (taken together with specific employment statuses) is provided in Goldthorpe and Hope (1974).

tude of β_1, and γ_1. It could, for example, be the case that a young person's chances of access to the service class are improved simply by acquiring more years of education, even if this does not lead to examination success. Alternatively, such time spent in education may be wasted in the sense that leaving school and embarking earlier on a career will yield a better chance of access to the service class.

(ii) $\gamma_1 + \gamma_2 > \beta_1 + \beta_2$. Remaining at school and failing increases the chances of entering the underclass. This means that there is a risk involved in choosing to continue to the next level of education.

(iii) $\gamma_2/\gamma_1 > 1$; $(\gamma_2/\gamma_1) \geq (\beta_2/\beta_1)$. Those who leave school immediately have a better chance of entry to the working class than to the service class. This may or may not be the case among those who remain at school and fail, though, if it is, their odds of entering the working class rather than the service class are no greater than those who leave school immediately.

(iv) $\alpha > 0.5$. Staying on at school and passing the examination makes entry to the service class more likely than entry to the working class.[5]

In the interests of realism, especially as regards (ii) and (iii) above, it ought to be noted that 'leaving' and entering the labour market need not in most educational systems be equated with a definitive ending of the individual's educational career. Taking this option could lead to further vocational courses pursued in conjunction with employment.

The Generation of Class Differentials

Given the model previously outlined, we can now turn to the question of explaining why differences exist across classes in the proportions of young people who make one kind of educational decision rather than another. For ease of exposition here we consider only two classes of origin, the service class, S, and the working class, W. In all of what follows we assume that these classes differ in only two ways. First—and it is here that we give recognition to 'primary' effects—children of the two classes differ in their average ability. Ability is taken to be normally distributed within each class with means $a_S > a_W$ and variance given by σ^2_a. Secondly, the two classes have different levels of resources, r, which they can use to meet c, the costs of education. Resources are taken to have a logistic distribution with mean values $r_S > r_W$ for the two classes and a common dispersion parameter, σ^2_r. Throughout, we make no other assumptions about differences between the classes. In particular, and as

[5] Strictly speaking, the mathematics of our model require a slightly weaker condition, namely that $\alpha \geq \gamma_1 / (\gamma_1 + \gamma_2)$. This imposes a condition on the magnitude of the difference in the chances of access to the service class as between remaining at school and passing the examination and leaving immediately. The conditional probability of access to the service class for those who leave immediately should not be greater than $\gamma_1 + \gamma_2$ times the conditional probability of access to the service class for those who remain at school and pass the examination. However, because of condition (iii), condition (iv) will always be met if $\alpha > 0.5$.

earlier noted, we do not suppose any class-specific cultural values or social norms nor any class differences in the subjective α, β, and γ parameters of our model.

We then propose three mechanisms through which class differentials in educational attainment may arise at the level of 'secondary' effects. Of these three, we would wish to stress the particular importance of the first, since this provides an account of how these differentials may be created and sustained through the apparently 'free' choices made by those in less advantaged classes. Our second and third mechanisms can be understood as accentuating the differing patterns of choice that derive from this initial source.

Relative risk aversion

We begin with an assumption regarding aspirations: that is, that families in both classes alike seek to ensure, so far as they can, that their children acquire a class position at least as advantageous as that from which they originate or, in other words, they seek to avoid downward social mobility. This means that the educational strategy pursued by parents in the service class is to maximize the chances of their children acquiring a position in this class. In terms of our model, their strategy is to maximize the probability of access to S^*. For working-class parents the implication is that they should seek for their children a place in either the working or the service class, since either meets the criterion of being at least as good as the class from which they originate. In terms of our model their strategy is then to maximize the probability of access to S^* or W^*, which is the same as minimizing the probability of access to U^*. This establishes families in both classes as having identical relative risk aversion: they want to avoid, for their children, any position in life that is worse than the one from which they start.

To see the consequence of these two strategies, maximize $pr(S^*)$ for those of service-class origins and minimize $pr(U^*)$ for those of working-class origins, let us assume, for the moment, that continuing in education is costless ($c = 0$). Then we find that whether or not a pupil believes it to be in his or her best interests to continue in education rather than leave depends on the value p_i (where i indicates the ith pupil) given by

$$p_{iS} = \frac{\pi_i \alpha + (1 - \pi_i)\beta_1}{\pi_i \alpha + (1 - \pi_i)\beta_1 + \gamma_1} \tag{1}$$

for the ith service-class pupil and by

$$p_{iW} = \frac{\pi_i + (1 - \pi_i)(\beta_1 + \beta_2)}{\pi_i + (1 - \pi_i)(\beta_1 + \beta_2) + (\gamma_1 + \gamma_2)} \tag{2}$$

for the ith working-class pupil.

Here we have allowed π to vary among pupils, but we have assumed the values of α, β, and γ to be common to all. If p takes a value greater than one-half, this indicates expected returns to remaining at school exceed those of leaving. Thus, without taking account, as yet, of the costs of pursuing the former strategy, pupils for whom $p_i > 0.5$ can be said to prefer to remain in education. Even if subjective expectations of future success, as captured by π, do not differ between the two classes, it will nevertheless be the case that, given conditions (i) to (iv) above, $p_{is} > p_{iw}$ for any value of π less than 1.[6]

This is proved as follows: $p_{is} > p_{iw}$ $\forall$ $\pi \leq 1$ if and only if

$$\frac{\pi\alpha + (1-\pi)\beta_1}{\gamma_1} > \frac{\pi + (1-\pi)(\beta_1 + \beta_2)}{(\gamma_1 + \gamma_2)}. \tag{3}$$

Taking the first term on the left-hand side of (3), we have

$$\frac{\pi\alpha}{\gamma_1} = \frac{\pi}{\frac{1}{\alpha}\gamma_1} > \frac{\pi}{\gamma_1 + \gamma_2} \tag{3a}$$

by conditions (iii) and (iv) in the text above. Taking the second term of the left-hand side of (3), we have

$$\frac{(1-\pi)\beta_1}{\gamma_1} \geq \frac{(1-\pi)(\beta_1 + \beta_2)}{(\gamma_1 + \gamma_2)} \tag{3b}$$

by conditions (ii) and (iii). Together (3a) and (3b) imply (3), which in turn implies $p_s > p_w$ as required.

This result establishes that, if continuing in education is costless and there are no class differences in the subjective probability parameters α, β, and γ, children from more advantaged class backgrounds will more strongly 'prefer' (in the sense of perceiving it to be in their best interests) to remain in school to a further level of education rather than leave.

The proportions in each class who prefer to stay are derived as follows. Assume that p has an unspecified distribution with means in each class p_s and p_w and dispersion parameters σ_{ps} and σ_{pw}. Because $p_{is} > p_{iw}$ for any common value of π, and assuming, for the moment, no class difference in the distribution of π, it follows that $p_s > p_w$. Then, given that only those pupils for whom p exceeds one-half prefer to stay at school, the proportions in each class preferring this outcome are given by the area under the unspecified distribution function above the point

$$z_s = \frac{\frac{1}{2} - p_s}{\sigma_{ps}}$$

for the service class and analogously for the working class.

Differences in ability and expectations of success

Thus far we have been assuming that the option of continuing in education is open to all pupils. But, of course, this is often not the case and successive

---

[6] Note that, whereas p_{iw} can take any value between zero and one, depending on the value of π, if $\beta_1 \geq \gamma_1$, then p_{is} will exceed one-half for all values of π.

levels of education may be open only to those who meet some criterion, such as a given level of performance in a previous examination. Let us assume, for the sake of simplicity, that this criterion can be expressed directly in terms of ability, so that, for example, a pupil may continue in education only if his or her ability level exceeds some threshold, k: that is, we impose the condition that a_i must be greater than k. Given our assumption regarding primary effects, that the mean level of ability is higher in the service class than in the working class but that both have the same variance in ability, it then follows that the proportion of service-class children who meet this condition exceeds the proportion of working-class children.

However, we might also suppose that pupils' own knowledge of their ability helps shape the subjective probability they attach to being successful in the next stage of education, which we labelled π_i. So we can write $\pi_i = g(a_i)$, where g indicates that π is a function of a. If we then denote by π_s^* and π_w^* the required minimum subjective probabilities compatible with continuing in education (these are the smallest values of π_i, for which $p_i > 0.5$), we can write the probability of continuing in education as

$$pr(a_i > k)pr(\pi_i > \pi^*|a_i > k)$$
$$= pr(a_i > k, \pi_i > \pi^*)$$
$$= pr(a_i > k, g(a_i) > \pi^*). \tag{4}$$

If

$$pr(g(a_i) > \pi^*) \le pr(a_i > k)$$

then (4) reduces to

$$pr(\pi_i > \pi^*).$$

If pupils' expectations about how well they will perform at the next level of education are upwardly bounded by how well they have performed in their most recent examination—for example, if there are no pupils who, although they have failed to exceed the threshold k, are nevertheless sufficiently optimistic about their future examination performance to wish to continue in education—then ability differences will be wholly captured in differences in the subjective parameter π. This will cause the average value of π to be lower among working- than service-class pupils because of the class difference in average ability levels.

Differences in resources

Thus far we have assumed education to be costless. If we relax this assumption, we need to take account of class differences in the resources that families in different locations in the class structure can devote to their children's education. Assume, therefore, that pupils can continue in education if and only if $r_i > c$, where r_i is the level of resources available for children's education in the ith family. Given that service-class families have, on average, greater resources than working-class families ($r_S > r_W$) and that resources have the same dispersion within each class, it follows that the proportion of service-class pupils for whom this resource requirement is met will exceed the proportion of working-class pupils.

We have now suggested three mechanisms that, taken together, give rise to class differentials in the proportions of children who choose to stay on in education. Our first mechanism shows how, solely because of the relative risk aversion that is seen as being common across classes, there will be a stronger preference among service- than among working-class pupils for remaining in education, given that no costs attach to doing so. Our second mechanism then allows for class differences in average ability levels and in turn in expectations of success. The effect of this is to introduce class differences in the values of π (the subjective probability of future educational success), which further widen class differences in the value of p and thus in the strength of the preference for staying on in education. Finally, our third mechanism takes account of the costs of continuing in education and allows for a further source of class differentials, the average resource levels available to meet these costs. The effect of this is to promote class differences via the proportion of families in each class whose resources exceed the costs of their children continuing in education or, more simply, who can afford to allow their children to continue.

How Important are Our Assumptions?

Throughout the foregoing exposition of our model we have made assumptions of two distinct kinds. First, there are assumptions that serve to restrict differences between classes, for which we have theoretical reasons; and, second, there are assumptions that we have introduced just to make our model more tractable. As regards the latter, it might reasonably be asked: how far are our results dependent upon these simplifying assumptions?

The assumption that the educational decision problem has three possible outcomes, each of which results in eventual entry to the labour market, is innocuous. In reality, the decision about whether or not to continue to educational level n may well be made with a view to gaining access to level $n + 1$: for example, a decision about whether to remain at school to sit certain examinations might be made in the light of possible entry to university. Such a situation could be represented through a decision tree such as that shown in Fig. 9.2 in which there are two branching points, labelled 'Choice 1' and 'Choice 2', both referring to decisions on whether or not to continue in education. Note that the second choice is open only to those who reach the node labelled P_1—that is, who pass the examination at the end of the previous level of education. In this model there are five educational outcome nodes, labelled L_1 (immediate leaving), F_1 (staying at the lower level but failing the examination), and, correspondingly, L_2, F_2, and P_2. These five nodes have associ-

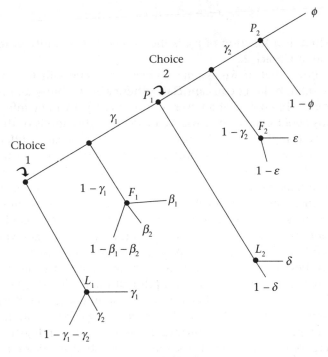

FIG. 9.2. A multiple decision tree

ated probabilities β, γ, δ, ε, and ϕ and there are two parameters measuring sub-jective beliefs about the chance of success at each level: π_1 relating to educational level one and π_2 relating to educational level two. Recall that anyone who passes the examination at the end of level 1 is assumed to have a zero probability of entering the underclass. This implies that for any outcome consequent on passing this examination there will be only one identified probability: that is, there will be only one value of δ, of ε, and of ϕ.

In this set-up the decision analysed in Fig. 9.1 could now be seen as Choice 1 embedded in a more realistic sequence of educational decisions. However, the situation is readily analysed using backward induction. We first solve the final decision in Fig. 9.2 (that is, the decision at Choice 2) in the same way as we analysed the decision in Fig. 9.1. This yields

$$p_{is2} = \frac{\pi_{i2}\phi + (1-\pi_{i2})\varepsilon}{\pi_{i2}\phi + (1-\pi_{i2})\varepsilon + \delta} \tag{5}$$

which is the value of p for the ith service-class pupil at Choice 2. If we assume that, at the time at which Choice 1 is made, pupils and their parents have formed the subjective expectation π_{i2}, then we can solve for p_{is2} in equation (5), and similarly for p_{iw2}. Having done this, we solve for α in equations (1) and (2), which, for pupils of either service- or working-class origins, is

$$\alpha_i = q_{i2}(\pi_{i2}\phi + (1 - \pi_{i2})\varepsilon) + (1 - q_{i2})\delta.$$

Here q_{i2}, which is a function of p_{i2}, is the expected probability of remaining in education at Choice 2.

Fig. 9.2 shows that, if we assume no class differences in the parameters δ, ε, and ϕ, then, holding constant class differences in ability and resources, class differences in choices at a lower educational level will be influenced by expectations about choices that will be made at higher levels of the system. However, these higher-level choices will, again net of class differences in resources, show less variation according to social class than will earlier ones. Not only will successive choices have reduced class differences in ability among those making these later choices, but the riskiness of making more ambitious educational choices will have been reduced or even eliminated. So, for example, in looking at Choice 2 in Fig. 9.2, we see that there is now no risk of demotion to the underclass: all the educational outcomes will serve to secure for children of working-class parents a position at least as good as that from which they originated. Under these circumstances, it seems reasonable to assume that, although service-class pupils will still be more likely than their working-class counterparts to choose to continue in education, the class difference should be lessened because this more ambitious educational option now carries with it no risk of downward mobility for working-class pupils. Indeed, were we to make finer distinctions in the labour-market outcomes in our model, we might find that, as we move to higher educational levels, the riskiness in choice comes to affect successively more advantaged classes.

The fact that our model allows only for a pass or fail outcome at the end of each educational level is similarly trivial. It would be easy to allow for three outcomes (for example, do well/do modestly/fail) or for a continuum of outcomes, without doing any violence to the model. Again, we have presented the choice to be made as staying in education versus leaving, but the basic approach represented by our model would apply equally well to other educational decisions that might be no less important, as, for example, the choice between following an academic or a vocational educational track. We could then consider four possible outcomes, defined as pass or fail in each track; and, in turn, there would be no difficulty in embedding this choice in a more complex set of sequential decisions such as that shown in Fig. 9.2.

One might also consider the possibility that the α, β, and γ parameters in the model of Fig. 9.1 should differ according to class origins, so reflecting class differences in beliefs about the returns to education. Although we have sought to minimize the extent of class differences in subjective parameters, there would be no difficulty in incorporating this modification into our model. In this case, the results would depend upon the exact nature of such differences, since what is important here is the pattern of relativities in the values of these parameters both within and between different class origins. For example, if we suppose that $\alpha_S > \alpha_W$ (the returns to staying in education and succeeding are believed greater in service- than in working-class families) and/or that $\beta_{1S} > \beta_{1W}$ (the chances of access to the service class among those who fail are

believed to be better for service- than for working-class children), then, referring to equation (3), it is clear that class differences in the proportions of
pupils who prefer to stay on in education will be greater. On the other hand,
if $\gamma_{1S} > \gamma_{1W}$, the effect will be indeterminate, depending upon the size of this
difference relative to the extent of class differences in the α and β parameters. For example, if $\gamma_{1S} > \gamma_{2W}$ (among those who leave school, service-class
children have a better chance of access to the service class than have working-
class children to the working class), then class differences in preferences will
be less marked. However, perhaps the most plausible class difference in
assumptions about returns to education is that concerning access to the
service class among young people whose chances would otherwise be diminished by educational failure. Here, service-class families may be in a better
position to compensate for such failure than working-class families by providing other channels through which their children could gain access to a
service-class destination (cf. Chapter 11). If this were the case, it would be
reflected in our model in a class difference in β_1, which, as we have seen, will
tend to exaggerate the extent of class differences in choice.

Finally, our assumptions that service-class families seek to maximize $pr(S^*)$
while working-class families seek to minimize $pr(U^*)$ imply that the former
do not differentiate between downward mobility to the working class and to
the underclass, while the latter attach no more positive weight to upward
mobility (into the service class) than to immobility. If, however, we do
suppose that such distinctions are drawn, does the basic result—namely, that
the preference for remaining in education rather than leaving is stronger
among service- than working-class pupils—still hold? As an example, assume
that service-class pupils attach weights $-x$, 0, and 1 to destinations in the
underclass, working class, and service class, respectively, and that working-
class pupils attach weights 0, 1, and x^* to these three destination classes, with
$x > 0$ and $x^* > 1$. In this case, the service class considers U^* to be less preferable than W^*, while the working class considers S^* to be preferable to W^*. In
this case $p_{iS} > p_{iW}$ holds only if

$$\frac{\pi\alpha + (1-\pi)\beta_1 - x(1-\pi)(1-\beta_1-\beta_2)}{\gamma_1 - x(1-\gamma_1-\gamma_2)} >$$
$$\frac{\pi + (1-\pi)(\beta_1+\beta_2) + (x^*-1)(\pi(\alpha-\beta_1)+\beta_1)}{\gamma_1 + \gamma_2 + (x^*-1)\gamma_1}. \tag{6}$$

Compared with equation (3), there is an extra term in both the numerator
and denominator for both classes in (6). In the case of the service class (the
left-hand side of equation (6)), the greater penalty attached to U^* makes both
the numerator (the pay-offs to choosing to stay) and denominator (the pay-
offs to choosing to leave) smaller, because both alternatives carry some possibility of ending up in U^*. However, providing that π is not small, the overall
effect will be to increase the probability of staying in education, because this
option provides a more advantageous trade-off between S^* and U^* than does
leaving. For the working class the extra terms in the equation will increase
the pay-offs to both staying and leaving, because in all cases there is at least

one path that leads to S^*, which now carries a greater reward. But, assuming $\beta_1 > \gamma_1$, the net effect will be to make staying more attractive than hitherto. For both classes, the larger the value of π, the greater the increase in the attractiveness of staying rather than leaving. Whether the effect will be a narrowing of class differences in p then depends on the actual configurations of the expected pay-offs to S^*, W^*, and U^*. The important considerations are the extent to which the chances of the extra return x^* counterbalance the risk associated with choosing to stay among the working class; and the extent to which the penalty of $-x$ attached to U^* makes the service class susceptible to the same kinds of risk associated with choosing to stay.

One situation in which class differences in p will narrow (though not necessarily be eliminated) is when $\pi < 1 - \gamma_3/\beta_3$ (where $\gamma_3 = 1 - \gamma_1 - \gamma_2$ and similarly for β_3). In this case the risk of entering U^* and receiving the very low pay-off of $-x$ will come to reduce p_{is} compared with its value under our earlier assumptions that the pay-offs to U^* and W^* were the same. But the extent to which this will reduce class differences in p is limited. This is because, under this new set-up, the increase in the probability of working-class pupils remaining at school depends upon the extent to which they benefit more from the extra return to S^* through remaining at school rather than leaving (so offsetting the riskiness of choice). Yet precisely when π is small the degree to which this is so is limited, so that, as π gets very small, their advantage arises solely because of our assumption that $\beta_1 > \gamma_1$.

The upshot of this is that, under these alternative assumptions about the weights attached to the various destination classes, there will exist a threshold value of π, say π^*, such that among young people for whom $\pi_i < \pi^*$, $p_{is} < p_{iw}$. For values of $\pi > \pi^*$, we find $p_{is} > p_{iw}$ as before, with the difference widening as we move to larger values of π. At the low values of π there is a very high expectation of failure should young people continue in education. But now failure is more costly for service-class than for working-class pupils because of the extra penalty associated with the greater downward mobility they risk experiencing. However, for parameter values that meet conditions (i) to (iv) given above, together with the assumption that $\beta_1 > \gamma_1$, it transpires that for any reasonable values of x^* and x, p^* will be less than zero. By reasonable we mean values of x^* that are less than 2 (so that, for members of the working class, the cost of downward mobility into U^* is greater than the benefits of upward mobility) and of x that are marginally greater than $x^* - 1$ (meaning that the cost of extra downward mobility into U^* for the service class is greater than the perceived desirability of the extra upward mobility into S^* on the part of the working class). These conditions on x and x^* are, in fact, further risk-aversion assumptions, albeit weaker than the ones with which we began this chapter. Young people and their families value upward mobility less than they fear downward.

Our original choice of pay-offs reflects our belief that educational decisions are driven by the desire of families to ensure that their children do not experience downward mobility. However, the central result of our risk-aversion assumption—namely, that children from more advantaged backgrounds will more strongly prefer to continue in education—is robust to other choices of pay-off, which seek to capture distinctions in the attractiveness of upward mobility rather than immobility and in the aversion to the amount of downward mobility.

Given this list of what is not essential to the model, it may then be asked what are those features of it that need to be preserved. We have in fact already indicated the answer to this question in noting that it is the first of the three mechanisms we have proposed—that of equal relative risk aversion—that basically drives the model and leads to its most novel and, perhaps, counter-intuitive results. More specifically, we may say that what the model crucially depends on is the general structure of the educational decision problem that we have set up, as this is constituted by our initial conditions (i) to (iv). What is essential is that there should be some measure of risk, in terms of eventual class of destination, that is attached to continuing in education or, more generally, to making certain more ambitious educational choices, relative to leaving education or taking less ambitious options. And then further, in order for the model to provide an explanation of class differences in the probabilities of the choices made, risk has in this respect to be unequally distributed across origin classes. Thus, in our model, riskiness is a cost imposed on the working class, but not the service class, through the possibility of their dropping into the underclass. This is why, with only two origin classes, we still have three destination classes, although it should be stressed that the notion of an underclass is not here of any particular importance in itself. All that is required is that there should be some outcome that can be considered as implying an inferior position to that from which children begin and that, for children of some class origins, this outcome should be less likely if they opt for less ambitious but 'safer' educational careers.[7]

Explaining Empirical Regularities

We may now seek to apply our model to the explanation of the empirical regularities that were set out in the introductory section, beginning with that of the widely observed persistence of class differentials in educational attainment in the context of an overall increase in educational participation rates. To account for the latter trend is fairly easy: the relative costs of education have declined over time in all economically advanced countries. As the period

---

[7] Of course, the risk of dropping into the underclass bears also on pupils of service-class origin. But, for these pupils, the more ambitious option of remaining at school entails no risk, relative to leaving, because their subjective probability of gaining access to the service class is greater even if they remain at school and fail than it would be if they left. This follows from condition (i) of our model. Put another way, the inferior outcome for service-class pupils is to end up in either the working class or the underclass; but, in contrast to the inferior outcome for working-class pupils, the risk of such an outcome is not reduced by taking the less ambitious educational option.

of compulsory schooling has been extended, the costs of successively higher levels of education have been reduced through the abolition of fees, the introduction of maintenance grants, soft loans, and so on. In our model this change is treated via the third mechanism suggested—the effect of class differences in resources—and is captured in a decline in the size of the parameter c. This will lead to an increase in the proportions of children from both service- and working-class origins continuing in education, providing, of course, that the preference for continuing (given by our p parameter) does not decline. However, far from p_i declining over time, it is more plausible to believe that there is a widespread increase in the desire to remain in full-time education, as educational credentials have taken on increasing importance in the labour market and in securing a relatively advantaged class position. Indeed, in so far as education is regarded as a 'positional' good (F. Hirsch 1976), p_i could be expected to rise steadily simply as a consequence of educational expansion itself.

At the same time, our model can provide an explanation of how, within a context of educational expansion, class differentials may none the less persist. To see this, recall that class differences in educational attainment are usually measured by odds ratios that compare the odds of continuing in education versus leaving for pairs of origin classes. Under our model, the odds ratio between the service and the working class is equal to

$$\frac{\phi_s/(1-\phi_s)}{\phi_w/(1-\phi_w)}$$

where we use ϕ_s to mean the proportion of service-class pupils who remain in education and similarly for ϕ_w. It is then possible to show (see the Appeddix) that, given a decline over time in c, together with an increase in the proportion of both service- and working-class pupils who consider it in their best interests to remain in education, the odds of continuing in education increase by a roughly constant amount for each class, and so preserve a similar constancy in the odds ratio. This tells us that, under these circumstances, a uniform decline in the costs of education—that is, uniform across classes—will result in the odds for children of all classes choosing to continue being multiplied by something like a common factor. So if, for example, some level of education is made free of charge (in the sense that fees are no longer levied), class differences in participation (as measured by odds ratios) at this level will remain more or less unchanged even though the overall participation rate will increase.

Our model also sheds some new light on the concept of 'maximally maintained inequality' in education (Raftery and Hout 1990; Hout et al. 1993). These authors argue that class differences in educational attainment will begin to decline only when participation in a given level of education of children of more advantaged backgrounds reaches saturation. In our model, such a reduction will occur once c declines to the value at which all members of the service class have resources that exceed it. At this point, all service-class families will possess resources that exceed the costs of remaining in education and thus the proportion in this class who choose to continue in education will be equal to the proportion who perceive it to be in their interests (i.e. for whom $p_i > 0.5$). Further reductions in c will then have no influence on the numbers of service-class children who choose to continue but will still increase the proportion of working-class children who do so. Under these conditions, the relevant odds ratio could be expected to move towards unity.[8] However, it should be recognized that, as understood in terms of our model, maximally maintained inequality does not imply that a decline in class differentials can commence only at the point at which all children of more advantaged class origins continue in education. Rather, this effect occurs once all such children whose p_i is greater than one-half continue; in other words, once all those who perceive it to be in their best interests to continue are able to act accordingly. It is true that in some instances the achievement of this latter condition will, in fact, give rise to 100 per cent continuation among children of more advantaged classes.[9] But further declines in c, even if they lead to $r_{iw} > c$ for all members of the working class, will not lead to equality in the proportions continuing in education in each class so long as there still remains a class difference in the proportion who prefer to continue.

It further follows from our model that class differentials in educational attainment will also respond to changes in the costs of education that, rather than being uniform, have a variable impact across classes. Such changes could be brought about directly through the selective subsidization of young people according to their class of origin, as occurred, for example, in some post-war Communist societies (cf. Chapter 11). However, essentially the same effect could follow from a general reduction in inequality of condition between classes. Specifically, if class differences in resources, r, become smaller, our model would predict that differentials in educational attainment, as measured by odds ratios, would in turn decline.

It is then in this way that the model may be seen as applying to the national case that most obviously deviates from the typical pattern of persisting class inequalities in education—that is, that of Sweden, in which, as earlier noted, a narrowing of such inequalities over the post-war decades is well attested. There is indeed further extensive evidence (cited in Chapter 8) that in this same period the average income levels of different classes in Sweden became more equal, while the degree of economic insecurity experienced by members of the working class was steadily reduced. And through time-series analysis, correlations can in fact be established between these latter tendencies and the growing equality in educational outcomes that are at all events consistent with the hypothesis of a causal influence (R. Erikson 1996).

---

[8] Though empirically this will be observed only if the proportion of service-class children who consider it in their best interests to remain in education does not change for other reasons. For example, given an increase over time in the importance of educational qualifications in obtaining jobs, we might see changes in the relative values of the α, β, and γ parameters causing the proportion for whom $p_i > 0.5$ to increase in both classes. Under these conditions a narrowing of the odds ratio will not necessarily follow.

[9] In our model this will be the case for the service class if (in addition to conditions (i) to (iv)) $\beta_1 \geq \gamma_1$, but it need not be so if this inequality does not hold.

As against the constancy in class differentials in educational attainment, to which exceptions are few, the decline in gender differentials that has occurred in virtually all advanced societies since the 1970s must appear as rather dramatic. Because gender differentials arise within rather than between families, neither changes in the costs of education nor in inequalities in resources among families are appropriate to explaining their reduction. In the light of our model, this may rather be seen as resulting from shifts in the perception of educational returns that have been prompted by changes in women's labour-market participation. It would be fair comment to say that the pattern of returns to different educational decisions that we have thus far envisaged would, for most of the twentieth century, be more applicable to young men than to young women. Until quite recently, it is likely that educational decisions in the case of girls were shaped in the main by the expectation that their primary social roles would be those of wife and mother, and that their class positions would therefore be determined more by whom they married than by how they themselves fared in the labour market. In so far as this was the case, then the relative returns to education for women would be somewhat different from those we have supposed in the exposition of our model: at all events, the returns associated with any particular educational decision would be less highly differentiated than for men. So, for example, young women of service-class origins could be thought best able to retain their position in this class through marriage; but to meet young service-class men did not necessitate that they themselves should acquire the educational qualifications that led to a service-class occupation. Rather, their qualifications had to be such as to provide them with employment that would bring them into contact with potential service-class husbands, and this requirement might be met through only relatively modest levels of educational attainment, leading to a job as, say, a secretary or a nurse. And within both the home and the educational system alike, as much emphasis was indeed placed on the acquisition of social and domestic skills as on skills that would have value in the labour market.

Such a flatter 'gradient' in the returns to different educational pathways would, if incorporated into our model, have two consequences. First, the proportion of women choosing to remain in education at each decision point would be smaller than the proportion of men; and, secondly, class differentials would tend to be less among women than among men. The former result follows from the lesser incentive to continue in successively higher levels of education that would be held out to women of all class origins alike; the latter comes about because the magnitude of the class differences among those choosing to remain in education (for given values of ability and resources) is directly proportional to the differences in returns associated with the various possible educational outcomes. If we consider equations (1) and (2) as earlier shown, then, as the difference between, say, α_1, β_1, and γ_1 diminishes, so the difference between p_{is} and p_{iw} will also diminish.

Since the early 1980s, we would suggest, the pattern of returns to education for women has drawn closer to that for men, as rates of women's labour-market participation and, especially, rates for married women have increased and as a woman's own employment has taken on greater significance in determining the standard of living enjoyed by her family and further, perhaps, her own class position. In other words, our model as expressed in Fig. 9.1 has come increasingly to apply to women: the 'gradient' in their returns to education has steepened. According to our model, then, such a change should have two effects: gender differentials in educational attainment should decline, as indeed they have,[10] and at the same time the magnitude of class differences among women should increase.

Empirical and Theoretical Implications of the Model

It was in order to account for the empirical regularities that we have just addressed, in particular, that of persisting class inequalities in education, that our model was developed. However, we earlier remarked that an advantage of the formal approach that we have adopted is that, as well as serving to clarify theoretical arguments that are advanced with explanatory intent, it also helps to bring out the wider implications that these arguments carry. In this concluding section, we consider a number of implications, both empirical and theoretical, that stem from our model.

The chief importance of empirical implications is that they provide opportunity for further testing of the model. In so far as the explanation that we have advanced of certain established empirical regularities would in turn lead to the expectation of other regularities, the possibility thus arises of further enquiry that could corroborate or undermine the model. In the course of the foregoing, at least three such implications of our model have emerged that would seem worthy of restatement here on account both of their apparent openness to test and of their own substantive interest:

---

[10] One respect in which gender differentials in education have proved relatively resistant to change is that of patterns of subject choice, with girls remaining under-represented in mathematics and some of the applied sciences. An explanation of this in the spirit of our model would be that, while women are nowadays much more likely to seek their own careers, they nevertheless anticipate quite lengthy breaks from the labour force or periods of part-time work arising for domestic reasons. They are therefore likely to choose those subjects that give access to careers that afford some flexibility in working arrangements or allow for career interruptions. So secretarial work, which provides a great deal of flexibility, is likely to be more attractive to girls than is, say, skilled manual work, although there is little difference in the level of educational attainment required by, or in the general desirability of, the two kinds of employment. Similar arguments might be made in respect of the choice between teaching or the law, on the one hand, and engineering or management, on the other. If women were better enabled, say, through adequate childcare provision, to maintain their availability for full-time employment over the life course, the expectation would then be that gender differences in subject choice would diminish far more rapidly than hitherto. Note that this explanation can again be set in contrast with one couched in terms of—in this case gender-specific—values and norms.

(i) Before they go on to a further level of education, children of less advantaged class backgrounds will require a higher expectation of success at that level—as indicated, say, by previous academic performance—than will children of more advantaged backgrounds.

(ii) As children proceed from lower to higher levels of the educational system, the pattern of choices that they make will (in addition to any continuing primary effects) lead to class differentials in participation becoming smaller.

(iii) As gender differentials in educational participation and attainment diminish over time, class differentials among women will increase from a level initially lower than that among men so as to approximate the male level or, in cases where class differentials are in general decline, will decline less than among men.

A good deal of evidence is in fact already available to lend support to at least the first two of these propositions.[11] However, it is not our concern here to enter into these empirical issues, and we would in any event hope that they are ones that others, including those who find our theoretical arguments unpersuasive, will be prompted to take up. We would also hope that others will seek to derive further empirical implications of our model than those we have ourselves identified, and in this way provide a still wider basis on which its testing can proceed.

As regards the theoretical implications of our model, we would see these as being of main significance in their bearing on explanatory strategy. The model represents children and their families as acting in a (subjectively) rational way—that is, as choosing among the different educational options available to them on the basis of evaluations of their costs and benefits and of the perceived probabilities of more or less successful outcomes. It then accounts for stability, or change, in the educational differentials that ensue by reference to a quite limited range of situational features. For example, in the case of persisting class differentials, the explanatory emphasis falls on similarly persisting inequalities in the resources that members of different classes can command in the face of the constraints and opportunities that their class positions typically entail. Class differences in demonstrated academic ability are also recognized, but not—as we have emphasized—class differences of a (sub)cultural character.

To the extent, then, that our model holds good—that is, that it can provide an adequate account of the regularities we have considered and that its further empirical implications are not rejected—the relatively parsimonious strategy of

[11] As regards the first point, there is clear evidence that, even when ability level is held constant, a strong association prevails between more advantaged class origins and children's choice of more ambitious educational options. This result has been obtained within a number of different educational systems, and appears little affected whether ability is determined by IQ or other 'scholastic aptitude' tests, by examination performance, or by teacher evaluation. See e.g., for Britain, Micklewright (1989) and Wadsworth (1991); for the USA, Sewell and Hauser (1976); for France, Duru-Bellat and Mingat (1989) and Duru-Bellat et al. (1992); for Sweden, Erikson and Jonsson (1993). As regards the second point, supporting evidence from research in a range of different societies—and various explanatory hypotheses, to which ours might be added—are discussed by Blossfeld and Shavit (1993).

the rational action approach is supported; and, we might add, in an area in which 'culturalist' theories of one kind or another have hitherto enjoyed great popularity—even if not great explanatory success. In turn, the case for attempting to pursue this strategy in other areas of sociological enquiry is strengthened.

Finally, though, we would wish to allude to certain theoretical implications that might be regarded as following from our model but that do not in fact do so. To begin with, we are not required to suppose that, in making educational choices, children and their parents in fact go through all the processes of ratiocination that the model might appear to attribute to them. We do take it to be the case that the actors in question have some knowledge of how their society works, have some concern for their own or for family interests, and seek to use the former to promote the latter. But we can at the same time accept that the decisions they make may only rarely result from any entirely explicit procedures rather than, say, 'emerging' over a period of time and, in all probability, reflecting also various non-rational influences. What underlies our approach is the idea that it is rational considerations that are, not the only, but the *main common* factor at work across individual instances, and that will therefore shape patterns of educational choices in aggregate and, in turn, the regularities that constitute our *explananda* (cf. Chapter 5). Our model then aims to represent these considerations in an 'idealized' way, so as to capture the key generative processes involved, rather than to represent decision-making as it actually occurs at the level of particular families.

Further, while we do not in explaining class differentials in education invoke systematic variation in values or derived norms, this does not mean that we have to deny their very existence. Thus, in so far as class-specific norms may be identified—which is an empirical issue—we could recognize them as serving as *guides* to rational action that have evolved over time out of distinctive class experience and that may substitute for detailed calculation when educational choices arise. Understood in this way, such norms could conceivably be of explanatory significance as inertial forces in cases where the structure of constraints and opportunities is changing. But what we would in fact expect—and the decline in gender differentials would, at least by analogy, lend support to the idea—is that norms, in being essentially epiphenomenal, would rather quickly come into line with patterns of action that display a rational adaptation to the circumstances that have come into being.

In sum, our model implies an explanatory strategy that is undoubtedly 'reductionist' so far as the relation of norms to rational action is concerned (cf. Elster 1991). However, we do not in this regard seek what Popper (1972: ch. 8) has criticized as reduction by fiat, but reduction only in so far as it is warranted by the empirical support that our theoretical arguments can obtain in the particular area in which they have been applied.[12]

[12] Elster (1991) criticizes several different versions of the argument that action taken in conformity with social norms is reducible to rational action. However, his efforts to show that no version entails that such a reduction is always possible are of greater philosophical than sociological interest. One could entirely agree with Elster, yet still wish to maintain that, in a particular instance of sociological explanation, a reductionist view could in fact be upheld.

APPENDIX

The Constancy of Class Differentials over Time

In this appendix we show in detail how our model can account for the widely observed approximate constancy of class differentials in educational participation rates in the context of increasing overall levels of participation.

Let ϕ_{St} be the proportion of service-class pupils continuing in education at time t, given costs c_i, and ϕ_{St+1} the proportion at time $t + 1$ (given costs c_{t+1}) and similarly for the working class. Then we require that

$$\phi_{St+1} > \phi_{St} \tag{A1a}$$

$$\phi_{Wt+1} > \phi_{Wt} \tag{A1b}$$

and

$$\frac{\phi_{St+1}/(1-\phi_{St+1})}{\phi_{Wt+1}/(1-\phi_{Wt+1})} \approx \frac{\phi_{St}/(1-\phi_{St})}{\phi_{Wt}/(1-\phi_{Wt})}. \tag{A2}$$

(A1a) and (A1b) say that overall participation rates increase in both classes over time; (A2) says that inequalities between them (measured as odds ratios) remain unchanged. Our model posits two conditions that must be met if a pupil is to continue in education: family resources must exceed the costs $(r_i > c)$; and it must be perceived as in the pupil's best interests to continue in education $(p_i > 0.5)$. If the costs of education decline over time from c_t to c_{t+1} $(c_t > c_{t+1} > 0)$, this leads to an increase in the probability of resources exceeding costs. Given the reasonable assumption that the values of p_i do not decline over time, (A1a) and (A1b) follow immediately.

Under the assumption that r has a logistic distribution, the probability of resources exceeding costs is given by

$$L(S,c_t) = \frac{\exp[-(c_t - r_s)/\sigma_r]}{1 + \exp[-(c_t - r_s)/\sigma_r]}. \tag{A3}$$

It is easy to demonstrate that the odds ratio as between the service and working classes

$$\frac{L(S,c_t)/(1 - L(S,c_t))}{L(W,c_t))/(1 - L(W,c_t))} \tag{A4}$$

is equal to

$$\exp[-(r_s - r_w)]$$

and thus does not depend upon the value of c_t (under the assumption that the dispersion parameter, σ, is common to both classes). It follows that, if the distribution of resources does not change over time, neither will the odds ratio (A4). However, the overall odds ratio between the two classes is equal to

$$\frac{\dfrac{p_{St}x_{St}}{1 - p_{St}x_{St}}}{\dfrac{p_{Wt}x_{Wt}}{1 - p_{Wt}x_{Wt}}} \tag{A5}$$

and similarly at time $t + 1$. Here, for convenience we use the abbreviations

$$p_{St} = pr\left(p_{St} > \frac{1}{2}\right)$$

$$x_{St} = pr(r_s > c_t)$$

and similarly for the working class.

To show that (A5) will be approximately constant over time despite change in c, we first rewrite it as

$$\frac{\dfrac{x_{St}}{(e_{St} - x_{St})}}{\dfrac{x_{Wt}}{(e_{Wt} - x_{Wt})}} \tag{A6}$$

where

$$e_{St} = \frac{1}{p_{St}}$$

and likewise for e_{Wt}. Note that if $e_{St} = e_{Wt} = 1$, then (A6) reduces to (A4). But given $e_{Wt} \geq e_{St}$, a decline in c over time will cause the odds ratio (A6) to decline rather than remain constant. However, recall our earlier argument that educational qualifications increase in importance over time and that this is reflected in an increase in the values of p in both classes. Then if e_S grows proportionately smaller than e_W over the interval t to $t + 1$, the tendency for (A6) to decline will be offset. In turn this will occur if

$$\frac{p_{St}/(1 - p_{St})}{p_{Wt}/(1 - p_{Wt})} > \frac{p_{St+1}/(1 - p_{St+1})}{p_{Wt+1}/(1 - p_{Wt+1})}$$

In words, the odds ratio in preferences for remaining in education increases as educational qualifications take on more importance in the labour market.

To summarize: our argument is that, given a decline in the costs of education, the proportions continuing in education in each class will increase, provided that there is no decline in the strength of preferences for so continuing. Thus, (A1a) and (A1b) will hold. We then argued that (A2) (approximate constancy in the between-class odds ratios of continuing in education) has held as the result of two processes that have had offsetting effects. The decline in the costs of education has a tendency to cause odds ratios to diminish, but the increasing importance of education (leading to a widespread increase in the strength of preference for continuing in education) has a tendency to cause odds ratios to widen. In the Swedish case, where odds ratios have declined, this can be explained as being due to the reinforcing of those factors pushing in this direction through the diminishing of class inequalities in resources.

10

Social Class and the Differentiation of Employment Contracts

M Y CONCERN here is with the theory of social class: I aim to contribute to the ultimate goal of explaining why social classes exist. However, I start out from a way of conceptualizing class, and in turn of making 'class' operational in empirical research, that I have developed, along with a number of colleagues, over the last twenty years. The fundamental idea that has been pursued is that class positions can be understood—in a way to be explained more fully below—as positions defined by *employment relations*. A 'class schema' has been progressively elaborated that differentiates class categories by reference to such relations, and that can be implemented in research through information on employment status and occupation.

This programme of work was undertaken as the basis for studies of social mobility envisaged within a class structural context (Goldthorpe and Llewellyn 1977; Goldthorpe 1987; Erikson *et al.* 1979; Erikson and Goldthorpe 1992*a*). However, the class schema, in one or other of its several versions, has subsequently become used in many other areas of research.[1] As a result, evidence of its *construct* validity has accumulated: that is, of its capacity to display associations or correlations of a theoretically expected kind with other variables: for example, as regards patterns of class voting (Heath *et al.* 1991; Evans *et al.* 1991, 1996) or class differentials in educational attainment (Jonsson 1993; Müller and Haun 1994; Jonsson *et al.* 1996) or in health (Bartley *et al.* 1996; Kunst 1996). One line of further research that is then prompted—but which is not my present concern—is that aimed at elucidating exactly how class, as conceptualized in terms of employment relations, exerts its influence on different dependent variables. What causal processes, ultimately at the level of social action, are involved? For example, just how does the incum-

This chapter has not been published previously. I am indebted to Sam Bowles, Richard Breen, Jerker Denrell, John Ermisch, Duncan Gallie, Dan Krymkowski and Aage Sørensen for comments on an earlier draft, and to Tony Atkinson, Meg Meyer and Karen O'Reilly for useful information and references.

[1] The schema is known, in consequence of its rather complex genesis, by several different names. In a British context it is usually referred to as the Goldthorpe schema; in an international context, as the EGP (Erikson–Goldthorpe–Portocarero) schema, the Erikson–Goldthorpe schema, or the CASMIN schema, after its use in the Comparative Analysis of Social Mobility in Industrial Societies Project.

bency of different class positions operate so as to produce the empirical regularities that are apparent in the association between class and party support
(cf. Evans 1993) or in that between class and educational choice (cf. Chapters 8 and 9 above)?

At the same time, the wider use of the schema has also encouraged
interest in its *criterion* validity: that is, in the extent to which, as opera-
tionalized through occupation and employment status, it does in fact capture
those differences in employment relations that it is, conceptually, supposed
to capture. The findings so far reported on this issue, mainly by Evans
(1992, 1996) and Evans and Mills (1998) and based on British data, indicate
that the schema does in general perform quite well, and these same authors
have more recently extended their research to newly capitalist eastern European nations (Evans and Mills 1999), again with encouraging results.[2] In particular, for individuals of employee status, occupation can, it appears, for the
most part serve as an adequate proxy for those features of their employment
relations that the schema takes as distinguishing class positions. In this way,
then, another line of further investigation is suggested and one that I shall
here seek to pursue: namely, that directed to the question of just why it should
be that different occupations do tend to be associated with differences in the
employment relations of those engaged in them—of the kind that I would in
turn see as implying different class positions.

In the conceptualization of class that underlies the schema (see further
Erikson and Goldthorpe 1992*a*: 35–47), basic distinctions are made among
employers, the self-employed, and employees: that is, among those who
buy the labour of others, those do not buy the labour of others but
neither sell their own, and those who do sell their labour to an employer or
employing organization. Why these three categories should exist is not itself
especially problematic, or at least not in the context of any form of society
that sustains the institutions of private property and a labour market.
However, in such societies in the modern world the third category, that of
employees, is numerically quite preponderant, usually accounting for some
85–90 per cent of the active population.[3] Thus, what is crucial to the class

---

[2] So far as the British case is concerned, much further evidence of the criterion validity of
the schema is in effect provided by a series of studies carried out as part of a review of official 'social classifications' by a committee appointed by the Economic and Social Research
Council, on behalf of the Office of National Statistics. The committee proposed, and ONS
subsequently accepted, a new 'Socio-Economic Classification' that takes over the conceptual
basis of the class schema, although with a revised algorithm for its implementation with
British occupational and employment status data. This classification was then itself subjected
to a series of tests of its criterion (and also construct) validity, which gave generally positive
results (see Rose and O'Reilly 1997, 1998).

[3] Why this very skewed distribution of individuals among the three categories should be
found *does* of course constitute a very significant problem: as Simon (1991) has put it, that
of why there are employing organizations and employees at all, rather than simply independent contractors or, alternatively, of why there is not just a single, encompassing organization. This problem is in fact centrally addressed by the organizational and transaction-cost
economics on which I draw later and is one of obvious relevance to understanding how class
structures of different 'shape' have evolved. However, it is not that with which I am here
concerned.

schema is the further level of distinction that is introduced, applying specifically to the employment relations *of employees*. This focuses on the form of regulation of their employment or, one might alternatively say, on the nature of their employment contracts, explicit and implicit.

In this regard, the main contrast that is set up is that between, on the one hand, the 'labour contract', supposed typically to operate in the case of manual and lower-grade nonmanual workers, and, on the other hand, the 'service relationship', as expressed in the kind of contract taken as typical for the professional, administrative, and managerial staffs of organizational bureaucracies, public and private.

Employment relationships regulated by a labour contract entail a relatively short-term and specific exchange of money for effort. Employees supply more-or-less discrete amounts of labour, under the supervision of the employer or of the employer's agents, in return for wages which are calculated on a 'piece' or 'time' basis. In contrast, employment relationships within a bureaucratic context involve a longer-term and generally more diffuse exchange. Employees render service to their employing organization in return for 'compensation', which takes the form not only of reward for work done, through a salary and various perquisites, but also comprises important prospective elements—for example, salary increments on an established scale, assurances of security both in employment and, through pensions rights, after retirement, and, above all, well-defined career opportunities.　(Erikson and Goldthorpe 1992a: 41)

It is recognized that these two basic forms of the regulation of employment may exist with degrees of modification and, further, that 'mixed' forms also occur—typically associated with positions intermediate between bureaucratic structures and rank-and-file workforces: for example, those of clerical or sales personnel or of lower-grade technicians and first-line supervisors. Table 10.1 summarizes the argument in relation to the categories of the class schema.

The main significance, for present purposes, of enquiries into the criterion validity of the class schema is then the following. They reveal that the regulation of employment of different occupational groupings of employees does in fact tend to follow the pattern indicated in Table 10.1. More specifically, when indicators of various relevant features of employment relations are considered for samples of the economically active population—concerning form of payment, perquisites, control of working time, security, opportunities for promotion, and so on—then occupations as differentiated in terms of these indicators are found to map onto the class categories distinguished by the schema in ways broadly consistent with its conceptual basis.[4] The question

---

[4] The indicators were derived from questions put to respondents concerning the methods by which they were paid (including arrangements regarding overtime and absences), the control of their working time, the period of notice they were required to give on leaving, the opportunities for promotion offered by their jobs, and so on. Various methods of analysis were used, including latent class analysis. Substantially better results than those reported could not, I believe, be expected given that difficulties in eliciting the precise information required from respondents would seem likely to have created a good deal of 'noise' in the data. For example, respondents reporting that they were paid weekly might in fact mean not that they had a fixed weekly wage but rather that, while being paid by the hour, they actually received their earnings weekly; being on an incremental scale might be confused with receiving annual cost-of-living increases; and respondents might report on their own *personal*

TABLE 10.1 *Categories of the class schema and supposed form of regulation of employment*

Class		Form of regulation of employment
I	Professionals, administrators and managers, higher-grade	Service relationship
II	Professionals, administrators and managers, lower-grade, and higher-grade technicians	Service relationship (modified)
IIIa	Routine nonmanual employees, higher grade	Mixed
IIIb	Routine nonmanual employees, lower-grade	Labour contract (modified)
IVabc	Small proprietors and employers and self-employed workers	
V	Lower-grade technicians and supervisors of manual workers	Mixed
VI	Skilled manual workers	Labour contract (modified)
VIIa	Nonskilled manual workers (other than in agriculture)	Labour contract
VIIb	Agricultural workers	Labour contract

Note: The class descriptions given should be understood as labels only. In any implementation of the schema, the detailed occupational groupings to be allocated to each class are fully specified. For Britain, see Goldthorpe and Heath (1992).

that arises is, 'therefore,' that of how this empirical regularity actually comes about. Why should there be such a tendency for individuals engaged in different kinds of work to have their employment regulated via different contractual arrangements and understandings?

In previous work (Goldthorpe 1982; see also 1995a), I have made some attempt at an answer to this question—with particular reference to the idea of the formation of a 'service class' or 'salariat'—but only in a brief and rather *ad hoc* fashion. Here, I aim at a more systematic and theoretically informed treatment. I draw on rational choice, or, as I would prefer to say, rational action theory (RAT), and in particular on such theory as deployed in recent organizational and personnel economics (see e.g. Milgrom and Roberts 1992; Lazear 1995) and in the 'new' institutional, especially transaction cost, economics (see e.g. Williamson 1985, 1996). I would not regard this cross-disciplinary 'borrowing' as in any way implying the abandonment of a sociological perspective (as is suggested, for example, by Pfeffer 1997: ch. 9). What is striking about the economics literature referred to is how much of it can

promotion chances rather than those generally associated with the jobs they held. Better-quality data could almost certainly be obtained directly from employers, provided that sampling problems could be overcome.

in fact be read as a more rigorous development—from the standpoint of a particular theory of action—of observations and insights already to be found in the industrial sociology of the later 1940s and 1950s.[5] Moreover, the version of RAT that is chiefly in use, at least in transaction-cost economics, is not the utility theory of neoclassical orthodoxy but a version in which the idea of objective rationality gives way to that of subjective, or 'bounded', rationality: that is, actors are seen as being, in Simon's words (1946/1961; cf. Williamson 1985: ch. 2), 'intendedly rational but only limitedly so'. As I have argued above (Chapter 6), this modification produces an obvious convergence with approaches to the theory of action that are central to the classic socio-logical tradition; and all the more so to the extent that rationality is seen as restricted not only by psychological, cognitive constraints on information processing but further by social constraints on the availability of information, or knowledge, itself.

Such efforts as sociologists have previously made to account for variation in the form of employment contracts (see e.g. Edwards 1979; Wright 1985, 1989, 1997: ch. 1) derive largely from Marxist 'political economy' (cf. Marglin 1974; K. Stone 1974; Bowles and Gintis 1976) and are in turn characterized by an almost exclusive emphasis on considerations of power and control. The basic assumption is that, under capitalism, the prime concern of employers will be to maximize the 'exploitation' of their workers: that is, to maximize the extraction of actual labour from employees' working time. Employers will thus in general aim to establish forms of contract that are to their greatest advantage in this regard in that they effectively 'commodify' labour. To the extent that variation in contracts does occur, it is then to be explained in terms of employers seeking to privilege their managerial and supervisory staffs as a means of buying their loyalty in the process of exploitation or to create conflicts of interest among employees as part of a larger strategy of 'divide and rule'. Organizational and transaction-cost economists have, however, been critical of such Marxist interpretations on both theoretical and empiri-cal grounds. The main counterclaim that they have advanced is that, rather than being seen as expressions of power and means of exploitation, most fea-tures of employment contracts are better understood in terms of efficiency: that is, as serving not only to ensure the viability of the enterprise within a competitive market context but further to increase the *total value* of the con-tract, to the benefit of all parties involved (see e.g. Milgrom and Roberts 1992: ch. 10; Williamson 1985: 206–11; 1994).

In what follows I aim to take up an intermediate position that avoids what I would see as ideologically induced weaknesses in the more extreme versions of both the 'exploitation' and 'efficiency' arguments.[6] I treat employment

---

[5] This statement may appear less surprising if certain common sources are recognized, most notably Barnard (1938) and Simon (1946/1961), and also a similar starting point in the cri-tique of the conceptualization of work, the firm, and employment relations within orthodox neoclassical economics.

[6] In particular, I seek to avoid, on the one hand, the self-indulgence of those Marxists who assume that in some future world the abolition of capitalist institutions will make possible

contracts primarily from the standpoint of employers, with whom the *initiative* in their design and implementation does at all events lie. I first set out what would appear to be certain general problems of the employment contract as such, and I then try to show how the different forms that this contract may take can be understood primarily as employers' responses to the more particular ways in which these problems arise in the case of employees involved in different kinds of work. I make the assumption that in this regard the 'central tendency' is for employers to act as rationally as they are able towards the goal of maintaining the viability and success of their organizations within the context of whatever constraints they may face. This may then lead them, depending on the specific circumstances that obtain, to view their contractual relations with employees in *either* zero-sum *or* positive-sum terms—just as employees may take a similarly varying view of their contractual relations with employers. In other words, I see no reason to treat the interests of employers and employees as being 'fundamentally' either in harmony or in conflict.[7]

General Problems of the Employment Contract

It is has for long been recognized by economists and sociologists alike that the employment contract has distinctive features (see e.g. Commons 1924; Simon 1951; Baldamus 1961). These stem basically from the fact that the labour that is bought by employers on the labour market cannot be physically separated from the individual persons who sell it. What is in effect bought and sold through the employment contract is not a commodity, or at least not in the sense of some definite, objective thing, but rather a social relationship. Employment contracts are contracts through which employees agree, in return for remuneration, to place themselves under the authority of the employer or of the employer's agents.[8] Further, though, employment

the production of 'new' men and women with preferences, orientations to work, and so on, such that present-world problems of efficiency will be entirely transcended; and, on the other hand, the Panglossian tendencies of those economists who assume that 'whatever is, is efficient' and fail to give due recognition to the conflictual or 'contested' aspects of employment relations.

[7] I do not assume, I should stress, that employers' rationality implies that they subject their contractual relations with employees to some continuous process of review and revision; only that they are ready to re-examine and modify these relations from the point of view of organizational effectiveness when prompted to do so by changing circumstances (cf. Osterman 1987; also Chapter 6 above). I also recognize that, although employers have the initiative in the design and implementation of employment contracts, they will typically act under various constraints. These are, of course, likely to include employee responses to their initiatives, whether of an individual kind or as expressed through trade unions or other representative organizations, and also whatever legislative and regulatory framework is imposed on employment relations by the state. The nature of such constraints can, however, be expected to show great variation by time and place. Thus, a focus on the actions of employers in dealing with highly generalized contractual problems would seem appropriate, given that my concern is with explaining broad probabilistic regularities in the association between forms of contract and types of work rather than the deviations from these regularities that will certainly be found.

[8] In what follows, 'employer' should be understood as also covering what is in fact the

contracts are in varying, but often substantial, degree implicit or in fact incomplete, and especially in regard to what employers may demand of employees and what in turn the obligations of employees are. Employers buy the right to tell employees what to do while at work, and minimum requirements may be formally laid down concerning, say, hours of work, working methods and procedures, and so on. But contracts rarely if ever seek to specify just how hard employees should work—what intensity of effort they should make—let alone what degree of responsibility, adaptability, or initiative they should be ready to show in their employer's interest. Such matters would indeed seem largely to defy formulation in explicit contractual terms.

From the employer's point of view, therefore, a major objective must be that not merely of *enforcing* the compliance of employees with the authority that they have in principle accepted but, further, that of *inducing* their maximum effort and cooperation in the performance of the work allocated to them. Another way of putting the matter would be to say that within the employment contract employees will always have some non-negligible amount of discretion; and that it will then be of obvious importance to employers and their agents to ensure that this discretion is as far as possible used in ways that support rather then subvert the purposes of the employing organization.

In the industrial sociology of the immediate post-war years, which had a strongly managerialist orientation, the problems arising in this regard were treated in terms of the degree of congruence prevailing between 'formal' and 'informal' organization—especially, that is, between employers' work rules and work-group values and norms. The greater the congruence that could be achieved, the higher, it was supposed, would be levels of employee 'motivation and morale'; and this goal was to be pursued through 'human-relations' policies, implemented by first-line managers and supervisors at the level of the work group—or, as critics would have it, through social-psychological manipulation.

In the economics literature previously referred to essentially the same issues are addressed, also in fact largely from the employer's standpoint, but in a different idiom. The key issue is taken to be that of how the employment contract may be most efficiently elaborated, not only in its explicit *ex ante* design, to which limitations clearly apply, but, more importantly perhaps, in its *ex post*, and possibly quite implicit, interpretation and actual day-to-day execution; or, that is, in the way in which it serves as the basis for the continuing regulation of employment relations over time.[9] At a minimum, the employer must be given protection against employee shirking or 'oppor-

---

more likely case of 'employing organization'. It should also be noted that throughout I use 'agent' only in (explicit or implicit) contradistinction to 'principal', and not as a synonym for 'actor'.

[9] The idea of 'implicit contracts' or of implicit provisions in contracts has taken on particular importance in the economics literature. Ehrenberg and Smith (1991: 409) refer in this connection to 'a set of shared, informal understandings about how firms and workers will respond to contingencies' and Gibbons (1997: 11) refers to 'an understanding backed by the parties' reputations instead of law'.

tunism'; but it is a further requirement that employee interests should as far as possible be aligned with those of the employer or, in other words, that appropriate incentive structures should be set in place. And at the same time transaction costs have to be taken into account: that is, the arrangements and procedures involved in actually implementing the contract must be cost-effective as compared with available alternatives.

The rational action theory that informs this latter approach does, I believe, endow it with greater intellectual coherence than that achieved by early industrial sociology. However, for my present purposes its most immediate attraction is that it leads naturally to recognition of the fact that employment contracts will need to take on different forms in relation to the different kinds of work task and work role that employees are engaged to perform.

Differentiation of the Employment Contract and Types of Work

What is to be explained here is, to repeat, the association between different occupational groupings of employees and the form of regulation of their employment that can, it appears, be empirically demonstrated on the lines indicated in Table 10.1. To this end, it is necessary to consider types of work analytically, and in a more abstract yet focused way than could be achieved by reliance on occupational designations themselves. The organizational and transaction-cost economics on which I draw would suggest two main dimensions in terms of which potential problems—or sources of 'contractual hazard'—from the employer's point of view can be identified (cf. Weakliem 1989):

   (i) the degree of difficulty involved in monitoring the work performed by employees: that is, the degree of difficulty involved both in measuring its quantity and also in observing and controlling its quality; and

  (ii) the degree of specificity of the human assets or human capital—skills, expertise, knowledge—used by employees in performing their work: that is, the degree to which productive value would be lost if these assets were to be transferred to some other employment.

In pursuing the explanatory task in hand, I shall therefore find it helpful to refer to the two-dimensional space described in Fig. 10.1. Work that falls into the lower-left quadrant of Fig. 10.1 is that which may be expected to give rise to fewest hazards for employers as regards the employment contract. The absence of serious work monitoring problems means that some kind of 'variable-pay' system can operate or, in other words, employees can be remunerated in direct relation to their productivity. And the absence of serious asset specificity problems means that no understandings need be entered into about the long-term continuation of the contract. No such understandings are required in order to provide employees with an incentive to acquire skills, etc., of specific value in their present employment and then to retain them in this employment. Under these conditions, the employment contract can

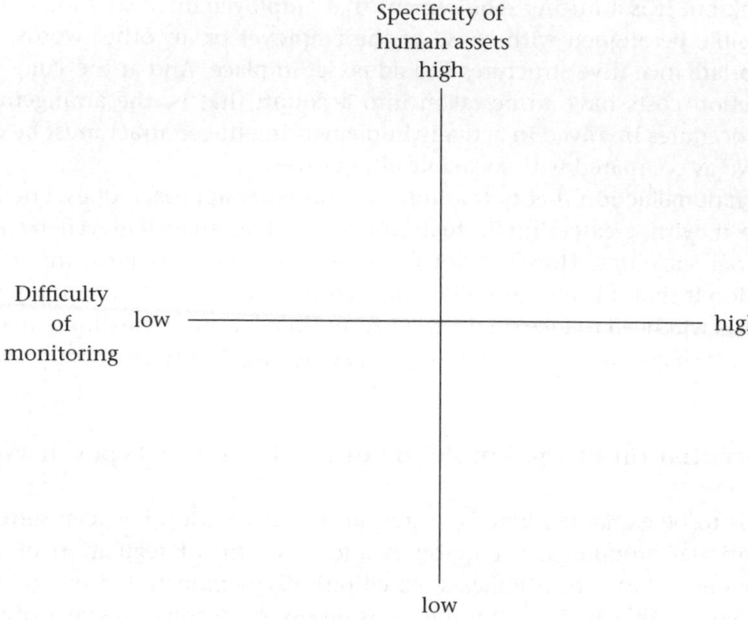

Specificity of
human assets
high

Difficulty
of   low ——————————————|—————————————— high
monitoring

low

FIG. 10.1. Dimensions of work as sources of contractual hazard

simply provide for discrete, short-term exchanges of money for effort, in the way characteristic of the labour contract as earlier described, and thus come in fact as close as is possible to a simple spot contract—albeit perhaps of a recurrent kind—for the purchase of a quantity of a commodity (cf. Kay 1993: ch. 4).

However, the question does then at once arise of why it is that, despite the evident advantages of the labour contract to employers, the occupational range of its application would appear, as is indicated in Table 10.1, to be rather restricted: that is, in its pure form to nonskilled manual occupations and, somewhat modified, to skilled manual and lower-grade nonmanual occupations. What will here be argued is that this limitation is to be explained in terms of various *concomitant* features of the kind of work in regard to which a labour contract proves viable.

The occupational restriction of the labour contract

Difficulties in measuring the quantity of work done by employees will be least, and a variable pay system will thus be most easily implemented, where measurement can be based on actual *output*. In this case, a direct link between work and pay can be established through piece rates of some kind. However, work that can be thus measured and remunerated is likely to have various other characteristics. To begin with, the measurement of work by output implies output that is of a specific, well-defined kind, and efficient payment by output implies a production process that is relatively simple: first, so that output can be clearly attributed to particular individuals or at most to small work groups and, secondly, so that the employer—as well as employees—can have reliable knowledge of how quickly the work can be done and can therefore set an appropriate rate of pay.[10] Moreover, since piece rates give an inducement to workers to concentrate on quantity of work at the expense of quality, it is important, from the employer's point of view, that the quality of the product as well as its quantity is easy to monitor—that is, to observe and assess—and likewise such other aspects of work quality as the use of tools, equipment, and raw materials (cf. Milgrom and Roberts 1992: 394–5). It could then be said that the kind of work with which piece rates are most likely to be associated is work in which workers, acting individually or in small groups, undertake physical (rather than mental) operations that lead in a fairly transparent way to discrete material (rather than symbolic) results. Typical piece-rate workers are in fact fruit and vegetable pickers, various kinds of loaders, fillers, and packers, and machinists in batch-production manufacturing industry.

It may also be possible for work to be more or less adequately measured by *input* in the sense of time spent at work, and thus for a variable pay system to operate through time rates, calculated, say, on an hourly or daily basis. Once more, though, for this to be the case—in effect, for time worked to be informative about output—restrictions would seem to apply to the nature of the work involved. If under piece rates the employer's main monitoring problem is that of quality, under time rates it becomes that of assessing and maintaining the level of worker effort. This problem will be least severe, and time rates thus most attractive to employers, where workers have in fact only limited autonomy in regard to their pace of work: where, for example, this is largely determined by technology, as in assembly-line or continuous-process production, or by the flow of customers or clients, as in the case, say, of checkout operators, ticket-sellers, or counter staff. Otherwise, it will be important that worker effort should be easily observable, and thus open to control through supervision; and this would then again tend to imply work activity

---

[10] If only workers have such knowledge, employers are exposed to opportunism. Workers may shirk in order to conceal this knowledge from their employer and in this way seek to get a higher rate of pay than they would if the employer were better informed (cf. Gibbons 1987, 1997). One has here a prime illustration of the similarity of concern but divergence of approach of the contemporary economics on which I draw and the industrial sociology of the 1940s and 1950s. In the latter, the restriction of output was recognized as a likely problem of piece-rate payment but was then represented as the outcome of a failure in 'communication' and 'human relations'—specifically, management had failed to build up work-group norms supportive of organizational goals. Interestingly, a yet earlier account of the phenomenon, that of Max Weber (1908), himself trained as an institutional economist, comes much closer in spirit to that of his present-day counterparts in treating the restriction of output under piece rates as in many circumstances an entirely rational strategy for workers to pursue.

with a clear physical component, even if not necessarily of a kind conventionally classified as 'manual' (cf. Fama 1991).

The payment of employees in return for discrete amounts of work done, whether by piece or time, is one defining element of the labour contract. The other is that the exchange is of a short-term nature in the sense that, while it may in fact be many times repeated, there is nothing in the contract itself, explicit or implicit, that is aimed at securing the relationship between employer and employee on a long-term basis. As earlier suggested, an employer is able to operate with such a contract where there is little to be gained in encouraging workers to invest in the acquisition of human assets specific to their present employment, and in turn little to be lost if employees should leave this employment—that is, the costs of labour turnover are slight. Here too, though, the argument may be made that, where such a situation prevails, there are likely to be further implications for the type of work that is involved.

Thus, while in principle a workforce with which no problems of human asset specificity arose could still be a skilled workforce—that is, one reliant simply on general purpose skills—it would seem empirically to be the case that, where general purpose skills are brought to particular employments, it tends to be both possible and advantageous for further, more specific skills, expertise, and knowledge to be developed around them.[11] Consequently, a situation in which employers need take no account of asset specificity in regard to their employees can be reckoned as most probably one in which employers are able to recruit the workers they require from a fairly homogeneous pool of labour, the individual members of which are substitutable for each other without serious loss of productive value on the basis simply of their physical capacities plus, perhaps, minimal literacy and numeracy.

In the light of the foregoing, then, what underlies the restriction of the occupational range of the labour contract should be more apparent. It is work with features that locate it in the lower-left quadrant of Fig. 10.1 that allows employers to resort to this form of regulation of employment. But work that is easily measured and otherwise monitored *and* that in itself offers little potential for the development of specific human capital will have other characteristics too. Its archetype can in fact be regarded as manual work of a non-skilled kind, or what might be thought of as labour in its most basic sense. It is, then, with such work that the labour contract can operate in its purest form or, in other words, that employers can take the 'commodification' of labour to its furthest possible point. Correspondingly, any extension of the labour contract beyond such work is likely to entail some departure from the

---

[11] Various authors have pointed out that general qualifications are valued by employers not only on account of the skills, expertise, and knowledge to which they directly attest but further, and perhaps primarily, as indicators of the individual's *capacity to learn*. Correspondingly, employees often report that in the course of their work they draw on their prior qualifications only to a surprisingly limited extent (see e.g. Thurow 1972; Wilensky and Lawrence 1980; Cohen and Pfeffer 1986; Bills 1988).

pure form in one direction or another. For example, where the monitoring of work is not entirely straightforward, as regards either quantity or quality, the strict principle of pay in return for discrete amounts of work done will need to be modified in some degree. Thus, a *weekly* wage with, perhaps, provision for overtime pay or time off 'in lieu' for work in excess of a given number of hours is a fairly common arrangement among more skilled manual and lower-grade nonmanual employees. And likewise such workers may be given certain privileges of seniority—such as pay guarantees or a 'first-in-last-out' under-standing in the case of redundancies—in circumstances where employers are compelled to recognize some need for the development and retention of human assets of an organization-specific kind (cf. Doeringer and Piore 1971; Weakliem 1989).

The full significance of these latter points can, however, be fully brought out only by changing perspective somewhat. Having begun by asking what accounts for the empirically observed restriction of the labour contract to manual and lower-grade nonmanual occupations, I shall next ask why it should be that, in the case of professional, administrative, and managerial occupations, this form of regulation of employment would appear to be effectively precluded and is typically replaced by what has been called the service relationship. Again, I shall seek to give an answer in terms of employ-ers' responses to the potential contractual hazards that are mapped out in Fig. 10.1 and, more specifically, as these intensify as one moves from the lower-left quadrant towards the upper right.

The rationale of the service relationship

The general problems of the employment contract, as outlined previously, are sometimes represented (e.g. Pratt and Zeckhauser 1984; Eggertsson 1990) as ones of a 'principal-agent' relationship: that is, of a relationship in which a principal (the employer) engages an agent (the employee) to act in the prin-cipal's interest in circumstances in which the principal cannot observe the agent's actions, nor share in all of the information guiding those actions. This representation may seem somewhat strained where it is possible for labour to be more or less commodified and some approximation to a spot contract is thus viable. However, it takes on special force where employees act in a pro-fessional, administrative, or managerial capacity.[12] Professionals are engaged to exercise specialized knowledge and expertise that they have obtained from a lengthy training; while administrators and managers are engaged to exercise the delegated authority of the employer. In both cases alike, there fore, the nature of the work tasks and work roles that are performed imply some asymmetry of information as between employer and employee

[12] It is in this connection of interest to note that, in the paper that in effect inaugurated transaction-cost economics, Coase (1937) draws attention to the legal distinction made in (then) current British law between an agent and a 'servant', which turns not on the absence or presence of a fixed wage or the payment of commission but rather 'on the freedom with which an agent may carry out his employment'.

and thus, for the latter, an area of autonomy and discretion into which monitoring by the employer cannot feasibly extend. Indeed, effective monitoring would here entail some kind of infinite regress. It would itself require precisely the kind of use of specialized knowledge and expertise and of delegated authority that creates the agency problem in the first place (cf. Simon 1991).

Where such difficulty in monitoring work arises, it then becomes especially important for the employer to gain the commitment of employees, which in turn implies designing and implementing a form of contract that can as far as possible ensure that their interests are, and remain, aligned with the goals of the organization as the employer would define them. In the case of profit-making organizations, one evident recourse is to link employee compensation to the economic success of the enterprise, as, for example, through stock awards or stock options or profit-related bonuses or other profit-sharing schemes. However, while these kinds of remuneration may often play a major part in the compensation of chief executive officers and other very senior personnel, they are difficult to extend at a similar level of importance throughout the staff hierarchy, and they would appear to have no very effective analogues in the case of employees in public-sector or non-profit-making bodies.[13]

Moreover, further circumstances may well obtain in which serious difficulties for any kind of performance-related pay system are created: that is, where employees are required—as professionals, administrators, and managers typically are—to carry out tasks, or roles, of a very diverse character. In such a situation, payment can scarcely be related equally to every aspect of the work that is undertaken. It will, rather, have to be linked to just one, or at most one or two, aspects—those for which performance indicators can most easily be devised being most likely to be chosen. But such arrangements hold dangers for employers. For the incentives offered will in this case serve not simply to induce greater effort on the part of employees but further to influence their *distribution* of effort, and of time and attention, *among* their different responsibilities. That is to say, those aspects of their work to which pay is in fact related will tend to be favoured at the expense of others, and to a degree that need not be optimal from the employer's point of view (cf. Holmström and Milgrom 1991). Employers may 'get what they pay for' in an all too literal sense (cf. Gibbons 1997). Moreover, given that work tasks *are* diverse, monitoring that is then specifically aimed at preventing such unintended consequences, or 'perverse effects', may well not be cost-effective, even if practical at all.

Since, therefore, in the employment of professionals, administrators, and

---

[13] Milgrom and Roberts (1992: 413) point out that, while in the late 1980s it was known that around 30% of all US firms operated profit-sharing schemes, the proportion of total employee income received through such schemes was very small, perhaps no more than 1%. Where close employee monitoring is not possible, profit-sharing and group-based bonus schemes are, of course, always likely to give rise to free-rider problems.

managers general principal-agent problems may often be compounded by the further ones posed by 'multi-task' agents, forms of employment contract in which either direct work monitoring or specific performance indicators provide the basis for pay would seem unlikely in the main to answer to employers' requirements. The alternative and generally more appropriate strategy will be for employers to seek to gain the commitment of their professional, administrative, and managerial personnel, or, in Simon's apt phrase (1991: 32), to shape their 'decision premises', through a form of contract with a quite different rationale—that is, one that relies on performance appraisal of only a broad and long-term, though perhaps comparative, kind and that then sets up, conditional upon such appraisal, the possibility of a steadily rising level of compensation throughout the course of the employee's working life. In this regard, the contract provides for compensation primarily through an annual salary that may be expected to increase both in accordance with an established scale and further, and more substantially, as the result of the employee's advancement through a career structure. Given the prospect of such an 'upward-sloping experience-earnings profile', as Lazear (1995: 39) has termed it, both effective incentives for employees *and* effective sanctions for the employer are created—and especially so if, as Lazear would argue (see also Lazear 1981), what is typically entailed is paying employees *less* than they are worth, in terms of their productivity, when they are young or at all events in the lower levels of the hierarchy and *more* than they are worth when they are older or in higher-level positions.

   On the one hand, the better employees perform (or at least are perceived to perform) in the pursuit of organizational goals, the further, and more rapidly, they will be promoted out of the levels at which they are 'underpaid' and into those at which they are 'overpaid'. On the other hand, because for most employees higher rewards will still lie ahead, and rewards that they have already in part earned through their previous underpayment, 'hasty quits' are discouraged and the threat of dismissal, as, say, in the case of manifest shirking or incompetence or of malfeasance, becomes a more potent one. Furthermore, appropriately constructed pensions schemes can also be seen as an integral part of such 'deferred-payment' contracts, encouraging employees to stay with their organizations up to the peak of the expected present value of benefits but then discouraging them from staying on too long (in the absence of a mandatory retiring age) in the phase when, relative to their productivity, they are being overpaid (Lazear 1995: 42–5).[14]

   In other words, the solution to the problem of agency, as it arises with professional, administrative, and managerial employees, is sought essentially in

---

[14] Empirical support for Lazear's theory can be found in Medoff and Abraham (1981) and Hutchens (1987). As Lazear notes (1995: 71), the upward-sloping experience-earnings profile would appear in many ways similar to an 'efficiency wage' or, as Marxists such as Wright (1997) would have it, a 'loyalty wage'. But, as Lazear also notes, a major difference is that 'deferred-payment' contracts need imply no breach of the principle of payment in accordance with marginal productivity—nor therefore involuntary unemployment; at the start of the earnings profile wages can be sufficiently low to clear markets.

the service relationship as this was described earlier. In place of any attempt at the immediate linking of performance and pay, the employment contract envisages, even if implicitly as much as explicitly, a quite diffuse exchange of service to the organization in return for compensation in which the prospective element is crucial; and, by the same token, the contract is understood as having a long-term rather than a short-term basis. The key connection that the contract aims to establish is that between employees' commitment to and effective pursuit of organizational goals and their career success and lifetime material well-being.[15]

So far in this subsection, I have concentrated on employers' contractual problems associated with work located towards the right of the horizontal dimension of Fig. 10.1: that is, those of monitoring. However, problems associated with work located towards the top of the vertical dimension are also relevant: that is, those of human asset specificity. I earlier suggested that these problems would be least demanding where employers could operate satisfactorily with workers who possessed no more than commonly available physical or cognitive capacities. In so far as a higher quality workforce is called for, the probability increases that there will be advantage to the employer in ensuring that any general purpose skills that employees bring with them are, as Williamson has put it (1985: 242), 'deepened and specialized' in the particular organizational contexts in which they are to be applied. And, where this is so, a form of contract that does nothing to help secure the employment relationship on a long-term basis will obviously be deficient: it will fail to provide incentives for employers to engage in the training, or for employees in the learning, from which they could alike benefit.

Problems of human asset specificity are not confined to professional, administrative, and managerial employees—as was indicated earlier and as will be seen further below. However, such problems may be thought to take on an importance in the case of these employees that is proportional to that of the organizational roles that they perform. That is to say, failure to provide for either the development or the retention of organization-specific skills, expertise, and knowledge on the part of professionals, administrators, and managers is likely to be especially damaging. Here again, then, the rationale of the service relationship, with its implication of continuing employment, is apparent. Through such a relationship, in contrast to one in which renewal

---

[15] The above differs from my earlier discussion of the service relationship (Goldthorpe 1982) chiefly in that it dispenses with the idea of 'trust' as being central to this relationship. I found my own increasing doubts in this regard expressed in a more cogent way than I was able to formulate myself in Williamson's critique (1996: ch. 10) of the concept of trust as applied in recent sociological work (e.g. Gambetta 1988; Coleman 1990). The gist of Williamson's argument (1996: 256) is that 'it is redundant at best and can be misleading to use the term "trust" to describe commercial exchange for which cost-effective safeguards have been devised in support of more efficient exchange. Calculative trust is a contradiction in terms.'

is entirely contingent, employers can more securely embark on costly training and 'planned-experience' programmes aimed at increasing employees'
organization-specific abilities, and employees can in turn more securely
devote the time and effort necessary to acquire such abilities. In other words,
it becomes possible for both the costs of and the returns on investments of
this kind to be shared between employers and employees (Milgrom and
Roberts 1992: 363; Lazear 1995: 74). The advantage of the long-term character of the service relationship as the basis of a solution to agency problems—
that is, via the rising worklife compensation curve—is therefore reinforced in
that at the same time the basis for a solution to asset specificity problems is
also provided.[16]

Mixed forms

Finally in this section some explanation should be attempted of the prevalence within certain occupational groupings—as indicated in Table 10.1—of
mixed forms of the employment contract: that is, of forms that, in various
ways, combine elements of both the labour contract and the service
relationship.

Referring back once more to Fig. 10.1, a tendency may be supposed, in the
light of the discussion so far, for empirical instances to be concentrated on
the lower-left to upper-right diagonal: or, in other words, for there to be some
correlation between the severity of the monitoring problems and of the
human asset specificity problems to which different kinds of work give rise.
None the less, instances lying off this diagonal can certainly be envisaged,
and the suggestion I would advance is that it is in terms of work thus located

---

[16] In this connection, it is of some interest to note that Savage and his associates (Savage
et al. 1992; Savage and Butler 1995) have argued, in critique of the idea of a 'service class',
that a line of class demarcation should be seen as falling between professionals, on the one
hand, and administrators and managers, on the other. This is on account of the different
kinds of asset that they typically possess—in the case of the former, *cultural* assets, and of
the latter, *organizational* assets. Professionals are then taken to be advantaged over administrators and managers in that cultural assets are less specific than organizational assets and
therefore more 'storable': that is, more readily accumulated in transferable form. This analysis can be related to, and may perhaps enhance, that which I have made in suggesting that
agency problems may be more acute than asset specificity problems among some kinds of
professional—such as, say, those employed in less senior positions in health, education, and
other state welfare services; while the converse situation may apply with some lower-level
administrators and managers whose decision-making role is more local than strategic. But
what, from the position I adopt, must tell against the claim that different class positions are
thus created is the fact that the service relationship would appear an appropriate response
to the contractual hazards that arise in either eventuality, even if certain features of this relationship are more fully expressed in some instances than in others. Moreover, Savage and
his colleagues seem to miss the key insight of transaction-cost economics that asset specificity gives rise to *bilateral* dependency. Thus, in so far as the assets that administrators and
managers acquire are of an organizationally specific kind, they may indeed be lost or much
diminished if these employees lose their jobs; but, at the same time, there will be costs to
employers who fail to retain employees with such assets. I have developed elsewhere
(Goldthorpe 1995a) a more general critique of the 'assets theory' of the differentiation of the
service class (see also Li 1997).

that the occupational distribution of mixed forms of the employment contract is to be explained. Work falling in the lower-right quadrant of Fig. 10.1—
that is, work that confronts employers with real difficulties of monitoring
but not of asset specificity—could be expected to lead to a form of contract
in which features entailing some departure from the exchange of discrete
amounts of money and effort characteristic of the labour contract would be
more apparent than ones directed towards furthering a long-term relationship. And, conversely, work falling in the upper-left quadrant, where asset
specificity problems are serious but not monitoring problems, could be
expected to lead to a form of contract in which a fairly specific money-for-
effort exchange is preserved but some understanding of the long-term nature
of the contract is at least implied.

Some empirical support for this argument can in fact be provided, and
indeed for a rather more precise version of it: namely, one that would asso-
ciate the first of the two situations outlined above primarily with routine nonmanual occupations in administration and commerce that exist, so to speak,
on the fringes of bureaucratic structures, and the second situation with
manual supervisory and lower-grade technical occupations.[17] Thus, routine
nonmanual employees—clerical workers, secretaries, and so on—would
appear to enjoy fixed salaries and also relatively relaxed or flexible time-
keeping arrangements almost to the same extent as the professionals, administrators, and managers with whom they typically work in ancillary roles,
although for the most part deploying only rather standardized skills (cf. Fama
1991). However, they are not to the same extent involved in career structures
within their employing organizations that would hold out the prospect of
steadily increasing rewards over the entire course of their working lives.[18]
Conversely, supervisors of manual workers and lower-grade technicians tend
to be paid weekly, with overtime pay and other adjustments being based on
the monitoring of hours worked, in much the same way as many of the rank-
and-file employees over whom they exercise direction and control. But their
distinctive value to their organizations is more often recognized through
agreements or understandings on employment and income security and also
perhaps through opportunities to progress up 'job ladders' that are based primarily on seniority—that is, in the manner provided for by the institutions

[17] Some findings of the validation exercises referred to in the text above and n. 2 point to
such a conclusion, as also do unpublished data on employment relations at the level of basic
ONS occupational groups resulting from the work of the ESRC committee described in n. 2,
and kindly made available to me by Karen O'Reilly.

[18] From this same point of view (as has been pointed out to me by Jerker Denrell), it is
then not surprising that secretarial and similar workers should often be engaged on a temporary basis via employment agencies. A further occupational group that is of interest in this
connection is that of sales personnel. With these employees, payment on the basis of a fixed
salary *plus* commission is often found. The rationale here would appear to be that while quantity of output, that is, sales made, can rather easily be measured, thus allowing piece-rate
payment, problems of monitoring 'quality' do also arise, notably as regards maintaining the
firm's reputation with its customers. I would, therefore, hypothesize that it is with the
employees of firms having least to lose in this respect—for example, firms selling double-
glazing or door and window frames—that the largest commission element will occur.

of the classic 'firm-internal' labour market (Doeringer and Piore 1971; Oster-man 1987).[19]

Taking this argument together with those previously advanced in this section of the chapter, it is then possible to give an overall representation of how the analytical dimensions of Fig. 10.1 are seen to relate to the empirical regularities implied in Table 10.1: that is, regularities in the association between different occupational groupings of employees and the form of regulation of their employment. This is done in Fig. 10.2. On the understanding that the regularities in question are to be regarded as only probabilistic, and that exceptions to them will thus certainly be found, this latter figure can stand as a summary of the explanation that is here offered of how they are in fact generated and sustained through employers' responses to the problems of contractual regulation that arise from the engagement of workers to undertake differing kinds of work.

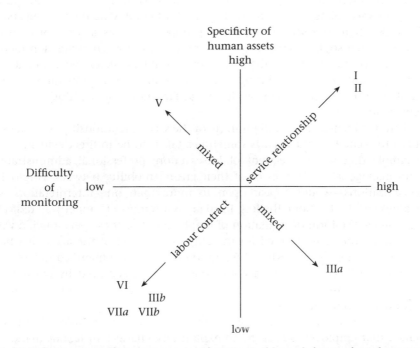

FIG. 10.2. Dimensions of work as sources of contractual hazard, forms of employment contract, and location of employee classes of the schema

[19] It should, however, be noted that the job ladders in question are typically much shorter than those available to professional, administrative, and managerial staff. Cf. the distinction made by Osterman (1987) between the 'industrial' and 'salaried' forms of internal labour markets.

New Employer Strategies and the Future of the Service Relationship

One objection that might be raised against the foregoing analysis—and to which a response should at least be outlined—is that it seeks to explain in very general theoretical terms a pattern of differentiation in employment contracts that could well prove specific to a particular historical era. Several authors have indeed already broached the question of the continuing viability of the service relationship under conditions of rapid change in technological and market conditions and of intensifying global competition that impose ever greater requirements of organizational 'flexibility' (e.g. Halford and Savage 1995); and others have gone further in maintaining that under these conditions the service relationship is actually being eroded, and in the public as well as the private sector as competitive tendering and other forms of 'market discipline' are increasingly imposed (e.g. Brown 1995). There is constant pressure, it is argued, to 'downsize' or 'de-layer' management structures, to buy in professional services rather than to provide them in-house, to engage staff on fixed-term contracts, and to introduce performance-related pay systems at all levels of employment. From this point of view, then, the service relationship appears not as a form of contract with a rather sophisticated underlying rationale but as an expression merely of a conventional status distinction that could be sustained as an aspect of 'organizational slack' during the long boom of the post-war years but that is now being swept aside in a far more demanding economic environment.[20]

Direct evidence of the undermining of the service relationship is in fact still hard to come by; and what is sometimes taken to be indirect evidence—for example, that of more frequent job losses among professional, administrative, and managerial employees or of their greater mobility between employing organizations—would appear open to more than one interpretation (see Gallie *et al.* 1998). None the less, in so far as attempts *are* under way radically to reshape the form of regulation of employment of these personnel, a valuable opportunity is afforded for the empirical testing of the account I have offered of the logic of the differentiation of employment contracts; and further clarification of this account may then be achieved by considering what would, from the point of view of empirical evaluation, have to be regarded as centrally at issue.

To begin with, it is entirely consistent with the general position that I have taken that employers *should try* to exploit any changes in labour market or

---

[20] A somewhat related argument is that advanced by Sørensen (1999; cf. also 1994, 1996) to the effect that, under competitive pressures, employers will seek to reduce problems of human asset specificity by the redesigning of jobs to allow them as far as possible to be carried out on the basis of general purpose skills. Sørensen sees the 'composite rents' to which asset specificity gives rise as a particular problem for employers, since the division of these rents can be settled, in Alfred Marshall's words, only by 'higgling and bargaining'—through which employers have no guarantee that they will get what they would regard as their fair share.

other economic conditions that might enable them to modify contracts of employment, explicitly or implicitly, in ways that would be to their advantage or, more specifically, that would reduce their contractual hazard. And it is further consistent that such modifications should then, all else being equal, be ones leading away from the service relationship and towards the discrete and short-term exchange of the labour contract; or, in other words, away from forms of the regulation of employment that presuppose a diffuse and continuing exchange and towards ones in which labour is to a greater degree commodified. As Breen (1997a) has observed, one can in this respect think of employers as seeking to transfer risk from themselves to their employees: that is, to free themselves from the inflexibility entailed by the 'quasi-generalized reciprocity' of the service relationship and to secure instead an 'asymmetric commitment' or in effect an *option* on the supply of labour, which they can then decline, if necessary, in order to avoid 'downside' risk while preserving the possibility of profiting from 'upside' risk. Evidence simply of employers being alert to the possibility of revising forms of contract in ways they would see as being in their interests is not, therefore, in itself, of any great consequence. What matters is how far employers are thus led actually to abandon the service relationship in cases where it had previously applied.

In this connection, it has also to be recognized that some of the strategies that employers may pursue in search of greater flexibility need have little or no impact on the service relationship *per se*, and indeed may even help to make this relationship *more* viable. Thus, by downsizing and de-layering management structures and also by buying in professional services, employers can hope to reduce the proportion of their total workforce to whom the service relationship is extended, and in turn the degree to which they are involved in 'quasi-generalized reciprocity'. Likewise, by creating greater flexibility in the employment of *other* grades of worker—as, say, by modifying features of internal labour markets for skilled manual workers (cf. Capelli 1995)—they may be better able to sustain the service relationship in the case of those employees for whom they would see it as specifically appropriate. In some influential models of the 'flexible firm' (e.g. J. Atkinson 1985) the emphasis is in fact on the *divergence* between the employment relations that apply with the 'core' and with the 'peripheral' workforce.[21]

What, therefore, emerges as the key question is that of how far in prevailing economic circumstances, and on what basis, employers do come to regard the service relationship itself as expressing a form of contract that they should aim in general to terminate rather than to preserve. And in so far as this relationship is in fact undermined in the case of professional, administrative, and managerial staff, as, say, through the introduction of short-term contracts or

---

[21] De-layering could perhaps make the service relationship more difficult to implement in that promotion opportunities would be reduced; but it would still be possible to maintain the upward-sloping earnings-experience profile by allowing incremental salary scales or appraisal-related pay increases to operate *within* given hierarchical levels (cf. Lazear 1995: 79–80).

performance-related pay, it will in turn be important to know just how employers then seek to handle those problems of work monitoring and of human asset specificity out of which, I have argued, the rationale of the service relationship and of its occupational range initially arise.

Breen, for example, has pointed out (1997a) that, despite employers' concern to offload risk within the employment contract onto their employees, there are still good grounds for supposing that the service relationship will prove durable since there is no other obvious solution to the agency problem deriving primarily from asymmetric information. Professionals, administrators, and managers are employees in regard to whom it is generally less important that the employment contract should provide for flexibility (from the employer's point of view) than that it should ensure that the employee has strong incentives to show commitment to organizational goals (see also Gallie *et al*. 1998: 312–13). And to this I would add that, even if improved techniques of monitoring may in some instances be capable of reducing agency problems (Halford and Savage 1995: 129), attempts at basing pay on performance will still threaten to give rise to 'perverse effects' in the way earlier noted where employees are engaged in work tasks of a multi-faceted kind.[22] In this respect, the requirements of contractual flexibility would seem to come into direct conflict with those of 'functional' flexibility (J. Atkinson 1985), which in fact lead to demands on employees to be ready to take on an ever-wider range of tasks and responsibilities.

What is perhaps more plausible than the idea of the general abandonment of the service relationship is the suggestion that, at least with some employee groupings, the 'deal' that it comprises may be reformulated: in particular, so that what the employee is offered, in return for commitment and a readiness to develop organization-specific assets, is an understanding not on continuity of employment but rather on continuity of *employability*. In this case, it falls to the employer to provide employees with training and experience that, as well as enhancing their organization-specific skills, expertise, and knowledge, will also equip them for future career progression in the external labour market. However, it is still far from clear that even this modification of the service relationship would necessarily be to the employer's advantage. The evident risk that the employer incurs is that, if investment is made in the development of human assets that are *not* organization specific and if the employees who benefit from this investment are not then retained, the returns on the investment will largely be lost: they will be divided between the employees and their *subsequent* employers. Again, then, the force of the original rationale of the service relationship is brought out.

In sum, for a compelling argument to be advanced that the service relationship is in general decline, two things would seem to be required: first, direct evidence—which, to repeat, is so far lacking—that employment con-

---

[22] As Holmström and Milgrom (1991) stress, the ultimate source of difficulty here lies in the diversity of tasks performed and in finding a way of appropriately relating pay to all of them, rather than in work monitoring and measurement *per se*.

tracts expressing this relationship are indeed being discontinued across the range of employee groupings for which they were previously typical; and, secondly, evidence—the need for which seems not even to have been appreciated—that such a change can be regarded as permanent, rather than being, say, a response merely to short-term economic exigencies or to the current vogue among management consultants, *because* the logic that previously underlay the service relationship has now ceased to apply or has in some way been transcended.[23] The analysis that I have earlier presented obviously leads me to the view that evidence of the latter kind at least will not be readily forthcoming.

In this chapter I have started from an empirical regularity that has emerged from attempts to assess the criterion validity of the class schema that colleagues and I have developed as a research instrument. At least for the British case, a pattern of association has been established, among employees, between their broad occupational grouping and the form of regulation of their employment. I have then suggested, drawing chiefly on theoretical ideas developed in both more and less orthodox branches of modern economics, how this regularity might be explained at the level of social action: that is, in terms of employers' rationally intelligible responses to the different problems that they face in devising and implementing employment contracts for workers engaged in different types of work—in particular, problems of work monitoring and of human asset specificity. I have also indicated how I believe that attempts at testing the explanation offered, within the contemporary economic context, might best be focused. To end with, I make two observations concerning what is and what is not implied by the central argument of the chapter for the more general understanding of the stratification of modern societies—on the assumption, of course, that the argument is basically sound. Since this assumption is, for the present at least, obviously open to challenge, the remarks will be brief, although they relate to large questions.

First, if the analysis I have presented is valid, it must follow that modern societies, at least in so far as they retain capitalist market economies of some kind, will have a relatively complex class structure as one of their concomitant and abiding features. In addition to the differentiation of employers, the self-employed and employees, the latter will themselves be differentiated in terms of the employment relations in which they are involved as a result of a highly generalized 'situational logic' that applies, and that will have its effects, across a wide range of institutional and cultural contexts. The further implication then is that, although such societies may well show variation in the historical evolution of their class structures—that is, in the rates of growth or decline of different classes and thus in their proportionate sizes—they will at the same time be characterized by a similar pattern of class-related social

---

[23] It might be added here that satisfactory evidence of the kind in question could not be derived merely from *ad hoc* case studies. Research based on representative samples both of employing organizations and of their employees would seem essential (see further Kalleberg 1990).

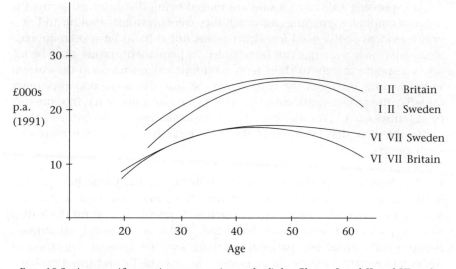

FIG. 10.3. Age-specific earnings curves (smoothed) for Classes I and II and VI and
VII, Britain and Sweden, men in full-time employment
Sources: Britain: *New Earnings Survey* (1992); Sweden: Level of Living Survey, 1990
(unpublished data).

inequalities. The form of these inequalities is likely to be no less complex than
the structure of class relations from which it derives, and therefore not capable
of adequate representation in any one-dimensional fashion. None the less, it
may still be said that, in so far as employees are involved in a service relationship rather than a labour contract, they will be advantaged not only (in
most cases) in their general level of income from employment but further in
that their incomes will be less subject to interruption or short-term fluctuation and will tend to follow a rising curve over the larger part of their
working lives.[24]

Secondly, though, it has to be recognized that the analysis advanced carries
no particular implications for the actual *degree* of inequality in rewards from

[24] It is in the case of intermediate classes that the problems of any one-dimensional ordering become most apparent. For example, while employees in manual supervisory and technical positions may have higher average earnings than employees in routine nonmanual
work, their earnings are likely to show more short-term variation; small employers and self-
employed workers are generally exposed to more insecurity than employees but have better
chances of accumulating capital, and so on. It has sometimes been seen as a disadvantage of
the class schema that my colleagues and I have developed that its categories cannot be fully
ordered in any unambiguous way. However, studies of its construct validity have shown its
capacity to reveal *both* marked class differences in regard to political partisanship, educational
choice, health, etc., as between the service class or salariat (Classes I and II) and the working
class (Classes VI and VII) *and* at the same time more subtle but still intelligible differences in
these respects involving the intermediate classes (Classes III, IV, and V) of a kind that would
often have been obscured by one-dimensional measures of inequality such as synthetic 'socio-
economic status' scales.

work (let alone in living standards more generally) that will be found among the members of different classes. There is indeed evidence to suggest that in this respect some significant cross-national variation can coexist with essentially the same pattern of class differentiation. An illustrative example is given in Fig. 10.3. From this it can be seen that in both Britain and Sweden age-specific earnings curves for (full-time male) employees in service-class and working-class positions show the same characteristic shapes: for the former, rising strongly up to around age 50—that is, revealing the expected 'upwards sloping profile'; for the latter, flattening out after age 30. However, at all ages, the gap between the two curves is narrower in the Swedish case than in the British.

An adequate explanation of this latter kind of finding would then need to be pursued on quite different lines from those that I have followed in the analyses above. Rather than being of a highly generalized character, such an explanation would have to give serious consideration to the effects of nationally specific features of, for example, industrial structure, trade union organization, collective bargaining institutions, and public policy, and might thus in the end take on far more of a historical than a sociological style (cf. Chapters 2 and 3). As will be seen in the chapter that follows, such a distinction between kinds of *explananda* and appropriate styles of explanation is of direct relevance when the attempt is made to account for further notable regularities—and deviations—that are by now fairly well established in the degree to which the class structures of modern societies display openness or fluidity: or, that is, in the degree to which individuals of differing class origins have equal chances of experiencing social mobility or immobility within these structures.

11

Outline of a Theory of Social Mobility

IT WOULD be widely recognized among sociologists that the field of social mobility research is that in which quantitative techniques of data collection and, especially, of data analysis have reached their highest levels of sophistication. However, such recognition could not be taken to imply approval. A series of articles by sociologists both within and outside the field could be cited in which it is charged that the concern with technique has become excessive and has had seriously detrimental consequences in at least two respects (for a recent example, see Miller 1998). On the one hand, it is held, the problems that are pursued by mobility researchers are to an undue degree chosen in the light of technique—that is, because they appear readily treatable via some favoured procedure; while, on the other hand, the preoccupation with quantitative analysis and the results that it produces has led to a crude empiricism and to an avoidance, or at least a disregard, of central theoretical issues.

As will be apparent from what I have written elsewhere (see especially Chapter 5), I can have some sympathy with this latter claim. Sociologists engaging in the quantitative analysis of social mobility, or indeed of other macrosocial phenomena, have, I believe, often shown an insufficient appreciation of the importance of theory; and, in particular, in failing to see that such analysis, no matter how sophisticated it may be, cannot itself substitute for theory in providing explanations of the empirical findings that it produces. At the same time, though, I would regard the former claim—that the range of problems treated in mobility research is unduly restricted by technical considerations—as being mistaken and indeed as betraying a lack of understanding of what has happened in the field. It is not in fact difficult to show how successive technical advances have permitted the more successful treatment of problems *that for long antedated them*. And, further, even if quantitatively oriented mobility researchers have neglected the need for their work

This chapter has not been published previously. In writing it, I have drawn on many discussions over the years with Robert Erikson, and I may well have taken over a number of ideas that were initially his. He also commented helpfully on an earlier draft of the essay, as did Richard Breen, Dominique Goux, Brendan Halpin, Gordon Marshall, Eric Maurin, Colin Mills, Walter Müller, and Aage Sørensen.

to be complemented by appropriate theory, this does not mean that the results of their analyses have been without theoretical significance. To the contrary, I would maintain, these results have led to the theoretical problems that arise within the field becoming defined with increasing clarity. In other words, in consequence of technically driven advances in mobility research over the last twenty years or so, it has become far more apparent than before just what a theory of social mobility should aim to do—or just what it is that such a theory should, and should not, seek to explain.

The major illustration of this argument is that provided by the application, from the 1970s onwards, of loglinear modelling to the analysis of standard mobility tables. Mobility researchers had from the first realized that where, as is virtually always the case, the marginal distributions of such tables—that is, those defining the 'origins' and 'destinations' of possible mobility traject-ories—were not identical, some amount of mobility would for this reason alone necessarily be displayed: it would not be arithmetically possible for all cases in the table to fall on the main diagonal. An issue that then came to attract much attention was that of how this 'structural' (or 'forced') mobility might be differentiated from that which could be thought of as occurring independently of any marginal discrepancies, in the form of mutually off-setting instances of 'exchange' (or 'circulation') mobility. The efforts made to resolve this matter were in one way or another based on an accounting iden-tity of the form:

$$\text{total mobility} - \text{structural mobility} \equiv \text{exchange mobility}$$

However, this approach did not lead to any very satisfactory outcome, pri-marily because it entailed an attempt at partitioning total mobility into two notional components that could actually be identified only at the supra-individual, or macrosocial, level, whereas the mobility table itself was a record of individual cases. Not until the introduction of loglinear modelling was the difficulty overcome—although not, it should be said, by the automatic appli-cation of this technique but rather by a new conceptualization that it prompted (Hauser *et al.* 1975; Goldthorpe *et al.* 1978). Instead of distin-guishing between structural and exchange mobility as two supposedly differ-ent components of total mobility, analysts using loglinear models were led to distinguish between *absolute* and *relative* mobility rates. The former were the total rates and inflow and outflow rates that could be derived from the stan-dard table by straightforward percentaging, while the latter were expressed by the odds ratios that defined the pattern of (net) association of origins and des-tinations within the table, and that in fact constitute the basic elements of loglinear models. Thus, in place of the identity given above, it became pos-sible to think of a set of relative rates in the form of odds ratios, when embod-ied within given marginal distributions, as then implying a set of absolute rates:

$$\text{marginal distributions, relative rates} \Rightarrow \text{absolute rates}$$

By means of loglinear modelling, therefore, mobility researchers were able to analyse mobility tables in a far more coherent way than hitherto. Specifically, they could separate out the impact on absolute rates, or on changes or differences in absolute rates, of marginal distributions or 'structural effects', on the one hand, and of relative rates or 'fluidity effects', on the other. Furthermore, and of chief importance for present purposes, the results to which such analyses gave rise turned out to be empirically rather surprising and at the same time theoretically highly consequential. This was especially so where *intergenerational* mobility was studied within a *class structural* context: that is, where individuals' class positions in adult life were compared with the class positions of their families of origin.[1] What was, in essence, revealed was that across modern societies absolute rates and patterns of intergenerational class mobility show considerable variation, both over time within a given society and from one society to another; but, further, that this variation results to an overwhelming extent from structural rather than from fluidity effects: that is, from differences in the ways in which class structures have evolved rather than from differences in 'underlying' relative rates.

In the light of these results, it was then first of all apparent that, if variation in absolute mobility rates and patterns was to be explained, this would have to be primarily by reference to factors that were exogenous rather than endogenous to processes of class stratification themselves: that is, to factors that determine the 'shapes' of class structures, in the sense of the proportionate sizes and the rates of growth or decline of different classes, rather than to factors that determine the propensities of individuals actually to retain or to change their positions within these structures. Moreover, it took little further enquiry to show that such exogenous factors were diverse—demographic, economic, political—and that they could, and did, interact in the histories of particular nations in many different ways (see e.g. Erikson and Goldthorpe 1992*a*: esp. ch. 6; Miles and Vincent 1993). It could, therefore, be understood why attempts that had previously been made to develop theory in this regard, as, say, by seeking to link variation in absolute rates to levels of economic development or 'modernization' or to types of political regime (e.g. Lipset and Zetterberg 1956; Fox and Miller 1965, 1966), had not fared well against empirical testing. And in turn most mobility researchers came to accept the view, implicitly if not explicitly, that variation in absolute rates cannot in fact usefully be regarded as systematic, and that explanations of such variation, whether over time or cross–nationally, will need to be provided far more in specific historical, than in general theoretical terms.

---

[1] Two long-standing traditions are evident in social mobility research: one in which mobility is studied in the context of a social hierarchy—of prestige, social status, 'socioeconomic', status, etc.—and one in which it is studied in the context of a class structure. Since the 1980s a revival of the class structural perspective has occurred (see further Goldthorpe 1985) and versions of the class schema referred to in the preceding chapter have become widely used as a basis for the construction of mobility tables. The findings of mobility research subsequently discussed in the text are, in my view, shown up more clearly and in greater detail in the class structural perspective, but they are still apparent enough in the former.

However, if, in this regard, the opportunity for developing theory would seem limited, the finding that emerges as the complement to that of the importance of structural effects in accounting for differences in absolute mobility rates—i.e. the finding of the very minor part that is played by fluidity effects or relative rates—does raise a major theoretical challenge; and, one may add, in direct contradiction to the suggestion of critics that the pursuit of technical innovation in mobility research has proved intellectually narrowing.[2] For what is, of course, implied by this further finding is that across modern societies, in all their historically created diversity, relative rates or chances of intergenerational class mobility, or what have become known as 'endogenous mobility regimes', display a substantial degree of stability or of *in*variance, both temporally and spatially. Here, in other words, one can identify a social regularity, or in effect a series of such regularities, that are empirically well established and yet of an entirely opaque kind: that is to say, no explanation of them is readily apparent. It is, therefore, difficult *qua* sociologist to avoid the question of how in fact it comes about that these regularities are created and sustained. And it is, moreover, clear that the kind of explanation that will here be required, rather than being one that is highly sensitive to context, will in the very nature of the case need to be to a significant extent context independent or, in other words, will need to be grounded in a theory of some generality.

My chief concern in this chapter is then to provide at all events a sketch of such a theory. First, though, in the section that follows, I indicate the problems that the regularities revealed in relative rates have created for the main pre-existing theory of mobility processes that, in some quarters, still retains a degree of support. Although this theory is, in my view, now invalidated and I aim to supersede it, I would none the less regard it as being a serious and, at least at the time of its first formulation, a by no means implausible one. As will be seen, I often find it helpful to develop my own theory in counterpoint to it.

Relative Rates and the Functionalist Theory of Mobility Processes

To repeat, the degree of stability or invariance in relative rates of intergenerational class mobility that is demonstrated in recent empirical research has two main aspects.

First of all, evidence of such stability emerges most strongly from studies

---

[2] Although the loglinear modelling of mobility tables is the most obvious case to take in order to make this point, it is by no means the only one available. Thus, the application of techniques of event history analysis has greatly advanced the study of intragenerational or worklife mobility and has raised many new theoretical issues, especially regarding the causation of such mobility (see esp. Blossfeld and Rohwer 1995a). Or, again, techniques of reformulating loglinear models of mobility tables as multinomial logit models for individual-level data (Breen 1994) have led to empirical analyses that have significantly moved forward the debate on meritocratic selection, or 'achievement' versus 'ascription' in mobility processes.

of mobility trends made within particular national societies. Whatever the basis of such studies—that is, whether they rely on quasi-cohort analyses or the repeated sampling of national populations—the recurrent finding is that relative mobility rates either remain essentially unaltered over decades, or change in only a very slow and usually rather uncertain fashion.[3] If for any nation trends in absolute rates were to be estimated from a statistical model that embodied entirely constant relative rates within the given marginal distributions of successive mobility tables, then, typically, the rates thus arrived at would, it seems, only rarely differ from those actually observed in such a way as to warrant sociological comment.

Secondly, comparative studies covering a wide range of national societies have revealed that across these societies relative mobility rates are characterized by a substantial commonality. This is a weaker regularity than that apparent in trends in such rates: cross-national differences do tend to show up that are not only of statistical but also of sociological significance. None the less, these differences can be largely understood as 'variations on a theme'. Even where relative rates indicate that nations differ in their general levels of fluidity, the patterns, or 'contours', of fluidity that they display often remain basically similar, and such variations in pattern as do occur are not of any major quantitative importance.[4]

These, then, are the empirical regularities that constitute the *explananda* that a theory of social mobility must primarily address. Since it would seem reasonable to suppose that temporal constancy and cross-national commonality are closely related phenomena, one theory should in fact be capable *mutatis mutandis* of explaining both.[5] As regards the further requirements that the theory will need to meet, these may be clarified by considering the

---

[3] References to most relevant studies carried out up to the 1990s can be found in Erikson and Goldthorpe (1992a), together with the results of comparative quasi-cohort analyses for nine nations. More recent studies of importance include Jonsson and Mills (1993), Ringdal (1994), Ishida (1995), Szelényi (1998), Yaish (1998), and Vallet (1999).

[4] The idea of a 'basic' similarity in relative mobility rates, at least across nations with market economies and nuclear family systems, originates with Featherman, Jones, and Hauser (1975). The 'FJH hypothesis' is refined and tested in Erikson and Goldthorpe (1992a) on the basis of a proposed 'core model' of social fluidity, taken to define the 'theme' around which variation is best seen as occurring. Subsequent studies of relevance include Jones, Kojima, and Marks (1994), Goldthorpe (1995b), Chan, Lui, and Wong (1995), Breen and Whelan (1996), and Goldthorpe, Yaish, and Kraus (1997).

[5] That is to say, it would seem improbable that these phenomena should be produced by quite different causal processes. However the degree of cross-national commonality in endogenous mobility regimes is brought about, one could expect the same processes to be involved, though perhaps reinforced by others, in creating the yet more marked temporal constancy. There are, in fact, various other kinds of regularity in relative rates of class mobility that one might also hope to bring within the scope of the same theory, although I do not attempt this here: for example, those arising from the tendency for essentially the same endogenous mobility regime to apply across different subpopulations within the same society. Thus, the relative class mobility rates of men and women are generally found to be very similar (whether women's class positions are taken to be determined by their own employment or, with married women, by their husbands') and such rates tend to be likewise similar across different geographical regions of national societies. In the case of racial or ethnic subpopulations, however—and for reasons that remain unclear—instances of both marked similarity and significant variation occur.

problems that recognition of the regularities described has posed for the one attempt previously made to give a general account of mobility processes within modern societies: that which forms a part of a yet more ambitious endeavour—elsewhere described as 'the liberal theory of industrialism' (Erikson and Goldthorpe 1992a: ch. 1, and Chapter 8 above)—and which has been most lucidly and systematically set out by Treiman (1970; see also Blau and Duncan 1967: ch. 12).

This account has a more or less explicitly functionalist character and I refer to it here accordingly.[6] It treats rates and patterns of social mobility in modern societies as in effect responses to the exigencies that stem from the dynamism of their technologies and economies. More specifically, and with particular relevance to relative rates of mobility,[7] it is argued that in such societies technological and economic advance creates an inexorably rising demand for highly educated and qualified personnel and thus requires that human abilities should be as efficiently utilized as possible wherever they may be located within the social structure. To this end, educational provision has to be expanded and educational institutions reformed so as to further equality of opportunity, and processes of selection within labour markets and work organizations have to become increasingly 'meritocratic': that is, increasingly governed by criteria of achievement rather than of ascription. In consequence of these changes, it is then maintained, education becomes crucial in mediating the association between individuals' class origins and destinations, and this association in turn *steadily weakens*: in other words, relative mobility rates become more equal or the level of social fluidity steadily rises. Underlying this theory, two key assumptions are to be noted. The first is that, prior to the exigencies of modern technologies and economies coming to exert their effects, human abilities were not in fact fully exploited—that is, were not allowed to develop into merit—at all events in the case of individuals of less advantaged social origins. The second is that under the pressure of these exigencies, both public policy in the field of education and the employment and personnel policies of employing organizations will change—indeed are forced to change—so as to allow merit to be more fully expressed and increasingly to determine the mobility chances of individuals whatever their social origins might be.

At an empirical level, the most obvious difficulty that confronts the functionalist theory is then the finding that, across modern societies, relative rates

---

[6] While it could equally well be labelled as the liberal theory, it is here its theoretical—i.e. functionalist—rather than its ideological character that I wish to stress. Other theories of mobility processes could be identified, but these are either not sufficiently general for present purposes or already clearly invalidated, as in the case of Marxist theories implying a pervasive 'proletarianization'.

[7] Although Treiman's (1970) statement of the theory antedates the distinction between absolute and relative mobility rates, it does in effect imply it, and no difficulty has therefore arisen in incorporating the distinction explicitly into later formulations. Similarly, although Treiman tends to suppose that mobility is studied in the context of a social hierarchy rather than of a class structure (see n. 1 above), the theory he expounds can be, and indeed has been, readily adapted to the latter approach (see e.g. Ganzeboom *et al.* 1989).

of intergenerational class mobility have not in fact shown any consistent tendency to become more equal but have, rather, displayed long-term stability, including over periods—notably the decades following the Second World War—in which economic development has been rapid and sustained. It is true that one comparative study, of which Treiman was a co-author (Ganzeboom *et al.* 1989), has claimed to reveal, within a basic cross-national similarity of relative rates, a slight but still 'worldwide' and 'secular' trend towards more equal relative rates, or greater fluidity, on the lines that the theory would predict. However, this claim has subsequently been called into question on various grounds and has failed to find support from alternative analyses carried out on the same data set (Jones 1992; Erikson and Goldthorpe 1992*a*: 100–1; Wong 1994). Probably the most that could be said empirically in favour of the theory is that, *if* in any national case some change in the general level of fluidity *is* detectable, it is usually one towards greater fluidity rather than less. But, for the theory to be confirmed, what is required is evidence of a trend in relative rates signalling increased fluidity that is indeed worldwide and secular; and the findings of mobility studies to date do not, on any reckoning, constitute evidence of this kind.[8]

Furthermore, the degree of cross-national commonality, as well as of temporal constancy, that is apparent in endogenous mobility regimes also creates a difficulty for the functionalist theory. What this would lead one to expect is that relative mobility rates will in fact vary a good deal across national societies and, further, that they will do so systematically: technologically and economically more advanced societies should display more equal relative rates, or greater fluidity, than those less advanced. But, in so far as cross-national differences in relative rates are revealed, it has not proved possible to show that this variation, when indicative of greater or less fluidity, is systematic in the way envisaged. Indeed, analysts both sympathetic to and sceptical of the functionalist theory would by now appear to be in agreement on the point that *even if* technological and economic dynamism do tend to promote greater fluidity within the class structures of modern societies, a range of other factors is also involved, including ones that have the capacity to create strong countervailing effects.[9]

The basic problem of the functionalist theory, it might therefore be said, is that the exigencies on which its explanatory power depends prove in fact to

---

[8] One problem is that of apparently contradictory findings that would in fact seem in large part to arise from analysts' ultimate decisions on the degree of comparability of different data sets or preferred models (see e.g., in the case of France, Goldthorpe 1995*b*; Goux and Maurin 1997; Vallet 1999). However, most damagingly for the functionalist theory, I would believe, are, first, cases such as those of Japan (Ishida 1995) or Israel (Yaish 1998), in which no increase in fluidity is apparent over periods of exceptionally rapid and sustained economic development; and, secondly, cases such as those of Hungary or Sweden, discussed later in the text, in which, after some apparent upturn in fluidity, this trend then faded out or was indeed reversed.

[9] From the former side, see especially the conclusions reached in Treiman and Yip (1989) and Simkus *et al.* (1990), and, from the latter, Erikson and Goldthorpe (1992*a*: ch. 12) and Wong (1994).

be insufficiently compelling. The theory is clearly supported to the extent that educational expansion and reform have everywhere been the concomitants of technological and economic advance. But, as noted, what the theory further requires is that education should then play a steadily more important role in promoting intergenerational mobility rather than immobility—in changing, rather than confirming, the class positions of families over generations; but, in this regard little indication is provided of just how the functional exigencies of a modern society might operate so as to give the required outcome. In so far as the theory is elaborated at all, it is simply to the effect that, while the association between education and class destinations may be expected to strengthen, as a result of meritocratic selection, that between class origins and education will be reduced, as a result of greater equality of educational opportunity—and to a sufficient degree that the overall association between individuals' origins and destinations will also weaken. However, what is not spelled out is how these relationships that are postulated at the level of variables are supposed to be produced, as they can only be produced, at the level of action and interaction among individuals. And, as described, the empirical evidence indicates that they are not so produced, at all events in any clear and consistent way.[10]

What would therefore seem necessary in a more successful theory is that, instead of seeking by appeal to functional exigencies to reduce social action to essentially epiphenomenal status,[11] the theory should have explicit microfoundations. More specifically, I would argue, it should aim to show how the regularities that *are* empirically demonstrable in relative mobility rates result ultimately from central tendencies in courses of action followed by individuals that, although constrained, can at the same time be seen as reflecting a degree of choice as regards both the goals towards which they are oriented and the ways in which these goals are pursued. I here opt, as in the preceding chapters, to proceed on the basis of rational action theory, and again on

[10] In this regard, it is also, of course, relevant to note the findings from which the analyses of Chapters 8 and 9 in effect begin: i.e. findings that suggest that in most modern societies class differentials in educational attainment have not in fact shown a consistent decline.

[11] All functionalist theories do in the end seek such a reduction. Essentially the argument is that any persisting feature of a 'social system' is to be explained by its function for that system—that is, by what it contributes to the system's self-maintenance and survival in an environment that is in some degree selective. In turn, it is because the system survives that the feature persists and thus can be taken as an *explanandum*. In all of this, social action is of little importance, since patterns of action that do not 'follow the script' laid down by functional exigencies will simply be eliminated. Thus, to take an example from economics, one can explain the fact that entrepreneurs maximize profits because, if they did not, they would not, on account of competitive pressures, be there to be observed in the first place. To analyse profit maximization as a form of action is, therefore, essentially redundant. Whether such an explanatory approach is a compelling one is disputed even in economics (see Chapter 6 above), where an appeal to the selectivity of competitive markets might in some contexts at least be plausible. So far as sociology is concerned, the potential of the approach seems to me even more limited. It should be noted that the functionalist theory of mobility processes says nothing about what will happen to societies where achievement does *not* progressively prevail over ascription. It does not specify any mechanism through which these societies will disappear so that lasting counter-examples to the theory are unlikely to be observed (cf. Breen 1997*b*).

the grounds that significant advantage is gained in so far as action can be treated as rational, at all events in a subjective sense, rather than as being explicable only in terms of actors' 'internalization' of the values of particular cultures or subcultures or their commitment to social norms. This consideration would in the present case seem especially important in view of the evident need to construct a theory of a rather high level of generality (see further Chapter 3).

I now wish to go on to outline a theory of the kind in question that starts from the idea of 'mobility strategies': that is, courses of action that are pursued by individuals of differing class backgrounds, typically, though not necessarily, in conjunction with their families of origin, in moving towards their own eventual class positions.[12] However, before I attempt to characterize such strategies in more detail and analyse their implications for relative mobility rates, I need first to take up the questions of the resources that are available for their pursuit and of the goals towards which they are directed.

Mobility Strategies: Resources and Goals

When social mobility is examined within the context of a class structure, this structure has to be seen as conditioning rates and patterns of intergenerational mobility in two different ways. First, and as earlier implied, the shape, and changes in the shape, of the structure in the sense simply of the proportionate sizes of different classes will determine the extent and nature of what might be called 'objective' mobility opportunities. Thus, for example, a structure in which higher-level class positions are expanding relative to lower-level ones could be said to offer increasing opportunities for entry into the former positions, regardless of the class origins of the individuals who actually take up these opportunities. In fact, as I have emphasized, empirical results clearly show that both temporal and cross-national shifts in absolute rates of intergenerational class mobility do very largely reflect the evolution of class structures, with changes or variation in relative rates making only a quite minor contribution.

Secondly, though, and more relevantly for the present concern with relative rates, class structures can also be seen as conditioning mobility via the

---

[12] The use of the concept of 'strategy' has been the subject of some debate, in British sociology at least, though not, in my view, of a very illuminating or helpful kind. I understand by a strategy a course of action, involving the use of resources, that is chosen in the pursuit of a given goal on the basis of some kind of cost-benefit evaluation. This implies a situation in which action is constrained but in which there are still at least two possible courses of action within the 'feasible set'. For my present purposes, it is of no consequence whether a strategy is chosen through some explicit decision-making procedure or only 'emerges' over time in a more or less implicit and piecemeal fashion. Nor indeed is it necessary, in order to explain the kind of probabilistic regularities with which I am concerned, that all relevant actors should actually have mobility strategies of the kind that I would attribute to them: only that such strategies represent central tendencies in action considered in aggregate and that deviations from these central tendencies are not systematic (see further Chapter 5).

typical attributes of the positions they comprise. In this case, what is affected is not the overall situation as regards mobility opportunities but, precisely, the relative chances of mobility that individuals of differing origins have within the class structure, whatever shape or pattern of change it may display. Different classes, considered as classes of origin, provide varying degrees and forms of advantage to those individuals who are born and grow up within them; or, one might say, from class to class, the resources that parents have available to help pursue their children's mobility strategies, or strategies that they themselves conceive on behalf of their children, will vary in both amount and kind, and such strategies will in this way be to a greater or lesser extent constrained. In short, the class structure not only creates more or less favourable ground for the mobility stakes; it also plays an important part in determining the runners' handicaps.[13]

The nature and significance of this second way in which class structure influences mobility can, I would argue, be best appreciated if class positions are understood as being differentiated in terms of employment relations (see further Chapter 10). An initial distinction has thus to be made among employers, self-employed workers, and employees. But more consequential, at least in the context of modern societies, are the further distinctions that can then be introduced within the numerically preponderant category of employees in regard to the form of regulation of their employment.

The major division here to be recognized is that between, on the one hand, a working class, comprising employees in broadly manual and lower-grade nonmanual occupations and, on the other hand, what has been termed a 'service class', or salariat, comprising professional, administrative, and managerial employees. The former are typically engaged by their employer or employing organization through a contract that implies a short-term and specific exchange of discrete amounts of labour in return for wages calculated on a piece or time basis. The latter are typically engaged through a contract that implies a longer-term and more diffuse exchange in which the employee renders service to the employing organization in return for compensation that as well as a salary and various perquisites also includes important prospective elements—regular salary increments, some expectation of continuity of employment, and, above all, career opportunities. Further employee classes may in turn be distinguished that are 'intermediate' between the working class and the service class in that the regulation of employment in their constituent positions tends to be of a mixed form, in which elements of both the 'labour contract' and the 'service relationship' occur. These would comprise routine nonmanual employees on the fringes, as it were, of professional,

---

[13] The foregoing argument does, of course, imply that the objective mobility opportunities provided by class structures are determined exogenously relative to the mobility strategies that individuals pursue. I would accept that this may not be entirely correct: that is, it is possible that the nature of the supply of individuals with differing attributes may influence demand for them and in turn the structure of class positions. However, the empirical indications are that, if such effects do occur, they are slight, and I therefore believe that making the assumption of exogeneity will not undermine the theory I suggest.

administrative, and managerial bureaucracies and employees in lower-grade technical or manual supervisory positions.

From this standpoint, it is, then, the service class that appears capable of conferring the greatest degree of advantage as a class of origin, and the working class the least, specifically in respect of the resources that their members can command by virtue of the class positions that they hold. What is important here is not simply that salaried professionals, administrators, and managers will have higher average earnings than rank-and-file wage-workers. The former have also to be regarded as being advantaged over the latter, through the form of regulation of their employment, in two other highly consequential ways: first, in that their incomes from employment will show less short-term fluctuation in relation to the amount of work performed and will be less subject to interruption as a result of unemployment, sickness, accident, and so on; and, secondly, in that their incomes will follow a rising curve until a much later stage in the course of their working lives, tending to peak in their fifties rather than their thirties. On all of these grounds, therefore, mobility strategies pursued from service-class origins are to be regarded as those least likely to be constrained by the availability of resources, while strategies pursued from working-class origins will be those most likely to be so constrained.

Matters become rather more complex when intermediate classes are brought into consideration, and especially when these are taken to include not just further employee classes, as referred to above, but also small employers and self-employed workers.[14] The advantages that such intermediate classes offer as classes of origin are not in fact readily ordered but can be better understood as differing qualitatively. For example, small employers and self-employed workers will typically be exposed to greater economic uncertainty and insecurity than members of intermediate employee classes but at the same time will have greater possibilities for the accumulation—and thus intergenerational transmission—of capital in some form. Or again, while employees in manual supervisory and technical positions may have higher average earnings than employees in routine nonmanual work, their earnings will tend to be more variable and perhaps to show less long-term progression.[15] Although, then, the mobility strategies of individuals of intermediate-class origins may be taken as somewhat less constrained than those of individuals of working-class origins, the degree of constraint is likely to vary greatly with the appropriateness of the kinds of resources available to the particular strategies that are conceived.

Viewing relative mobility rates in a class structural context defined in terms of employment relations is by now of proven value in empirical research.

[14] Small employers are theoretically best understood as employers whose businesses are not incorporated. In modern societies, most larger enterprises, in terms of numbers employed, and so on, are incorporated, so that, even if ownership remains with particular individuals or families, those owners who also work for the enterprise will have the status of employees.
[15] The nature and rationale of this difference are further discussed in Chapter 10.

Such an approach would be widely accepted as in various respects more revealing than that in which mobility is treated simply within a one-dimensional hierarchy of, say, prestige or 'socioeconomic' status (see e.g. Erikson and Goldthorpe 1992a; Ishida et al. 1995; Hendrickx and Ganzeboom 1998; Western, 1999). What, though, for present purposes is of added significance is the possibility that the approach may be given a more developed theoretical basis. That is, by arguing, as I sought to do in the preceding chapter, that, among the body of employees, the association that exists between the kind of work they carry out and the typical form of regulation of their employment is the outcome of decisions made by employers that have a clear rationale in considerations of organizational effectiveness. For, if this argument holds good—if the differentiation of class positions among employees can indeed be understood as deriving from employers' attempts to deal with such highly generalized organizational problems as work monitoring and human asset specificity—then this in itself gives grounds for expecting that endogenous mobility regimes will, through the class structural effects bearing on them, tend towards uniformity. The shapes of class structures, determining the overall distribution of mobility opportunities and in turn conditioning absolute mobility rates, may vary widely over time and place; but what might be called the principle of differentiation of these structures, as it constrains individuals' mobility strategies and in turn conditions relative mobility rates, could be thought to have a far more enduring character.[16]

Mobility strategies pursued from different class origins will then be backed by varying levels and kinds of resources. It has, though, further to be recognized that such strategies may differ in the goals towards which they are directed. In so far as the question of individuals' goals has been previously taken up by analysts of mobility processes, two contrasting views can be identified. The first—and it is this that would seem to be taken over in the functionalist theory—is that the goals that individuals pursue can be treated as always and everywhere the same. On account of universal psychological impulses, defined as 'ego-needs' or whatever, individuals aim to move, so far as they can, from positions that are less desirable to positions that are more desirable in terms of the various rewards that they offer (see e.g. Lipset and Zetterberg 1956; Kelley et al. 1981). The second view is that individuals' orientations towards social mobility, even within more advanced societies, show wide, subculturally determined, variation. In particular, it has been suggested, working-class subcultures may be inimical to the 'success ethic' that more generally prevails in such societies, either because these subcultures embody alternative values to that of individual achievement—for example, values of family or community solidarity—or simply because they engender fatalism

---

[16] The theory I outline to attempt to explain regularities in relative rates of class mobility could, of course, in this regard be linked to some other theory than my own of why class structures are differentiated as they are—provided that this alternative theory had a similar degree of generality.

and a 'poverty' of aspirations (see e.g. Hyman 1954; Rosen 1956; Richardson 1977).

However, it is possible to suggest an alternative approach to this question that is at least as compatible with the empirical evidence as is either of the foregoing views,[17] and that would appear to offer greater explanatory potential. This approach requires that mobility orientations should be thought of as being basically similar across different social classes but at the same time as involving *priorities*, so that, given the differing degrees of constraint that are imposed by class origins, some systematic variation may indeed be observed in the actual goals that are pursued. More specifically, the suggestion is that what should be treated as common to individuals of all class backgrounds alike is a concern, in the first place, to maintain a class position that is no less desirable than that of their parents or, in other words, *to avoid downward class mobility*. A concern to secure a more desirable class position, or, that is, to achieve upward class mobility, is then to be regarded as a secondary objective, even if, perhaps, a still important one.[18]

If mobility is envisaged as occurring within a single, well-defined hierarchy of positions and if, further, educational attainment, understood in a linear, 'more or less' fashion, is taken to be the crucial determinant of mobility chances, then the issue of priorities in mobility orientations may well appear of little consequence. For in this case the *same* mobility strategy, that of maximizing educational attainment, could be regarded as equally appropriate to improving the individual's chances both of avoiding downward and of achieving upward mobility: more education is always better. However, if mobility is envisaged as occurring within the more complex context of a class structure, if factors other than education are accepted as significantly influencing mobility chances, and if educational systems are in any event seen as diversified—that is, as providing options not just for more or less education but also for education of differing kinds—then a quite different perspective is gained. It is now at least conceivable that the strategies that would best serve to ensure that individuals of a given class origin maintain their class positions intergenerationally need not be the same as those that would best serve to promote their chances of upward mobility; and, it might be added,

---

[17] Data in the form of individuals' own expressions of their ambitions, aspirations, etc., are notoriously difficult to interpret. One basic problem is that of knowing the degree to which such expressions are already conditioned by a recognition of likely constraints—i.e. represent 'adaptive preferences'.

[18] This position is derived in part from what has become known as the structural theory of aspirations (see further Keller and Zavalloni 1964, and Chapter 8 above) and it can also be expressed in terms of identical *relative* risk aversion across classes (see further Chapter 9). From a psychological standpoint, it is highly consistent with 'prospect theory', as developed by Kahneman and Tversky (1979), according to which the slope of individuals' utility curves is steeper in the 'domain of losses' than in the 'domain of gains'. However, I would see no need to accept the view of these authors that, simply because their theory is incompatible with standard expected utility theory, it must *ipso facto* imply action of an irrational or at least non-rational kind. See further Chapter 6 above and also the general critique of Kahneman and Tversky's 'heuristics and biases' programme advanced by Gigerenzer and his associates (e.g. Gigerenzer 1996; Gigerenzer and Todd 1999).

that those strategies that would be optimal for pursuing 'short-range' upward mobility need not be the same as those that would be optimal for pursuing mobility of a more ambitious 'long-range' kind. In other words, in this perspective the possibility can be recognized that significant choices of strategy may have to be made, implicitly if not explicitly, and ones that will entail differing degrees of risk. In pursuing one goal, the chances of realizing another may be jeopardized.

In so far as such situations do in fact arise, then—to repeat—the basic assumption that I would propose, and that will underlie the analysis that follows, is that the tendency will be for the avoidance of mobility downwards to be given priority over the achievement of mobility upwards. Thus, while individuals will not be supposed, as in the functionalist theory, all to have an equal commitment to the goal of social advancement, neither will individuals of working-class or other less advantaged backgrounds be supposed either to reject this goal or to be effectively precluded from pursuing it as a result of their subcultural conditioning.

Mobility Strategies and 'Class Competition'

If it is supposed that individuals engage in mobility strategies, subject to resource constraints and directed towards goals as outlined above, the problem to be addressed is then the following: how does it come about that this purposive action is consistent with—indeed results in—individuals' actual chances of class mobility, considered relative to their origins, revealing the degree of constancy and commonality that is apparent in the empirical evidence?

In treating this problem, it may be helpful to note a further way in which relative mobility rates, as expressed via odds ratios, can be interpreted—as an alternative, that is, to viewing them as an indicator of the level of social fluidity. Such rates can also be seen as indicating the state of competition, or in fact of a whole series of competitions, between individuals of one rather than another class origin to achieve—or to avoid—one rather than another class destination. Thus, in the simplest case in which only two classes are distinguished—say, A, comprising the more desirable positions, and B—the one odds ratio calculable could be taken to show the state of competition between individuals originating in class A and those originating in class B seeking to gain for themselves positions in class A rather than in class B. The closer the value of such an odds ratio to unity, the more equal is the competition to which it refers, in the sense that individuals' destinations are in a lesser degree dependent upon their origins.[19] In terms of this interpretation, the key issue

---

[19] My use here of the idea of 'class competition' should not be taken to imply that I envisage competition as occurring between classes understood as collective actors. Nor, despite my further use of the idea of mobility strategies, do I suppose that what has become known as 'strategic rationality' is involved—i.e. that actors from different classes are engaged in a game

can then be expressed as that of why the state of class competition is so difficult to change. More specifically, it may be asked: if, as proponents of the functionalist theory, and indeed most other sociologists, would believe, a significant amount of unexploited ability does exist among the members of less advantaged classes, why have educational expansion and reform and generally increased pressure for meritocratic selection not produced some consistent movement towards more equal class competition—and to a greater degree in more economically advanced societies than in those less advanced? Or, in other words, why in modern societies should not an increasing proportion of more able children from less advantaged origins come to compete with greater success for more desirable class positions, at the same time as an increasing proportion of less able children from more advantaged origins lose out in their efforts to escape less desirable positions?

In seeking answers to these questions, it will be a useful and, I believe, a not too misleading simplification to regard mobility strategies as being of two main kinds: that is, strategies 'from below' and strategies 'from above'. The former are strategies pursued from less advantaged class origins, which, following the discussion of the preceding section, will be taken as origins in the working class or in the various classes which, in terms of the typical employment relations of their members, were considered as intermediate. The latter are those strategies pursued from more advantaged class origins or, that is, from origins in the service class or salariat of professional, administrative, and managerial employees. I will now examine these two kinds of strategy in turn with the aim of providing theoretical accounts or narratives that can show them to be capable of generating the empirical regularities in relative mobility rates that require explanation and at the same time to be rational, and thus intelligible, responses by individuals to the situations in which they find themselves. As these narratives are developed, I will note already available evidence relevant to assessing their validity and also ways in which they might be subjected to further empirical test.

Mobility strategies pursued from below are those most likely to entail difficult choices, and the difficulty tends to be compounded in that such strategies will also be those that are most constrained by the availability of resources. If individuals' mobility orientations are in general directed towards maintaining their class positions intergenerationally as their first priority, then, for individuals of less advantaged class origins, a conflict may well arise between seeking this goal and seeking that of upward mobility. In particular, while an effective strategy for upward mobility, or at all events for upward mobility into a service-class position, could be taken to entail a high level of

against each other (in contrast, for example, to the approach taken by Goux and Maurin 1997). Rather, I see the competition in question as involving a game 'against society' in which these actors are *concurrently* involved. Thus, although the degree of success of actors from one class background must ultimately constrain the degree of success of those from another (as discussed further in the text below), the rationality that guides mobility strategies can still be taken to be simply 'parametric'—i.e. as assuming a constant environment—rather than involving considerations of what other actors may or may not do.

educational attainment, this need not be a requirement of the most reliable strategy for class stability. This point is most readily brought out in the case of the children of small employers and self-employed workers. For these individuals, the maintenance of their class positions might well appear to be best guaranteed through their direct inheritance of family businesses as 'going concerns' or through the intergenerational transmission of capital that could enable them to start up enterprises of their own. There is in fact clear cross-national evidence that the propensity for intergenerational class stability within the 'petty bourgeoisie' is relatively high, at least for men (R. V. Robinson 1984; Erikson and Goldthorpe 1992a), and further that the part played by educational qualifications in sustaining this stability is in fact quite negligible (Ishida et al. 1995).[20]

However, the issue of the importance of education also arises with individuals originating in less advantaged employee classes and, perhaps, more acutely, for pursuing educational attainment beyond a certain point might in their case be seen not only as contributing little to a strategy of class stability but even as carrying some threat to its success. At least for children of working-class origins, the safest option for maintaining their positions inter-generationally—in, say, the skilled rather than the nonskilled working class or in relatively continuous employment of some kind as against the possibility of becoming long-term or recurrently unemployed—could be regarded as that of leaving mainstream education relatively early and of taking up vocational training, whether full-time or in conjunction with some appropriate kind of employment.[21] Moreover, such a strategy might also appear to give good chances of modest upward mobility into intermediate-class, especially manual supervisory or lower technical, positions. In contrast, a strategy of continuing with general education could be seen as involving significant risk, at least if not carried through to the point at which relatively high-level qualifications could be achieved, and most obviously through the possibility of actual failure (cf. Chapters 8 and 9). More evidence of a direct kind on the ways in which individuals of less advantaged class origins do in fact conceive and implement mobility strategies would certainly be illuminating. But evid-

---

[20] In the case of the daughters of the petty bourgeoisie, in contrast, education would seem, at least up to the very recent past, to have played an important part in mobility strategies conducted within the marriage market. In fact the main way in which the pattern of women's relative class mobility chances via marriage deviates overall from men's chances via employment is that, while the sons of the petty bourgeoisie are significantly more likely to be themselves found in this class through their employment than are their 'sisters' to marry into it, the daughters of the petty bourgeoisie are more likely to marry into the service class than are their 'brothers' to gain access to a service-class occupation (see further Erikson and Goldthorpe 1992a: Chapter 7). I do not, however, in this chapter seek to treat class mobility via marriage markets in any systematic way.

[21] As is here implied, I suppose the possibility of downward mobility, that is, into the ranks of the long-term or recurrently unemployed, even for members of the class of nonskilled wage-workers. Whether or not this should be regarded as itself class mobility, that is, into a yet more disadvantaged class—for example, an 'underclass' of some kind—or rather as mobility out of the class structure altogether, as implied by the loss of any kind of stable employment relationship, is an interesting conceptual issue but not one that much affects the argument regarding mobility strategies.

ence does exist to show that, in so far as class stability is prioritized, reservations about the value of mainstream education as against vocational training could claim a degree of realism. Müller and Shavit (1998), in reviewing research findings on the transition from education to employment in thirteen advanced societies, are led directly to question the idea that more—general—education is *always* better. In this regard they note *inter alia* that the completion of vocational courses usually gives individuals the best chance of entering skilled rather than nonskilled work and, further, that it is quite often the case that the probability of being found in unemployment is lower for those with vocational qualifications than for those with more academic education of a comparable or even a somewhat higher level.

Moreover, in making educational choices as part of mobility strategies from below, individuals are also likely to be pushed towards options of a less ambitious kind—that is, ones more relevant to the achievement of class stability than of decisive upward mobility—simply through the economic constraints that their class origins impose. Although reform programmes have in most modern societies removed or substantially reduced the direct costs of education, at least up to secondary level, the opportunity costs of remaining outside the labour market are, of course, still present; and the successful passage of students through tertiary education is still often facilitated by, even if it does not actually demand, parental economic support in some form or other. The costs in question can then be expected to be of greater consequence for individuals the less advantaged their class origins, and in particular, I would argue, in determining the time horizons that frame their choices. For children from class backgrounds where family income is liable to show significant fluctuation and parental earning power peaks early, educational options that offer relatively short-term pay-offs can be expected to prove more attractive than ones from which the economic rewards, though potentially larger, are longer delayed and carry greater risk of not being successfully completed. Evidence of such restricted time horizons has in fact been found in a number of studies of educational and occupational aspirations, and especially among children of working-class origin. In earlier work at least, this finding was then usually provided with a culturalist interpretation: that is, as indicating a lack of 'achievement values' or, more specifically, a culturally induced inability to 'defer gratification' (e.g. Schneider and Lysgaard 1953; Rosen 1956). However, as Sørensen has observed (1999), to the extent that an investment is threatened by uncertainty, as, say, over the adequacy of the resources available to back it, then to apply in effect a high discount rate to future returns may be considered as entirely rational.[22]

To see mobility strategies pursued from below as being characterized by

---

[22] In studies of the kind referred to in the text, a contrast is sometimes drawn between the short time horizons of the working class and the often much more extended ones of the 'lower middle class', with the emphasis again being placed on subcultural influences in view of the fact that the (current) income levels of these classes may appear rather similar. But this is again to neglect the importance of differences in employment relations and their implications for both the stability of incomes and their life-course trajectories.

tensions and constraints in the ways suggested is also consistent with empirical evidence that I have previously cited (see Chapters 8 and 9) in attempting to explain persisting class differentials in educational attainment. That is, the recurrent finding that, even when academic ability is held constant, children of more advantaged class origins are still more likely to continue to higher educational levels than those of less advantaged origins. This finding need not imply an unresponsiveness on the part of the latter to the widening opportunities for long-range upward mobility via education that may result from class structural change. These children may indeed still increase their take-up of such opportunities at a similar rate to others. However, the implication that is here of importance is that the 'release' of previously unexploited ability that in the functionalist theory of mobility processes represents the main driving force behind steadily increasing social fluidity—or more equal class competition—does not in fact occur in the quite unrestrained way that the theory would assume. Even supposing that educational systems do operate on strictly meritocratic principles—that there are no class-linked 'ability handicaps' consciously or unconsciously imposed by teachers or academic administrators—the very nature of the class structure, the basis on which class positions are differentiated, is still capable of inhibiting this release. That is, by creating circumstances in which individuals pursuing mobility strategies from below can have good reasons, in the light of perceived costs and benefits, for not attempting to use educational channels to the fullest extent that would be open to them and that their ability would warrant.[23]

Finally, a point needs to be made about the potential in mobility strategies from below of ascription as opposed to achievement: or, that is, of the part that may be played in such strategies not by individual ability, or at least not by the kind that is typically expressed and developed through educational attainment, but rather by resources and attributes deriving from specific family backgrounds. The point is the seemingly obvious one that, in so far as ascription in this sense is involved, its importance will tend to be greater in strategies aimed essentially at class stability rather than at major social advancement (cf. Goux and Maurin 1997). In turn, then, where the possibility of using ascriptive resources or attributes is present, this will be a further factor favouring the adoption of mobility strategies of a relatively conservative kind. An illustration has already been provided in the case of the high propensity for stability within the class of small employers and self-employed

---

[23] In practice, 'ability handicaps', rather than being simply imposed by teachers or administrators, are often exerted more subtly via discussion or 'consultations' involving children and their parents. Any biases that teachers or administrators may have regarding the suitability of children from less-advantaged backgrounds for more ambitious educational options are thus likely to be reinforced by diffidence in this respect that these children and their parents may display. For an insightful analysis of this process within the French school system, see Duru-Bellat, Jarousse, and Mingat (1992). Also important here may be differences in the degree of knowledge that parents of differing class background have of the educational institutions in which their children are involved and of the formal regulations and informal conventions that govern their operation (see further Erikson and Jonsson 1996a).

workers, facilitated by the possibility of passing on businesses or capital across generations. However, cultural and social resources could also be involved: for example, in the form of traditions of family employment in certain kinds of work, such as skilled trades or specialized branches of commerce, that endow individuals brought up within these traditions with knowledge and capacities or with contacts and networks that may be of as great a labour-market value as formal qualifications that are 'achieved' through the educational system.

I turn now to consider mobility strategies as pursued from above: that is, by individuals originating in the service class or salariat. These individuals, and their families of origin, face a situation the logic of which is in fact relatively straightforward. The maintenance of their class position intergenerationally is the one obvious goal to which their strategies should be directed, and it is in their case far clearer than in that of individuals pursuing strategies from below that to seek to maximize attainment within the educational mainstream will be an appropriate course of action to follow.[24] In modern societies the most reliable means of gaining entry into the professional, administrative, and managerial positions of the service class has undoubtedly become that of acquiring formal qualifications of degree level (Müller and Shavit 1998). Service-class families can then in general be expected to give their offspring every encouragement and support to continue in full-time education beyond the minimum leaving age, to take up more academic options in secondary education, and to continue through to the tertiary stage. In other words, their strategy will be that of translating their children's ability as far as ever possible into educational attainment. And, as earlier indicated, a tendency is in fact empirically well established for children from more advantaged class origins to be ready to proceed to higher educational levels where children of similar ability, but from less advantaged origins, would be reluctant to do so.

Within service-class families, moreover, pursuing a strategy of this kind is rather unlikely to be constrained by inadequate resources. What is important in this regard is not only the relatively high level and stability of service-class incomes but also the fact that, at the same time as children are passing through the crucial secondary and tertiary stages of their educational careers, parental earning power will be moving towards its highest point. Thus, long-term investment in education is encouraged, and it is possible that the direct and indirect costs involved may be absorbed without any detrimental effect on established family living standards. However, there are indications of various kinds that, even if some degree of sacrifice is involved, parents are still ready to commit substantial resources to improving their children's

[24] Just as I would suppose the possibility of downward mobility even for members of the class of nonskilled wage-workers, so I would suppose the possibility of upward mobility even for members of the service class—that is, into élite positions *within* this class. Again, the conceptual issue might be debated of the nature of this mobility but, for present purposes, the important point is that maximizing educational attainment would be equally relevant to strategies aimed at such advancement as to those aimed at maintaining class stability.

chances of educational success: for example, by buying homes in high-status residential areas that provide good-quality state schools, by supplementing state education with private tuition, or by opting out of the state system altogether and placing their children in private educational institutions. The availability of resources for such action thus gives children from more advantaged backgrounds a clear competitive edge in, supposedly, meritocratic competition. It is thus that, to quote Halsey (1977: 184), 'ascriptive forces find ways of expressing themselves as "achievement"'.

Moreover, in the light of such possibilities, one can also better understand the tendency for these children to be pushed to the very limits of their academic ability—or even beyond; or the tendency, as Gambetta has put it (1987: 171), in the context of his Italian study, for them to be 'light-heartedly' exposed to the possibility of failure. For, if failure occurs, further resources can then be deployed: second, or third, attempts at relevant qualifications can be underwritten, or alternative courses or institutions explored. In other words, a range of possibilities exist for what in French discussion has been aptly referred to as *récupération*—in marked contrast to the situation faced by children pursuing strategies from below, and backed by fewer resources, where failure in a relatively ambitious educational option might well leave them and their families less well placed than if they had never attempted it.[25]

It will, of course, in some proportion of cases occur that children from more advantaged class origins still do not perform well enough educationally to obtain the credentials that would essentially ensure their class stability. However, where a strategy based on educational achievement thus fails, despite all forms of parental support, ascription may still serve to compensate in yet more direct ways. In the case of children from more, as from less advantaged origins, ascriptive resources and attributes will be chiefly of value in providing routes to class stability; but with, of course, the important difference that, in the context of strategies from above, stability is the *same* goal as that sought via education and not, as in the context of strategies from below, quite possibly a different one.

Thus, children from service-class families may be able to use 'connections' within the occupational and wider social milieux of their parents in order to find openings for employment that would not be available to those from other backgrounds and that their own educational attainments and qualifications might scarcely justify. There seems no reason to believe that the functional exigencies of modern societies have eliminated such practices, or indeed even plain nepotism. However, probably of more general importance is the fact that various ascriptive attributes of these children—that is, attributes deriving directly from their upbringing in particular family and class contexts—could themselves represent 'merit', if not perhaps as understood in the functionalist theory, then at all events in the no less cogent sense of having

---

[25] It is, I think, likely that, within different 'fractions' of the service class—for example, the professional, administrative, or managerial—different forms of educational *récupération* will be typical. More investigation of this issue would be rewarding.

economic value in the eyes of an employer.[26] For example, this could be the case with personal features, such as general appearance or accent, with aspects of lifestyle, or with manners, *savoir faire*, and other social skills. In many branches of the expanding services sectors of modern economies, such attributes might be thought to be as much in demand as high-level cognitive ability—for example, in quality sales, public relations and promotions, hotels and restaurants, travel and tourism—and, together with only rather ordinary educational attainments, could then provide the basis for successful careers or at very least for avoiding downward mobility of an extreme kind. Further research on the 'refuge' occupations of children of advantaged class origins whose educational performance is weak would certainly be apposite. But from several enquiries undertaken into the actual extent of 'merit selection' in modern societies, the clear implication is that ability and educational attainment do play a less important part in mediating intergenerational stability within the service class than they do in mediating upward mobility into this class (see e.g. Goux and Maurin 1997; Breen and Goldthorpe 1999, forthcoming).

The foregoing characterization of mobility strategies, from below and from above, taken together with the idea of relative mobility rates as reflecting class competition in the sense suggested, does then point to an explanation for the very limited extent of variation found in these rates that would run on the following lines.

Class structures generate unequal resources, and thus unequal advantages, among families differently located within them, in ways that reflect the adaptation of employment relations to highly generalized problems of work organization. Thus, the class structural constraints that bear on the mobility strategies in which individuals engage can themselves be seen as making for temporal constancy and cross-national commonality in endogenous mobility regimes. Further, though, there are no evident grounds for supposing that either the exigencies invoked by the functionalist theory of mobility processes or indeed any other factors generally operative in modern societies are tending significantly to modify these constraints: that is, so as to lead individuals of different class origins to change the choices they make of the goals at which their mobility strategies are aimed or of the means by which these strategies are pursued in such ways that systematic changes might in turn be brought about in relative mobility chances, whether in the direction of greater equality or otherwise.

On the one hand, individuals of less advantaged class origins may still have good reason not to seek to exploit the possibilities offered by educational expansion and reform, and thus to engage in meritocratic competition for more desirable class positions, in the manner that the functionalist theory

---

[26] There is indeed a strong argument to the effect that, in the context of a market economy, it is only merit in this latter sense that can count. See, for example, the position taken up by Hayek (1960, 1976) and developed in Goldthorpe (1996), Breen (1998), and Breen and Goldthorpe (forthcoming).

would envisage. Given the constraints to which they and their families of origin are subject, they may, rather, favour strategies aimed primarily at achieving class stability, or only modest advancement, and even when their ability would be consistent with more ambitious educational and occupational aspirations. On the other hand, and likewise with good reason, individuals of more advantaged origins largely do engage in such competition, via the educational system, while however being at the same time able to draw on family economic resources in order to raise their chances of educational success to some extent independently of their ability, or, in the event of failure, to exploit other aspects of their family backgrounds so as still to qualify themselves for positions that would avert a *déclassement* of any radical kind. In sum, while those pursuing strategies from below may show some reluctance to participate in meritocratic competition, those following strategies from above do so far more readily, even aggressively, *and* on terms that are clearly weighted in their favour. Moreover, as observed, in the case of strategies from below a reliance on ascription rather than achievement typically implies a choice between goals, in effect in favour of stability rather than mobility, whereas in the case of strategies from above no such choice is involved: stability is the one goal to be pursued by means of achievement or ascription, so that the latter can in fact complement the former or, if need be, serve as substitute for it.

The constraints imposed by the class structure, one might then say, induce rationally adaptive responses from the individuals subject to them—their mobility orientations and the related courses of action that they follow—that serve to reinforce and to perpetuate the effects of these constraints on the mobility regime. However, arguing thus, I would again wish to stress, in no way entails underwriting the idea that among individuals of less advantaged class origins culturally grounded resistance exists to the idea of upward mobility.[27] It is not precluded that a sizeable proportion of such individuals—indi-

---

[27] An issue that could seriously be raised here, as it was previously in regard to the problem of class differentials in educational attainment (see Chapters 8 and 9), is that of how far individuals' responses to the conditions under which they must act are *over*-adaptive, as, say, in the case of individuals of less advantaged class origins who may in their educational and occupational choices 'sell themselves short'. Moreover, in so far as there is over-adaptation, it can in turn be asked how far it is possible for this to be brought within the scope of rational action theory. For example, if it is the case that the average ability of children of working-class origins who go on to some higher educational level is above that of children of more advantaged origins who make the same transition, then the information most immediately available to the former, within their primary social networks, local communities, etc., is likely be biased in a way that will help to perpetuate excessive caution. And this would then seem a good example of the process emphasized by Boudon (1996, 1998) whereby beliefs may be formed through quite rational processes although ones that prove to be misleading in the particular context of their use (see further Chapter 6). Breen (1999) explores a different approach to the rational formation of mistaken beliefs, including beliefs about mobility chances: that of Bayesian learning theory, in which the possibility arises of actors becoming trapped in a 'confounded learning equilibrium'. What both approaches have in common is a concern to endogenize belief formation into rational action theory and thus actually to *explain* socially structured differences in beliefs rather than merely redescribing them as aspects of subcultures. As both Boudon and Breen appreciate, the main challenge ahead is to develop ways in which such explanations can be empirically tested.

viduals, it would be expected, of relatively high ability—will engage in competition for more desirable class positions and, moreover, where the number of these positions is growing, will perhaps do so with increasing relative success. What *is*, however, implied is that any potential impact on the state of class competition that might in this way arise will tend always to be in some significant degree offset by individuals of more advantaged origins likewise exploiting the favourable conditions that prevail so as to improve their chances of preserving their class positions and of avoiding mobility downwards. And the degree of success that *they* thus achieve will, of course, itself operate as a constraint on the extent to which those pursuing mobility strategies from below aimed at upward mobility of a long-range kind can in fact achieve their goals.[28]

A scenario on the lines here envisaged would indeed appear often to be approximated in modern societies, and it may here be helpful to illustrate it by means of British data (see further Goldthorpe 1987: ch. 9). As of the early 1970s, the chances of men of service-class, intermediate-class, and working-class origins respectively being found in service-class positions showed disparity ratios of approximately $4:2:1$, while their chances, or risks, of being found in working-class positions were more or less in the reverse ratios of $1:2:4$. By the late 1980s, the former disparities had moved to something closer to $3:1.5:1$: that is, men of working-class origins did improve their relative chances of access to what could be regarded as the most desirable class positions. But, at the same time, the latter disparities also changed, to around $1:3:5$: that is, men of service-class origins improved *their* relative chances of avoiding the least desirable class positions. And disparity ratios changing on the pattern in question would then imply odds ratios remaining little altered, or moving in marginally different directions, rather than showing any general shift towards unity so as to indicate a greater equality in the state of class competition overall.[29]

For odds ratios actually to manifest such an increase in equality, it would be necessary for individuals of less advantaged class origins to make, as it were, gains on one front—that is, in either the positive competition for more desirable, or the negative competition for less desirable, positions—*without* losing out to a more or less similar extent to individuals of more advantaged origins on the other front. However, in so far as mobility strategies from below and from above do tend to be pursued under the constraints and according

---

[28] A clear contrast here arises, it may be noted, with the case of class differentials in educational attainment, in that the expansion of higher-level educational provision has to a large extent been demand led, so that the tendency of children of more advantaged class origins to maintain or increase their take-up of opportunities has not itself seriously limited the possibilities for children of less advantaged origins doing likewise.

[29] An odds ratio is the product of two complementary disparity ratios. Thus, in the example given, the odds ratio for the chances of men of service-class origins being found in service-class rather than working-class positions as against the same chances for men of working-class origins changes only from $(4/1) (4/1) = 16$ in the first period to $(3/1) (5/1) = 15$ in the second (using the precise disparity ratios results in no significant change in the odds ratio). The other odds ratios implied in the example can be calculated in the same manner.

to the rationales that I have suggested, there would seem little basis on which one might expect an outcome of this kind to be systematically generated.

Change and Variation in Relative Rates

It is the degree of temporal constancy and cross-national commonality in relative rates of intergenerational class mobility that poses the main theoretical challenge in the field of mobility research. However, as I have recognized throughout, such rates do reveal some amount of change and variation, and it is therefore pertinent to ask to what extent the theory that has been outlined in the foregoing as a basis for explaining their tendency towards invariance can be appropriately extended so as to account also for instances where this tendency does not prevail. In so far as the theory can be so extended, further opportunities for its empirical testing will arise.

In this regard, it would seem important to distinguish sharply between change or variation in relative rates that implies greater or less social fluidity—or greater or less equality in class competition—and that which does not. In the former case, the odds ratios expressing relative rates will differ in being in general further from or closer to unity, while in the latter case they will simply differ in other ways. Of course, in actual instances in which relative mobility rates are shown to change over time or to vary across societies, both kinds of change or variation are likely to be in evidence, although it is then possible for them to be statistically separated.

In so far as change or variation in relative rates do *not* imply greater or less fluidity overall—and in fact most of the difference observed is usually in the pattern rather than the level of fluidity—I would see it as falling outside the scope of the theory I have suggested and, most probably, outside that of any other theory that has aspirations to generality. This is because the available empirical evidence would strongly indicate that, in accounting for change or variation of this kind, specific historical factors will have to play a dominant part, whether in the form of events or sequences of events that impact on relative rates or of long-established institutional or cultural influences that bring distinctive elements into their pattern within particular societies (Erikson and Goldthorpe 1992*a*: esp. chs. 3, 5).[30] However, in so far as relative rates change or vary in ways that do imply differences in the general level of fluidity, the theory should have relevance. Since it represents in effect an attempt to explain why relative rates show a high degree of resistance to change or variation and in particular to any movement in the direction of greater fluidity, it should be able to specify the conditions under which this

---

[30] Thus, for example, the widely differing agrarian histories of modern societies have exerted clearly traceable effects on the detail of their mobility regimes, though not ones necessarily implying greater or less fluidity overall, through to the end of the twentieth century. Similar effects may also derive from the differing historical formation of educational and vocational training systems.

resistance will be weakened. More specifically, the theory sees the degree of invariance of relative rates of intergenerational class mobility as being grounded in the nature of the class structure itself: that is, in the way in which this structure, in creating systematic inequalities in the resources available to families in one generation, thus influences the goals and conditions the pursuit of mobility strategies in the next. If, therefore, the tendency towards invariance is to some extent modified so that fluidity increases—or indeed decreases—what the theory would lead one to expect is that some corresponding modification should have occurred either in the inequalities that are generated by the class structure itself or in the effects that these inequalities exert on mobility strategies. In short, it could be taken as one main implication of the theory that, in so far as *inequality of opportunity*, as indicated by odds ratios for relative class mobility chances, does show temporal change or cross-national variation, this will be associated with corresponding change or variation in class-linked *inequality of condition*.

In empirical research that is relevant to testing the theory via this implication, one approach that has been followed is to exploit the fact that, while national class structures may be seen as differentiated according to common principles, some significant variation can still occur in the extent of economic inequality as represented by the distribution of personal or family incomes (see further Chapter 10). In a cross-national comparative perspective, then, the question can be raised of how far such income inequality is associated with inequality in relative class mobility chances. An early study of twenty-four nations (Tyree *et al.* 1979) produced results to suggest that such an association is in fact present: nations with more equal income distributions tended to show (for men) more equal relative rates of intergenerational class mobility or, that is, higher levels of social fluidity. This finding is then essentially confirmed by a later analysis, limited to fifteen nations but using generally more reliable data and more advanced techniques (Erikson and Goldthorpe 1992*a*: ch. 12). Greater equality in relative mobility chances here again proves to be associated with greater equality in the distribution of income—although not, it may be added, with measures of educational equality or of level of economic development.

Such results are then encouraging for the theory that has been outlined; but evident 'small *N*' problems (cf. Chapter 3) and also persisting difficulties over data comparability mean that their confirmatory significance should not be exaggerated. Of perhaps greater importance are studies of changes over time in relative rates that have been made within individual nations and especially in cases where high-quality data and evident theoretical interest fortunately coincide. Two such cases are those of Hungary and Sweden over the middle decades of the twentieth century.

The Hungarian case is of interest as one that gives opportunity to investigate relative mobility rates in a society under a Communist regime openly committed to transforming the class structure and the general pattern of social inequality. A series of analyses, using data from mobility surveys carried out in Hungary in 1973 and 1984, have led to largely, even if not entirely, similar empirical findings (see esp. Andorka 1990; Simkus *et al.* 1990; Erikson and Goldthorpe 1992*a*; Wong and Hauser 1992; Szelényi 1998). First, over the early years of Communist rule, social fluidity would appear to have increased. For men and women who were born in the inter-war years and who entered employment during the 1940s and 1950s, relative mobility chances became somewhat more equal. There are, moreover, grounds for claiming that this was, in part at least, the outcome of various forms of state intervention aimed at 'destratification'. The old landowning and capitalist classes were eliminated, and in the context of a command economy inequalities in family incomes and resources generally were reduced. Further, a policy of creating a 'people's intelligentsia' led to formal discrimination in educational selection in favour of the children of peasants and workers and against children from 'bourgeois' or other supposedly privileged backgrounds. At the same time, relatively strict relationships were established between educational credentials and type of employment. What is then of particular significance is evidence that the increase in social fluidity came about through an improvement in the relative chances of upward mobility of the children of peasants and workers that went *together with* a fall in the propensity for intergenerational stability within the professional, administrative, and managerial salariat—the latter being a phenomenon that would seem rarely to have been observed in the context of a modern liberal democracy.[31]

Secondly, though, results from the Hungarian case quite consistently show that, in the later years of Communist rule, whatever trend there may earlier have been towards more equal class competition levelled out and, by the end of the Communist era, had if anything been reversed, with propensities for intergenerational stability within the salariat and indeed most other classes becoming much firmer. This development may in turn be associated with major shifts in state policy that date from the period of so-called normalization, following the uprising of 1956. The new understanding with the intelligentsia sought by Kádár led to the abandonment of at least all 'negative' forms of educational discrimination and also allowed for a widening of income differentials that were subsequently much accentuated as the economy became increasingly 'marketized'.

The interest of the Swedish case lies in the fact that it too is one in which a concerted political effort was made to create a more egalitarian form of society, although via electoral politics or the 'democratic translation' of the class struggle (Korpi 1983). Over the period from the mid-1930s to the 1970s, in which the Swedish Social Democratic Party was more or less continuously in power, the development of a distinctive form of political economy and of

---

[31] It should be noted that, of the authors cited, Szelényi is the one most sceptical about the effectiveness of policies of destratification and comments on the 'almost eerie constancy' (1998: p. viii) in relative rates of class mobility in Hungary over half a century. But even she recognizes evidence of some decline in the intergenerational stability of managers, if not professionals, during the earlier years of Communist rule.

a comprehensive welfare state together resulted in a degree of equality in incomes and living standards across social classes that by comparative standards was rather exceptional, while in the post-war years the educational system was expanded and reformed with the specific aim of maximizing equality of opportunity. Evidence from repeated national surveys would then indicate that class differentials in educational attainment were indeed reduced, with children of working-class and farm origins in particular 'closing the gap' on children of service-class origins (cf. Chapter 8), and, further, that for several decades relative mobility chances likewise moved towards generally greater equality (R. Erikson 1983; Jonsson 1991). By the 1970s Sweden was characterized by a higher level of fluidity than most other modern societies, chiefly on account of a low propensity for immobility in all classes alike (Erikson and Goldthorpe 1992*a*).

However, more recent survey evidence reveals that, from the 1970s onwards, at the same time as the 'Swedish model' of economic and social policy lost its coherence, the tendency towards more equal relative rates weakened and then, at least among men, disappeared (Jonsson and Mills 1993; Jonsson 1996). It is, moreover, of interest to note that the role played by educational reform and indeed increasing educational equality in promoting greater social fluidity appears throughout to have been somewhat problematic. Rather than a 'tightening bond' being evident between educational attainment and class position, as might have been anticipated, their association would seem if anything to have become somewhat looser over time. And of perhaps special significance is the finding that, while the proportion of service-class members with higher education continued to grow, over the period in which the trend towards greater social fluidity faded out educational attainment become of relatively *decreasing* importance as a factor creating intergenerational stability within this class (Jonsson 1991, 1996).

Both the Hungarian and the Swedish cases thus lend further support to the idea that, for greater equality of opportunity, in the sense of more equal relative rates of class mobility, to be achieved, inequalities of condition deriving from the class structure itself will need to be in some way modified or countered in their effects. At the same time, though, these cases could also be taken to point to a further conclusion: namely, that, in order thus to create the conditions under which more equal relative rates might be expected, political intervention that is both forceful and sustained will be necessary. In particular, the effectiveness of educational reform alone is called into question, unless, perhaps, taken to the lengths of class-related discrimination that could scarcely find acceptance in a liberal democratic context. In other words, the resistance to change that endogenous mobility regimes can exert— or, at all events, to change in the direction of more equal class competition— is underlined, and likewise the capacity of these regimes to reassert themselves.

A further question that is then, of course, prompted, and that suggests one other way in which the theory that has been proposed might be open to test, is that of whether this resistance would in fact be similarly strong to change in the *opposite* direction, that is, towards more unequal relative rates. The theory clearly implies that this would *not* be the case. Given the increased class-linked inequalities of condition that would promote such a trend, individuals pursuing mobility strategies from below would face greater constraints and greater risks in engaging in competition for more desirable class positions, while those pursuing strategies from above would be yet more advantaged in the resources that they could use so as, by one route or another, to ensure their class stability.

During the years of the 'long boom' that followed the Second World War, income distributions in most modern societies, in apparent conformity with the 'Kuznets hypothesis' (Kuznets 1955), became somewhat more equal, and at the same time most governments extended citizens' rights to social welfare—a process that T. H. Marshall (1947) aptly described as one of 'class abatement'. It is then against this background, I would suggest, that one can best understand the fact previously noted that, in so far as changes in relative mobility rates have been shown up in research to date, they do more often point to increasing than to decreasing fluidity. However, in the decades following the long boom, trends in income distributions in more advanced societies have shown a good deal of cross-national variation and in a number of cases, most strikingly so far in the UK and the USA, a shift towards greater inequality is apparent (Gottschalk and Smeeding 1997; A. B. Atkinson 1998). At the same time social welfare provision has almost everywhere been subject to retrenchment. Assuming, therefore, that these tendencies are not rapidly reversed, which would seem unlikely, the prediction from the theory that I have outlined must evidently be that, by the early decades of the twenty-first century, mobility research will in fact be discovering instances of social fluidity in decline.[32]

I have argued that recent technical advances in social mobility research have not had the intellectually narrowing effect that various critics have claimed. I have sought to show how, in at least one major respect, they have in fact led to empirical findings that have greatly clarified just what the focus of theoretical effort in the field should now be: that is, to explain the degree of temporal constancy and cross-national commonality that are revealed in relative rates of intergenerational mobility, especially as viewed in a class structural context. The application of loglinear modelling to the analysis of standard mobility tables and the conceptual distinction that this has allowed between absolute and relative mobility rates has made it possible to see that it is the latter rather than the former that pose the central challenge to theory construction. The extent of change and variation in absolute rates, which is

---

[32] One caveat that I might be allowed to make here is the following: that in such research it will be of special importance that due attention is given to data quality and in particular to problems that may arise from non-response to surveys becoming increasingly class biased, and thus leading to a serious under-representation of individuals located at the base of the class structure or in the 'underclass' of the long-term or recurrently unemployed. Neglect of this potential problem could easily lead to a real decline in fluidity not being shown up in survey data.

considerable, can be shown overwhelmingly to reflect the differing ways in which the class structures of particular societies have evolved, and will therefore require explanation far more of a historical than a theoretical kind: that is, explanation in which the invocation of contingencies and singularities will play a crucial role. In contrast, the degree of invariance over time and place displayed by relative rates, or endogenous mobility regimes, clearly calls for theoretical explanation and at a level of generality that can transcend the specificities of particular temporal or societal contexts.

I have sought to make a start on the development of such an explanation and have opted for one that is grounded in a theory of action, in contrast to the functionalist grounding of the most important attempt previously made to account for what were believed to be—mistakenly, as it now appears—the main trends and patterns of relative mobility rates observable in modern societies. I do not intend here to recapitulate my outline theory but simply to make two final remarks for the benefit of potential critics and of those who might try to take the theory further (these categories being, I would hope, largely overlapping).

First, I have attempted to preserve coherence by relying throughout on rational action theory. It might at various points have been possible to give my argument at least a more immediate plausibility by shifting ground and treating action as, say, being ultimately shaped by individuals' adherence to cultural values or social norms. But this would, in fact, have been of little value if no more than *ad hoccery* were involved. I would, therefore, invite anyone inclined to improve the theory through such eclecticism to see their theoretical task as then extending to justification for so doing.

Secondly, I have also attempted to indicate wherever possible the existing empirical evidence that I would regard as having relevance for the theory and also ways in which further research could serve to test the theory more specifically. It would be only reasonable to expect that either the revision of old findings or the production of new ones will sooner or later create problems for the theory.[33] But when this occurs I would urge that theoretical efforts should none the less continue, whether on similar lines or different ones, in order to provide explanations of the highly significant results that social mobility research has produced and will, I believe, continue to produce, rather than the field being allowed to lapse back into a condition of more or less unleavened empiricism, for which it could indeed be rightly criticized.

[33] For example, there are indications from 'revisionist' research currently in progress that in the decades after the Second World War very slight but steady increases in social fluidity occurred—together with reductions in class differentials in education—in France and also perhaps in (the former West) Germany, on something like the Swedish pattern. If findings to this effect were to be confirmed (I do not believe that they are, as yet, secure) then an evident theoretical puzzle would arise. While my own theory would need, at all events, modification and extension, it would at the same scarcely be satisfactory to suppose simply that the functionalist theory might operate in some nations but not in others.

12

Sociology and the Probabilistic Revolution, 1830–1930: Explaining an Absent Synthesis

As I NOTED at the outset, the chapters in this collection are ordered into three main groups, which could be labelled as 'critical', 'programmatic', and 'illustrative'. From a reading of the chapters in this order, an increasingly clear idea can, I hope, be gained of the kind of sociology that I would see as offering the best prospects for the future of the discipline. This is a sociology that is concerned with establishing and explaining phenomena that can be described in some way or other by reference to social regularities of a probabilistic kind—their formation, continuity, interrelation, change, disruption, and so on. As regards establishing such phenomena, and also determining their precise form, I would attach main importance to statistical methods of data collection and analysis as being the most reliable and versatile of those available to the sociologist. As regards explaining such phenomena, I would, from the standpoint of methodological individualism, seek a basis in the theory of action, and give rational action theory a privileged, if not necessarily exclusive, role. And finally, as regards the testing of explanations, I would again see statistical analysis as having a major role to play and, most fundamentally, as providing a well-developed logic of inference for empirical but non-experimental science that can be appropriately extended for use with qualitative as well as quantitative data.

If a sociology of the kind in question could be successfully developed, several significant advantages might then be expected to follow. First, the lack of integration of research and theory—the long-standing scandal of sociology—could at last be overcome. It would no longer be supposed that statistical technique alone is capable of providing sociological explanations or, in other words, that 'variable sociology' can be complete in itself, while at the same time theory could no longer claim autonomy from the findings of empirical research but would be called upon to demonstrate its explanatory power. Secondly, vexatious differences between 'scientific' and 'humanistic'

This chapter has not been published previously. For comments on earlier drafts, I am indebted to David Cox, Lorraine Daston, Alain Desrosières, Daniel Krymkowski, Gordon Marshall, Karl Ulrich Mayer, and Wout Ultee.

conceptions of sociology could be transcended. It would be apparent that sociology can, and ultimately needs to, combine the collection and analysis of data in ways informed by statistical science with efforts to make the results that emerge both explicable and at the same time intelligible: statistics and hermeneutics are complementary. And, finally, a major contribution could in this way be made to a new sociological mainstream, capable of replacing the current, largely spurious pluralism that does sociology little credit in the context of the social sciences or the humanities and indeed bodes ill for its future as an academic discipline of any sort.

I recognize, however, that to argue in this vein does raise at least one rather obvious question. If a sociology on the lines that I would advocate does hold out such promise, why is it that it has been so very slow to make its appearance?[1] More specifically, why is it that through most of the history of sociology the statistical treatment of social data, on the one hand, and the theory of social action, on the other, have been concerns pursued for the most part separately from each other and by individuals or 'schools' with, apparently, rather little in common. One answer that might be given is that this divergence is not at all accidental: that inherent problems have faced, and will continue to face, any sociology that seeks to achieve a synthesis of these concerns, since they reflect what are ultimately incompatible understandings of the nature of sociology or even, perhaps, of society itself. Alternatively, though, it might be held that the difficulties that stood in the way of such a synthesis in the past were contingent rather than necessary— the result, say, of specific institutional or intellectual circumstances, or even perhaps in some cases of the courses of personal histories and their intersection, which could, in principle, have been otherwise and which at all events need not be taken as indicative of problems of any fundamental and abiding kind.

In this concluding chapter, my aim is then to consider which of these views comes nearer to the truth. I pursue this aim through an essay on the history of sociology in its key formative period from, roughly, the 1830s through to the 1930s, and with special reference to the cases of France, England, and Germany. I realize, of course, that a more complete treatment would require the inclusion also of the USA, as in the course of the twentieth century American sociology came to achieve, at least in numerical and organizational terms, a position of international dominance. I do not in fact attempt this here, if only so as to keep the text to a reasonable length. However, my reading of the relevant literature leads me to believe that the conclusions that are to be drawn from the American case do not in fact differ in their essentials from those I reach on the basis of the European experience; and I am confirmed in this view by various secondary analyses and, above all, by the insightful remarks of Coleman (1986a) on the historical—and indeed continuing—

---

[1] Although marred by the limitations of available data and techniques (see further Chapter 8 above), Boudon's *Education, Opportunity and Social Inequality* (1974) could be taken as a key pioneering work in sociology in the style in question.

failure in American sociology to bring quantitative research and the theory of social action into any coherent and productive relationship.[2]

One other preliminary remark is in order. The history that follows is, quite openly, history written from the standpoint of the present and specifically in order to address a current issue. The reader should therefore be warned that there are more than the usual dangers of bias and distortion—of 'Whig history' or, more likely perhaps, of what Bulmer (1981) has referred to as 'inverse Whig history', which represents the past not as leading inexorably to a glorious present but rather as a catalogue of errors that can only now be recognized as such. I have sought to document my arguments fairly extensively so that those who do not find my interpretations acceptable should at all events be able to pin down just where differences arise.[3]

Sociology and the Probabilistic Revolution

In order to provide an essential context for the discussion of my three national cases, I need first of all to take up a topic that is in fact almost entirely neglected in standard histories of sociology: the initially important, but later faltering, involvement of sociology in what has become known as the 'probabilistic revolution' in scientific thinking (Krüger et al. 1987a,b; Gigerenzer et al. 1989).[4] That is, the revolution that, to paraphrase Hacking (1987: 45), led from a conception of the world at the end of the eighteenth century in which it was 'deemed to be governed by stern necessity and universal laws' to one established by around 1930 in which the world was 'run at best by laws of chance'.

At the beginning of the nineteenth century, probability theory had two main, though quite different, areas of application. On the one hand, within the 'moral sciences' of the Enlightenment, it served as the calculus through which rational individuals could—and should—form their beliefs and direct their actions wherever situations of risk or uncertainty arose. Thus, probability theory was urged (with varying degrees of success) as providing the proper basis for the settlement of interrupted games of chance, for deciding the terms of life-insurance policies, annuities, and other aleatory contracts, and for

---

[2] Also relevant are Bernert (1983) and Bannister (1987) on the reception of the new English statistics in American sociology, the early Columbia school, and the work of William F. Ogburn; Boudon (1971) on Lazarsfeld and his problems with Weber's understanding of social action; and Turner and Turner (1990) and Ross (1991) more generally.

[3] In view of my earlier critical remarks on sociologists' uses of historical materials (Chapter 2), I should make it clear that for my present purposes my primary sources are texts from the period with which I am concerned and it is on these that I chiefly rely. Where I refer to secondary sources—i.e. commentaries etc. on these texts—I do so as a convenience and it can be taken that, unless otherwise indicated, I share their authors' interpretation of the texts to which they refer.

[4] One exception is S. P. Turner (1985). This work does, however, suffer from having been written before the publication of most of the remarkable series of studies on the history of the probabilistic revolution (including those cited in the text) that emerged from the 1982–3 programme of the Zentrum für interdisziplinäre Forschung of the University of Bielefeld.

fixing the ground rules for jury verdicts and electoral procedures. This tradition can be seen as reaching its culmination in the work of Condorcet, the 'last of the *philosophes*', but now recognized as one of the founders of the present-day theory of 'social choice' (Baker 1975). On the other hand, in a number of non-experimental natural sciences, especially astronomy and geodesy, probability theory was used as a means of handling observational error and arriving at 'best estimates' in the measurement of the properties of physical objects or systems. Mathematicians of the calibre of Gauss and Laplace provided the ultimate rationale and refinement of techniques that had, however, been applied by working scientists in a rule-of-thumb fashion for many decades previously (see further Stigler 1986: pt. one).

It is, then, not a little surprising to find that, when, from around 1830 to 1860, sociology and probability theory came together in a relatively brief but highly influential period of synergy, it was in fact from the theory's application in this *latter* field that inspiration derived. The 'social mathematics' of Condorcet were almost entirely ignored; it was the 'social physics' of Adolphe Quetelet, the Belgian astronomer-turned-sociologist, that were central (cf. Daston 1987).

As an astronomer, Quetelet was familiar with what he and his colleagues knew as Laplace's 'error law' or 'error curve' or, in modern terminology, the normal distribution. Astronomers were well aware of the fallibility both of their instruments and of their own senses, and had for long sought to improve their measurements by making many equivalent observations of a phenomenon of interest (for example, the position of a star) and then calculating the *mean* of the values recorded as the best approximation to the true value. The error curve of probability theory was of key importance in legitimating this procedure. If deviations from the mean value—that is, what were to be treated as errors—proved to be distributed around the mean in accordance with this curve, the validity of taking the mean as the best estimate was confirmed. It became possible to regard errors as resulting from many different 'accidental' causes that, in the mean, were in effect cancelled out. However, if deviations were not so distributed, a more problematic situation was indicated in which the observations made were for some reason or other not equivalent or in which they were influenced by systematic rather than merely random sources of error; and, in these circumstances, their mean value could stand as no more than an arbitrary arithmetical result.[5]

Quetelet's scientific interests seem first to have moved beyond astronomy when he noted that much anthropometric data—measurements of individuals' physical features and capacities, such as height, weight, or strength—showed distributions very similar to the error curve. It was, he suggested, as if Nature were 'aiming' at a true value, represented by the mean, but, because

---

[5] It is also of interest to note that the extension of this use of the error curve to situations where two quantities were being measured simultaneously led to the method of estimation through 'least squares' long before it was applied to the choice of the best fitting regression line (see Stigler 1986: ch. 1).

of various accidental influences, was subject to inaccuracy, or error, in the same way as a marksman shooting at a target. But Quetelet made his crucial step, so far as social science was concerned, by then going on to discover, or at all events to propose, a similar phenomenon in the case of demographic and, further, of 'moral' statistics—the statistics of marriage, illegitimacy, suicide, or crime. Like many others before him, Quetelet was impressed by the fact that such moral statistics, considered as, say, annual rates for some national or regional population, or in some other ratio form, showed a high degree of stability. But what distinguished his position was his suggestion that, if one traced out the variation in such rates or ratios around a mean value for a large number of observations, what tended to be revealed was again the error curve.

Where this was the case, Quetelet then argued, the mean values could be taken as expressing distinctive features of the population or society to which they referred; or, alternatively, distinctive 'propensities' (*penchants*) of its individual members: that is, their propensities to marry, have illegitimate children, kill themselves, or resort to crime. In other words, from these values one could be said to learn not just about the 'average man' (*l'homme moyen*) of the society in some purely arithmetical sense but also, because the means were ones derived from observations distributed according to the error curve, about the 'typical man' (*l'homme type*). In turn, then, Quetelet maintained, it was on such 'true' mean values that scientific attention should focus. For these values would be purely influenced by, and would thus facilitate the identification of, those causal factors at work that were of a *constant* or, possibly, a *systematically varying* kind; whereas actually observed rates would, in addition, be influenced by a wide range of accidental causes of no particular interest. Thus, from astronomical observations, through anthropometric data to moral statistics, the same logic was pursued: where true means were to be found, as guaranteed by the error curve, true values were represented.[6]

The work of Quetelet has then to be seen as the first attempt at the study of regularities in social action that combined the use of extensive descriptive statistics with some elements of probability theory. However, in its own day it proved to have a wider significance still. The regularities to which Quetelet's efforts pointed were ones of a radically new kind—more so than he himself was able to appreciate. They were not the deterministic regularities of eighteenth-century science that could be directly explained in terms of 'laws' of nature or of society, despite Quetelet's repeated references to the latter. Rather, they were probabilistic regularities, observable only at the level of the aggregate or 'mass', and relating to phenomena that, when viewed more locally, appeared as being inherently underdetermined.

The significance of such regularities was in fact most rapidly grasped and effectively exploited by the physical scientists whom Quetelet had always

---

[6] I draw here mainly on Quetelet (1835/1842, 1846, 1869). However, tracing exactly the development of Quetelet's thought is hindered by the extensive but fragmented nature and often complex publication history of his work. A new critical edition is badly needed.

sought to emulate. That is, in the development of the kinetic theory of gases and of 'statistical physics' more generally that set the probabilistic revolution on its triumphant way. Remarkably (cf. Porter 1982, 1986: ch. 5; Gigerenzer *et al.* 1989: ch. 2) *both* of the leading figures in the field, Clerk Maxwell and Ludwig Boltzmann, were crucially, though independently, influenced by Quetelet. Both acknowledged his work on moral statistics as providing the basic model of how a higher-level order could emerge, and become open to study, from out of lower-level processes that, whether ultimately subject to deterministic laws or not, proved to be practically untreatable from this point of view. Thus, the rather ironic situation arose that, while Quetelet aimed always to base his social science on the methods of physics in its classical era, those who in the mid-nineteenth century were creating a new physics felt free to take their lead from the insights of Quetelet's social science. As Krüger (1987: 80) has remarked, at this point 'the familiar hierarchy of the disciplines loses meaning'.

By 1860, Quetelet's own original work was virtually completed. He had, however, large numbers of devoted followers throughout Europe, and his ideas were to remain a major focus of commentary and critique within statistics for at least two decades more. Correspondingly, sociology continued to be one of the main subject-matter areas with reference to which key issues were pursued. Two such issues can, for present purposes at least, be taken as of main importance.

First, as moral statistics steadily increased in both quantity and quality, and were seized upon by the disciples of Quetelet, doubts began to be voiced about the main postulate of his approach to the analysis and interpretation of such data: that is, that series of moral statistics revealed a long-term stability, in the sense that short-term deviations from their mean values conformed to the error curve. The enthusiasts of *Queteletismus*, still more than Quetelet himself, were, as Hacking has put it (1990: 113), ready to accept 'any empirical distribution that came up in a hump' as being that which they wished to find. But work in the 1870s by more critically minded statisticians, such as Émile Dormoy in France and Wilhelm Lexis in Germany, on evaluating dispersion in statistical series led to increased questioning in this regard. In the light of the tests that were developed, the indications were in fact that most series of moral statistics showed greater dispersion in their distributions than would be expected under the error curve (Porter 1986: 240–55; Desrosières 1993: 116–21). Thus, the idea that mean values captured general population characteristics that were causally specific was subverted. It seemed rather the case that rates of moral statistics calculated for a national society were a composite of those specific to a number of different collectivities within that society, each of which was subject to its own particular set of causal processes.

In fact, Quetelet had always shown an awareness of this problem of 'heterogeneity'[7] and in many of his analyses had recognized, at least implicitly,

---

[7] This awareness went back in fact to an early episode in Quetelet's career—the forceful critique by de Keverberg of Laplace's 'ratio' method for estimating the size of national populations that Quetelet had endorsed (Stigler 1986: 163–9).

that just a single 'average individual' would be quite inadequate to represent an entire society. A whole series of average men—and average women—further specified by age, ethnicity, occupation, social class, and so on, might need to be distinguished before true average rates could be isolated. Indeed, in pursuing this line of argument, Quetelet was led to produce, notably in his studies of crime rates (see esp. 1835/1942: pt. 3), some recognizable, though primitive, exercises in *multivariate* analysis.[8] And in this way he then himself anticipated what in the later nineteenth century was to mark the decisive break with *Queteletismus*: that is, the movement, as Desrosières has put it (1993: ch. 4), away from 'the statistics of the average' and towards 'the statistics of relationships'.

This movement was, however, yet more powerfully driven by debate on the second major issue that arose from Quetelet's work: that of the significance that should be attached in moral and other social statistics to deviations from mean values, regardless of whether these followed the error curve or not. As noted at the outset, the probabilistic ideas that informed Quetelet's social science were ones developed in order to deal with observational problems in the physical sciences. But the analogies that Quetelet was then forced to imply between true means and best estimates in, say, astronomy and in the study of regularities in social action were clearly open to question. Just what was the validity of regarding deviations from the mean in the case of moral statistics as being 'error' in the same sense as deviations from the mean in the case of observations of celestial bodies?

An incisive treatment of the matter was eventually provided by Edgeworth (1885), who insisted that 'observations' and 'statistics' should be clearly distinguished. Observations could be understood as more or less accurate representations of the attributes of some given object—'different copies of one original'; but statistics, at least of the kind analysed by social scientists, had their own autonomy—'different originals affording one "generic portrait"'. Thus, in the former case, true means as guaranteed by the error curve could indeed be regarded as the best approximation to true values, and deviation as being mere error; but in the latter case even true means could be no more than useful summaries, and deviations from them had to be seen not as error but as genuine *variation*, which could in fact claim a greater reality, and interest, than the mean itself.

Indeed, for some time before Edgeworth's intervention, researchers in various fields had been using the error curve in ways that were inspired by Quetelet's work but which led them clearly beyond his preoccupation with population means. Most notably, Galton, in his pioneering studies of heredity (1869, 1889a), realized the potential of the error curve from Quetelet's sociological applications, but used it as more than simply a method of determining 'types' (cf. chapter 4 above). For Galton, it became the basis for examining variation in, and the intergenerational transmission of, individual

---

[8] Quetelet in effect treated as causally relevant those attributes that, if ignored in the categorization of data, revealed a lack of homogeneity in producing average rates that were clearly not 'true' ones. For critical commentary, see Stigler (1987).

characteristics within populations. As a committed hereditarian, Galton stressed the degree of family likeness that was shared by parents and their off-spring across a wide range of characteristics. But, by studying the relations between 'error-curve' distributions, he made the important finding that a class of parents with a similar value on a given characteristic—for example, height—would have offspring with a mean value in this regard that differed from their own, and that would in fact show 'regression' closer to the mean value for the population as a whole. Then in further work, also on Quetelet-ian lines, in the field of anthropometry, Galton developed the concept of 'correlation' and recognized it as being, formally, an extension of that of regression.

Galton's analytic efforts in dealing with his substantive problems proved in fact to be of far greater consequence than these problems themselves. They marked the first breakthrough in what was to become a collective intellectual achievement of a quite outstanding kind (see esp. Stigler 1986: chs. 8–10; also Porter 1986: chs. 5, 9). Through the subsequent work of Edgeworth and then, crucially, of Karl Pearson and George Udny Yule, Galton's initial understand-ing of regression and correlation as specifically biological phenomena was transformed into the idea of regression and correlation as *general statistical methods* for treating the connection between two, and then, in principle, any number of variables, *of any kind whatever*. In this way, the foundations were established of multivariate statistical analysis as it is practised today, and indeed of what Stigler (1986: 361) has aptly described as 'a unified logic of empirical science', the significance of which went far beyond that of its com-ponent techniques.

However, paradoxically, at the same time as the 'new English statistics' were being thus created, the period of vital engagement of sociology in the prob-abilistic revolution was coming to its close. The application of probability theory to social data had played a central role in the recognition of a new kind of regularity—probabilistic regularity—and hence of a new kind of sci-entific *explanandum*, unknown to the classical determinists of the eighteenth century. And sociology had remained an important subject-matter area for the initial attempts at using probability theory in turn as the basis of estab-lishing and analysing such regularities, and of making and testing inferences about the processes through which they were generated. But, by the end of the nineteenth century, even as the full potential of this project was becom-ing apparent, sociology and statistics began to draw apart. The subject-matter areas in which the new statistics became most effectively deployed were, first of all, evolutionary biology and then psychology and economics. In the early decades of the twentieth century, biometrics, psychometrics, and economet-rics came into being and were energetically developed, but without any soci-ological equivalent.[9]

[9] When the terms 'sociometry' and 'sociometrics' eventually made their appearance, it was with reference not to a statistical methodology adapted to the needs of sociology but rather to an approach to the study of primary social relations. Sociology's failure to respond

It cannot be supposed that what is here revealed is simply a declining interest in sociology on the part of statisticians, preoccupied, say, with demonstrating the value of their discipline to the 'harder' sciences. The makers of the new statistics, Galton, Edgeworth, Pearson, and Yule alike, were extraordinarily wide-ranging in their intellectual interests, and on numerous occasions showed themselves ready enough to try to apply their expertise to social, and indeed sociological, issues.[10] However, as will later be shown, their efforts in this regard found scant appreciation in the sociological circles of the day. Often they were not well understood and, whether understood or not, tended to meet with a response that was at best lukewarm. Furthermore, the tendency of sociologists to distance themselves from the new statistics meant that, even where they sought to maintain the tradition of Quetelet in using descriptive statistical data on patterns of social action as an empirical resource, they were increasingly ill-equipped to exploit the analytical opportunities that such data afforded. And neither then were they well positioned to integrate their empirical work with the development of a theory of action consistent with probabilistic thinking and offering some explanatory purchase in regard to the substantive problems with which they were concerned.

Why, then, did such a situation arise, and persist for more than half a century?

France

France could be regarded as Quetelet's intellectual homeland; but the reception of his ideas there, and especially on the part of sociologists, was perhaps less favourable than in any other European country. To begin with, Quetelet greatly angered Auguste Comte, the founder of 'positivist philosophy', by taking the term *physique sociale*, in which Comte had priority, to describe the new science that he sought to base on the analysis of statistical data. Comte then coined the word *sociologie* in an effort to ensure that no confusion between his work and that of Quetelet should arise. But far more was involved here than personal rivalry. For not only did Comte lack all interest in the kind of empirical enquiry in which Quetelet engaged; he repeatedly and vehemently opposed any suggestion that probability theory could have a useful,

positively to the new English statistics in the same way as the other disciplines referred to meant that, when in the course of the twentieth century interest in quantitative analysis revived, there was for some time a far from satisfactory dependence upon previously established '-ometrics'. As earlier noted (Chapter 1), it is only quite recently that sociologists have managed to free themselves from this dependence by developing techniques more suited to the kinds of data and problem with which they typically deal.

[10] This point is unfortunately obscured in the work of MacKenzie (1981), who, apparently in his concern to validate the 'strong programme' in the sociology of science, puts too great an emphasis on the eugenicist preoccupations of the English statisticians—as, perhaps, contemporaries were also inclined to do (see text below and n. 27). As MacKenzie does acknowledge, while Galton and Pearson were leaders of the eugenicist movement, Edgeworth was never seriously involved and Yule tended to be hostile.

or indeed a valid, application in the study of society. All attempts, whether in the style of Quetelet or of Condorcet, 'à rendre positives les études sociales d'après une subordination chimérique à l'illusoire théorie mathématique des chances' (Comte 1830–42/1908: iv. 270–1; cf. ii. 192) were to be rejected out of hand. Moreover, the main arguments that Comte levelled against a statistically grounded sociology were ones that remained influential in France for many decades after his death.

On the one hand, Comte upheld a theory of science (cf. Heilbron 1995: chs. 11–13) of a strongly anti-reductionist character. Each of the sciences that had reached the 'positive' stage had, he insisted, created its own specific methodology. Mathematics, or more precisely geometry and mechanics, had become part of the proper methodology of astronomy, and could also play some role in physics. But, in the more complex science of chemistry, mathematical reasoning had little place, and in biology and sociology, which were more complex still, had no place at all. The complexity to which Comte here referred was that deriving from the degree of interdependence of the phenomena that these latter sciences treated. This meant in effect that biology and sociology had to follow what would later be called a 'holistic' approach. Their concern must be with the study of organisms or societies as such, aimed at the discovery of the principles that govern their integration and their development. So far, then, as sociology was concerned, its evidential basis had to be found not in data on patterns of individual action occurring within societies but rather in the recorded history of societies, or of entire civilizations, considered as entities in themselves. Indeed, so thoroughgoing was Comte's holism that, as Aron (1965–7: i. 83) has aptly observed, its logical conclusion, from which Comte did not in fact resile, was that the ultimate goal of sociology should be the understanding of human history in its totality, 'regarded as the history of a single people'.

On the other hand, though, Comte opposed the introduction of probabilistic thinking into sociology through an argument that appealed to the unity of science rather than to its differentiation: namely, that 'le calcul de chances' offended against the idea of deterministic law that was fundamental to every science, no matter what its methodology (cf. Hacking 1990: ch. 17). Comte adhered always to the eighteenth-century view, which the probabilistic revolution was destined to transform, that invoking chance simply testified to ignorance. It was, he contended, open to sociology to establish laws of human society and of the movement of human history—of 'social statics' and 'social dynamics'—that would be no less strict in their determinism than those of astronomy or physics. And indeed Comte believed that he had himself succeeded in formulating the most important of these laws, the 'law of the three stages', which showed how the development of human societies was necessarily governed by the progress, no less necessary, of the human mind. Moreover, Comte's determinism, allied with his holism, then led him in turn to an extreme anti-individualistic position—in effect, as Kolakowski (1972: 87) has noted, to a virtual refusal 'to ascribe a reality to the human individual'.

Consequently, at the same time as Comte's sociology excluded any notion of the social world as probabilistic, it also excluded any serious consideration of human agency: the reality of chance and the reality of choice were together denied (cf. Daston 1987).

Comte's attack on probabilistic thinking does not appear to have had any very widespread impact. In the larger scientific context, it became rather quickly outmoded. However, in the development of sociology, and in France in particular, a Comtean legacy can clearly be traced: most consequentially, in the work of Durkheim and then of the Durkheimian school, which remained pre-eminent up to the time of the Second World War (cf. T. N. Clark 1973).[11]

In understanding the significance of this legacy, the key text is undoubtedly Durkheim's *Suicide* (1897/1952). This work has been widely regarded as a great pioneering study in quantitative sociology, pointing the way to twentieth-century achievements. However, such a view is not a little misleading. At least as regards the creation of a sociology in which the statistical analysis of regularities in social action is combined with the explanation and understanding of such action at the individual level, *Suicide* made no contribution, nor was it intended to. It can in fact be far better seen as exemplifying several of the more serious intellectual barriers that help explain why such a project was for so long delayed.

To begin with, *Suicide* does not display any major advances in the application of statistical technique in sociological work. Durkheim differed from Comte in that he recognized the need for detailed empirical research, and saw official statistics as being in this respect a valuable resource. But, in his treatment of such data, Durkheim did not go much beyond the moral statisticians who had preceded him, and in some ways his analyses could be reckoned as less sophisticated than those of Quetelet.[12] This is all the more remarkable in that by the time of the writing of *Suicide* the early work of the English statisticians was available and, at least to some extent, actually known to Durkheim. Already in *The Division of Labour* (1893/1933: bk. II, ch. 4) he had discussed, approvingly if not with full understanding, Galton's analyses of regression towards the mean.[13] None the less, in *Suicide* Durkheim made no

---

[11] An implication of moving thus directly from Comte to Durkheim is neglect of Tocqueville, who is in fact regarded by Aron, Boudon, and others as one of the great representatives of the individualistic tradition in sociology and thus set in contrast with Durkheim. However, Tocqueville's influence on the development of sociology, in France or elsewhere, would appear, at least until recently, to have been rather slight.

[12] For example, Durkheim did not show Quetelet's concern with the question of whether deviations from average suicide rates were normally distributed; nor did he give as much attention as had Quetelet to problems of the reliability and validity of official statistics. It is in fact these latter problems that most immediately undermine Durkheim's analyses (see e.g. Day 1987; van Poppel and Day 1996). Durkheim's own criticisms (1897/1952: 300–4) of Quetelet's work are not easy to follow but could be taken to imply some misunderstanding of the ideas of *l'homme moyen* and *l'homme type*, as distinguished in the text above.

[13] Selvin (1976) gives other reasons for supposing that Durkheim was probably aware of English statistical work but neglects the actual reference to Galton. On Durkheim's failure to grasp the point of Galton's argument, see Desrosières (1985) and Hacking (1990: 178).

use of the derived concept of correlation, which would have been well suited to his purposes and would indeed have saved him from a number of serious errors.

One possible reason for this disregard is that Durkheim, in true Comtean fashion, believed that sociology should, like any other science, have its own distinctive methods, and therefore did not wish it to be seen as overly dependent upon statistics, a field, moreover, in which he had no evident expertise. But of surely greater significance was the further Comtean insistence on determinism that runs through *Suicide* and that makes it—received opinion notwithstanding—in most respects a profoundly *anti*-statistical work.

Thus, contrary to appearances, the method on which Durkheim chiefly relies in analysing the connection between rates of suicide in different populations and other of their characteristics is not statistical at all but rather a *logical* procedure designed to establish relations of a quite deterministic kind: that is, John Stuart Mill's method of 'concomitant variation' (cf. Boudon 1967: ch. 2). Before a link between suicide and another population characteristic can be claimed, Durkheim typically requires (and especially when attacking the theories of rival authors) what would in modern terms be called a *perfect* rank-order correlation. By this criterion, he is, for example, led to deny (1897/1952: bk. 1, chs. 1, 2) that *any* connection exists between the suicide rate and the proportion of German-speakers in data from the Austrian provinces, or again between the suicide rate and the consumption of alcohol in data for the French *départements*—although, in both cases, a fairly strong, if far from perfect, correlation is in fact present (Selvin 1976; Skog 1991; cf. Desrosières 1985). For Durkheim, in other words, dependencies between social variables had to be either total or non-existent; no intermediate position could be recognized.

Furthermore, Durkheim's commitment to deterministic rather than probabilistic thinking emerges strongly at a theoretical as well as a technical level: that is, in the way in which he seeks to explain those constancies and variations in suicide rates that he accepts as being well established. For the authors who first discovered regularity in moral statistics, this appeared as a clear manifestation of divine providence: the pioneering work of J. P. Süssmilch of 1741 bears the title *Die göttliche Ordnung* (see H. Westergaard 1932: ch. 7). Quetelet remained to a large extent under the sway of this tradition of 'explanation from above', even though appealing not to divine power but rather to that of the 'social system'. He did, however, at the same time attempt, and at the cost of some ambivalence, to accommodate individual action. As well as recognizing free will as one of the accidental causes that produced variation around stable average rates, he was, as earlier noted, also ready to interpret both constancy and systematic variation in rates as expressing individual 'propensities' to act.[14] In contrast, Durkheim, following the programme of *The*

---

[14] Quetelet saw such propensities as explaining why individuals might act differently in similar circumstances. However, he seems never to have reached any settled view about whether propensities were to be understood as biological, psychological, or social.

Rules of Sociological Method (1895/1938), reverted to a position of macro-to-micro determinism of a quite uncompromising kind.

In taking up suicide as a subject for study, Durkheim's very purpose was to show how this apparently most private act could not be understood, in the *rate*, as opposed to the *incidence*, of its occurrence, by reference to the attributes of individuals, such as, say, their material circumstances or mental states. Rates of suicide, and indeed of the different types of suicide that Durkheim distinguished, had to be seen as determined by 'realities' that were entirely external to and independent of the individual. These realities took the form of what Durkheim called suicidogenic 'currents' or 'impulses' that bore off their victims at a rate directly proportional to the strength with which they operated at particular times and in particular societies and their various milieux. In other words, what Durkheim had in mind here were not simply *conditions* of action that might influence individual decisions on whether or not to commit suicide but rather 'real, living, active forces' in which causal power inhered and to which individuals were subject (see 1897/1952: esp. bk. 2, ch. 1; bk. 3, ch. 1).

As several commentators have observed, Durkheim could not himself always sustain the 'radical disjunction' (Lukes 1975: 213) that he wished to set up between the explanation of suicide rates and of individual acts of suicide. Especially in his more detailed discussions of how rates of egoistic, altruistic, and anomic suicide are determined by the differing intensities of primary social relations and of moral regulation, Durkheim tends to move down from the level of suicidogenic currents and to treat statistical associations between suicide rates and specific social situations in terms of individuals' subjective responses. That is to say, he *does* refer, and despite his own prohibitions (e.g. 1897/1952: 43, 297), to the meanings that suicide carries for individuals and in turn to their motives and intentions in either killing themselves or being resistant to this course of action (see esp. Douglas 1967: ch. 2; also Aron 1965–7: ii. ch. 5; Lukes 1975: ch. 9).

However, what, for present purposes, is important is that still at no stage does Durkheim come to contend seriously with the idea that statistically demonstrated regularities in suicide rates might be explained in a way quite different from that which his methodological programme would require. That is, not deterministically, by appeal to the operation of macrosocial forces external to and independent of individuals—and indeed of an altogether mysterious character (cf. Aron 1965–7: ii. 87–91)—but rather probabilistically, as the outcome of individual actions varying around some central tendency under a range of conditions that are more or less constant over time but differ, perhaps, from one population or subpopulation to another. At just one point in *Suicide* (1897/1952: 305–6) does Durkheim contemplate this possibility, with reference to the work of Moritz Drobisch (1867). Durkheim here clearly sees the import of the probabilistic argument—perhaps all too clearly. With this argument, he writes, 'One need not assume that they [potential suicides] yield to a superior influence; but merely that they reason generally in the same way when confronted by the same circumstances.' But he at once proceeds to a rejection that is based, first, on an entirely question-begging assertion—that we already *know* that the circumstances associated with suicides 'are not their real causes'—and, secondly, on the quite fallacious claim that, if suicides did come about in this way, then suicide rates could not display the kinds of regularity that are apparent.

In sum, it was not for Durkheim conceivable that, in accounting for these regularities, no effect of a societal power existing over and above individuals need be invoked, but only the actions of individuals themselves, aggregated through the 'laws of chance' (cf. Oberschall 1987: 117; Hacking 1990: 177–8). Ironically, in his concern to make sociology a true Comtean science, dealing in holistic and deterministic causation rather than the uncertainties of human action and its interpretation, Durkheim failed to grasp one of the most potent ideas of the science of his day: that the operation of chance at one level could play a crucial role in the creation of order—of a kind—at a higher, emergent level.

After *Suicide*, Durkheim's interest in the use of statistical data waned. Work that he started on crime rates, intended, it seems, to form the basis of a sequel, was never completed (Lukes 1975: 257). From the later 1890s Durkheim's main substantive concerns came in fact to centre on systems of *représentations collectives* as the ultimate source of the moral regulation of societies; and the approach he pursued was primarily an evolutionary one, in the sense that he sought to identify the original, or at least the most 'elementary', expressions of the ideational and institutional phenomena that he wished to study, most famously, of course, in *The Elementary Forms of the Religious Life* (1912/1915). The empirical materials to which he chiefly resorted were then those of comparative history and, increasingly, ethnography, despite the strong reservations about the reliability of the latter that he had previously voiced.[15]

Moreover, this shift in the focus of Durkheim's work exerted a powerful influence on the Durkheimian school in the process of its formation around *L'Année sociologique*, the first volume of which appeared in 1898. Up to the time of Durkheim's death in 1917 and the disruption of the school in consequence of the First World War, most of Durkheim's closer associates, such as Mauss, Hubert, and Hertz, also concentrated their attention on 'archaic' rather than modern societies, and established strong ties with the emerging discipline of social anthropology (Karady 1981, 1983; see also T. N. Clark 1973: app. 2). In contrast, some others associated with the *Année* whose sociological interests directed them towards research in the society of their own day and of a more quantitative kind tended to be marginalized. For instance, the concerns of Paul Lapie with the role of education in social mobility (Lapie

---

[15] Parsons (1937) has argued that also at this stage Durkheim began to move towards a voluntaristic theory of action and even a Weberian notion of *Verstehen*. This view would, however, seem difficult to sustain. Even if, by the time of *The Elementary Forms of Religious Life*, Durkheim had come to adhere to some kind of idealist position, there is little indication that he was led to accord any greater autonomy to individuals in relation to *représentations collectives* than in relation to the normative constraints of the institutional order that he had stressed in his earlier work.

was the inventor of the mobility table) were apparently deemed 'not sociolo-gizable', on the grounds that they were too much related to 'psychology' (Besnard 1983a; see also Cherkaoui 1983)—or, one might say, to individual life events and courses of action that ideational and institutional structures conditioned but did *not* determine. For the true Durkheimians, *any* individ-ualistic approach threatened to compromise the autonomy of their new dis-cipline by implying psychological foundations.

This is not, of course, to say that the Durkheimian school was entirely monolithic. Both before and after the war, there were those who strove 'from within' to free it from some of the rigidities that, in the name of Comtean science, it had imposed upon itself. However, their efforts remained crucially lacking in the degree of confidence and coherence that would have been needed in order to give French sociology a radically new orientation. Thus, Bouglé (1896, 1899), under the influence of both French and German neo-Kantianism, was ready to question the dogma that required that the expla-nation of 'social facts' should be given always in terms of 'preceding social facts' (Durkheim 1895/1938: 110) rather than of the actions of individuals and their consequences. But, although in the 1930s some of his students moved, in various directions, away from Durkheimian orthodoxy (Stoetzel 1957), Bouglé himself had no apparent interest in, nor perhaps the ability to take up, the possibilities offered by new statistical thinking for translating his theoretical ideas into research and data analysis (cf. Vogt 1983).

Conversely, Simiand and Halbwachs kept in close touch with 'official' stat-isticians in France (Desrosières, 1996) and also monitored the development of the new statistics in England and elsewhere, with advantage to their own empirical studies (e.g. Simiand 1907, 1932; Halbwachs 1930/1978, 1933). Both clearly favoured statistical over the ethnographic methods of the other Durkheimians—Simiand (1932) inveighing against the 'superstition de l'étude d'origine' and the 'tissu d'anecdotes' often involved in its pursuit (Desrosières 1985: 306), while Halbwachs upheld statistical analysis as the only means of *reliably* identifying social regularities (Craig 1983: 283). Further, both Simiand and Halbwachs saw in emerging multivariate techniques a vital substitute for experimental methods in the testing of explanatory theory. However, their work did not bring into being any distinctively new style of sociological analysis. While their lack of more general influence may in some degree be attributable to personal characteristics and circumstances, neither in fact showed any tendency to waver in the defence of the essentials of Durkheim's meta-theoretical stance.[16] Indeed, they could together be ranked among their master's most faithful adherents in regarding the regularities that statistical

---

[16] This is apparent even in their reception of the new statistics. Thus Halbwachs, from his early study of Quetelet (Halbwachs 1912), through a primer on probability theory written with the mathematician Maurice Fréchet (Fréchet and Halbwachs 1924), to some of his last essays, returned always to the argument that the application of statistical models in soci-ology must be limited by the fact that individual actions are not 'independent' of each other but, rather, influenced by shared beliefs and norms. However, as Lazarsfeld has pointed out (1961), this is no serious objection; for in so far as such interdependence is known to exist, it too can be statistically modelled if appropriate changes in underlying assumptions are made—as, for example, in well-known 'contagion' models (see also Oberschall 1987).

or other research revealed as being expressions of a supra-individual reality *sui generis*, which were then to be accounted for at this same level and *not* by resort to theories formulated in the perspective of actors themselves (cf. Desrosières 1991; 1993: 267–71).[17] It was, moreover, chiefly on this account that they followed Durkheim into a polemical 'imperialism' that sought to represent other social sciences and various humanistic disciples as being ultimately subordinate to sociology (cf. T. N. Clark 1973: ch. 6; Besnard 1983*b*; Craig 1983) and that blinded them, often, it must be said, in a rather embarrassing fashion, to the degree of success that an anti-deterministic and individualistic approach had elsewhere achieved, most notably, perhaps, in economics and historiography.

In sum, even though challenged in particular respects, and in some decline in the later 1920s and 1930s, the Durkheimian school still managed to maintain an intellectual influence too powerful to allow the emergence in France of any fundamentally different version of sociology, in which the concept of social action would provide the focus for statistical analysis and theoretical understanding alike.[18]

England

Quetelet's work was viewed far more positively and exerted a far wider influence in England than in France. Quetelet was a frequent visitor to England and enjoyed the respect of leading figures in English science, such as Herschel and Whewell. Moreover, as earlier noted, it was in England in the later nineteenth century that, starting from Quetelet's exploitation of the error curve in his *physique sociale*, modern methods of multivariate statistics were created. It might, therefore, appear that England represented an unusually favourable context for the integration of sociology within the probabilistic revolution. And all the more so, perhaps, since the country had also a strong tradition of economics that, by the time in question, could offer a relatively well-developed model of 'micro-to-macro' analysis, in which regularities observable at an aggregate, societal level were theoretically explained by reference to individual action. However, from this standpoint, the actual progress of sociology turned out to be as disappointing in England as in France—in part for similar, but in part too for rather different, reasons.

In England as well as France the influence of Comte stood for long as a barrier to statistical thinking in sociology. John Stuart Mill and Herbert

---

[17] It is, incidentally, for this reason that criticism of Durkheim's and likewise of Halbwachs's own work on suicide (1930/1978) for relying largely on 'ecological' rather than individual-level correlations is scarcely to the point (cf. Isambert 1973; S. P. Turner 1985: 135–8), and notwithstanding Halbwachs's concerns to go somewhat beyond Durkheim in reconciling sociological and psychiatric explanations of suicide.

[18] As T. N. Clark has observed (1973: 200), the 'non-Durkheimian alternatives', such as the highly eclectic 'international sociology' promoted by René Worms or the remnants of Le Playism, were in fact 'most dismal'.

Spencer, dominant figures of the Victorian era, tended alike to play down their intellectual debt to Comte on account, it would seem, of their strong disagreement with him on political issues (Abrams 1968: 53–8). None the less, both were fully committed to the Comtean faith that the concept of deterministic law, the foundation of the natural sciences, was, in principle at least, equally applicable to the study of society. In his early years, Mill indeed followed Comte in attacking probability theory—'the real opprobrium of mathematics' (Mill 1843/1973–4: vii. 538); and, although he was ready, as was Spencer, to accept the regularities revealed by moral and other social statistics as data of some significance, this was always from a strictly deterministic position. Such regularities were to be understood as the outcome, albeit perhaps complex, of the operation of invariable laws that it was the task of sociology to discover.[19] Furthermore, Mill and Spencer were also at one with Comte in believing that the ultimate concern of sociology must be not with the laws of social statics but, rather, with those of social dynamics: the laws according to which one state or form of society succeeded another over the course of human history. In turn, then, for them, as for Comte, the empirical materials—and regularities—of crucial interest were those provided not by statistics but by historical, and also in Spencer's case, ethnographic enquiry.

The major scientific issue on which Mill and Spencer differed from Comte was that of the relation between sociology and psychology. Comte refused even to allow psychology a place in the structure of positivist science; there was no space between the claims of sociology and biology. Mill and Spencer, in contrast, were both sufficiently under the sway of the English individualistic tradition to wish to have sociological laws ultimately grounded in psychological ones, in the sense of 'laws of human nature'. However, what must still be recognized is that no relaxation of their determinism was here entailed of a kind that might have allowed a theory of social action, as distinct from social behaviour, to emerge.

The linkage between sociological and psychological laws envisaged by Mill (1843/1973–4: viii, bk. vi, chs. 3–8) was highly complicated and, perhaps not surprisingly, remained no more than programmatic.[20] For Spencer, matters were simplified by his evolutionism and, more specifically, by his adherence

[19] Both Mill, in his later work, and Spencer tended to refer in this regard to the work of Buckle (1857), which was important in disseminating Quetelet's ideas, rather than to Quetelet's own writings. Mill's difficulties with probability theory are indicated by the number of changes he made in passages dealing with this topic over the successive editions of *A System of Logic*. His initial hostility to it was, however, perhaps more related to its use in the manner of Condorcet than of Quetelet.

[20] Various intermediary 'special sciences' were involved, the most important being, apparently, 'ethology'—the science of human character and its modification by circumstance—on which, however, Mill has little of substance to say. Economics was another special science: that concerned with the behaviour of individuals, *given* that they seek to increase their wealth and are able to compare the efficacy of different means to that end. Mill supposed that the conclusions of economics would need ultimately to be qualified in the light of sociology, but appears never to have contemplated the possibility that sociology might proceed on the basis of a generalization of the methodology of economics. For further relevant commentary on the limitations of Mill's conception of human action, see Ryan (1970: 162–6).

to a theory of evolution of an unreservedly Lamarckian kind (Peel 1971: ch. 6). On this basis, he was able to integrate 'individualism' and 'holism' in an apparently seamless way. As societies struggled to survive and grow, evolutionary processes—ones of increasing social differentiation and integration—worked themselves out at an institutional level; but at the same time accommodative changes occurred, and were intergenerationally transmitted, in the behaviour patterns of individuals and indeed in human nature itself (Spencer 1873/1961: esp. ch. 3). Thus, without denying a role to psychology, Spencer's explanatory approach could still remain essentially 'macro-to-micro', being, in effect, a pioneering version of structural-functionalism (cf. Burrow 1966: ch. 6; Abrams 1968; Peel 1971: ch. 7) reliant on a *highly* 'oversocialized conception of man' (Wrong 1961). The individual was to be viewed 'as one whose will is a factor in social evolution and yet as one whose will is a product of all antecedent influences, social included'.[21]

An important methodological implication of this position was, then, that, while the relevance of individual action was acknowledged in principle, *in the actual practice of empirical enquiry* institutions could be the almost exclusive focus of attention—as indeed they were throughout the volumes of Spencer's *Principles of Sociology* (1876–97). Because the process of social evolution was taken to guarantee what Spencer called (after Comte) a 'consensus' between the institutions of a society and the social character of its members (1873/1961: 47), all patterns of action, or rather behaviour, could be taken as, so to speak, instancing the presence of some institution or other. And, conversely, an adequate account of the institutional structure of a society could then stand as at very least an adequate synopsis of the behavioural regularities that its members displayed. In other words, the need for any direct statistical demonstration of these regularities was circumvented: an obvious convenience, one might add, so far as a wide-ranging treatment of historical and preliterate societies was concerned.

With Spencer there in fact originated a distinctive English tradition of sociology *defined as* the study of social institutions in comparative and evolutionary or developmental perspective. L. T. Hobhouse, who occupied the first chair in sociology in a British university—at the London School of Economics from 1907 to 1929—stood clearly in this tradition (e.g. 1906, 1924), even while striving to produce a version of social evolutionism more 'moralized' than that of Spencer and in turn more congenial to collectivist politics (cf.

---

[21] Several authors (see esp. J. H. Turner 1985) have noted the extent to which Spencer's work prefigures that of the later Parsons—despite Parsons having begun his first major treatise (1937: 3) with the rhetorical question: 'Who now reads Spencer?'; and also that differences between Spencer and Durkheim on the nature of social order are in fact fewer than Durkheim sought to make out. It is of further interest to note that, at one point where Spencer does specifically address the problem of social action and its interpretation (1873/1961: ch. 6), he is chiefly concerned to show that this is more or less insuperable, at all events where actors from remote 'races' or 'civilizations' are concerned: 'we must represent their thoughts and feelings in terms of our own' but 'in so representing them we can never be more than partially right, and are frequently very wrong'. Thus, such 'automorphic' interpretation can never be of great scientific value.

Collini 1979). And his successor, Morris Ginsberg, upheld the tradition, if more through exposition than continuing research, until after the Second World War.

For present purposes, it need further be noted about this tradition only that its representatives' lack of enthusiasm for statistical methods was apparent even in the pursuit of their analyses at the level of institutions. In 1888 in a paper to the Anthropological Institute, Edward Tylor presented evidence of correlations (or what he called 'adhesions') among elements of economic and familial institutions across almost four hundred societies (Tylor 1889). Galton, at that time President of the Institute and himself an experienced ethnographer, questioned the validity of Tylor's analyses (Galton 1889b) on the grounds of a probable lack of independence among his cases resulting from— to use a later term—'cultural diffusion', and thus initiated what remains well known in comparative sociology as 'Galton's problem' (cf. Chapter 3 above). But what is less well known is that Galton also offered encouraging suggestions about how Tylor might deal with the problem and in other ways improve his statistical work, as, for example, through what would now be called tests of significance.[22] Tylor did not, apparently, ever seek to follow this advice. However, what is far more remarkable is that when, a quarter of a century later, Hobhouse, Wheeler, and Ginsberg in their *Material Culture and Social Institutions of the Simpler Peoples* (1915) carried out analyses similar in form to Tylor's, they were content simply to follow his methods (see also Ginsberg 1965). They made no reference whatever to Galton or to any of those who had followed him in transforming statistical thinking and technique—although they did regret that more had not been done to extend *Tylor's* methods to other issues! Perhaps the most plausible explanation that can be advanced for this almost studied disregard is that Hobhouse could not dissociate the new statistics from the eugenics movement that Galton had in effect initiated and Pearson promoted, and to which Hobhouse was strongly opposed (Collini 1979: ch. 6).[23]

The other major tradition in the early history of English sociology, apart from that of comparative and evolutionary institutionalism, was represented by the study of social problems and policy—with particular reference to issues of poverty and 'the condition of the working class'. Such enquiry, though

---

[22] Tylor's foray into comparative institutionalism was something of a departure from his main concern with cultural issues. It is possible that Galton's response to Tylor's work was intended as an implicit reproach to Spencer in regard to his *Descriptive Sociology* (Spencer *et al.* 1873–1934), a multi-volume compilation of ethnographic extracts, largely undertaken by research assistants and continued after Spencer's death, which is often regarded as the prototype for the Yale Human Relations Area Files, Spencer made no attempt at all at the statistical analysis of his data, despite being ready to advance claims that would appear to entail such analysis.

[23] However, another serious possibility is that neither Hobhouse nor his collaborators were equipped to understand the new statistics. One of the few other pieces of empirical research in which Ginsberg was involved was a study of social mobility (1929) that is also technically very limited and that again ignores valuable leads in earlier statistical work, in this case by Pearson (e.g. 1904) of a kind that were quite readily detachable from the latter's eugenicist preoccupations.

extending back to the 'political arithmeticians' of the seventeenth century (cf. R. Stone 1997), revived strongly in the 1830s in association with a growing enthusiasm for the collection of statistical data and the organization of local statistical societies, and also at this time had rather close links with political economy (Abrams 1968; Cullen 1975). But, despite these seemingly promising beginnings, the proponents of this tradition, too, proved more or less immune to the attractive opportunities for the empirical analysis of social data and their theoretical understanding that the probabilistic revolution afforded. In this case, the barrier was not determinism but rather a crude and unreflecting empiricism.

To begin with, the leaders of the 'statistical movement', anxious to avoid its disruption by political dissension, especially in regard to the 'principles' of political economy, represented the role of statistics as being simply that of the production of *facts*, in numerical form, and not consideration of what these facts implied or how they might be explained. Thus, when in 1833 a statistical section was created within the British Association for the Advancement of Science, its President went out of his way to stress that, should statistics once transgress its proper concern with matters of fact, 'that instant will the foul Daemon of discord find its way into our Eden of philosophy' (Cullen 1975: 79). And when, the following year, the Statistical Society of London (the forerunner of the Royal Statistical Society) was established, it adopted the quite explicit motto of *Aliis Exterendum*—'It is for others to thresh out our results'. In this context, then, the study of social problems could rarely rise above unfocused, even if often profuse, description; and, in so far as investigators were bold enough to consider policy questions, they did so with little in the way of intervening analysis.

Furthermore, given the prevalence of this 'Gradgrind' view of the role of statistics in social research, there was little incentive for its practitioners to keep abreast of technical advances. Indeed, there was resistance to what was called the 'mathematicization' of statistics—that is, the grounding of statistical analysis in probability theory (Lecuyer 1987); and over the course of the nineteenth century technical standards of social research using statistics would appear, if anything, to have declined rather than improved (cf. Cole 1972; Oberschall 1987). Consequently, by the time the tradition of 'social problems and policy' research reached its culmination with the poverty surveys of Booth (1889–1903) and Rowntree (1901) at the turn of the century, a wide gulf had opened up between the conception of statistics that this work embodied and that which informed the new English statistics, concurrently emerging as one of the great achievements of the probabilistic revolution.

In this regard, the most revealing episode is the clash that occurred between Booth and Yule over whether a connection existed between pauperism and poor relief policy: specifically, the giving of relief outdoors rather than indoors (that is, in workhouses). Booth had denied any such connection, but Yule (1895), using the new technique of correlation, demonstrated that across English poor law unions the higher the proportion of out-relief, the higher, on average, was the rate of pauperism. From Booth's reply (1896), it was apparent that he suffered from exactly the same difficulty as Durkheim in understanding correlation. He conceded that Yule had shown what he called a 'general' relation between out-relief and pauperism, but not, he insisted, a 'regular' one—by which he meant simply that the correlation was not perfect. To this Yule (1896: 613–14) made the obvious counter that a perfect correlation was scarcely to be expected wherever 'one quantity (e.g. pauperism) is a function of a great many others' and that the important point, both analytically and in respect of policy, was whether there was any correlation *at all*.

In a later paper (1899) Yule then took up another of Booth's objections (which he had in fact anticipated) that the correlation revealed might be spurious, with levels both of out-relief and of pauperism being determined by some other factor, such as, say, the actual amount of poverty. This paper was of major technical importance in that it marked the final stage in the freeing of the ideas of correlation and regression from the particular biological contexts in which Galton had first developed them, and in turn illustrated their applicability to social data (Stigler 1986: 345–58).[24] But the paper also represented, and still represents, a notable piece of quantitative sociology. Yule established that his correlation held up when several likely confounding factors were allowed for and also that it persisted when *changes* in levels of out-relief and pauperism were considered. Furthermore, while clearly concerned with the use of regression in treating 'causal' questions regarding variation in pauperism, Yule was none the less aware that his analysis could in itself establish only association, not causation (see esp. 1899: n. 25; and cf. Freedman, forthcoming, and Chapter 7 above), and indeed appeared to recognize that in the end the explanation of the regularities he displayed would need to be given in terms of the patterns of action of the different parties involved—the poor, paupers, poor law administrators, and so on. His paper, he emphasized, was, as it stood, incomplete and raised many issues to which he hoped to return.[25]

However, he received little encouragement to do so. Booth chose not to pursue the controversy, perhaps because he now felt out of his depth (despite being a former President of the Royal Statistical Society) and, as Selvin (1976) has suggested, preferred the intellectually less demanding world of 'newspaper editorials and Royal Commissions'. And when in 1905 such a Commission was appointed to consider reform of the Poor Laws, with Booth as a member and responsible for statistics, Yule's work was almost entirely

[24] More specifically, in this and a more technical paper (1897), Yule showed that the coefficient of correlation was not as closely dependent as had been previously supposed on the bivariate normal distribution and also described and applied the technique of what later became known as multiple regression.

[25] It is thus evident that Yule wished to think in terms of causation, even while recognizing that this was not necessarily implied by association, in marked contrast to Pearson, who, under the influence of the new 'critical' positivism of Mach, dismissed the idea of causation as a mere 'fetish' for which that of association, or more specifically correlation, should be substituted (cf. Chapter 7 above).

ignored.[26] In fact, the tradition of research into poverty and working-class social conditions continued in the narrowly descriptive mode already established in the 1830s through to the mid-twentieth century. Although methods of data collection were significantly advanced, notably with Bowley's introduction of probability theory into sampling (Bowley 1906, 1926; Bowley and Burnett-Hurst 1915), the opportunities for improving analytical procedures, following on Yule's lead, were disregarded, and explanations of poverty and its consequences, if they were attempted at all, remained of a very limited kind (cf. Kent 1985).[27]

Indeed, in so far as any significant development of the tradition did occur, it went in a clearly anti-statistical *and* anti-analytical direction. The studies of Sidney and Beatrice Webb (e.g. B. Webb 1891; Webb and Webb 1894, 1897) represented a shift of interest away from the social conditions of the working class to its social institutions—cooperatives, trade unions, and local governmental bodies. And with this work, institutionalism and 'the cult of the facts' were powerfully combined. Beatrice Webb numbered both Spencer and Booth among her mentors, and Spencer taught her, she recalled (1926: 38), 'to look on all social institutions exactly as if they were plants or animals' and to describe and classify them accordingly. In their textbook on methods of social research (Webb and Webb 1932), the Webbs gave only one rather hesitant chapter to statistics, which they still understood essentially as a means of univariate description. The creation of the 'statistics of relationships' over the preceding three decades was simply ignored. They did, however, echo the Spencerian lesson. 'The only right way to approach the subject-matter of sociology', they wrote (1932: 41), 'is not to focus the enquiry upon discovering the answer to some particular question' but to choose 'a particular social institution', treat it as if it were 'the type-specimen of a plant or some species of animal' and 'to acquire all possible information about it'. Their faith then was not only that 'the facts would speak for themselves' (cf. Kent 1981: ch. 3) but further, following Spencer, that establishing the facts about social institutions was in effect the same thing as establishing the regularities present in social action.

[26] The main reference to it came in the form of a critical submission from the economist, A. C. Pigou, on which see the apt remarks of Stigler (1986: 356). After his work on pauperism Yule largely abandoned the social sciences and worked in a variety of other subject-matter areas, making pioneering contributions to the 'statistics of attributes' that led eventually to loglinear modelling techniques.

[27] It might seem especially strange that Bowley, a leading expert in economic statistics, should not have applied his abilities to data analysis as well as data collection. Indeed, as Kent (1985: 66) has observed, in his statistics textbook Bowley (1910) made no mention at all of the work of Galton, Pearson, or Yule—although he did, very briefly, in an earlier work. (In *his* textbook Yule (1911) reciprocated by failing to refer to Bowley.) It could be, as Kent suggests, that the issue of eugenics was again the divisive one; but, if so, Yule suffered guilt by association. Conflict over eugenics would again seem the most likely explanation for the fact that the group around Lancelot Hogben at the LSE in the 1930s who sought to revive the 'political arithmetic' tradition (Hogben 1938) also used the new statistics to only a very limited extent.

In England the emergence of a version of sociology capable of exploiting the new technical and theoretical possibilities that the probabilistic revolution offered was not blocked, as it was in France, by an already well-entrenched school of sociology, inimical to developments in this direction. Sociology in the early decades of the twentieth century remained a quite ill-defined enterprise, and indeed one fragmented to a yet greater extent than the foregoing account has been able to bring out (see further Abrams 1968; Halliday 1968; Bulmer 1985). The disputatious history of the Sociological Society (founded in 1903) and the highly variegated contents of its journal, the *Sociological Review*, stand in marked contrast with the degree of intellectual coherence achieved by the Durkheimian school and *L'Année sociologique*. None the less, the same negative outcome, from the standpoint of this essay, is to be observed in England as in France.

Perhaps the most notable comparative point here is that, even though sociology was more loosely understood and organized in England than in France, it does not appear to have been any more open to new intellectual influences or better able to build positive relationships with neighbouring disciplines. As already indicated, English sociologists, or proto-sociologists, showed little appreciation of the transformation of statistics that was being achieved in their own country—far less in fact than did Simiand and Halbwachs. And at the same time they would appear to have been no more inclined than were the 'imperialistic' Durkheimians to respond to current work in other social sciences or the humanities that could have afforded them theoretical perspectives better suited to a probabilistic world than those they carried over in effect from the early nineteenth century.

Thus, for example, the efforts of Alfred Marshall (1890) to widen utility theory as a theory of action by elaborating the idea of 'wants' and relating it to that of 'activities' had a large, if undeveloped, sociological potential but one that aroused no interest at all within the English sociological community—although it was, of course, later seized upon by Talcott Parsons (1937) as the starting point of his own theoretical odyssey. Similarly, Collingwood's attempts (1946/1993) to set the rational reconstruction of 'processes of action', rather than the 'external' narration of events, at the core of historiography was highly suggestive as regards alternative possibilities for explanation in sociology, but found no resonance among its English practitioners. And it is in turn then scarcely surprising that for most established scholars, including Marshall and Collingwood themselves, sociology should have remained a highly dubious undertaking, veering unpersuasively between grandiose but ill-supported claims of deterministic laws of society in the manner of Comte and Spencer and fact gathering and classifying of an essentially mindless kind.[28]

---

[28] On Marshall's views, see Soffer (1978: 106–8). Dismissive references to Comte and Spencer are scattered throughout Collingwood (1946/1993). Also relevant in this regard (see further Chapter 2 above) is the scathing attack launched on Spencer by Maitland (1911).

Germany

In Germany the main reception of Quetelet's ideas was of a later date than in France or England, and followed their popularization through the work of Buckle (1857), which first appeared in German translations in the 1860s. However, the debate that then ensued was in general of a more sophisticated and penetrating kind than occurred elsewhere, and formed an important strand within the complex *Methodenstreiten* that were a feature of the social sciences and humanities in Germany (cf. Desrosières 1996). The crucial issue was that of the significance, scientific and philosophical, that should be attached to the social regularities that Quetelet and his followers were able to display and, in particular, when these were viewed from the standpoint of the Kantian dualism of 'the realm of necessity' and 'the realm of freedom'. Did the demonstration of such regularities in the statistics of marriage, illegitimacy, suicide, or crime mean that the realm of necessity extended to human society? And, if so, did this then further mean that ideas of the freedom of human will and of the moral determination of individual conduct were illusory?

The answers offered to these questions were diverse (Porter 1986: esp. ch. 6; 1987; Hacking 1990: esp. ch. 15). Most, and including those that were of major consequence for the development of sociology, entailed rejection of at least the larger claims of *Queteletismus*, but often on the basis of arguments that were of an appreciative as well as a critical kind. In fact, with benefit of hindsight, it could be said that in the period here under review it was in Germany that the implications of the probabilistic revolution for the nature of the social sciences were most seriously considered and, in turn, that the possibility of a sociology capable of assimilating these implications, both methodological and theoretical, came closest to realization—even though, in the end, this was not achieved.

German philosophic and academic traditions, and notably those expressed in the distinction between *Geisteswissenschaften* and *Naturwissenschaften*, in themselves entailed a far greater resistance than in France or England to the idea that deterministic law could hold a similar place in the study of society to that which it held in the study of the natural world. For this reason, sociology as understood by Comte, or later Spencer, gained only a relatively limited following in nineteenth-century Germany and was the subject of many forceful attacks (Aron 1936). In turn, the most typical reaction of German social scientists to the regularities demonstrated by the Queteletians was not to seize upon these as manifesting the operation of underlying social laws but, rather, to emphasize their purely empirical character and to insist on the difference between such empirical regularities and true laws that carried causal force. Moreover, from this position it could further be argued that, since no law had been established, there could be no question of the curtailment of the autonomy of the individual. It was 'statistical fatalism', not free will, that was illusory.

At the same time, though, such a position did not lead to acceptance of a radical individualism of the kind that was associated in Germany with the English utilitarian tradition—and thus again with supposedly deterministic laws, in this case those of political economy. The most significant group in the German reception of Quetelet was made up of adherents of the 'historical school' of economics, often also members of the Verein für Sozialpolitik, founded in 1872, who stood opposed to both the principles and practice of laissez-faire and who had in fact already established their own tradition of descriptive statistics in the course of their critique of 'abstract' economic theory. For these thinkers, Queteletian statistics pointed a way to greater analytical rigour; but, given their dominant socio-political concerns with the growing differentiation and tensions of German society as rapid industrialization took hold, a focus on population averages appeared to them inadequate. Although out of quite different interests, they followed Galton in insisting on the importance of *variation* as well as means, but with the emphasis on variation at the level of subpopulations, or social collectivities, rather than of individuals.

The key role in this regard was played by Wilhelm Lexis, one of the founders of the Verein. As earlier noted, Lexis's work on dispersion (1877, 1879) led to serious doubts over whether series of moral statistics could be regarded as showing merely random fluctuations around their mean values. This work was, however, more than just technical in ambition. The indication that such series were almost all 'supernormal'—that is, displayed greater dispersion than would be expected under the normal curve—led Lexis to argue, following in fact Quetelet's own logic, that the rates or ratios examined were actually a summation of ones that should have been regarded as specific to a number of component collectivities in which differing levels or trends over time were present. In other words, if the recorded statistics of marriage, illegitimacy, suicide, or crime, were to be properly understood, they must be treated in an appropriately disaggregated form—by age, sex, occupation, region, etc., and also period. Statistics, in Lexis's view (1875, 1877), should aim to establish for each of the many social groupings that together made up a modern society their own 'probability schemes' (*Chancensysteme*) in regard to different kinds of act or life event, and then to trace out the nature of change in these differing probabilities. In this way, statistics could provide the 'natural-scientific foundation' for the social sciences (cf. Porter 1986: 247–53) and free them from dependence on either spurious 'laws' or analyses of an entirely abstract kind.

Moreover, Lexis also drew significance from a negative result: that none of the series that he examined proved to be 'subnormal'—that is, to show *less* dispersion than if it were indeed normal. Here the important point was that, if, in the various kinds of action represented by the statistics in question, all individuals within a society were alike subject to some constraining supra-individual force, then subnormality is what might have been expected, as it would be if a particular action was required of certain individuals by law in the sense of a statute—as, say, entering military service at a given age. Conversely, in the absence of subnormality, there would seem little reason why regularities in social statistics should not be seen as resulting simply from individuals acting, probabilistically, in similar ways in so far as they found themselves in similar circumstances—just as in fact Drobisch had suggested in the case of regularities in suicide rates, to Durkheim's uncomprehending disapproval (see further Porter 1986: 248–9; Wise 1987; Gigerenzer et al. 1989: 52–3).

Finally, though, Lexis acknowledged (1874/1903: ch. 10) that statistical analysis could not in itself provide causal accounts of patterns of human action. To arrive at such accounts, social scientists would need to complement the empirical results obtained through the natural science methodology of statistics with some form of understanding (Verständnis) of the subjective mental states of actors and of their motivations. In economics, Lexis argued, the causal explanation and the understanding of action alike derived from the postulate that individuals pursued their material interests to the best of their ability. On this basis, models of rational action could be constructed and their adequacy in relation to statistically established empirical regularities could in turn be assessed (cf. Oberschall 1965: 48–9).[29] Some appropriate generalization of this procedure, Lexis appeared to believe, would represent the best way ahead for the other social sciences.

With Lexis, then, one has at least an outline sketch of a kind of sociology in which the quantitative analysis of patterns of social action and the attempt at their explanation and interpretation would be combined. However, little in fact developed from Lexis's writings in this regard. His own substantive interests lay chiefly in economics and demography, and he would in any event seem to have become steadily less adventurous intellectually as his academic career progressed (Schumpeter 1954: 852–3). Moreover, from the 1870s through to the 1890s other unfavourable conditions supervened.

On the one hand, this was the period in which in Germany positivist conceptions of sociology, and in particular different versions of Social Darwinism, achieved their greatest prominence, even though confined largely to the fringes of the academic community. Not only were their proponents themselves little interested in either statistics or the theory of social action, but, further, their 'naturalistic' excesses had the effect of arousing the hostility of the mandarin defenders of the Geisteswissenchaften against sociology in general.[30] On the other hand, and, in the long view, yet more damagingly,

---

[29] Although Lexis rejected, along with other members of the German historical school, the idea of general and deterministic laws in economics, he none the less differed from its more extreme representatives in seeing theoretical models as being necessary if economists were to go beyond mere description, statistical or institutional.

[30] Of particular significance and influence in this respect was Dilthey's Einleitung in die Geisteswissenschaften (1883/1959). It has, however, subsequently become apparent, largely from Dilthey's Nachlass, that he had a long-standing interest in the work of Quetelet and in fact took up a position on the possible linking of statistical and interpretative accounts of social action broadly similar to that formulated by Lexis and, later, Max Weber (see Ermarth 1978: 297–303).

German statistics fell into decline. Representatives of the older German tradition of statistics as a form of state bookkeeping (*Universitätsstatistik*) resisted the introduction of probability theory and the conception of statistics as a general methodology for empirical research (Lazarsfeld 1961; Schad 1972: 22–5), while the successors of Lexis reacted by concentrating more on mathematical problems of probability theory itself than on those of its application, at all events outside the physical sciences (Porter 1986: 253–5). Thus, statistics in Germany languished, in notable contrast with the situation in England, where major theoretical advances were made largely in consequence of the pursuit of substantive concerns in the social and biological fields.

It was not in fact until the first decade of the twentieth century that the possibility returned that something on the lines of Lexis's programme, or indeed a yet more ambitious project, might be accomplished: that is, with the attempt, led by Max Weber, to create in Germany a sociology quite distinct in its conception from that of Comte or Spencer and that would impose both strong empirical *and* explanatory-cum-interpretative requirements.[31]

From an early stage in his career, and while still working primarily as an economic and legal historian, Weber took up a number of methodological positions (1903–6/1975; 1904/1949; 1906/1949; 1907/1977; 1908/1975) that crucially shaped his understanding of what sociology could, and could not, hope to achieve and how it should proceed. To begin with, he rejected the idea that sociology should aim at the formulation of deterministic laws and in particular developmental or evolutionary laws claiming to provide some cognitive grasp on the general movement of human history. From this point of view, Weber thus came into opposition not only with Comte and Spencer and their intellectual heirs but likewise with Marx and the Marxist theoreticians of the German labour movement. Further, Weber was sceptical of what could be gained from 'organic' analogies in the study of societies that led to explanations of their institutional or other structural features in functional terms (see also 1922/1968: 14–15). He insisted, rather, that sociology must rely on causal explanations of a probabilistic kind that were given 'micro-to-macro' in terms of individual action and its consequences, and can indeed claim priority in the assertion of the principle of methodological individualism (Udehn 1994: ch. 1; Ringer 1997) and in the more or less explicit counterposing of—to use Boudon's (1987) distinction—the 'individualistic' against the 'nomological' paradigm in sociology (see esp. 1913/1981: 158–9).

Thus, for Weber, social institutions could not be the ultimate units of sociological analysis, nor their description an adequate substitute for the study of social action itself, for institutions were no more than the products of action; and, while they in turn obviously conditioned action, they did not

---

[31] There is little evidence of any close intellectual ties between Weber and Lexis, although in 1896 they sat alongside each other as the two academic participants in a governmental committee concerned with the reform of the German stock exchange (Marianne Weber 1926/1975: 197–8); and it is evident from Weber's correspondence that he had a high regard for Lexis.

determine it: they implied only the probability that given forms of action by individuals would occur. At the same time, though, Weber made it abundantly clear that adopting such an individualistic approach did *not* entail the grounding of sociology in a naturalistic psychology (1908/1975, 1913/1981). To the contrary, if sociological explanation had, as Weber believed, to entail the 'interpretative understanding' of action, this must derive from the sociologist's reconstruction of the meanings with which actors themselves subjectively endowed their actions in the particular kinds of situation under study (Ringer 1997: esp. ch. 4).

For a basic model of such 'explanatory interpretation' (*erklärendes Verstehen*), which could make action intelligible at the same time as giving it causal force, Weber in fact, in much the same way as Lexis, looked to economic analysis (Lachmann 1970: ch. 1; Ringer 1997; Swedberg 1998: ch. 2). Here, a major advantage existed in so far as attention focused on action of an instrumentally rational (*Zweckrational*) type, which was that most open to intelligible reconstruction through the demonstration of logical links between actors' goals, their beliefs, and the courses of action they then in fact followed (see esp. 1903–6/1975: 186–91; 1913/1981: 151–6). But, again like Lexis, Weber regarded the explanatory strategy involved—the providing of causal narratives at the level of action—as being capable of generalization from instrumentally rational action to other types, such as 'value-rational' (*Wertrational*) action and even perhaps, at the limit, to action determined by tradition or habit or by actors' emotional states.[32]

However, while Weber can thus be seen as upholding the idea of sociology as a *Geisteswissenschaft*, he did at the same time insist that it must also have a secure foundation in empirical research, and—like Halbwachs—attached a particular importance to research findings in statistical form as the most reliable means by which social regularities could be displayed. As is by now well documented (Lazarsfeld and Oberschall 1965; Oberschall 1965; Käsler 1988), over the first two decades of his academic life Weber was involved in a series of field studies of the German working classes, both agricultural and industrial, that were aimed at the collection and analysis of quantitative data. These studies are of great, but much neglected, interest in their own right.[33] They

---

[32] Thus, an example that Weber several times took up (e.g. 1922/1968: 10–11, 18–19) is that of 'Gresham's Law'—actually, an empirical generalization to the effect that, when a coinage becomes debased, 'the bad money drives out the good' from circulation. Weber notes that in seeking to account for this regularity modern economists do not in fact aim to subsume it under some higher-level 'covering' law but rather to explain it *and* to render it intelligible as the outcome of rational action on the part of individuals. The causal narrative is a very simple one: it 'makes sense' under conditions of debasement to trade with bad coin and hold onto good. However, another empirical regularity Weber considers (e.g. 1904–5/1930: 59–60) is that revealed when workers, under certain conditions, work *less* as their rates of pay increase (the 'backward sloping supply curve for labour'). In this case, the regularity could be seen as deriving from traditionally determined action but this might also be rendered intelligible if a traditional standard of living, strictly delimiting workers' economic wants, was accepted as a situational factor.

[33] Their neglect, notably by 'interpreters' of Weber entirely reliant on such of his work as is available in English translation, has indeed often led to very partial, if not distorted, accounts.

represent important contributions to the German debate on 'the social question', which was of a wider-ranging kind than the concurrent British debate on poverty, and have also to be seen (cf. Marianne Weber 1926/1975: 367; Käsler 1988) in the context of Weber's larger concerns with the changing nature of work and of employment relations and class formation under capitalism. They are thus closely allied with his major historical study of the same period, *The Protestant Ethic and the Spirit of Capitalism* (1904–5/1930), which does indeed at various points draw on them.[34] Further, though, it is this body of research that would appear to provide the main basis for Weber's most explicit statements on the essential complementarity in sociological analysis of the demonstration of empirical, probabilistic regularities in social action and its consequences and their explanatory interpretation. Passages such as the following are of particular note (1922/1968: 12; see also 18–19, and 1913/1981: 151, 157):

If adequacy in respect to meaning is lacking, then no matter how high the degree of uniformity and how precisely . . . [the] probability [of a course of action] can be numerically determined, it is still an incomprehensible statistical probability . . . On the other hand, even the most perfect adequacy on the level of meaning has causal significance from a sociological point of view only insofar as there is some proof for the existence of a probability that action in fact normally takes the course which has been held to be meaningful.[35]

Here, Weber's position on the articulation of research and theory does in fact come very close to that from which this chapter started out. Social regularities that are empirically established need to be causally explained and also made intelligible by reference to the patterns of action through which they are created and sustained, with the idea of rationality playing a central role in the reconstruction of the subjective meaning of such action. At the same time, the whole point of elaborating theories and models of action is that they should be put to explanatory use in relation to empirical findings. It is, therefore, of evident interest to ask why in Germany at least *some* sociology did not develop that could be regarded as an expression of Weber's vision, and all the more so since it is clear that Weber himself engaged in a serious attempt to promote such a development.

In 1909, around the time when Weber first came to designate himself as a 'sociologist', he played a prominent role in the founding of the Deutsche

---

[34] Weber in fact begins this study by referring to a regularity in German official statistics, which, he claims, is confirmed in a more detailed study of Baden by one of his students and on which he then in various ways elaborates: namely, 'that business leaders and owners of capital, as well as the higher grades of skilled labour, and even more the higher technically and commercially trained personnel of modern enterprises, are overwhelmingly Protestant' (cf. Hernes 1989 and, for a more sceptical view, Hamilton 1996: ch. 3). Moreover, the general *explanandum* of the study—the 'spirit of capitalism'—can itself be understood as referring to recurrent patterns of action: that is, those in which individuals engage in relation to work and money (cf. G. Marshall 1980, 1982: ch. 2).

[35] It should be noted that Weber began writing the work here cited as early as 1909 or 1910 (Marianne Weber 1926/1975: 418–19) and that an early version of the opening section was published a few years later (Max Weber 1913/1981).

Gesellschaft für Soziologie (DGfS) and became its Treasurer (Käsler 1988: 15). The main objective of Weber and his associates in this venture was to create an alternative context for large-scale social research to the Verein für Sozialpolitik (under the auspices of which much of Weber's empirical work had hitherto been carried out), and one within which the emphasis could be placed firmly on a 'value-neutral' linkage of research to *theory* rather than to social problems and policy (cf. Roth 1968; Weyembergh 1971; Hennis 1996: ch. 3). At the same time, Weber was anxious to promote greater cooperation between sociologists and statisticians, and encouraged the organization of a new German statistical society, intended to have close relations with its sociological counterpart (Schad 1972: 22–3). At the inaugural meeting of the DGfS in 1910, Weber outlined his ideas that it should serve as a collaborative 'workshop' and seek to raise funds for major empirical investigations. As an initial research programme, he suggested studies of three topics: voluntary associations, social mobility, and—his own current concern—the sociology of the press (Oberschall 1965: 109; Schad 1972: 42–3).

However, from these apparently promising beginnings, little of any substance emerged, and after the second meeting of the DGfS in 1912 Weber withdrew in evident frustration (Marianne Weber 1926/1975: 420–5). His subsequent efforts at developing a sociology aiming at 'the interpretive understanding of social action and thereby . . . a causal explanation of its course and consequences' (1922/1968: 4) were pursued entirely through his historically based studies—with, it seems, some relief on his part but also, it should be added, some clear methodological reservations.[36] Weber's personality appears not to have been well suited to organizational activity of the kind he attempted, and misunderstandings over the idea of 'value-neutral' sociology persisted. But behind the failure of the DGfS initiative two further problems can be identified.

First, as Weber bitterly complained, other eminent figures in the association proved unwilling to abandon their individual scholarship in order to participate in empirical research of a kind that called for collaboration.[37] In this regard, the traditions of the German university system may perhaps be seen as an obstacle, although in other new disciplines, notably psychology, they would appear to have been far more successfully adapted.

Secondly, and more seriously, among the membership of the DGfS at large

---

[36] These chiefly concerned the difficulties inherent in using 'secondary' historical sources as the major empirical resource for sociological analysis and especially where this went beyond institutional description to the level of individual action. Weber was acutely aware, and to an extent that commentators have usually failed to bring out—exceptions are Roth (1968) and G. Marshall (1982)—of the fallibility of such sources, of the problem of conflicting accounts, and, above all, of the ever-present possibility that on theoretically crucial issues secondary works might have nothing to say simply because 'primary' evidence did not exist (cf. also Marianne Weber 1926/1975: 331–2, and the discussion in Chapter 2 above).

[37] When Weber felt disqualified from continuing as director of the research into the press because of his involvement in a lawsuit with a newspaper, he was unable to find anyone ready to take over from him even though he had already secured financial support for the project (Marianne Weber 1926/1975: 423–4, 429–39).

there was a lack of expertise in the conduct of social research and especially in so far as quantification was involved. Weber himself from the time of his earliest field studies had expressed worries about how to deal with issues of both data collection and data analysis—especially multivariate analysis—and about the difficulty of obtaining appropriate guidance (Lazarsfeld and Oberschall 1965).[38] Moreover, this problem was deepened in that the attempt to create an alliance with the statisticians did not succeed. As earlier noted, the more conservative of the latter still regarded their discipline as itself a kind of social science and thus tended to see sociology as a potential competitor (Schad 1972: 17–35), while the more progressive, who understood statistics as a general methodology based on probability theory, appear for the most part to have adopted a rather unhelpful attitude towards the sociologists' efforts. Thus, in 1911, just when Weber's work with the DGfS was at a crucial stage, von Bortkiewicz, perhaps the most distinguished student of Lexis but a man noted for his negative temperament (Schumpeter 1954: 851), sharply criticized reports from a study of industrial workers that Weber had led for the Verein, pointing out, among other failings, inadequacies in sample size and representativeness and also elementary computational errors. Weber made an uncomfortable reply in which he felt obliged to play down, to an undue degree, what the study had achieved (Verein für Sozialpolitik 1912; Oberschall 1965: 130–1; Käsler 1988: 72–3).

Viewed in this way, the failure in the years before the First World War to create a *verstehende Soziologie* that had also a secure quantitative basis then largely foreshadows the situation that developed in the Weimar period. Chairs in sociology were for the first time established in German universities, but this institutional advance did little to further the intellectual coherence of the discipline. As Aron observed (1936: 167), in order to establish a claim to a chair, it seemed necessary for every aspirant to produce his own 'system' of sociology—typically expressed in foundational terms, though with little reference to genuine theoretical issues, let alone to actual research. And, as the political tensions of Weimar heightened, the ideological content of such discussions of 'method' became increasingly apparent (cf. Ringer 1969: 227–53).

Not surprisingly, then, the more serious attempts that were made to advance research were essentially divorced from theory, and vice versa. For example, Tönnies, one of the co-founders with Weber of the DGfS, enthusiastically pursued empirical—and quantitative—studies on a wide range of issues, but under the rubric of 'sociography' and without any relation to

---

[38] It would seem fairly clear that Weber himself had no serious knowledge of statistics. Some commentators have been led to speculate otherwise on account of the frequent references in his work to 'probability', 'likelihood', or 'chances'. However, these should rather be seen as reflecting Weber's *legal* training. In Weber's day, the concept of probability played a key role in German jurisprudential theory: i.e. in the determination of individual responsibility, or 'liability', for particular outcomes under given sets of conditions (Turner and Factor 1981, 1994). Thus, while Weber readily invoked the concept of probabilistic regularity and viewed causality in probabilistic rather than deterministic terms, there are still no grounds for supposing that he was technically equipped to translate these ideas into research design or the analysis of quantitative data.

theoretical ideas, even his own. The earlier aspiration of seeking the greater integration of research and theory, Tönnies now believed, had been premature. He was also disinclined to renew Weber's plan of involving statisticians more constructively in sociological work. He showed no interest himself in acquiring knowledge of the new statistics, and relied in his sociography on techniques of correlation and multivariate analysis that were of a highly idiosyncratic, and in fact largely inadequate, kind (Oberschall 1965: 52–62; Schad 1972: 46–8, 66–73).

Conversely, the most sustained effort at elaborating the conception of a *verstehende Soziologie* was that made by Schutz (1932/1967). This was, however, aimed at giving such a sociology what Schutz believed to be a more secure philosophical—that is, phenomenological—basis, rather than at clarifying further how *erklärendes Verstehen* was to be applied in, and ultimately tested by, empirical research. Indeed, the 'phenomenological turn' in the reception of Weber's work served to make these matters appear considerably more rather than less problematic. As Colin Campbell (1996: esp. 31–7) has observed, Schutz extended Weber's understanding of what makes action 'social' so as to require that it involve not simply the actor 'taking account' in a general way of the action of others but indeed engaging continuously in the interpretation of the meaning of the action of all specific 'others' who were encountered. Thus, rather than the focus of sociological attention falling on the micro-to-macro link—on how social regularities are generated through central tendencies in action and interaction that can be understood as deriving from social situations of a particular type—it had in effect to be confined to the micro-level: that is, to the processes through which actors, as themselves micro-sociologists, 'make sense' together. Moreover, even at this level, it remained unclear just how Schutz and his followers envisaged that their supposed theoretical refinements of Weber's approach should be incorporated into substantive sociological enquiry.[39]

In sum, by the time of the Nazi accession to power in 1933, and the devastation of German sociology that followed, it could, from the standpoint of this chapter, be said that the high promise of the period around 1910 had in fact already been dissipated.

The questions that have motivated this chapter were posed at the outset as follows. Why was a version of sociology aiming to combine the quantitative analysis of probabilistic social regularities with their explanatory interpretation on the basis of a theory of social action so slow to appear? How far is this retardation to be understood as reflecting difficulties inherent in the

---

[39] Whether there is any serious warrant for a phenomenological reading of Weber I would in fact regard as highly debatable. Weber's neglect of the way in which the subjective meanings of actions are actually formed—from which Schutz begins—may well have been quite deliberate: that is, because Weber simply did not believe that direct access to 'other minds' was possible and, as Hollis (1987: 7–8) has suggested, saw the 'rational' reconstruction of action as providing the essential interpretative bridge. For an illuminating commentary on the directly opposing developments (or distortions?) of Weber's ideas by Schutz and by Parsons, see Wagner (1983: 74–9).

project itself or, rather, historically specific barriers of an institutional or an intellectual kind or even perhaps still more contingent factors? In the light of the foregoing review of the early development of sociology in France, England, and Germany, I would now venture these answers.

To begin with, there is little indication that, in so far as a sociology of the kind in question was envisaged, its progress was impeded by serious internal contradictions. It is true that Quetelet and his followers had only an uncertain grasp of the significance of the probabilistic regularities in social life that they were able to demonstrate, and often regarded them as being but the (imperfect) manifestation of deterministic laws operating at a supra-individual level—the position that Mill and Spencer in England and the Durkheimians in France readily took up in direct opposition to probabilistic thinking.

However, within the German tradition of the *Geisteswissenschaften*, Lexis and then Weber saw such an explanation of social regularities as being neither necessary nor indeed appropriate, and outlined a quite different approach: that is, one of a 'micro-to-macro' rather than 'macro-to-micro' kind that gave causal force to the typical or 'central' courses of action pursued by collectivities of individuals within social situations of a given type. Thus, quite consistently, probabilistic regularities were addressed from the standpoint of probabilistic causation; and in turn the way was opened for sociological explanation to be grounded ultimately in the interpretation of individual action, through which it might at the same time be rendered intelligible.

The period in which this approach originated corresponded with that in which in England the new statistics were created—the ideal complement, it might be thought, so far as empirical enquiry was concerned, allowing, on the one hand, more reliable and revealing analyses of the character of social regularities and, on the other, more rigorous testing of hypotheses regarding their generation that might be formulated at the level of action. However, despite the eminent suitability of a marriage of research and theory on this basis, the historical fact remains that it did not take place. It is on external barriers, I would then maintain, that attention has chiefly to focus.

As regards the development of sociology at large, much of interest has been written on the problems of 'institutionalization' that the emergent discipline faced as it struggled for acceptance by both academia and governments (e.g. Abrams 1968; Oberschall 1972). None the less, as regards the particular issues to which this chapter is directed, such problems do not stand out as being ones of major significance. The failure to achieve a sociology that could in both research and theory exploit the potential of the probabilistic revolution was common to France, England, and Germany alike, despite very evident differences in the structuring of their academic and scientific communities and in the extent and manner in which sociology was accommodated. It could not, for example, be claimed that institutionalized rivalry between statisticians and sociologists was a generally adverse factor. As noted, such rivalry did indeed arise to some extent in the German case; but, in France, Simiand and Halbwachs were able to sustain a dialogue with statisticians even across quite sharply drawn organizational boundaries, while in England the loose institutionalization of *both* disciplines clearly did not make for a high level of cooperation or even interaction. In accounting for the failure in question, I would then believe, far greater weight has to be given to intellectual than to institutional factors. Three intellectual barriers can be identified, as follows.

The first and most serious, at least in France and England and for at time in Germany also, was the Comtean legacy or, in other words, the positivist conception of science. In this conception, the goal of all sciences, whatever their specific methodologies, was the formulation of deterministic laws, and probabilistic thinking was thus viewed with hostility or at least great suspicion. Moreover, the sociology elaborated within positivist science was one that, largely on account of analogies drawn with biology, sought to take total societies or at all events their constituent institutions as its basic units of analysis, and to discover the laws that governed societal integration and long-term developmental, or evolutionary, trajectories. It followed, therefore, that sociological explanation proceeded always in a macro-to-micro fashion. If individual action and interaction were considered at all, they could be given little more than epiphenomenal status. Further, the essential empirical materials of such a sociology were ones that could serve to illustrate the functioning and change of institutions across the widest conceivable range of societies, and that had therefore to be largely derived from (what were taken to be) the pre-established findings of history or ethnography. No particular interest or privilege attached to the *direct* study of patterns of social action (as opposed to their inference from institutional descriptions) that would call for research in contemporary societies and of a kind likely to employ methods of data collection and analysis that the new statistics of the probabilistic revolution could inform. Thus, at virtually every point, the positivist version of sociology stood opposed to one in which the idea of social action would be central, as the focus of both research and theory, and in which, to revert to Boudon's distinction, the nomological would be replaced by the individualistic paradigm. The particular significance of the German case is that it reveals how the radical rejection of the Comtean legacy was a necessary condition for such an alternative sociology even to be programmatically envisaged—although not, of course, by any means a sufficient one for its realization.[40]

Secondly, the barrier of positivism was in certain instances reinforced by that of an extreme empiricism. Where, on the one hand, such empiricism was associated with statistical work, as was most notably the case in mid-nineteenth century England but also and for a somewhat longer period in Germany, it restricted statistics, at best, to a form of numerical social descrip-

[40] In this perspective it is, of course, rather remarkable that from the 1960s onwards sociological analysis using quantitative methods and conducted on the basis of methodological individualism has itself been routinely condemned as 'positivistic'. Responsibility for this historically and philosophically unhelpful and indeed misleading use of the term must, I believe, rest largely with members of the Frankfurt school who initiated the *Postivismusstreit* (cf. Chapter 1).

tion and, at worst, to a mindless 'cult of the facts'. It was, in other words, inimical to the development of statistics into a general scientific methodology, based on probability theory, which sociologists could then use in establishing and analysing social regularities and in testing the theoretically grounded explanations of these regularities that they might advance. Where, on the other hand, empiricism was associated with the idea of sociology as the study of social institutions, again as best exemplified in the English case and above all in the work of the Webbs, it resulted in such study being progressively divorced from the evolutionary theory that had initially inspired it and becoming another, qualitative form of descriptivism, lacking at least any explicit analytical or theoretical concerns.

Thirdly, the creation of a sociology in which the concept of social action played a central role was also impeded by psychologism, and in two different ways. It was, above all, a fear of psychologism—a fear that the autonomy of sociology might appear to be undermined by a dependence on 'laws of human nature'—that led the Durkheimians, following Comte, to reject any kind of sociological explanation that referred ultimately to the action of individuals, and to insist that 'social facts' be accounted for exclusively in terms of other 'social facts'. But, conversely, a recognition that sociological explanation could not in the end avoid reference to individual attributes and conduct led to the argument, as found in Mill and Spencer, that sociology did indeed need a specific psychology—in effect, a science of human behaviour—as its foundation. Only in the German tradition of the *Geisteswissenschaften*, and in particular through the work of Max Weber, was the crucial point eventually established that adopting the principle of methodological individualism in sociology did not in fact imply psychologism. Instead of the individualistic paradigm being associated with the idea of making individual behaviour explicable by subsuming it under general psychological laws, it could rather be associated with that of making individual action intelligible by placing it within its social context.

These intellectual barriers were indeed formidable. Finally, though, I would wish to argue that it ought not to be supposed that in any of the national cases reviewed the appearance of a sociology allying the quantitative analysis of social regularities with their explanation via a theory of social action was *inevitably* precluded. For this would be to discount factors of a yet more contingent kind than those I have so far considered but which are quite often in evidence. In their nature, such factors do not lend themselves to systematic treatment. They do, however, tend to prompt, and may in turn be highlighted by, counterfactual speculation.

For example, it is, as earlier remarked, a curious feature of the French case that Simiand and Halbwachs, the two sociologists of the early twentieth century who were perhaps best informed about the new statistics, should have remained throughout their academic careers committed, even militant, Durkheimians. It would be difficult to maintain that this could not have been otherwise. And it is not in turn absurd to contemplate the question of what might have happened in French sociology in the inter-war years if the attachment of these two individuals to the Durkheimian school had been weaker or, alternatively, if others who were more ready to question its disregard for a theory of action had chosen to acquire a similar degree of statistical sophistication.

Similarly, to turn to the English case, the attempts made by the creators of the new statistics themselves to show its value to various kinds of sociological enterprise surely did not *have* to be spurned in quite the way that they were. Conflicts of ideology, especially over eugenics, may well have played some part here. But, even if the rejection of Galton and Pearson by the evolutionary institutionalists is left aside, it cannot be regarded as unthinkable that 'poverty' research, with stronger intellectual leadership than that provided by Booth, might have developed into a more serious form of applied sociology; that is, might have drawn more readily on advances in data analysis, especially following on Yule's intervention, and in this way have been better equipped to move beyond 'the cult of the facts' to pursue explanations of its empirical findings of a theoretically grounded kind.

Finally, in Germany above all a situation that was, in the years prior to the First World War, in many respects highly favourable to a new sociology linking quantitative and interpretative concerns must be seen as being marred at least as much by a conjunction of particularities as by more systematic difficulties, whether institutional or intellectual. How might German sociology have developed, one is tempted to ask, if Weber had had the proclivity and capacity for academic mobilization of a Durkheim, and if his quest for guidance and cooperation from statisticians could have met with the response of a Yule rather than a von Bortkiewicz?

All such 'what if . . .' questions of historical possibility are of course in one sense vain: what happened, happened. None the less, they do still serve to bring out that the issue to which this chapter has been addressed—that of why a sociology more responsive to the probabilistic revolution in its conception of both research and theory did not earlier develop—has itself to be answered in probabilistic terms. There were indeed substantial barriers in the way of such a development, and it did not in fact occur. But from the vantage point of, say, the late nineteenth century, the situation was surely far more open than it might now appear in retrospect. Other things could have happened than actually did if individuals had acted and interacted in different ways. In other words, even in this relatively early period, the kind of sociology in the interests of which this chapter is written was neither inconceivable nor unrealizable. However, it must of course by the same token be accepted that, even if today there are encouraging signs that such a sociology is at last beginning to take recognizable shape, its eventual success is still by no means guaranteed.

REFERENCES

Abbott, A. (1992a), 'What Do Cases Do? Some Notes on Activity in Sociological Analysis', in C. C. Ragin and H. S. Becker (eds.), *What is a Case?* (Cambridge: Cambridge University Press).

—— (1992b), 'From Causes to Events: Notes on Narrative Positivism', *Sociological Methods and Research*, 20: 428–55.

—— (1997), 'On the Concept of Turning Point', *Comparative Social Research*, 16: 85–105.

—— (1998), 'The Causal Devolution', *Sociological Methods and Research*, 27: 148–81.

Abell, P. (1992), 'Is Rational Choice Theory a Rational Choice of Theory?', in J. S. Coleman and T. J. Fararo (eds.), *Rational Choice Theory: Advocacy and Critique* (Newbury Park, Calif.: Sage).

Åberg, R., Selén, J., and Tham, H. (1987), 'Economic Resources', in R. Erikson and R. Åberg (eds.), *Welfare in Transition* (Oxford: Clarendon Press).

Abrams, P. (1968), *The Origins of British Sociology* (Chicago: University of Chicago Press).

—— (1980), *Historical Sociology* (Bath: Open Books).

Adorno, T. W., *et al.* (1976), *The Positivist Dispute in German Sociology* (London: Heinemann).

Agassi, J. (1975), 'Institutional Individualism', *British Journal of Sociology*, 26: 144–55.

Alexander, J. C. (1998), *Neofunctionalism and After* (Oxford: Blackwell).

Allardt, E. (1990), 'Challenges for Comparative Social Research', *Acta Sociologica*, 33: 183–93.

Amenta, E., and Poulsen, J. D. (1994), 'Where to Begin: A Survey of Five Approaches to Selecting Independent Variables for Qualitative Comparative Analysis', *Sociological Methods and Research*, 23: 22–53.

Anderson, M. (1971), *Family Structure in Nineteenth Century Lancashire* (Cambridge: Cambridge University Press).

Anderson, P. (1974a), *Passages from Feudalism to Antiquity* (London: New Left Books).

—— (1974b), *Lineages of the Absolutist State* (London: New Left Books).

Andorka, R. (1990), 'Half a Century of Trends in Social Mobility in Hungary', in J. L. Peschar (ed.), *Social Reproduction in Eastern and Western Europe* (Nijmegen: Institute for Applied Social Sciences).

Appleby, L., and Starmer, S. (1987), 'Individual Choice Under Uncertainty: A Review of Experimental Evidence Past and Present', in J. D. Hey and P. J. Lambert (eds.), *Surveys in the Economics of Uncertainty* (Oxford: Blackwell).

Aron, R. (1936), *La Sociologie allemande contemporaine* (Paris: Presses Universitatires de France).

—— (1965–7), *Main Currents in Sociological Thought*, 2 vols. (London: Weidenfeld & Nicolson).

Arrow, K. J. (1984), 'The Economics of Agency', in J. W. Pratt and R. J. Zeckhauser (eds.), *Principals and Agents: The Structure of Business* (Boston: Harvard Business School Press).

Arum, R., and Hout, M. (1998), 'The Early Returns: The Transition from School to Work in the United States', in Y. Shavit and W. Müller (eds.), *From School to Work* (Oxford: Clarendon Press).

——, and Shavit, Y. (1995), 'Secondary Vocational Education and the Transition from School to Work', *Sociology of Education*, 68: 187–204.

Atkinson, A. B. (1998), 'Equity Issues in a Globalizing World: The Experience of OECD Countries', typescript.

——Rainwater, L., and Smeeding, T. S. (1995), 'Income Distribution in Advanced Economies: Evidence from the Luxembourg Income Study (LIS)', LIS Working Paper 120.

Atkinson, J. (1985), 'The Changing Corporation', in D. Clutterbuck (ed.), *New Patterns of Work* (Aldershot: Gower).

Baert, P. (1998), *Social Theory in the Twentieth Century* (Cambridge: Polity Press).

Baker, K. M. (1975), *Condorcet: From Natural Philosophy to Social Mathematics* (Chicago: University of Chicago Press).

Baldamus, W. (1961), *Efficiency and Effort* (London: Tavistock).

Banks, O. (1971), *The Sociology of Education*, 2nd edn. (London: Batsford).

Bannister, R. C. (1987), *Sociology and Scientism: The American Quest for Objectivity, 1880–1940* (Chapel Hill, NC: University of North Carolina Press).

Barnard, C. (1938), *The Functions of the Executive* (Cambridge, Mass.: Harvard University Press).

Barnes, B. (1995), *The Elements of Social Theory* (London: UCL Press).

Baron, J. N., and Hannan, M. T. (1994), 'The Impact of Economics on Contemporary Sociology', *Journal of Economic Literature*, 32: 1111–46.

Barry, B. (1970), *Sociologists, Economists and Democracy* (London: Collier-Macmillan).

Bartley, M., *et al.* (1996), 'Measuring Inequalities in Health: An Analysis of Mortality Patterns Using Two Social Classifications', *Sociology of Health and Illness*, 18: 455–74.

Basmann, R. L. (1988), 'Causality Tests and Observationally Equivalent Representations of Econometric Models', *Journal of Econometrics*, 39: 7–21.

Becker, C. (1955), 'What are Historical Facts?', in H. Meyerhoff (ed.), *The Philosophy of History in Our Time* (New York: Doubleday).

Becker, G. (1976), *The Economic Approach to Human Behavior* (Chicago: Chicago University Press).

Becker, H. S. (1992), 'Cases, Causes, Conjunctures, Stories and Imagery', in C. C. Ragin and H. S. Becker (eds.), *What is a Case?* (Cambridge: Cambridge University Press).

Bell, C., and Newby, H. (1981), 'Narcissism or Reflexivity in Modern Sociology?', *Polish Sociological Bulletin*, 1: 5–19.

Berk, R. A. (1988), 'Causal Inference for Sociological Data', in N. J. Smelser (ed.), *Handbook of Sociology* (Newbury Park, Calif.: Sage).

Bernert, C. (1983), 'The Career of Causal Analysis in American Sociology', *British Journal of Sociology*, 24: 230–54.

Berry, B. J. L. (1970), 'Some Methodological Consequences of Using the Nation as a Unit of Analysis in Comparative Politics', Social Science Research Council, New York, Committee on Comparative Politics.

Besnard, P. (1983a), 'The "*Année Sociologique*" Team', in P. Besnard (ed.), *The Sociological Domain* (Cambridge: Cambridge University Press).

——(1983b), 'The Epistemological Polemic: François Simiand', in P. Besnard (ed.), *The Sociological Domain* (Cambridge: Cambridge University Press).

Bierstedt, R. (1959), 'Toynbee and Sociology', *British Journal of Sociology*, 10: 95–104.

Bills, D. B. (1988), 'Credentials and Capacities: Employers' Perceptions of the Acquisition of Skills', *Sociological Quarterly*, 29: 439–49.

Björklund, A., and Kjellström, C. (1994), 'Avkastingen på Utbildning i Sverige 1968 till 1991', in R. Erikson and J. O. Jonsson (eds.), *Sorteringen i Skolan* (Stockholm: Carlsson).

Blalock, H. M. (1984), 'Contextual-Effects Models: Theoretical and Methodological Issues', *Annual Review of Sociology*, 10: 353–72.

Blau, P. M., and Duncan, O. D. (1967), *The American Occupational Structure* (New York: Wiley).

Blaug, M. (1991), 'Afterword', in N. de Marchi and M. Blaug (eds.), *Appraising Economic Theories* (Aldershot: Elgar).

—— (1992), *The Methodology of Economics*, 2nd edn. (Cambridge: Cambridge University Press).

Blossfeld, H.-P., and Huinink, J. (1991), 'Human Capital Investments or Norms of Role Transition? How Women's Schooling and Career Affect the Process of Family Formation', *American Journal of Sociology*, 97: 143–68.

——, and Prein, G. (1998) (eds.), *Rational Choice Theory and Large-Scale Data Analysis* (Boulder, Colo.: Westview Press).

——, and Rohwer, G. (1995*a*), *Techniques of Event History Modeling: New Approaches to Causal Analysis* (Hillsdale, NJ: Erlbaum).

———— (1995*b*), 'West Germany', in H.-P. Blossfeld (ed.), *The New Role of Women: Family Formation in Modern Society* (Boulder, Colo.: Westview Press).

——, and Shavit, Y. (1993), 'Persisting Barriers: Changes in Educational Opportunities in Thirteen Countries', in Y. Shavit and H.-P. Blossfeld (eds.), *Persistent Inequality: Changing Educational Attainment in Thirteen Countries* (Boulder, Colo.: Westview Press).

Booth, C. (1889–1903), *Life and Labour of the People of London* (London: Macmillan).

—— (1896), 'Poor Law Statistics', *Economic Journal*, 6: 70–4.

Boudon, R. (1967), *L'Analyse mathématique des faits sociaux* (Paris: Plon).

—— (1971), 'La Metasociologie de Lazarsfeld', in *La Crise de sociologie* (Geneva: Droz).

—— (1974), *Education, Opportunity and Social Inequality* (New York: Wiley).

—— (1976), 'Comment on Hauser's Review of *Education, Opportunity and Social Inequality*', *American Journal of Sociology*, 81: 1175–87.

—— (1982), *The Unintended Consequences of Social Action* (London: Macmillan).

—— (1987), 'The Individualistic Tradition in Sociology', in J. C. Alexander *et al.* (eds.), *The Micro-Macro Link* (Berkeley and Los Angeles: University of California Press).

—— (1989), *The Analysis of Ideology* (Cambridge: Polity Press).

—— (1990), 'Individualism or Holism in the Social Sciences', in P. Birnbaum and J. Leca (eds.), *Individualism* (Oxford: Clarendon Press).

—— (1994), *The Art of Self-Persuasion* (Cambridge: Polity Press).

—— (1996), 'The "Cognitivist Model": A Generalized "Rational-Choice" Model', *Rationality and Society*, 8: 123–50.

—— (1998), 'Social Mechanisms Without Black Boxes', in P. Hedström and R. Swedberg (eds.), *Social Mechanisms* (Cambridge: Cambridge University Press).

Bouglé, C. (1896), *Les Sciences sociales en Allemagne* (Paris: Alcan).

—— (1899), *Les Idées égalitaires* (Paris: Alcan).

Bourdieu, P. (1973), 'Cultural Reproduction and Social Reproduction', in R. K. Brown (ed.), *Knowledge, Education and Cultural Change* (London: Tavistock).

Bourdieu, P., and Passeron, J.-C. (1970), *La Reproduction* (Pairs: Éditions de Minuit).

—, and Wacquant, L. (1992), *An Invitation to Sociology* (Chicago: University of Chicago Press).

Bowles, S., and Gintis, H. (1976), *Schooling in Capitalist America* (London: Routledge).

Bowley, A. L. (1906), 'Address to the Economic Science and Statistics Section of the British Association for the Advancement of Science', *Journal of the Royal Statistical Society*, 47: 607–25.

—(1910), *An Elementary Manual of Statistics* (London: Macdonald & Evans).

—(1926), 'Measurement of the Precision Obtained in Sampling', *Bulletin of the International Statistical Institute*, 22, Supplement: 6–62.

—, and Burnett-Hurst, A. R. (1915), *Livelihood and Poverty* (London: Bell).

Bradford Hill, A. (1937/1991), *Principles of Medical Statistics*, 12th edn. (London: Arnold).

—(1965), 'The Environment and Disease: Association or Causation?', *Proceedings of the Royal Society for Medicine*, 58: 295–300.

Bradshaw, Y., and Wallace, M. (1991), 'Informing Generality and Explaining Uniqueness: The Place of Case Studies in Comparative Research', in C. C. Ragin (ed.), *Issues and Alternatives in Comparative Social Research* (Leiden: E. J. Brill).

Breen, R. (1994), 'Individual Level Models for Mobility Tables and other Cross-Classifications', *Sociological Methods and Research*, 23: 147–73.

—(1997a), 'Risk, Recommodification and Stratification', *Sociology*, 31: 473–89.

—(1997b), 'Inequality, Economic Growth and Social Mobility', *British Journal of Sociology*, 48: 429–49.

—(1998), 'The Persistence of Class Origin Inequalities among School Leavers in the Republic of Ireland, 1984–1993', *British Journal of Sociology*, 49: 275–98.

—(1999), 'Beliefs, Rational Choice and Bayesian Learning', typescript.

—, and Goldthorpe, J. H. (1999), 'Class Inequality and Meritocracy: A Critique of Saunders and an Alternative Analysis', *British Journal of Sociology*, 50: 1–27.

——(forthcoming), 'Class, Mobility and Merit: The Experience of Two British Birth Cohorts', *European Sociological Review*.

—, and Whelan, C. T. (1996), *Social Mobility and Class in Ireland* (Dublin: Gill & Macmillan).

Brooks, C. (1994a), 'Class Consciousness and Politics in Comparative Perspective', *Social Science Research*, 23: 167–95.

—(1994b), 'The Selectively Political Citizen?', *Sociological Methods and Research*, 22: 419–59.

Brown, P. (1995), 'Cultural Capital and Social Exclusion: Some Observations on Recent Trends is Education, Employment and the Labour Market', *Work, Employment and Society*, 9: 29–51.

Brunton, D., and Pennington, D. H. (1954), *Members of the Long Parliament* (London: Allen & Unwin).

Bryant, C. G. A. (1995), *Practical Sociology* (Cambridge: Polity Press).

Bryant, J. M. (1994), 'Evidence and Explanation in History and Sociology', *British Journal of Sociology*, 45: 3–19.

Bryman, A. (1988), *Quantity and Quality in Social Research* (London: Routledge).

—(1994), 'The Mead/Freeman Controversy: Some Implications for Qualitative Researchers', *Studies in Qualitative Methodology*, 4: 1–27.

Buckle, T. H. (1857), *History of Civilisation in England* (London: J. W. Parker).

Bulmer, M. (1981), 'Quantification and Chicago Social Science in the 1920s: A Neglected Tradition', *Journal of the History of the Behavioral Sciences*, 17: 312–31.

——(1985) (ed.), *Essays on the History of British Sociological Research* (Cambridge: Cambridge University Press).

Bunge, M. (1979), *Causality and Modern Science* (New York: Dover).

Burawoy, M. (1989), 'Two Methods in Search of Science: Skocpol versus Trotsky', *Theory and Society*, 18: 759–805.

——(1998), 'Critical Sociology: A Dialogue between Two Sciences', *Contemporary Sociology*, 27: 12–20.

Burgess, R. G. (1984), *In the Field* (London: Allen & Unwin).

Burrow, J. W. (1966), *Evolution and Society: A Study in Victorian Social Theory* (Cambridge: Cambridge University Press).

Busch, A. (1993), 'The Politics of Price Stability: Why the German-Speaking Nations are Different', in F. G. Castles (ed.), *Families of Nations: Patterns of Public Policy in Western Democracies* (Aldershot: Dartmouth).

Bynner, J. (1991), 'Transitions to Work', in D. Ashton and G. Lowe (eds.), *Making their Way* (Milton Keynes: Open University Press).

Caldwell, B. J. (1991), 'Clarifying Popper', *Journal of Economic Literature*, 29: 1–33.

Calhoun, C. (1996), 'The Rise and Domestication of Historical Sociology', in T. J. McDonald (ed.), *The Historic Turn in the Human Sciences* (Ann Arbor: University of Michigan Press).

Campbell, C. (1996), *The Myth of Social Action* (Cambridge: Cambridge University Press).

Campbell, M. (1942), *The English Yeoman* (New Haven: Yale University Press).

Capelli, P. (1995), 'Rethinking Employment', *British Journal of Industrial Relations*, 33: 563–602.

Carr, E. H. (1961), *What is History?* (London: Macmillan).

Castles, F. G. (1978), *The Social Democratic Image of Society* (London: Routledge).

——(1993a), 'Introduction', in F. G. Castles (ed.), *Families of Nations: Patterns of Public Policy in Western Democracies* (Aldershot: Dartmouth).

——(1993b) (ed.), *Families of Nations: Patterns of Public Policy in Western Democracies* (Aldershot: Dartmouth).

Cautrès, B. (1995), 'Mobilité sociale et comportement électoral: Modèles sociologiques et modélisations statistiques', *Revue française de sociologie*, 36: 185–224.

Chan, T. W., Lui, T. L., and Wong, T. W. P. (1995), 'A Comparative Analysis of Social Mobility in Hong Kong', *European Sociological Review*, 11: 135–55.

Cherkaoui, M. (1983), 'Education and Social Mobility: Paul Lapie's Pathbreaking Work', in P. Besnard (ed.), *The Sociological Domain* (Cambridge: Cambridge University Press).

Clark, J. C. D. (1986), *Revolution and Rebellion* (Cambridge: Cambridge University Press).

Clark, T. N. (1973), *Prophets and Patrons: The French University and the Emergence of the Social Sciences* (Cambridge, Mass.: Harvard University Press).

Clifford, J. (1988), *The Predicament of Culture: Twentieth Century Ethnography, Literature and Art* (Cambridge, Mass.: Harvard University Press).

——, and Marcus, G. E. (1986) (eds.), *Writing Culture: The Poetics and Politics of Ethnography* (Berkeley and Los Angeles: University of California Press).

Clifford, P., and Heath, A. F. (1993), 'The Political Consequences of Social Mobility', *Journal of the Royal Statistical Society*, Series A, 156: 51–61

Clogg, C. C. (1992), 'The Impact of Sociological Methodology on Statistical Methodology', *Statistical Science*, 7: 183–207.

——, and Haritou, A. (1997), 'The Regression Method of Causal Inference and a Dilemma Confronting this Method', in V. R. McKim and S. P. Turner (eds.), *Causality in Crisis?* (Notre Dame, Ind.: University of Notre Dame Press).

Clubb, J. M. (1980), 'The "New" Quantitative History: Social Science or Old Wine in New Bottles?', in J. M. Clubb and K. Scheuch (eds.), *Historical Social Research* (Stuttgart: Klett-Cotta).

Coase, R. H. (1937), 'The Nature of the Firm', *Economica*, NS 4: 386–405.

Cohen, A. P. (1984), 'Informants', in R. F. Ellen (ed.), *Ethnographic Research* (London: Academic Press).

Cohen, P. C. (1976), 'Rational Conduct and Social Life', in S. I. Benn and G. W. Mortimore (eds.), *Rationality and the Social Sciences* (London: Routledge).

Cohen, Y., and Pfeffer, J. (1986), 'Organizational Hiring Standards', *Administrative Science Quarterly*, 31: 1–24.

Cole, S. (1972), 'Continuity and Institutionalization in Science: A Case Study of Failure', in A. Oberschall (ed.), *The Establishment of Empirical Sociology* (New York: Harper & Row).

——(1996), 'Voodoo Sociology: Recent Developments in the Sociology of Science', in P. R. Gross, N. Levitt, and M. W. Lewis (eds.), *The Flight from Science and Reason* (New York: New York Academy of Sciences).

Coleman, J. S. (1964), *Introduction to Mathematical Sociology* (New York: Free Press).

——(1986a), 'Social Theory, Social Research and a Theory of Action', *American Journal of Sociology*, 91: 1309–35.

——(1986b), *Individual Interests and Collective Action* (Cambridge: Cambridge University Press).

——(1990), *Foundations of Social Theory* (Cambridge, Mass.: Belknap Press).

——, and Fararo, T. J. (1992), 'Introduction', in J. S. Coleman and T. J. Fararo (eds.), *Rational Choice Theory: Advocacy and Critique* (Newbury Park, Calif.: Sage).

Collier, D. (1998), 'Comparative-Historical Analysis: Where Do We Stand?', *APSA Comparative Politics Section Newsletter* (Summer), 1–7.

Collingwood, R. G. (1946/1993), *The Idea of History*, 2nd edn. (Oxford: Oxford University Press).

Collini, S. (1979), *Liberalism and Sociology* (Cambridge: Cambridge University Press).

Collins, R. (1996), 'Can Rational Action Theory Unify Future Social Science?', in J. Clark (ed.), *James S. Coleman* (London: Falmer Press).

Commons, J. R. (1924), *Institutional Economics* (Madison: University of Wisconsin Press).

Comte, A. (1830–42/1908), *Cours de philosophie positive* (Paris: Schleicher Frères).

Converse, P. A. (1964), 'The Nature of Belief Systems in Mass Publics', in D. Apter (ed.), *Ideology and Discontent* (New York: Free Press).

——(1970), 'Attitudes and Non-Attitudes: Continuation of a Dialogue', in E. R. Tufte (ed.), *The Quantitative Analysis of Social Problems* (Reading, Mass.: Addison-Wesley).

Cook, T. D., and Campbell, D. (1979), *Quasiexperimentation* (Chicago: Rand McNally).

Cox, D. R. (1990), 'Role of Models in Statistical Analysis', *Statistical Science*, 5: 169–74.

——(1992), 'Causality: Some Statistical Aspects', *Journal of the Royal Statistical Society*, Series A, 155: 291–301.

——, and Wermuth, N. (1993), 'Linear Dependencies Represented by Chain Graphs', *Statistical Science*, 8: 204–18.

————(1996), *Multivariate Dependencies* (London: Chapman Hall).

Craig, J. E. (1983), 'Sociolgoy and Related Disciplines between the Wars: Maurice Halbwachs and the Imperialism of the Durkheimians', in P. Besnard (ed.), *The Sociological Domain* (Cambridge: Cambridge University Press).

Cressey, D. R. (1953), *Other People's Money* (New York: Free Press).

Cullen, M. (1975), *The Statistical Movement in Early Victorian Britain* (New York: Harvester).

Daston, L. J. (1987), 'Rational Individuals versus Laws of Society: From Probability to Statistics', in L. Krüger, L. J. Daston, and M. Heidelberger (eds.), *The Probabilistic Revolution*, i. *Ideas in History* (Cambridge, Mass.: MIT Press).

Davidson, D. (1976), 'Psychology as Philosophy', in J. Glover (ed.), *The Philosophy of Mind* (Oxford: Oxford University Press).

——(1980), *Essays on Actions and Events* (Oxford: Clarendon Press).

Davies, R., Heinesen, E., and Holm, A. (1999). 'The Relative Risk Aversion Hypothesis of Educational Choice', paper presented at the conference of the European Society for Population Economics, Turin.

Davis, J. A. (1985), *The Logic of Causal Order* (Beverly Hills, Calif.: Sage).

——(1994), 'What's wrong with Sociology?', *Sociological Forum*, 9: 179–97.

Day, L. H. (1987), 'Durkheim on Religion and Suicide—a Demographic Critique', *Sociology*, 21: 449–61.

De Graaf, N. D., and Heath, A. F. (1992), 'Husbands' and Wives' Voting Behaviour in Britain: Class-Dependent Mutual Influence of Spouses', *Acta Sociologica*, 35: 311–22.

——, and Ultee, W. (1990), 'Individual Preferences, Social Mobility and Electoral Outcomes', *Electoral Studies*, 9: 109–32.

——Nieuwbeerta, P., and Heath, A. F. (1995), 'Class Mobility and Political Preferences: Individual and Contextual Effects', *American Journal of Sociology*, 100: 997–1027.

De Graaf, P. M., and Ganzeboom, H. G. B. (1993), 'Family Background and Educational Attainment in the Netherlands for the 1891–1960 Birth Cohorts', in Y. Shavit and H.-P. Blossfeld (eds.), *Persistent Inequality: Changing Educational Attainment in Thirteen Countries* (Boulder, Colo.: Westview Press).

Dennis, N., Henriques, F., and Slaughter, C. (1956), *Coal is Our Life* (London: Eyre & Spottiswoode).

Denzin, N. K. (1989), *Interpretive Interactionism* (Newbury Park, Calif.: Sage).

——(1990), 'Reading Rational Choice Theory', *Rationality and Society*, 2: 172–89.

——(1997), *Interpretive Ethnography* (Thousand Oaks, Calif.: Sage).

——, and Lincoln, Y. S. (1994) (eds.), *Handbook of Qualitative Research* (Thousand Oaks, Calif.: Sage).

Desrosières, A. (1985), 'Histoire de formes: Statistiques et sciences sociales avant 1940', *Revue française de sociologie*, 26: 277–310.

——(1991), 'The Part in Relation to the Whole: How to Generalise? The Prehistory of Representative Sampling', in M. Bulmer, K. Bales, and K. K. Sklar (eds.), *The Social Survey in Historical Perspective, 1880–1940* (Cambridge: Cambridge University Press).

——(1993), *La Politique des grands nombres* (Paris: La Découverte).

——(1996), 'Quetelet et la sociologie quantitative: Du piédestal à l'oubli', paper presented at the Quetelet Bicentenary Colloquium, Brussels.

Devine, F. (1998), 'Class Analysis and the Stability of Class Relations', *Sociology*, 32: 23–42.

Dilthey, W. (1883/1959), *Einleitung in die Geisteswissenschaften* in *Gesammelte Schriften*, i. (Stuttgart: Teubner).

DiPrete, T., and Forristal, J. D. (1994), 'Multilevel Models: Methods and Substance', *Annual Review of Sociology*, 20: 331–57.

Doeringer, P., and Piore, M. (1971), *Internal Labor Markets and Manpower Analysis* (Lexington: Heath).

Dogan, M. (1994), 'Use and Misuse of Statistics in Comparative Research', in M. Dogan and A. Kazancigil (eds.), *Comparing Nations* (Oxford: Blackwell).

Douglas, J. (1967), *The Social Meanings of Suicide* (Princeton: Princeton University Press).

Dray, W. (1993), *Philosophy of History*, 2nd edn. (Englewood Cliffs, NJ: Prentice Hall).

Drobisch, M. (1867), *Die moralische Statistik und die menschliche Willensfreiheit* (Leipzig: Voss).

Duncan, O. D. (1975), *Introduction to Structural Equation Models* (New York: Academic Press).

——(1982), 'Rasch Measurement and Sociological Theory', Hollingshead Lecture, Yale University.

——(1984), *Notes on Social Measurement* (New York: Russell Sage).

——(1992), 'What If?', *Contemporary Sociology*, 21: 667–8.

Durkheim, E. (1893/1933), *The Division of Labour in Society* (Glencoe, Ill.: Free Press).

——(1895/1938), *The Rules of Sociological Method* (Glencoe, Ill.: Free Press).

——(1897/1952), *Suicide* (London: Routledge & Kegan Paul).

——(1912/1915), *The Elementary Forms of the Religious Life* (London: Allen & Unwin).

Duru-Bellat, M., and Mingat, A. (1989), 'How do French Junior Secondary Schools Operate? Academic Achievement, Grading and Streaming of Students', *European Sociological Review*, 5: 47–64.

——Jarousse, J.-P., and Mingat, A. (1992), *De l'orientation en fin de cinquième au fonctionnement du collège* (Dijon: Presses de l'Université de Bourgogne).

Edgeworth, F. Y. (1885), 'Observations and Statistics: An Essay on the Theory of Errors and the First Principles of Statistics', *Transactions of the Cambridge Philosophical Society*, 14: 138–69.

Edwards, R. (1979), *Contested Terrain: The Transformation of the Workplace in the Twentieth Century* (London: Heinemann).

Eells, E. (1991), *Probabilistic Causality* (Cambridge: University of Cambridge Press).

Eggertsson, T. (1990), *Economic Behavior and Institutions* (Cambridge: Cambridge University Press).

Ehrenberg, R. G., and Smith, R. S. (1991), *Modern Labor Economics: Theory and Public Policy* (New York: Harper Collins).

Eisenstadt, S. N. (1963), *The Political Systems of Empires* (New York: Free Press).

Elster, J. (1979), *Ulysses and the Sirens* (Cambridge: Cambridge University Press).

——(1983a), *Explaining Technical Change* (Cambridge: Cambridge University Press).

——(1983b), *Sour Grapes* (Cambridge: Cambridge University Press).

——(1985), *Making Sense of Marx* (Cambridge: Cambridge University Press).

——(1986a), 'Introduction', in J. Elster (ed.), *Rational Choice* (Oxford: Blackwell).

——(1986b) (ed.), *The Multiple Self* (Cambridge: Cambridge University Press).

——(1989a), *The Cement of Society* (Cambridge: Cambridge University Press).

——(1989b), *Nuts and Bolts for the Social Sciences* (Cambridge: Cambridge University Press).

——(1989c), *Solomonic Judgments* (Cambridge: Cambridge University Press).

——(1990), Interview in R. Swedberg (ed.), *Economics and Sociology* (Princeton: Princeton University Press).

——(1991), 'Rationality and Social Norms', *Archives européennes de sociologie*, 32: 109–29.

——(1993), 'Some Unresolved Problems in the Theory of Rational Behavior', *Acta Sociologica*, 36: 179–90.

Erikson, K. (1966), *Wayward Puritans* (New York: Wiley).

Erikson, R. (1983), 'Changes in Social Mobility in Industrial Nations: The Case of Sweden', *Research in Social Stratification and Mobility*, 2: 165–95.

——(1996), 'Can We Account for the Change in Inequality of Educational Opportunity?', in R. Erikson and J. O. Jonsson (eds.), *Can Education be Equalized? The Swedish Case in Comparative Perspective* (Boulder, Colo.: Westview Press).

——(1998), 'Thresholds and Mechanisms', in H.-P. Blossfeld and G. Prein (eds.), *Rational Choice Theory and Large-Scale Data Analysis* (Boulder, Colo.: Westview Press).

——, and Goldthorpe, J. H. (1992*a*), *The Constant Flux: A Study of Class Mobility in Industrial Societies* (Oxford: Clarendon Press).

————(1992*b*), 'The CASMIN Project and the American Dream', *European Sociological Review*, 8: 283–305.

——, and Jonsson, J. O. (1993), *Ursprung och Utbildning* (Stockholm: Statens Offentliga Utredningar).

————(1994*a*), 'Ökade Löneskillnader—Ett Sätt att ta till vara Begåvningsreserven', *Ekonomisk Debatt*, 22: 581–94.

————(1994*b*) (eds.), *Sorteringen i Skolan* (Stockholm: Carlsson).

————(1996*a*), 'Explaining Class Inequality in Education: The Swedish Test Case', in R. Erikson and J. O. Jonsson (eds.), *Can Education be Equalized? The Swedish Case in Comparative Perspective* (Boulder, Colo.: Westview Press).

————(1996*b*) (eds.), *Can Education be Equalized? The Swedish Case in Comparative Perspective* (Boulder, Colo.: Westview Press).

——Goldthorpe, J. H., and Portocarero, L. (1979), 'Intergenerational Class Mobility in Three Western European Societies', *British Journal of Sociology*, 30: 415–41.

Ermarth, M. (1978), *Wilhelm Dilthey: The Critique of Historical Reason* (Chicago: University of Chicago Press).

Esping-Andersen, G. (1985), *Politics against Markets* (Princeton: Princeton University Press).

——(1990), *The Three Worlds of Welfare Capitalism* (Princeton: Princeton University Press).

Esser, H. (1993), 'The Rationality of Everyday Behaviour: A Rational Choice Reconstruction of the Theory of Action by Alfred Schutz', *Rationality and Society*, 5: 47–57.

——(1996), 'What is Wrong with "Variable Sociology"?', *European Sociological Review*, 12: 159–66.

Etzioni, A. (1988), *The Moral Dimension: Toward a New Economics* (New York: Free Press).

Evans, G. (1992), 'Testing the Validity of the Goldthorpe Class Schema', *European Sociological Review*, 8: 211–32.

——(1993), 'Class, Prospects and the Life-Cycle: Explaining the Association between Class Position and Political Preferences', *Acta Sociologica*, 36: 263–76.

——(1996), 'Putting Men and Women into Classes: An Assessment of the Cross-Sex Validity of the Goldthorpe Class Schema', *Sociology*, 30: 209–34.

——(1999) (ed.), *The End of Class Politics? Class Voting in Comparative Context* (Oxford: Clarendon Press).

——, and Mills, C. (1998), 'Identifying Class Structures: A Latent Class Analysis of the Criterion-Related and Construct Validity of the Goldthorpe Class Schema', *European Sociological Review*, 14: 87–106

————(1999), 'Are there Classes in Post-Communist Societies? A New Approach to Identifying Class Structure', *Sociology*, 33: 23–46.

——Heath, A. F., and Payne, C. (1991), 'Modelling the Class/Party Relationship 1964–87', *Electoral Studies*, 10: 99–117.

————(1996), 'Class and Party Revisited: A New Method for Estimating Changes in Levels of Class Voting', *British Elections and Parties Yearbook, 1995* (London: Frank Cass).

Fama, E. F. (1991), 'Time, Salary, and Incentive Payoffs in Labor Contracts', *Journal of Labor Economics*, 9: 25–44.

Fararo, T. J. (1996), 'Foundational Problems in Theoretical Sociology', in J. Clark (ed.), *James S. Coleman* (London: Falmer Press).

Farmer, M. K. (1982), 'Rational Action in Economic and Social Theory: Some Misunderstandings', *Archives européennes de sociologie*, 23: 179–97.

————(1992), 'On the Need to Make a Better Job of Justifying Rational Choice Theory', *Rationality and Society*, 4: 411–20.

Farr, J. (1983), 'Popper's Hermeneutics', *Philosophy of the Social Sciences*, 13: 157–76.

————(1985), 'Situational Analysis: Explanation in Political Science', *Journal of Politics*, 47: 1085–107.

Featherman, D. L., and Spenner, K. I. (1990), 'Class and the Socialization of Children: Constancy, Chance or Irrelevance?', in E. M. Hetherington, R. M. Lerner, and M. Perlmutter (eds.), *Child Development in Life-Span Perspective* (Hillsdale, NJ: Erlbaum).

————Jones, F. L., and Hauser, R. M. (1975), 'Assumptions of Social Mobility Research in the US: The Case of Occupational Status', *Social Science Research*, 4: 329–60.

Feigl, H. (1953), 'Notes on Causality', in H. Feigl and M. Brodbeck (eds.), *Readings in the Philosophy of Science* (New York: Appleton-Century Crofts).

Fetterman, D. (1998), *Ethnography* (Thousand Oaks, Calif.: Sage).

Fielding, N. (1981), *The National Front* (London: Routledge).

Fischer, C. (1982), *To Dwell Among Friends* (Chicago: Chicago University Press).

Fisher, R. A. (1935), *The Design of Experiments* (Edinburgh: Oliver and Boyd).

Flora, P., and Alber, J. (1981), 'Modernization, Democratization, and the Development of Welfare States in Western Europe', in P. Flora and A. J. Heidenheimer (eds.), *The Development of Welfare States in Europe and America* (New Brunswick, NJ: Transaction Books).

Fogel, R. W., and Elton, G. R. (1983), *Which Road to the Past?* (New Haven: Yale University Press).

Fox T. G., and Miller, S. M. (1965), 'Economic, Political and Social Determinants of Mobility', *Acta Sociologica*, 9: 76–93.

————(1966), 'Occupational Stratification and Mobility: Inter-Country Variations', in R. Merritt and S. Rokkan (eds.), *Comparing Nations* (New Haven: Yale University Press).

Frank, R. H. (1990), 'Rethinking Rational Choice', in R. Friedland and A. F. Robertson (eds.), *Beyond the Marketplace* (New York: Aldine de Gruyter).

Fréchet, M., and Halbwachs, M. (1924), *Le Calcul des probabilités à la portée de tous* (Paris: Dunod).

Freedman, D. A. (1983), 'Structural-Equation Models: A Case Study', Technical Report No. 22, Department of Statistics, University of California, Berkeley.

————(1985), 'Statistics and the Scientific Method', in W. Mason and S. Fienberg (eds.), *Cohort Analysis in Social Research* (New York: Springer).

————(1991), 'Statistical Analysis and Shoe Leather', *Sociological Methodology*, 21: 291–313.

————(1992a), 'As Others See Us: A Case Study in Path Analysis', in J. P. Shaffer (ed.), *The Role of Models in Nonexperimental Social Science: Two Debates* (Washington: American Educational Research Association and American Statistical Association).

—— (1992*b*), 'A Rejoinder on Models, Metaphors and Fables, in J. P. Shaffer (ed.), *The Role of Models in Nonexperimental Social Science: Two Debates* (Washington: American Educational Research Association and American Statistical Association).

—— (1997), 'From Association to Causation via Regression' in V. R. McKim and S. P. Turner (eds.), *Causality in Crisis?* (Notre Dame, Ind.: University of Notre Dame Press).

—— (forthcoming), 'From Association to Causation: Some Remarks on the History of Statistics', *Statistical Science*.

Frey, B. (1992), *Economics as a Science of Human Behavior* (Boston: Kluwer).

Friedman, D., and Hechter, M. (1988), 'The Contribution of Rational Choice Theory to Macrosociological Research', *Sociological Theory*, 6: 201–18.

—— ——, and Kanazawa, S. (1994), 'A Theory of the Value of Children', *Demography*, 31: 375–401.

Friedman, M. (1953), *Essays in Positive Economics* (Chicago: University of Chicago Press).

Frisby, D. (1976), 'Introduction to the English Translation', in T. W. Adorno *et al.*, *The Positivist Dispute in German Sociology* (London: Heinemann).

Fritzell, J. (1993), 'Income Inequality Trends in the 1980s: A Five Country Comparison', *Acta Sociologica*, 36: 47–62.

Froude, J. A. (1884), *Short Studies on Great Subjects*, i (London: Longmans).

Furlong, A. (1992), *Growing Up in a Classless Society?* (Edinburgh: Edinburgh University Press).

Gähler, M. (1998), *Life After Divorce* (Stockholm: Swedish Institute for Social Research).

Gallie, D., White, M., Cheng, Y., and Tomlinson, M. (1998), *Restructuring the Employment Relationship* (Oxford: Clarendon Press).

Gallie, W. B. (1964), *Philosophy and the Historical Understanding* (London: Chatto & Windus).

Galton, F. (1869), *Hereditary Genius* (London: Macmillan).

—— (1889*a*), *Natural Inheritance* (London: Macmillan).

—— (1889*b*), 'Comment' on E. B. Tylor, 'On a Method of Investigating the Development of Institutions; Applied to Laws of Marriage and Descent', *Journal of the Anthropological Institute*, 18: 270.

Galtung, J. (1979), 'Om Makrohistoriens Epistemologi og Metodologi: en Skisse', in Nordisk Fagkonferanse for Historik Metodelaere, *Makrohistorie* (Oslo: Universitetsforlaget).

Gambetta, D. (1987), *Were They Pushed or Did They Jump? Individual Decision Mechanisms in Education* (Cambridge: Cambridge University Press).

—— (1988) (ed.), *Trust: Making and Breaking Co-operative Relations* (Cambridge: Cambridge University Press).

Ganzeboom, H. G. B., Luijkx, R., and Treiman, D. J. (1989), 'Intergenerational Class Mobility in Comparative Perspective', *Research in Social Stratification and Mobility*, 8: 3–55.

Garrett, G., and Lange, P. (1991), 'Political Responses to Interdependence: What's Left for the Left?', *International Organization*, 45: 539–64.

Gellner, E. (1992), *Postmodernism, Reason and Religion* (London: Routledge).

Geweke, J. (1984), 'Inference and Causality in Economic Time Series', in Z. Griliches and M. D. Intriligator (eds.), *Handbook of Econometrics*, ii (Amsterdam: North Holland).

Gibbons, R. (1987), 'Piece-Rate Incentive Schemes', *Journal of Labor Economics*, 5: 413–29.

——(1997), 'Incentives and Careers in Organizations', in D. M. Kreps and K. F. Wallis (eds.), *Advances in Economics and Econometrics: Theory and Applications* (Cambridge: Cambridge University Press).

Gibson, Q. (1976), 'Arguing from Rationality', in S. I. Benn and G. W. Mortimore (eds.), *Rationality and the Social Sciences* (London: Routledge).

Giddens, A. (1979), *Central Problems in Social Theory* (London: Macmillan).

——(1984), *The Constitution of Society* (Cambridge: Polity Press).

——(1987), *Social Theory and Modern Sociology* (Cambridge: Polity Press).

Gigerenzer, G. (1996), 'On Narrow Norms and Vague Heuristics', *Psychological Review*, 103: 592–6.

——, and Todd, P. M. (1999), *Simple Heuristics that Make Us Smart* (New York: Oxford University Press).

——Swiftink, Z., Porter, P., Daston, L., Beatty, J., and Krüger, L. (1989), *The Empire of Chance* (Cambridge: Cambridge University Press).

Ginsberg, M. (1929), 'Interchange between Social Classes', *Economic Journal*, 39: 554–65.

——(1965), 'Introduction to the 1965 Reprint', in L. T. Hobhouse, G. C. Wheeler, and M. Ginsberg, *The Material Culture and Social Institutions of the Simpler Peoples* (London: London School of Economics).

Glaser, B. G., and Strauss, A. L. (1967), *The Discovery of Grounded Theory* (Chicago: Aldine).

Glass, G. V., McGaw, B., and Smith, M. L. (1981), *Meta-Analysis in Social Research* (Beverly Hills, Calif.: Sage).

Glymour, C. (1986), 'Comment: Statistics and Metaphysics', *Journal of the American Statistical Association*, 81: 964–6.

Goldfrank, W. (1972), 'Reappraising Le Play', in A. Oberschall (ed.), *The Establishment of Empirical Sociology* (New York: Harper Row).

Goldstone, J. A. (1997), 'Methodological Issues in Comparative Macrosociology', *Comparative Social Research*, 16: 107–20.

Goldthorpe, J. H. (1962), 'The Relevance of History to Sociology', *Cambridge Opinion*, 28: 26–9.

——(1971), 'Theories of Industrial Society', *Archives européennes de sociologie*, 12: 263–88.

——(1979), 'Intellectuals and the Working Class in Modern Britain', Fuller Memorial Bequest Lecture, University of Essex.

——(1982), 'On the Service Class: its Formation and Future', in A. Giddens and G. Mackenzie (eds.), *Social Class and the Division of Labour* (Cambridge: Cambridge University Press).

——(1984) (ed.), *Order and Conflict in Contemporary Capitalism* (Oxford: Clarendon Press).

——(1985), 'On Economic Development and Social Mobility', *British Journal of Sociology*, 36: 549–73.

——(with Llewellyn, C. and Payne, C.) (1987), *Social Mobility and Class Structure in Modern Britain*, 2nd edn. (Oxford: Clarendon Press).

——(1992*a*), 'Employment, Class and Mobility: A Critique of Liberal and Marxist Theories of Long-Term Social Change', in H. Haferkamp and N. J. Smelser (eds.), *Social Change and Modernity* (Berkeley and Los Angeles: University of California Press).

——(1992*b*), 'The Theory of Industrialism and the Irish Case', in J. H. Goldthorpe and C. T. Whelan (eds.), *The Development of Industrial Society in Ireland* (Oxford: British Academy).

——(1994), 'The Uses of History in Sociology—A Reply', *British Journal of Sociology*, 45: 55–77.

——(1995*a*), 'The Service Class Revisited', in T. Butler and M. Savage (eds.), *Social Change and the Middle Classes* (London: UCL Press).

——(1995*b*), 'Le "Noyau dur": fluidité sociale en Angleterre et en France dans les années 70 et 80' *Revue française de sociologie*, 36: 61–79.

——(1996*a*), 'Class and Politics in Advanced Industrial Societies', in D. J. Lee and B. S. Turner (eds.), *Conflicts over Class* (London: Longmans).

——(1996*b*), 'Problems of "Meritocracy"', in R. Erikson and J. O. Jonsson (eds.), *Can Education be Equalized? The Swedish Case in Comparative Perspective* (Boulder, Colo.: Westview Press).

——(1997*a*), 'The Integration of Sociological Research and Theory', *Rationality and Society*, 9: 405–26.

——(1997*b*), 'A Response to the Commentaries', *Comparative Social Research*, 16: 121–32.

——, and Heath, A. F. (1992), 'Revised Class Schema, 1992', JUSST Working Paper 13, Nuffield College, Oxford.

——, and Hope, K. (1974), *The Social Grading of Occupations* (Oxford: Clarendon Press).

——, and Llewellyn, C. (1977), 'Class Mobility in Modern Britain: Three Theses Examined', *Sociology*, 11: 257–87.

——, and Marshall, G. (1992), 'The Promising Future of Class Analysis: A Response to Recent Critiques', *Sociology*, 26: 381–400.

——Payne, C., and Llewellyn, C. (1978), 'Trends in Class Mobility', *Sociology*, 12: 441–68.

——Yaish, M., and Kraus, V. (1997), 'Class Mobility in Israeli Society: A Comparative Perspective', *Research in Social Stratification and Mobility*, 15: 3–28.

Gomm, R., Foster, P., and Hammersley, M. (1999), 'From One to Many, but How? Theory and Generalisation in Case Study Research', typescript.

Goodin, R., and Le Grand, J. (1987), *Not Only the Poor: The Middle Classes and the Welfare State* (London: Allen & Unwin).

Goody, J. (1996), *The East in the West* (Cambridge: Cambridge University Press).

Gottschalk, P., and Smeeding, T. M. (1997), 'Cross-National Comparisons of Earnings and Income Inequality', *Journal of Economic Literature*, 35: 633–87.

Goux, D., and Maurin, E. (1997), 'Meritocracy and Social Heredity in France', *European Sociological Review*, 13: 159–77.

Granger, C. W. J. (1969), 'Investigating Causal Relations by Econometric Models and Cross-Spectral Methods', *Econometrica*, 37: 424–38.

——(1986), 'Comment', *Journal of the American Statistical Association*, 81: 967–8.

Green, D. P., and Shapiro, I. (1994), *Pathologies of Rational Choice Theory: A Critique of Applications in Political Science* (New Haven: Yale University Press).

Griffin, L. J. (1992), 'Temporality, Events, and Explanation in Historical Sociology', *Sociological Methods and Research*, 20: 403–27.

Gross, P. R., and Levitt, N. (1994), *Higher Superstition* (Baltimore: Johns Hopkins University Press).

————, and Lewis, M. W. (1996) (eds.), *The Flight from Science and Reason* (New York: New York Academy of Sciences).

Hacking, I. (1987), 'Was There a Probabilistic Revolution 1800–1930?', in L. Krüger, L. J. Daston, and M. Heidelberger (eds.), *The Probabilistic Revolution*, i. *Ideas in History* (Cambridge, Mass.: MIT Press).

——(1990), *The Taming of Chance* (Cambridge: Cambridge University Press).

Halaby, C. N., and Weakliem, D. L. (1989), 'Worker Control and Attachment to the Firm', *American Journal of Sociology*, 95: 549–91.

Halbwachs, M. (1912), *La Théorie de l'homme moyen* (Paris: Alcan).

Halbwachs, M. (1930/1978), *The Causes of Suicide* (London: Routledge).

——(1933), *L'Évolution des besoins dans les classes ouvrières* (Paris: Alcan).

Halford, S., and Savage, M. (1995), 'The Bureaucratic Career: Demise or Adaptation?, in T. Butler and M. Savage (eds.), *Social Change and the Middle Classes* (London: UCL Press).

Hall, J. (1985), *Powers and Liberties* (Harmondsworth: Penguin).

Halliday, R. (1968), 'The Sociological Movement, the Sociological Society and the Genesis of Academic Sociology in Britain', *Sociological Review*, 16: 377–98.

Halpin, B. (1999), 'Simulation in Sociology' *American Behavioral Scientist*, 42: 1488–1508.

Halsey, A. H. (1977), 'Towards Meritocracy? The Case of Britain', in J. Karabel and A. H. Halsey (eds.), *Power and Ideology in Education* (New York: Oxford University Press).

——Floud, J., and Anderson, C. A. (1961) (eds.), *Education, Economy and Society* (New York: Free Press).

——Heath, A. F., and Ridge J. M. (1980), *Origins and Destinations* (Oxford: Clarendon Press).

Hamilton, R. F. (1996), *The Social Misconstruction of Reality* (New Haven: Yale University Press).

Hammel, E. A. (1980), 'The Comparative Method in Anthropological Perspective', *Comparative Studies in Society and History*, 22: 145–55.

Hammersley, M. (1989), *The Dilemma of Qualitative Method: Herbert Blumer and the Chicago Tradition* (London: Routledge).

——(1991), *Reading Ethnographic Research* (London: Longman).

——(1992), *What's Wrong with Ethnography?* (London: Routledge).

——(1999), 'Not Bricolage but Boatbuilding', *Journal of Contemporary Ethnography*, 28: 574–85.

——, and Atkinson, P. (1995), *Ethnography* (London: Routledge).

Handl, J. (n.d.), 'Heiratsomobilität und berufliche Mobilität von Frauen', VASMA Project Working Paper, 8, Institüt für Sozialwissenschaften, University of Mannheim.

Hands, D. W. (1985), 'Karl Popper and Economic Methodology: A New Look', *Economics and Philosophy*, 1: 83–100.

Hansen, M. H. (1987), 'Some History and Reminiscences of Survey Sampling', *Statistical Science*, 2: 180–90.

Harsanyi, J. C. (1969), 'Rational-Choice Models of Political Behavior vs. Functionalist and Conformist Theories', *World Politics*, 22: 513–38.

Hart, N. (1994), 'John Goldthorpe and the Relics of Sociology', *British Journal of Sociology*, 45: 21–30.

Hauser, R. M. (1973), 'Socioeconomic Background and Differential Returns to Education', in L. C. Solmon and P. J. Taubman (eds.), *Does College Matter?* (New York: Academic Press).

——(1976), 'On Boudon's Model of Social Mobility', *American Journal of Sociology*, 81: 911–28.

——Koffel, J. N., Travis H. P., and Dickinson, P. J. (1975), 'Temporal Change in Occupational Mobility: Evidence for Men in the United States', *American Sociological Review*, 40: 279–97.

Hausman, D. M. (1992), *The Inexact and Separate Science of Economics* (Cambridge: Cambridge University Press).

Hayek, F. (1960), *The Constitution of Liberty* (London: Routledge).

——(1976), *Law, Legislation and Liberty* (London: Routledge).

Heath, A. F., Curtice, J., Evans, G., Jowell, R., Field, J., and Witherspoon, S. (1991), *Understanding Political Change* (Oxford: Pergamon).

Hechter, M. (1983) (ed.), *The Microfoundations of Macrosociology* (Philadelphia: Temple Press).

——(1987), *Principles of Group Solidarity* (Berkeley and Los Angeles: University of California Press).

——(1994), 'The Role of Values in Rational Choice Theory', *Rationality and Society*, 6: 318–33.

——(1998), 'Is There a Future for Rational Choice Theory in Macrosociological Research?', in H.-P. Blossfeld and G. Prein (eds.), *Rational Choice Theory and Large-Scale Data Analysis* (Boulder, Colo.: Westview Press).

——, and Kiser, H. (1995), 'A Proposal for Conducting Theory-Driven Historical Research', Working Paper 31, Department of Sociology, University of Stockholm.

Hedström, P. (1996), 'Rational Choice and Social Structure: On Rational Choice Theorizing in Sociology', in B. Wittrock (ed.), *Social Theory and Human Agency* (London: Sage).

——, and Swedberg, R. (1996), 'Rational Choice, Empirical Research and the Sociological Tradition', *European Sociological Review*, 12: 127–46.

————(1998a), 'Social Mechanisms: An Introductory Essay', in P. Hedström and R. Swedberg (eds.), *Social Mechanisms* (Cambridge: Cambridge University Press).

————(1998b), 'Rational Choice, Situational Analysis, and Empirical Research', in H.-P. Blossfeld and G. Prein (eds.), *Rational Choice Theory and Large-Scale Data Analysis* (Boulder, Colo.: Westview Press).

————(1998c) (eds.), *Social Mechanisms* (Cambridge: Cambridge University Press).

Heilbron, J. (1995), *The Rise of Social Theory* (Cambridge: Polity Press).

Helm, D. (1984), 'Predictions and Causes: A Comparison of Friedman and Hicks on Method', *Oxford Economic Papers*, 36: 118–34.

Hendrickx, J., and Ganzeboom, H. G. B. (1998), 'Occupational Status Attainment in the Netherlands, 1920–1990: A Multinomial Logistic Analysis', *European Sociological Review*, 14: 387–403.

Hennis, W. (1996), *Max Webers Wissenschaft vom Menschen* (Tübingen: J. C. B. Mohr).

Hernes, G. (1989), 'The Logic of *The Protestant Ethic*', *Rationality and Society*, 1: 123–62.

——(1992), 'We are Smarter than We Think', *Rationality and Society*, 4: 421–36.

Hexter, J. H. (1958/1961), 'Storm over the Gentry', in *Reappraisals in History* (London: Longmans).

Hibbs, D. A. (1991), 'Market Forces, Trade Union Ideology and Trends in Swedish Wage Dispersion', *Acta Sociologica*, 34: 89–102.

Hicks, A. M. (1994), 'Introduction to Pooling', in T. Janoski and A. M. Hicks (eds.), *The Comparative Political Economy of the Welfare State* (Cambridge: Cambridge University Press).

Hirsch, F. (1976), *Social Limits to Growth* (Cambridge, Mass.: Harvard University Press).

Hirsch, P., Michaels, S., and Friedman, R. (1987), ' "Dirty Hands" versus "Clean Models": Is Sociology in Danger of being Seduced by Economics', *Theory and Society*, 16: 317–36.

Hirshleifer, J. (1985), 'The Expanding Domain of Economics', *American Economic Review*, 75: 53–68.

Hobhouse, L. T. (1906), *Morals in Evolution* (London: Allen & Unwin).

——(1924), *Social Development* (London: Allen & Unwin).

Hobhouse, L. T., Wheeler, G. C., and Ginsberg, M. (1915), *The Material Culture and Social Institutions of the Simpler Peoples* (London: Chapman & Hall).

Hogarth, R. M., and Reder, M. W. (1986) (eds.), *Rational Choice* (Chicago: University of Chicago Press).

Hogben, L. T. (1938) (ed.), *Political Arithmetic* (London: Allen & Unwin).

Holland, P. (1986a), 'Statistics and Causal Inference', *Journal of the American Statistical Association*, 81: 945–60.

——(1986b), 'Rejoinder' *Journal of the American Statistical Association*, 81: 968–70.

——(1988), 'Causal Inference, Path Analysis, and Recursive Structural Equation Models', *Sociological Methodology*, 18: 449–84.

——(1992), 'It's the Interplay that's Important', *Statistical Science*, 7: 198–201.

Hollis, M. (1977), *Models of Man* (Cambridge: Cambridge University Press).

——(1987), *The Cunning of Reason* (Cambridge: Cambridge University Press).

——(1994), *The Philosophy of Social Science* (Cambridge: Cambridge University Press).

Holmström, B., and Milgrom, P. (1991), 'Multitask Principal-Agent Analyses: Incentive Contracts, Asset Ownership, and Job Design', *Journal of Law, Economics and Organization*, 7: 25–51.

Homans, G. C. (1961), *Social Behavior* (New York: Harcourt, Brace & World).

Honigman, J. J. (1973), 'Sampling in Ethnographic Fieldwork', in R. Naroll and C. Cohen (eds.), *Handbook of Method in Cultural Anthropology* (New York: Columbia University Press).

Hope, K. (1984), *As Others See Us: Schooling and Social Mobility in Scotland and the United States* (Cambridge: Cambridge University Press).

——(1992), 'Barren Theory or Petty Craft? A Response to Professor Freedman', in J. P. Shaffer (ed.), *The Role of Models in Nonexperimental Social Science: Two Debates* (Washington: American Educational Research Association and American Statistical Association).

Hopkins, T. K. (1987), 'World-System Analysis: Methodological Issues', in B. H. Kaplan (ed.), *Change in the Capitalist World Economy* (Beverly Hills, Calif.: Sage).

——and Wallerstein I. (1981), 'Structural Transformations of the World Economy', in R. Rubinson (ed.), *Dynamics of World Development* (Beverly Hills, Calif.: Sage).

Hough, R. (1959), *Admirals in Collision* (London: Hamish Hamilton).

Hout, M., Raftery, A. E., and Bell, E. O. (1993), 'Making the Grade: Educational Stratification in the United States, 1925–1989', in Y. Shavit and H.-P. Blossfeld (eds.), *Persistent Inequality: Changing Educational Attainment in Thirteen Countries* (Boulder, Colo.: Westview Press).

Huber, E., Ragin, C. C., and Stephens, J. D. (1993), 'Social Democracy, Christian Democracy, Constitutional Structure and the Welfare State', *American Journal of Sociology*, 99: 711–49.

Huber, J. (1995), 'Institutional Perspectives on Sociology', *American Journal of Sociology*, 101: 194–216.

Hutchens, R. M. (1987), 'A Test of Lazear's Theory of Delayed Payment Contracts', *Journal of Labor Economics*, 5: S153–70.

Hutchison, T. W. (1988), 'The Case for Falsification', in N. de Marchi (ed.), *The Popperian Legacy in Economics* (Cambridge: Cambridge University Press).

Hyman, H. (1954), 'The Value Systems of Different Classes', in R. Bendix and S. M. Lipset (eds.), *Class, Status and Power* (Glencoe, Iu.: Free Press).

Isambert, F.-A. (1973), 'Durkheim et la statistique écologique', in *Une nouvelle civilisation? Hommage à Georges Friedmann* (Paris: Gallimard).

Ishida, H. (1995), 'Intergenerational Class Mobility and Reproduction', in H. Ishida (ed.), *Social Stratification and Mobility: Basic Analysis and Cross-National Comparison* (Tokyo: SSM Research Series).

——Müller, W., and Ridge, J. M. (1995), 'Class Origin, Class Destination, and Education: A Cross-National Study of Ten Industrial Nations', *American Journal of Sociology*, 60: 145–93.

Jankowski, M. S. (1991), *Islands in the Street* (Berkeley and Los Angeles: University of California Press).

Janoski, T., and Hicks, A. M. (1994) (eds.), *The Comparative Political Economy of the Welfare State* (Cambridge: Cambridge University Press).

Jarvie, I. C. (1964), *The Revolution in Anthropology* (London: Routledge).

——(1972), *Concepts and Society* (London: Routledge).

Johnson, J. C. (1990), *Selecting Ethnographic Informants* (Newbury Park, Calif.: Sage).

Jones, F. L. (1992), 'Common Social Fluidity: A Comment on Recent Criticisms', *European Sociological Review*, 8: 255–9.

——Kojima, H., and Marks, G. (1994), 'Comparative Social Fluidity: Trends over Time in Father-to-Son Mobility in Japan and Australia, 1965–1985', *Social Forces*, 72: 775–98.

Jonsson, J. O. (1988), *Utbildning, Social Reproduktion och Social Skiktning* (Stockholm: Institutet för Social Forskning).

——(1991), 'Education, Social Mobility and Social Reproduction in Sweden: Patterns and Changes', in E. J. Hansen *et al.* (eds.), *Scandinavian Trends in Welfare and Living Conditions* (Armonck, NY: Sharpe).

——(1993), 'Persisting Inequalities in Sweden?' in Y. Shavit and H.-P. Blossfeld (eds.), *Persisting Inequality: Changing Educational Attainment in Thirteen Countries* (Boulder, Colo.: Westview Press).

——(1995), 'A Note on the Differential Incentive to Continue in Higher Education', Swedish Institute for Social Research, Stockholm.

——(1996), 'Stratification in Post-Industrial Society: Are Educational Qualifications of Growing Importance?', in R. Erikson and J. O. Jonsson (eds.), *Can Education be Equalized?: The Swedish Case in Comparative Perspective* (Boulder, Colo.: Westview Press).

——and Gähler, M. (1997), 'Family Dissolution, Family Reconstitution, and Children's Educational Careers: Recent Evidence for Sweden', *Demography*, 34: 277–93.

——and Mills, C. (1993), 'Social Class and Educational Attainment in Historical Perspective', *British Journal of Sociology*, 44: 213–47, 403–28.

————and Müller, W. (1996), 'A Half Century of Increasing Educational Openness? Social Class, Gender and Educational Attainment in Sweden, Germany and Britain', in R. Erikson and J. O. Jonsson (eds.), *Can Education be Equalized? The Swedish Case in Comparative Perspective* (Boulder, Colo.: Westview Press).

Kahneman, D., and Tversky, A. (1979), 'Prospect Theory: An Analysis of Decision under Risk', *Econometrica*, 47: 263–91.

Kalleberg, A. J. (1990), 'The Comparative Study of Business Organizations and their Employees: Conceptual and Methodological Issues', *Comparative Social Research*, 12: 153–75.

Kangas, O. (1991), *The Politics of Social Rights: Studies on the Dimensions of Sickness Insurance in 18 OECD Countries* (Stockholm: Swedish Institute for Social Research).

——(1994), 'The Politics of Social Security: on Regressions, Qualitative Comparisons, and Cluster Analysis', in T. Janoski and A. M. Hicks (eds.), *The Comparative Political Economy of the Welfare State* (Cambridge: Cambridge University Press).

Karady, V. (1981), 'French Ethnology and the Durkheimian Breakthrough', *Journal of the Anthropological Society of Oxford*, 12: 165–76.

——(1983), 'The Durkheimians in Academe: A Reconsideration', in P. Besnard (ed.), *The Sociological Domain* (Cambridge: Cambridge University Press).

Käsler, D. (1988), *Max Weber* (Cambridge: Polity Press).

Katz, J. (1997), 'Ethnography's Warrants', *Sociological Methods and Research*, 25: 391–423.

Katznelson, I. (1992/3), 'Refuse to Choose!', *Clio*, 3: 1–2.

Kay, J. (1993), *The Foundations of Corporate Success* (Oxford: Oxford University Press).

Keller, S., and Zavalloni, M. (1964), 'Ambition and Social Class: A Respecification', *Social Forces*, 43: 58–70.

Kelley, J., Robinson, R. V., and Klein, H. S. (1981), 'A Theory of Social Mobility, with Data on Status Attainment in a Peasant Society', *Research in Social Stratification and Mobility*, 1: 27–66.

Kendall, P. L., and Lazarsfeld, P. F. (1950), 'Problems of Survey Analysis', in R. K. Merton and P. F. Lazarsfeld (eds.), *Continuities in Social Research: Studies in the Scope and Method of 'The American Soldier'* (Glencoe, Ill.: Free Press).

Kent, R. (1981), *A History of British Empirical Sociology* (Aldershot: Gower).

——(1985), 'The Emergence of the Sociological Survey', in M. Bulmer (ed.), *Essays on the History of British Sociological Research* (Cambridge: Cambridge University Press).

Kerr, C. (1983), *The Future of Industrial Societies* (Cambridge, Mass.: Harvard University Press).

——*et al.* (1973), *Industrialism and Industrial Man*, 2nd edn. (Cambridge, Mass.: Harvard University Press).

Kiaer, A. N. (1895), 'Observations et expériences concernant des dénombrements représentatifs', *Bulletin of the International Statistical Institute*, 9: 176–83.

——(1901), 'Sur les méthodes représentatives ou typologiques', *Bulletin of the International Statistical Institute*, 13: 66–70.

King, G. (1986), 'How Not to Lie with Statistics: Avoiding Common Mistakes in Quantitative Political Science', *American Journal of Political Science*, 30: 666–87.

——Keohane, R. O., and Verba, S. (1994), *Designing Social Inquiry* (Princeton: Princeton University Press).

——————(1995), 'The Importance of Research Design in Political Science', *American Political Science Review*, 89: 475–81.

Kirk, J., and Miller, M. L. (1986), *Reliability and Validity in Qualitative Research* (Beverly Hills, Calif.: Sage).

Kiser, E., and Hechter, M. (1991), 'The Role of General Theory in Comparative-Historical Sociology', *American Journal of Sociology*, 97: 1–30.

——————(1998), 'The Debate on Historical Sociology: Rational Choice Theory and its Critics', *American Journal of Sociology*, 104: 785–816.

Klima, R. (1972), 'Theoretical Pluralism, Methodological Dissension and the Role of the Sociologist', *Social Science Information*, 11: 69–108.

Koertge, N. (1975), 'Popper's Metaphysical Research Program for the Human Sciences', *Inquiry*, 18: 437–62.

——(1979), 'The Methodological Status of Popper's Rationality Principle', *Theory and Decision*, 10: 83–95.

——(1998) (ed.), *A House Built on Sand* (New York: Oxford University Press).

Kolakowski, L. (1972), *Positivist Philosophy* (Harmondsworth: Penguin).

Korpi, W. (1983), *The Democratic Class Struggle* (London: Routledge).

——(1989), 'Power, Politics, and State Autonomy in the Development of Social Citizenship: Social Rights during Sickness in Eighteen OECD Countries since 1930', *American Sociological Review*, 54: 309–28.

Kreager, P. (1993), 'Anthropological Demography and the Limits of Diffusionism', *Proceedings of the International Population Conference*, Montreal, 4: 313–26.

Krüger, L. (1987), 'The Slow Rise of Probabilism: Philosophical Arguments in the Nineteenth Century', in L. Krüger, L. J. Daston, and M. Heidelberger (eds.), *The Probabilistic Revolution*, i. *Ideas in History* (Cambridge, Mass.: MIT Press).

——Daston, L. J., and Heidelberger, M. (1987*a*) (eds.), *The Probabilistic Revolution*, i. *Ideas in History* (Cambridge, Mass.: MIT Press).

——Gigerenzer, G., and Morgan, M. S. (1987*b*) (eds.), *The Probabilistic Revolution*, ii. *Ideas in the Sciences* (Cambridge, Mass.: MIT Press).

Kruskal, W., and Mosteller, F. (1980), 'Representative Sampling, IV: The History of the Concept in Statistics', *International Statistical Review*, 48: 169–95.

Kuhn, T. (1962), *The Structure of Scientific Revolutions* (Chicago: University of Chicago Press).

Kunst, A. E. (1996), *Socioeconomic Inequalities in Morbidity and Mortality in Europe: A Comparative Study* (Rotterdam: Department of Public Health, Erasmus University).

Kuznets, S. (1955), 'Economic Growth and Income Inequality', *American Economic Review*, 45: 1–28.

Lachmann, L. M. (1970), *The Legacy of Max Weber* (London: Heinemann).

Lakatos, I. (1970), 'Falsification and the Methodology of Scientific Research Programmes', in I. Lakatos and A. Musgrave (eds.), *Criticism and the Growth of Knowledge* (Cambridge: Cambridge University Press).

Lane, M. (1972), 'Explaining Educational Choice', *Sociology*, 6: 255–66.

Langlois, R. N. (1986), 'Rationality, Institutions and Explanation', in R. N. Langlois (ed.), *Economics as Process* (Cambridge: Cambridge University Press).

Latour, B. (1987), *Science in Action* (Milton Keynes: Open University Press).

——and Woolgar, S. (1979), *Laboratory Life* (Beverly Hills, Calif.: Sage).

Latsis, S. J. (1976), 'A Research Programme in Economics', in S. J. Latsis (ed.), *Method and Appraisal in Economics* (Cambridge: Cambridge University Press).

Lazarsfeld, P. F. (1959), 'Problems of Methodology', in R. K. Merton, L. Broom, and L. S. Cottrell (eds.), *Sociology Today: Problems and Prospects* (New York: Basic Books).

——(1961), 'Notes on the History of Quantification in Sociology—Trends, Sources and Problems', *Isis*, 52: 277–333.

——and Oberschall, A. (1965), 'Max Weber and Empirical Social Research', *American Sociological Review*, 30: 185–99.

——and Rosenberg, M. (1955) (eds.), *The Language of Social Research* (New York: Free Press).

——Pasanella, A. K., and Rosenberg, M. (1972) (eds.), *Continuities in the Language of Social Research* (New York: Free Press).

Lazear, A. P. (1981), 'Agency, Earnings Profiles, Productivity and Hours Restrictions', *American Economic Review*, 71: 606–20.

314   References

——(1995), *Personnel Economics* (Cambridge, Mass.: MIT Press).
Le Play, F. (1855/1877–9), *Les Ouvriers européens* (Paris: Imprimerie Impériale).
Lecuyer, B.-P. (1987), 'Probability in Vitae and Social Statistics: Quetelet, Farr, and the Bertillons', in L. Krüger, L. J. Daston, and M. Heidelberger (eds.), *The Probabilistic Revolution*, i. *Ideas in History* (Cambridge, Mass.: MIT Press).
Levi, M. (1997), 'A Model, a Method, and a Map: Rational Choice in Comparative Historical Analysis', in M. I. Lichbach and A. S. Zuckerman (eds.), *Comparative Politics* (Cambridge: Cambridge University Press).
Lewis, O. (1951), *Life in a Mexican Village: Tepoztlan Revisited* (Urbana, Ill.: University of Illinois Press).
Lexis, W. (1874/1903), "Naturwissenschaft und Sozialwissenschaft', in *Abhandlungen zur Theorie der Bevölkerungs- und Moralstatistik* (Jena: Fisher).
——(1875), *Einleitung in die Theorie der Bevölkerungsstatistick* (Strassburg: Trübner).
——(1877), *'Theorie der Massenerscheinungen in der menschlichen Gesellschaft* (Freiburg: Wagner).
——(1879), 'Über die Theorie der Stabilität statistischer Reihen', *Jahrbücher Für Nationalökonomie und Statiskik*, 32: 60–98.
Li, Y. (1997), 'The Service Class: Theoretical Debate and Empirical Value', D. Phil. thesis, Oxford.
Lieberson, S. (1985), *Making It Count* (Berkeley and Los Angeles: University of California Press).
——(1992), 'Small Ns and Big Conclusions: An Examination of the Reasoning in Comparative Studies Based on a Small Number of Cases', in C. C. Ragin and H. S. Becker (eds.), *What is a Case?* (Cambridge: Cambridge University Press).
——(1994), 'More on the Uneasy Case for Using Mill-Type Methods in Small-N Comparative Studies', *Social Forces*, 72: 1225–37.
Liebow, E. (1967), *Tally's Corner* (London: Routledge).
Lindenberg, S. (1982), 'Sharing Groups: Theory and Suggested Applications', *Journal of Mathematical Sociology*, 9: 33–62.
——(1983), 'Utility and Morality', *Kyklos*, 36: 450–68.
——(1985), 'An Assessment of the New Political Economy: Its Potential for the Social Sciences and Sociology in Particular', *Sociological Theory*, 3: 99–114.
——(1989), 'Choice and Culture: The Behavioral Basis of Cultural Impact on Transactions', in H. Haferkamp (ed.), *Social Structure and Culture* (Berlin: de Gruyter).
——(1990), 'Homo Socio-Economicus: The Emergence of a General Model of Man in the Social Sciences', *Journal of Institutional and Theoretical Economics*, 146: 727–48.
——(1992), 'The Method of Decreasing Abstraction', in J. S. Coleman and T. J. Fararo (eds.), *Rational Choice Theory: Advocacy and Critique* (Newbury Park, Calif.: Sage).
——(1998), 'Choice-Centred versus Subject-Centred Theories in the Social Sciences: The Influence of Simplification on Explananda', in H.-P. Blossfeld and G. Prein (eds.), *Rational Choice Theory and Large-Scale Data Analysis* (Boulder, Colo.: Westview Press).
——and Frey, B. (1993), 'Alternatives, Frames and Relative Prices: A Broader View of Rational Choice Theory', *Acta Sociologica*, 36: 191–205.
——and Wippler, R. (1978), 'Theorienvergleich: Elemente der Rekonstruktion', in K. O. Hondrich and J. Matthes (eds.), *Theorienvergleich in den Sozialwissenschaften* (Darmstadt: Luchterhand).
Lindesmith, A. (1948), *Opiate Addiction* (Bloomington, Ind.: Principia).

Lipset, S. M., and Zetterberg, H. L. (1956), 'A Theory of Social Mobility', *Transactions of the Third World Congress of Sociology*, iii (London: International Sociological Association).

Lockwood, D. (1960), 'The "New Working Class"', *Archives européennes de sociologie*, 1: 248–69.

——(1981), 'The Weakest Link in the Chain? Some Comments on the Marxist Theory of Action', *Research in the Sociology of Work*, 1: 435–81.

——(1992), *Solidarity and Schism* (Oxford: Clarendon Press).

Lukes, S. (1975), *Émile Durkheim: His Life and Work* (London: Peregrine).

Lustick, I. S. (1996), 'History, Historiography, and Political Science: Multiple Historical Records and the Problem of Selection Bias', *American Political Science Review*, 90: 605–17.

McClintock, C. C., Brannon, B., and Maynard-Moody, S. (1983), 'Applying the Logic of Sample Surveys to Qualitative Case Studies: The Case Cluster Method', in J. Van Maanen (ed.), *Qualitative Methodology* (Beverly Hills, Calif.: Sage).

MacIntyre, A. (1962), 'A Mistake about Causality in Social Science', in P. Laslett and W. G. Runciman (eds.), *Philosophy, Politics and Society* (Oxford: Blackwell).

MacKenzie, D. A. (1981), *Statistics in Britain, 1865–1930* (Edinburgh: Edinburgh University Press).

Mackie, J. L. (1974), *The Cement of the Universe: A Study of Causation* (Oxford: Clarendon Press).

McKim, V. R., and Turner, S. P. (1997) (eds.), *Causality in Crisis?* (Notre Dame, Ind.: Notre Dame University Press).

McMichael, P. (1990), 'Incorporating Comparison Within a World-Historical Perspective: An Alternative Comparative Method', *American Sociological Review*, 55: 385–97.

Maitland, F. M. (1911), 'The Body Politic', in *Collected Papers*, ed. H. A. L. Fisher (Cambridge: Cambridge University Press).

Mann, J. M. (1986), *The Sources of Social Power* (Cambridge: Cambridge University Press).

——(1994), 'In Praise of Macro-Sociology', *British Journal of Sociology*, 45: 37–54.

Manning, P. K. (1982), 'Analytic Induction', in R. B. Smith and P. K. Manning (eds.), *Qualitative Methods* (Cambridge, Mass.: Ballinger).

Manski, C. F. (1993), 'Adolescent Econometricians: How Do Youth Infer the Returns to Schooling?', in C. T. Clotfelter and M. Rothschild (eds.), *Studies of Supply and Demand in Higher Education* (Chicago: Chicago University Press).

March, J. G. (1978), 'Bounded Rationality, Ambiguity, and the Engineering of Choice', *Bell Journal of Economics*, 9: 587–608.

Mare, R. D. (1981), 'Change and Stability in Educational Stratification', *American Sociological Review*, 46: 72–87.

Marglin, S. (1974), 'What Do Bosses Do?', *Review of Radical Political Economics*, 6: 60–112.

Marsh, C. (1982), *The Survey Method: the Contribution of Surveys to Sociological Explanation* (London: Allen & Unwin).

Marshall, A. (1890), *Principles of Economics* (London: Macmillan).

Marshall, G. (1980), *Presbyteries and Profits: Calvinism and the Development of Capitalism in Scotland* (Oxford: Clarendon Press).

——(1982), *In Search of the Spirit of Capitalism* (London: Hutchinson).

Marshall, T. H. (1947), *Citizenship and Social Class* (Cambridge: Cambridge University Press).

——(1963), *Sociology at the Crossroads* (London: Heinemann).

Mason, W. M. (1991), 'Problems in Quantitative Comparative Analysis: Ugly Ducklings are to Swans as Ugly Scatter Plots are to . . . ?', in J. Huber (ed.), *Macro-Micro Linkages in Sociology* (Newbury Park, Calif.: Sage).

Medoff, J. L., and Abraham, K. G. (1981), 'Are Those Paid More Really More Productive? The Case of Experience', *Journal of Human Resources*, 16: 186–216.

Merton, R. K. (1987), 'Three Fragments from a Sociologist's Notebook: Establishing the Phenomenon, Specified Ignorance and Strategic Research Materials', *Annual Review of Sociology*, 13: 1–28.

Meyer, J. W. (1987), 'The World Polity and the Authority of the Nation-State', in G. M. Thomas *et al.*, *Institutional Structure* (Newbury Park, Calif.: Sage).

Micklewright, J. (1989), 'Choice at Sixteen', *Economica*, 56: 25–39.

——Pearson, M., and Smith, S. (1988), 'Unemployment and Early School Leaving', Institute for Fiscal Studies, London.

Miles, A. (1993), 'How Open was Nineteenth-Century British Society? Social Mobility and Equality of Opportunity, 1839–1914', in A. Miles and D. Vincent (eds.), *Building European Society* (Manchester: Manchester University Press).

——and Vincent, D. (1993), 'The Past and Future of Working Lives', in A. Miles and D. Vincent (eds.), *Building European Society* (Manchester: Manchester University Press).

Miles, M. B. (1983), 'Qualitative Data as an Attractive Nuisance', in J. Van Maanen (ed.), *Qualitative Methodology* (Beverly Hills, Calif.: Sage).

——and Huberman, A. M. (1984), *Qualitative Data Analysis* (Beverly Hills, Calif.: Sage).

Milgrom, P., and Roberts, J. (1992), *Economics, Organization and Management* (London: Prentice-Hall).

Mill, J. S. (1843/1973–4), *A System of Logic Ratiocinative and Inductive*, in *Collected Works of John Stuart Mill*, ed. J. M. Robson (Toronto: University of Toronto Press).

Miller, R. (1998), 'The Limited Concerns Social Mobility Research', *Current Sociology*, 46: 145–63.

Mitchell, J. C. (1983), 'Case and Situation Analysis', *Sociological Review*, 31: 187–211.

Moore, B. (1966), *The Social Origins of Dictatorship and Democracy* (Boston: Beacon Press).

Mouzelis, N. (1994), 'In Defence of "Grand" Historical Sociology', *British Journal of Sociology*, 45: 31–6.

Müller, W., and Haun, D. (1994), 'Bildungsungleichheit im Sozialen Wandel', *Kölner Zeitschrift für Soziologie und Sozialpsychologie*, 46: 1–42.

——and Karle, W. (1993), 'Social Selection and Educational Systems in Europe', *European Sociological Review*, 9: 1–23.

——and Shavit, Y. (1998), 'The Institutional Embeddedness of the Stratification Process: A Comparative Study of Qualifications and Occupations in Thirteen Countries', in Y. Shavit and W. Müller (eds.), *From School to Work* (Oxford: Clarendon Press).

Murphey, M. G. (1973), *Our Knowledge of the Historical Past* (Indianapolis: Bobbs Merrill).

Murphy, J. (1981), 'Class Inequality in Education: Two Justifications, One Evaluation but No Hard Evidence', *British Journal of Sociology*, 32: 182–201.

——(1990), 'A Most Respectable Prejudice: Inequality in Educational Research and Policy', *British Journal of Sociology*, 41: 29–54.

Naroll, R. (1970), 'Galton's Problem', in R. Naroll and R. Cohen (eds.), *A Handbook of Method in Cultural Anthropology* (New York: The Natural History Press).

Need, A., and De Jong, U. (1999), 'Educational Differentials in the Netherlands: Testing Rational Action Theory', Markt Dag NSV, Utrecht.

Neyman, J. (1934), 'On the Two Different Aspects of the Representative Method: The Method of Stratified Sampling and the Method of Purposive Selection', *Journal of the Royal Statistical Society*, 97: 558–606.

Ní Bhrolcháin, M. (forthcoming), ' "Divorce Effects" and Causality in the Social Sciences', *European Sociological Review*.

——Chappell, R., and Diamond, I. (1994), 'Scolarité et autres caractéristiques sociodémographiques des enfants de mariages rompus', *Population*, 6: 1585–1612.

Nichols, E. (1986), 'Skocpol on Revolution: Comparative Analysis vs. Historical Conjuncture', *Comparative Social Research*, 9: 163–86.

Oakeshott, M. (1933), *Experience and its Modes* (Cambridge: Cambridge University Press).

Oberschall, A. (1965), *Empirical Social Research in Germany, 1848–1914* (The Hague: Mouton).

——(1972) (ed.), *The Establishment of Empirical Sociology* (New York: Harper and Row).

——(1987), 'The Two Empirical Roots of Social Theory and the Probability Revolution', in L. Krüger, G. Gigerenzer, and M. S. Morgan (eds.), *The Probabilistic Revolution*, ii. *Ideas in the Sciences* (Cambridge, Mass.: MIT Press).

O'Connell, P. J. (1994), 'National Variation in the Fortunes of Labor: A Pooled and Cross-Sectional Analysis of the Impact of Economic Crisis in the Advanced Capitalist Nations', in T. Janoski and A. M. Hicks (eds.), *The Comparative Political Economy of the Welfare State* (Cambridge: Cambridge University Press).

O'Connor, J. S., and Brym, R. J. (1988), 'Public Welfare Expenditure in OECD Countries', *British Journal of Sociology*, 39: 47–68.

Olson, M. (1965), *The Logic of Collective Action* (Cambridge, Mass.: Harvard University Press).

Opp, K.-D. (1998), 'Can and Should Rational Choice Theory be Tested by Survey Research? The Example of Explaining Collective Political Action', in H.-P. Blossfeld and G. Prein (eds.), *Rational Choice Theory and Large-Scale Data Analysis* (Boulder, Colo.: Westview Press).

Orloff, A. S., and Skocpol, T. (1984), 'Why Not Equal Protection? Explaining the Politics of Public Spending in Britain, 1900–1911, and the United States, 1890s–1920', *American Sociological Review*, 49: 726–50.

Orum, A. M., Feagin, J. R., and Sjoberg, G. (1991), 'Introduction', in A. M. Orum, J. R. Feagin, and G. Sjoberg (eds.), *A Case for the Case Study* (Chapel Hill, NC: University of North Carolina Press).

Osterman, P. (1987), 'Choice of Employment Systems', *Industrial Relations*, 26: 46–67.

Pahl, R. (1993), 'Does Class Analysis without Class Theory have a Promising Future? A Reply to Goldthorpe and Marshall', *Sociology*, 27: 253–8.

Pampel, F. C., and Williamson, J. B. (1989), *Age, Class, Politics, and the Welfare State* (Cambridge: Cambridge University Press).

Papanicolaou, J., and Psacharopoulos, G. (1979), 'Socioeconomic Background, Schooling and Monetary Rewards in the United Kingdom', *Economica*, 46: 435–9.

Parsons, T. (1937), *The Structure of Social Action* (Glencoe, Ill.: Free Press).

Pearson, K. (1892), *The Grammar of Science* (London: Black).

——(1904), *On the Theory of Contingency and its Relation to Association and Normal Correlation* (London: Drapers' Company Research Memoirs).

Peel, J. D. Y. (1971), *Herbert Spencer: The Evolution of a Sociologist* (London: Heinemann).

Penrose, L. S. (1946), 'The Elementary Statistics of Majority Voting', *Journal of the Royal Statistical Society*, 109: 53–7.

Persson, I. (1990) (ed.), *Generating Equality in the Welfare State: The Swedish Experience* (Oslo: Norwegian University Press).

Petit, P. (1975), 'Rendement de l'enseignement supérieur et origine sociale', *Revue économique*, 26: 587–64.

Pfeffer, J. (1997), *New Directions for Organization Theory* (Oxford: Oxford University Press).

Phelps Brown, H. (1977), *The Inequality of Pay* (Oxford: Oxford University Press).

Piore, M. (1983), 'Qualitative Research Techniques in Economics', in J. Van Maanen (ed.), *Qualitative Methodology* (Beverly Hills, Calif.: Sage).

Pissarides, C. A. (1981), 'Staying on at School in England and Wales', *Economica*, 48: 345–63.

Platt, J. (1988), 'What Can Case Studies Do?', *Studies in Qualitative Methodology*, 1: 1–23.

Popper, K. R. (1945/1966), *The Open Society and its Enemies*, 2nd edn. (London: Routledge).

——(1957), *The Poverty of Historicism* (London: Routledge).

——(1972), *Objective Knowledge* (Oxford: Clarendon Press).

——(1976a), 'The Logic of the Social Science', in T. W. Adorno *et al.*, *The Positivist Dispute in German Sociology* (London: Heinemann).

——(1976b), *Unended Quest* (London: Fontana).

——(1994), *The Myth of the Framework* (London: Routledge).

Porter, T. M. (1982), 'A Statistical Survey of Gases: Maxwell's Social Physics', *Historical Studies in the Physical Sciences*, 8: 77–116.

——(1986), *The Rise of Statistical Thinking, 1820–1900* (Princeton: Princeton University Press).

——(1987), 'Lawless Society: Social Science and the Reinterpretation of Statistics in Germany, 1850–1880', in L. Krüger, L. J. Daston, and M. Heidelberger (eds.), *The Probabilistic Revolution*, i. *Ideas in History* (Cambridge, Mass.: MIT Press).

Portocarero, L. (1987), *Social Mobility in Industrial Societies: Women in France and Sweden* (Stockholm: Almqvist & Wicksell).

Pratt, J. W., and Zeckhauser, R. J. (1984), 'Principals and Agents', in J. W. Pratt and R. J. Zeckhauser (eds.), *Principals and Agents: The Structure of Business* (Boston: Harvard Business School Press).

Przeworski, A. (1987), 'Methods of Cross-National Research, 1970–83: An Overview', in M. Dierkes, H. N. Weiler, and A. B. Antal (eds.), *Comparative Policy Research* (Berlin: WZB-Publications).

——and Teune, H. (1970), *The Logic of Comparative Social Inquiry* (New York: Wiley).

Quadagno, J. S. (1987), 'Theories of the Welfare State', *Annual Review of Sociology*, 13: 109–28.

——and Knapp, S. J. (1992), 'Have Historical Sociologists Forsaken Theory?', *Sociological Methods and Research*, 20: 481–507.

Quetelet, A. (1835/1842), *A Treatise on Man and the Development of his Faculties* (Edinburgh: Chambers).

——(1846): *Lettres à S.A.R. le Duc Régnant de Saxe-Coburg-Gotha, sur la théorie des probabilités, appliquée aux sciences morales et politiques* (Brussels: Hayez).

——(1869), *Physique sociale* (Brussels: Muquardt).

Raftery, A. E., and Hout, M. (1990), 'Maximally Maintained Inequality: Expansion, Reform and Opportunity in Irish Education, 1921–1975', ISA Research Committee on Social Stratification and Mobility, Madrid.

Ragin, C. C. (1987), *The Comparative Method* (Berkeley and Los Angeles: University of California Press).

—— (1991), 'Introduction: Cases of "What is a Case?"', in C. C. Ragin and H. S. Becker (eds.), *What is a Case?* (Cambridge: Cambridge University Press).

—— (1994*a*), *Constructing Social Research* (Thousand Oaks, Calif.: Pine Forge Press).

—— (1994*b*), 'Introduction to Qualitative Comparative Analysis', in T. Janoski and A. M. Hicks (eds.), *The Comparative Political Economy of the Welfare State* (Cambridge: Cambridge University Press).

—— (1997), 'Turning the Tables: How Case-Oriented Research Challenges Variable-Oriented Research', *Comparative Social Research*, 16: 27–42.

Ramirez, F. O., and Boli, J. (1987), 'Global Patterns of Educational Institutionalization', in G. M. Thomas *et al.* (eds.), *Institutional Structure* (Newbury Park, Calif.: Sage).

Redfield, R. (1930), *Tepoztlan: A Mexican Village* (Chicago: University of Chicago Press).

Renier, G. J. (1950), *History: Its Purpose and Method* (London: Allen & Unwin).

Richardson, C. J. (1977), *Contemporary Social Mobility* (London: Francis Pinter).

Ringdal, K. (1994), 'Intergenerational Class Mobility in Post-War Norway: A Weakening of Vertical Barriers?', *European Sociological Review*, 10: 273–88.

Ringer, F. (1969), *The Decline of the German Mandarins* (Cambridge, Mass.: Harvard University Press).

—— (1997), *Max Weber's Methodology: The Unification of the Cultural and Social Sciences* (Cambridge, Mass.: Harvard University Press).

Ritzer, G. (1975), *Sociology: A Multiple Paradigm Science* (Boston: Allyn & Bacon).

Robbins, L. (1932/1949), *The Nature and Significance of Economic Science*, 2nd edn. (London: Macmillan).

Robinson, R. V. (1984), 'Reproducing Class Relations in Industrial Capitalism', *American Sociological Review*, 49: 182–96.

Robinson, W. S. (1951), 'The Logical Structure of Analytic Induction', *American Sociological Review*, 16: 812–18.

Rogosa, D. (1992), 'Causal Models do not Support Scientific Conclusions: A Comment in Favour of Freedman', in J. P. Shaffer (ed.), *The Role of Models in Nonexperimental Social Science: Two Debates* (Washington: American Educational Research Association and American Statistical Association).

Rose, D., and O'Reilly, K. (1997) (eds.), *Constructing Classes: Towards a New Social Classification for the UK* (London: Economic and Social Research Council and Office for National Statistics).

—— —— (1998), *The ESRC Review of Government Social Classifications* (London: Office for National Statistics and Economic and Social Research Council).

Rosen, B. (1956), 'The Achievement Syndrome: A Psychocultural Dimension of Social Stratification', *American Sociological Review*, 21: 203–11.

Rosenbaum, P. R. (1995), *Observational Studies* (New York: Springer).

Ross, D. (1991), *The Origins of American Social Science* (Cambridge: Cambridge University Press).

Roth, G. (1968), 'Introduction', in Max Weber, *Economy and Society*, ed. G. Roth and C. Wittich (Berkeley: University of California Press).

Rowntree, S. (1901), *Poverty: A Study of Town Life* (London: Macmillan).

Rubin, D. B. (1974), 'Estimating Causal Effects of Treatments in Randomized and Non-randomized Studies', *Journal of Educational Psychology*, 66: 688–701.

—— (1977), 'Assignment to Treatment Groups on the Basis of a Covariate', *Journal of Educational Statistics*, 2: 1–26.

—— (1986), 'Comment: Which Ifs Have Causal Answers?', *Journal of the American Statistical Association*, 81: 961–2.

——(1990), 'Formal Models of Statistical Inference for Causal Effects', *Journal of Statistical Planning and Inference*, 25: 279–92.

Rueschemeyer, D. (1991), 'Different Methods—Contradictory Results? Research on Development and Democracy', in C. C. Ragin (ed.), *Issues and Alternatives in Comparative Social Research* (Leiden: E. J. Brill).

Rueschemeyer, D., and Stephens, J. D. (1997), 'Comparing Historical Sequences—A Powerful Tool for Causal Analysis', *Comparative Social Research*, 16: 55–72.

——Stephens, E. H., and Stephens, J. D. (1992), *Capitalist Development and Democracy* (Cambridge: Polity Press).

Runciman, W. G. (1983), *A Treatise on Social Theory: I—The Methodology of Social Theory* (Cambridge: Cambridge University Press).

Rutter, M. (1981), 'Epidemiological/Longitudinal Strategies and Causal Research in Child Psychiatry', *Journal of the American Academy of Child Psychiatry*, 20: 513–44.

——(1994), 'Beyond Longitudinal Data: Causes, Consequences, Changes and Continuity', *Journal of Consulting and Clinical Psychiatry*, 62: 928–40.

Ryan, A. (1970), *The Philosophy of John Stuart Mill* (London: Macmillan).

Salmon, W. C. (1980), 'Probabilistic Causality', *Pacific Philosophical Quarterly*, 61: 50–74.

Sartori, G. (1994), 'Compare Why and How', in M. Dogan and A. Kazancigil (eds.), *Comparing Nations* (Oxford: Blackwell).

Savage, M., and Butler, T. (1995), 'Assets and the Middle Classes in Contemporary Britain', in T. Butler and M. Savage (eds.), *Social Change and the Middle Classes* (London: UCL Press).

——et al. (1992), *Property, Bureaucracy and Culture: Middle-Class Formation in Contemporary Britain* (London: Routledge).

Schad, S. P. (1972), *Empirical Social Research in Weimar-Germany* (Paris: Mouton).

Scheff, T. J. (1992), 'Rationality and Emotion: Homage to Norbert Elias', in J. S. Coleman and T. J. Fararo (eds.), *Rational Choice Theory: Advocacy and Critique* (Newbury Park, Calif.: Sage).

Scheuch, E. K. (1989), 'Theoretical Implications of Comparative Survey Research: Why the Wheel of Cross-Cultural Methodology Keeps on being Reinvented', *International Sociology*, 4: 147–67.

Schmidt, M. G. (1993), 'Gendered Labour Force Participation', in F. G. Castles (ed.), *Families of Nations: Patterns of Public Policy in Western Democracies* (Aldershot: Dartmouth).

Schmitter, P. C. (1991), 'Comparative Politics at the Crossroads', working paper, Instituto Juan March, Madrid.

Schneider, L., and Lysgaard, S. (1953), 'The Deferred Gratification Pattern', *American Sociological Review*, 18: 142–9.

Schoemaker, P. J. (1982), 'The Expected Utility Model: Its Variants, Purposes, Evidence and Limitations', *Journal of Economic Literature*, 30: 529–63.

Schumpeter, J. A. (1954), *History of Economic Analysis* (London: Routledge).

Schutz, A. (1932/1967), *The Phenomenology of the Social World* (New York: Northwestern University Press).

——(1960), 'The Social World and the Theory of Social Action', *Social Research*, 27: 203–21.

Searle, J. R. (1993), 'Rationality and Realism: What is at Stake?', *Daedalus* (Fall), 55–83.

——(1995), *The Construction of Social Reality* (London: Allen Lane).

Selvin, H. C. (1976), 'Durkheim, Booth and Yule: The Non-Diffusion of an Intellectual Innovation', *Archives européennes de sociologie*, 17: 39–51.

Sen, A. K. (1977), 'Rational Fools: A Critique of the Behavioural Foundations of Economic Theory', *Philosophy and Public Affairs*, 6: 317–44.

—— (1986), 'Prediction and Economic Theory', *Proceedings of the Royal Society of London*, A407: 3–23.

—— (1987), 'Rational Behaviour', in J. Eatwell, M. Milgate, and P. Newman (eds.), *The New Palgrave: A Dictionary of Economics*, iv (London: Macmillan).

Seng, Y. P. (1951), 'Historical Survey of the Development of Sampling Theories and Practice', *Journal of the Royal Statistical Society*, Series A, 114: 214–31.

Sewell, W. H., and Hauser, R. M. (1976), 'Causes and Consequences of Higher Education: Models of the Status Attainment Process', in W. H. Sewell, R. M. Hauser, and D. L. Featherman (eds.), *Schooling and Achievement in American Society* (New York: Academic Press).

Shavit, Y., and Blossfeld, H.-P. (1993) (eds.), *Persistent Inequality: Changing Educational Attainment in Thirteen Countries* (Boulder, Colo.: Westview Press).

—— and Müller, W. (1998) (eds.), *From School to Work* (Oxford: Clarendon Press).

Silver, C. (1982) (ed.), *Frédéric Le Play on Family, Work and Social Change* (Chicago: Chicago University Press).

Silverman, D. (1993), *Interpreting Qualitative Data* (London: Sage).

Simiand, F. (1907), *Le Salaire des ouvriers des mines de charbon en France* (Paris: Société Nouvelle).

—— (1932), *Le Salaire: l'Évolution sociale et la monnaie* (Paris: Alcan).

Simkus, A., *et al.* (1990), 'Changes in Social Mobility in Two Societies in the Crux of Transition: A Hungarian–Irish Comparison, 1943–73', *Research in Social Stratification and Mobility*, 8: 33–78.

Simmel, G. (1900/1978), *The Philosophy of Money* (New York: Free Press).

—— (1905/1977), *The Problems of the Philosophy of History* (New York: Free Press).

Simon, H. A. (1946/1961), *Administrative Behavior* (New York: Macmillan).

—— (1951), 'A Formal Theory of the Firm', *Econometrica*, 19: 293–305.

—— (1954), 'Spurious Correlation: A Causal Interpretation', *Journal of the American Statistical Association*, 49: 467–92.

—— (1982), *Models of Bounded Rationality* (Cambridge, Mass.: MIT Press).

—— (1983), *Reason in Human Affairs* (Oxford: Blackwell).

—— (1991), 'Organizations and Markets', *Journal of Economic Perspectives*, 5: 25–44.

—— and Iwasaki, Y. (1988), 'Causal Ordering, Comparative Statics, and Near Decomposability', *Journal of Econometrics*, 39: 149–73.

Skocpol, T. (1979), *States and Social Revolutions* (Cambridge: Cambridge University Press).

—— (1982), 'Rentier State and Shi'a Islam in the Iranian Revolution', *Theory and Society*, 11: 265–83.

—— (1984), 'Emerging Agendas and Recurrent Strategies in Historical Sociology', in T. Skocpol (ed.), *Vision and Method in Historical Sociology* (Cambridge: Cambridge University Press).

—— (1986), 'Analyzing Causal Configurations in History: A Rejoinder to Nichols', *Comparative Social Research*, 9: 187–94.

—— (1994), *Social Revolutions in the Modern World* (Cambridge: Cambridge University Press).

—— and Somers, M. (1980), 'The Use of Comparative History in Macrosocial Inquiry', *Comparative Studies in Society and History*, 22: 174–97.

Skog, O.-J. (1991), 'Alcohol and Suicide—Durkheim Revisited', *Acta Sociologica*, 34: 193–206.

Smeeding, T. M., O'Higgins, M., and Rainwater, L. (1990), *Poverty, Inequality and the Distribution of Income in Comparative Perspective* (London: Wheatsheaf).

Smelser, N. J. (1976), *Comparative Methods in the Social Sciences* (Englewood Cliffs, NJ: Prentice-Hall).

——(1992), 'The Rational Choice Perspective: A Theoretical Assessment', *Rationality and Society*, 4: 381–410.

Smith, H. L. (1990), 'Specification Problems in Experimental and Non-Experimental Social Research', *Sociological Methodology*, 20: 59–91.

Snow, D. A., and Anderson, L. (1991), 'Researching the Homeless', in J. R. Feagin, A. M. Orum, and G. Sjoberg (eds.), *A Case for the Case Study* (Chapel Hill, NC: University of North Carolina Press).

——and Morrill, C. (1993), 'Reflections on Anthropology's Ethnographic Crisis of Faith', *Contemporary Sociology*, 22: 8–11.

Sobel, M. E. (1981), 'Diagonal Mobility Models', *American Sociological Review*, 46: 893–906.

——(1985), 'Social Mobility and Fertility Revisited', *American Sociological Review*, 50: 699–712.

——(1995), 'Causal Inference in the Social and Behavioral Sciences', in G. Arminger, C. C. Clogg, and M. E. Sobel (eds.), *Handbook of Statistical Modeling for the Social and Behavioral Sciences* (New York: Plenum Press).

——(1996), 'An Introduction to Causal Inference', *Sociological Methods and Research*, 24: 353–79.

Soffer, R. N. (1978), *Ethics and Society in England: The Revolution in the Social Sciences, 1870–1914* (Berkeley and Los Angeles: University of California Press).

Sokal, A., and Bricmont, J. (1997), *Intellectual Impostures* (London: Profile Books).

Somers, M. R. (1998), ' "We're No Angels": Realism, Rational Choice and Relationality in Social Science', *American Journal of Sociology*, 104: 722–84.

Sørensen, A. B. (1994), 'Firms, Wages, and Incentives', in N. J. Smelser and R. Swedberg (eds.), *Handbook of Economic Sociology* (Princeton: Princeton University Press).

——(1996), 'The Structural Basis of Social Inequality', *American Journal of Sociology*, 101: 1333–65.

——(1998), 'Theoretical Mechanisms and the Empirical Study of Social Processes' in P. Hedström and R. Swedberg (eds.), *Social Mechanisms* (Cambridge: Cambridge University Press).

——(1999), 'Employment Relations and Class Structures', typescript.

Spånt, R. (1979), *The Distribution of Income in Sweden, 1920–1976* (Stockholm: Swedish Institute for Social Research).

Spencer, H. (1861/1911), *Essays on Education* (London: Dent).

——(1873/1961), *The Study of Sociology* (Ann Arbor: University of Michigan Press).

——(1876–97), *The Principles of Sociology* (London: Williams & Norgate).

——(1904), *An Autobiography* (London: Williams & Norgate).

——*et al.* (1873–1934), *Descriptive Sociology* (London: various publishers).

Spradley, J. P. (1980), *Participant Observation* (New York: Holt, Rinehart & Winston).

Stake, R. E. (1978), 'The Case Study Method of Social Inquiry', *Educational Researcher*, 7: 5–8.

Stevens, S. S. (1946), 'On the Theory of Scales of Measurement', *Science*, 103: 677–80.

Stewart, A. (1998), *The Ethnographer's Method* (Thousand Oaks, Calif.: Sage).

Stigler, S. M. (1986), *The History of Statistics: the Measurement of Uncertainty before 1900* (Cambridge, Mass.: Harvard University Press).

——(1987), 'The Measurement of Uncertainty in Nineteenth-Century Social Science', in L. Krüger, L. J. Daston, and M. Heidelberger (eds.), *The Probabilistic Revolution*, i. *Ideas in History* (Cambridge, Mass.: MIT Press).

Stimson, J. A. (1985), 'Regression in Space and Time: A Statistical Essay', *American Journal of Political Science*, 29: 914–47.

Stinchcombe, A. L. (1968), *Constructing Social Theories* (New York: Harcourt Brace).

——(1993), 'The Conditions of Fruitfulness of Theorizing about Mechanisms in Social Science', in A. B. Sørensen and S. Spilerman (eds.), *Social Theory and Social Policy: Essays in Honor of James S. Coleman* (Westport, Conn.: Praeger).

Stoecker, R. (1991), 'Evaluating and Rethinking the Case Study', *Sociological Review*, 39: 88–112.

Stoetzel, J. (1957), 'Sociology in France: An Empiricist View', in H. Becker and B. Boskoff (eds.), *Modern Sociological Theory* (New York: Holt, Rinehart & Winston).

Stone, K. (1974), 'The Origins of Job Structures in the Steel Industry', *Review of Radical Political Economics*, 6: 61–97.

Stone, L. (1987), *The Past and Present Revisited* (London: Routledge).

Stone, R. (1997), *Some British Empiricists in the Social Sciences, 1650–1900* (Cambridge: Cambridge University Press).

Strauss, A., and Corbin, J. (1990), *Basics of Qualitative Research* (Newbury Park, Calif.: Sage).

Swedberg, R. (1998), *Max Weber and the Idea of Economic Sociology* (Princeton: Princeton University Press).

Suppes, P. (1970), *A Probabilistic Theory of Causality* (Amsterdam: North Holland).

Sutherland, S. (1992), *Irrationality* (London: Penguin).

Szelényi, S. (1998), *Equality by Design: The Grand Experiment in Destratification in Socialist Hungary* (Stanford, Calif.: Stanford University Press).

Sztompka, P. (1988), 'Conceptual Frameworks in Comparative Inquiry: Divergent or Convergent?', *International Sociology*, 3: 207–18.

Tawney, R. H. (1912), *The Agrarian Problem in the Sixteenth Century* (London: Longmans).

——(1941/1954), 'The Rise of the Gentry, 1558–1640' (with a 'Postscript'), in E. M. Carus-Wilson (ed.), *Essays in Economic History* (London: Arnold).

Taylor, M. (1988) (ed.), *Rationality and Revolution* (Cambridge: Cambridge University Press).

Teune, H. (1997), 'Stories, Observations, Systems, Theories', *Comparative Social Research*, 16: 73–83.

Therborn, G. (1993), 'Beyond the Lonely Nation-State', in F. G. Castles (ed.), *Families of Nations: Patterns of Public Policy in Western Democracies* (Aldershot: Dartmouth).

Thurow, L. C. (1972), 'Education and Economic Inequality', *Public Interest*, 28 (Summer), 66–81.

——(1983), *Dangerous Currents: The State of Economics* (New York: Vintage).

Tilly, C. (1997), 'Means and Ends of Comparison in Macrosociology', *Comparative Social Research*, 16: 43–53.

Tilton, T. (1990), *The Political Theory of Swedish Social Democracy* (Oxford: Clarendon Press).

Toulmin, S. (1970), 'Reasons and Causes', in R. Borger and F. Cioffi (eds.), *Explanation in the Behavioural Sciences* (Cambridge: Cambridge University Press).

Treiman, D. J. (1970), 'Industrialization and Social Stratification', in E. O. Laumann (ed.), *Social Stratification: Research and Theory for the 1970s* (Indianapolis: Bobbs Merrill).

Treiman, D. J., (1975), 'Problems of Concept and Measurement in the Comparative Study of Occupational Mobility', *Social Science Research*, 4: 183–230.

——and Yip, K.-B. (1989), 'Educational and Occupational Attainment in 21 Countries', in M. L. Kohn (ed.), *Cross-National Research in Sociology* (Newbury Park, Calif.: Sage).

Tsebelis, G. (1990), *Nested Games: Rational Choice in Comparative Politics* (Berkeley and Los Angeles: University of California Press).

Turner, J. H. (1985), *Herbert Spencer* (Beverly Hills, Calif.: Sage).

Turner, S. P. (1985), *The Search for a Methodology of Social Science* (Dordrecht: Reidel).

——and Factor, R. A. (1981), 'Objective Possibility and Adequate Causation in Weber's Methodological Writings', *Sociological Review*, 29: 5–28.

————(1994), *Max Weber: The Lawyer as Social Thinker* (London: Routledge).

——and Turner, J. H. (1990), *The Impossible Science: An Institutional Analysis of American Sociology* (Newbury Park, Calif.: Sage).

Tylor, E. B. (1989), 'On a Method of Investigating the Development of Institutions; Applied to Laws of Marriage and Descent', *Journal of the Anthropological Institute*, 18: 245–69.

Tyree, A., Semyonov, M., and Hodge, R. W. (1979), 'Gaps and Glissandos: Inequality, Economic Development, and Social Mobility in 24 Countries', *American Sociological Review*, 44: 410–24.

Udehn, L. (1994), *Methodological Individualism: A Critical Appraisal* (Uppsala: Uppsala Universitet, Sociologiska Institutionen).

Ultee, W. (1991), 'How Classical Questions were Enriched', in H. Becker, F. L. Leeuw, and K. Verrips (eds.), *In Pursuit of Progress: An Assessment of Achievements in Dutch Sociology* (Amsterdam: SISWO).

Usui, C. (1994), 'Welfare State Development in a World System Context: Event History Analysis of First Social Insurance Legislation among 60 Countries, 1880–1960', in T. Janoski and A. M. Hicks (eds.), *The Comparative Political Economy of the Welfare State* (Cambridge: Cambridge University Press).

Vallet, L.-A. (1999), 'Quarante années de mobilité sociale en France', *Revue française de sociologie*, 40: 3–64.

van den Berg, A. (1998), 'Is Sociological Theory Too Grand for Social Mechanisms?', in P. Hedström and R. Swedberg (eds.), *Social Mechanisms* (Cambridge: Cambridge University Press).

van Poppel, F., and Day, L. H. (1996), 'A Test of Durkheim's Theory of Suicide—without Committing the "Ecological Fallacy"', *American Sociological Review*, 61: 500–7.

Vidich, A. J., and Lyman, S. M. (1994), 'Qualitative Methods: Their History in Sociology and Anthropology', in N. K. Denzin and Y. S. Lincoln (eds.), *Handbook of Qualitative Research* (Thousand Oaks, Calif.: Sage).

Vogel, J. (1987), *Det Svenska Klassamhället* (Stockholm: Statistika Centralbyrån).

Vogt, W. P. (1983), 'Durkheimian Sociology versus Philosophical Rationalism: The Case of Célestin Bouglé', in P. Besnard (ed.), *The Sociological Domain* (Cambridge: Cambridge University Press).

Verein für Sozialpolitik (1912), *Verhandlungen der Generalversammlung in Nürnberg, 1911* (Leipzig: Dunker & Humblot).

von Wright, G. H. (1971), *Explanation and Understanding* (London: Routledge).

——(1972), 'On So-Called Practical Inference', *Acta Sociologica*, 15: 39–53.

Wadsworth, M. E. J. (1991), *The Impact of Time: Childhood, History and Adult Life* (Oxford: Clarendon Press).

Wagner, H. R. (1983), *Alfred Schutz: An Intellectual Biography* (Chicago: University of Chicago Press).

Wallerstein, I. (1974–89), *The Modern World System*, 3 vols. (New York: Academic Press).

Walsh, W. H. (1974), 'Colligatory Concepts in History', in P. Gardiner (ed.), *The Philosophy of History* (Oxford: Oxford University Press).

Watkins, J. W. N. (1963), 'On Explaining Disaster', *Listener*, 10 Jan., 69–70.

——(1970), 'Imperfect Rationality', in R. Borger and F. Cioffi (eds.), *Explanation in the Behavioural Sciences* (Cambridge: Cambridge University Press).

Weakliem, D. L. (1989), 'The Employment Contract: A Test of the Transaction Cost Theory', *Sociological Forum*, 4: 203–26.

——and Heath, A. F. (1994), 'Rational Choice and Class Voting', *Rationality and Society*, 6: 243–70.

Webb, B. (1891), *The Cooperative Movement in Great Britain* (London: Sonnenschein).

——(1926), *My Apprenticeship* (London: Longmans).

Webb, S., and Webb, B. (1894), *The History of Trade Unionism* (London: Longmans).

————(1897), *Industrial Democracy* (London: Longmans).

————(1932), *Methods of Social Study* (London: Longmans).

Weber, Marianne (1926/1975), *Max Weber: A Biography* (New Brunswick, NJ: Transaction Books).

Weber, Max (1903–6/1975), *Roscher and Knies: The Logical Problems of Historical Economics* (New York: Free Press).

——(1904/1949), ' "Objectivity" in Social Science and Social Policy', in *The Methodology of the Social Sciences* (Glencoe, Ill.: Free Press).

——(1904–5/1930), *The Protestant Ethic and the Spirit of Capitalism* (London: Allen & Unwin).

——(1906/1949), 'A Critique of Eduard Meyer's Methodological Views', in *The Methodology of the Social Sciences* (Glencoe, Ill.: Free Press).

——(1907/1977), *Critique of Stammler* (New York: Free Press).

——(1908), 'Zur Psychophysik der industriellen Arbeit', *Archiv für Sozialwissenschaft und Sozialpolitik*, 27: 730–70.

——(1908/1975), 'Marginal Utility Theory and "The Fundamental Law of Psychophysics" ', *Social Science Quarterly*, 56: 21–36.

——(1913/1981), 'Some Categories of Interpretative Sociology', *Sociological Quarterly*, 22: 145–80.

——(1922/1968), *Economy and Society* (Berkeley and Los Angeles: University of California Press).

Weir, M., and Skocpol, T. (1985), 'State Structures and the Possibilities for "Keynesian Responses" to the Great Depression in Sweden, Britain and the United States', in P. Evans, D. Rueschemeyer, and T. Skocpol (eds.), *Bringing the State Back In* (New York: Cambridge University Press).

Westergaard, H. (1932), *Contributions to the History of Statistics* (London: King).

Westergaard, J., and Resler, H. (1975), *Class in a Capitalist Society* (London: Heinemann).

Western, M. (1999), 'Class Attainment among British Men: A Multivariate Extension of the CASMIN Model of Intergenerational Class Mobility', *European Sociological Review*, 15: 431–54.

Weyembergh, M. (1971), *Le Volontarisme rationnel de Max Weber* (Brussels: Académie Royale de Belgique).

Whyte, W. F. (1943), *Street Corner Society* (Chicago: Chicago University Press).

Wickham-Crowley, T. P. (1992), *Guerrillas and Revolution in Latin America* (Princeton: Princeton University Press).

Wilensky, H. L., and Lawrence, A. T. (1980), 'Job Assignment in Modern Societies: A Re-Examination of the Ascription-Achievement Hypothesis', in A. H. Hawley (ed.), *Societal Growth: Processes and Implications* (New York: Free Press).

Williamson, O. E. (1985), *The Economic Institutions of Capitalism* (New York: Free Press).

—— (1994), 'The Economics and Sociology of Organizations: Promoting a Dialogue', in G. Farkas and P. England (eds.), *Industries, Firms and Jobs* (New York: Aldine De Gruyter).

—— (1996), *The Mechanisms of Governance* (New York: Oxford University Press).

Willis, P. (1977), *Learning to Labour* (Farnborough: Saxon House).

Wise, M. N. (1987), 'Do Sums Count? On the Cultural Origins of Statistical Causality', in L. Krüger, L. J. Daston, and M. Heidelberger (eds.), *The Probabilistic Revolution*, i. *Ideas in History* (Cambridge, Mass.: MIT Press).

Wolf, F. M. (1986), *Meta-Analysis: Quantitative Methods for Research Synthesis* (Beverly Hills, Calif.: Sage).

Wong, R. S.-K. (1994), 'Postwar Mobility Trends in Advanced Industrial Societies', *Research in Social Stratification and Mobility*, 13: 121–44.

—— and Hauser, R. M. (1992), 'Trends in Occupational Mobility in Hungary under Socialism', *Social Science Research*, 21: 419–44.

Wright, E. O. (1985), *Classes* (London: Verso).

—— (1989), 'Rethinking, Once Again, the Concept of Class Structure', in E. O. Wright *et al.* (eds.), *The Debate on Classes* (London: Verso).

—— (1997), *Class Counts* (Cambridge: Cambridge University Press).

Wrong, D. (1961), 'The Oversocialized Conception of Man in Modern Sociology', *American Sociological Review*, 26: 183–93.

Yaish, M. (1998), 'Opportunities, Little Change: Class Mobility in Israeli Society, 1974–1991', D. Phil. thesis, Oxford.

Yin, R. K. (1994), *Case Study Research* (Thousand Oaks, Calif.: Sage).

Yule, G. U. (1895), 'On the Correlation of Total Pauperism with Proportion of Out-Relief, I: All Ages', *Economic Journal*, 5: 603–11.

—— (1896), 'On the Correlation of Total Pauperism with Proportion of Out-Relief, II: Males over 65', *Economic Journal*, 6: 613–23.

—— (1897), 'On the Theory of Correlation', *Journal of the Royal Statistical Society*, 60: 812–54.

—— (1899), 'An Investigation into the Causes of Changes in Pauperism in England, Chiefly during the Last Two Intercensal Decades', *Journal of the Royal Statistical Society*, 62: 249–95.

—— (1911), *An Introduction to the Theory of Statistics* (London: Griffin).

Zaret, D. (1978), 'Sociological Theory and Historical Scholarship', *American Sociologist*, 13: 114–21.

Zelditch, M. (1971), 'Intelligible Comparisons', in I. Vallier (ed.), *Comparative Methods in Sociology* (Berkeley and Los Angeles: University of California Press).

Zellner, A. (1988), 'Causality and Causal Laws in Economics', *Journal of Econometrics*, 39: 7–21.

Znaniecki, F. (1934), *The Method of Sociology* (New York: Farrar & Rhinehart).

Zonabend, F. (1992), 'The Monograph in European Ethnography', *Current Sociology*, 40: 49–54.

NAME INDEX

SUBJECT INDEX

ability 188, 190–1, 202
absent synthesis, historical reasons 26, 259–94
  England 274–81
  France 267–74
  Germany 282–94
  sociology and probabilistic revolution 261–7
absolute mobility rates 231–2, 241, 257
achievement 174, 233 n., 235, 247, 249
  see also meritocracy
agency problems 147, 217–19, 221, 226
agrarian economies 48, 62, 128, 253 n.
agricultural research 142, 148, 159
American Sociological Association (ASA) 10 n.
analytic induction 88, 115
anthropometry 262–3, 266
ascription 162, 174, 233 n., 235, 247–9, 251
aspirations 158, 169–71
association 138–9, 152
astronomy 262–3, 265, 268
Austria 270
averages 71–2

behavioural economics 123–4, 126
Beveridge Plan 54
biology 266, 268, 275, 285, 292
biometrics 17, 100 n., 140, 266
Bismarckian social policy 54
black-box problem 15–16, 48, 57–64, 135, 149
Boolean algebra 51–2
bounded rationality 119–22, 127–8, 131–2, 135–6, 210
Britain 112, 252, 257
  Beveridge Plan 54
  education differentials 169, 177, 185, 202 n.
  and employment 207, 209, 217 n., 227–9
  poverty surveys 70, 73 n.
  sociological community 28, 34, 37–8, 56 n., 238 n.
  see also England; Scotland
British Association for the Advancement of Science 278
British Journal of Sociology 13–14, 28 n.

Calvinism 34, 36
capitalism 34, 36, 58, 61 n., 162, 210
CASMIN (Comparative Analysis of Social Mobility in Industrial Societies Project) 206 n.
causation 16, 137–60, 271, 291
  causal-path analysis 96, 98–9, 140–2
  as consequential manipulation 21, 138, 142–51, 157, 159
  and ethnography 81–2, 87–90, 92
  as generative process 21, 138, 149–51, 157, 159–60
  as robust dependence 21, 138–43, 149–52, 159
chemistry 268
Chicago tradition 50 n.
Chinese revolution 55, 60
Christian Democracy 51 n.–2 n.
class:
  competition 162, 253
  decomposition 161–2, 178
  differentials: educational 22–4, 147, 153, 161–81, 204–5; generation of 188–92, model of decisions 185–8, 192–7, 201–3, RAT and 164–7, 172–8, *see also* education; employment contracts 206–29
  formation 161–3, 178, 287
  mobility 26, 161–2, 169, 180 n., 242
  schema 24, 209, 227
  stability 26, 103, 161, 164, 175, 251
  stratification 164, 232
  voting 18, 112, 155, 163, 206–7
cognitive:
  psychology 124, 131
  relativism 8 n., 16 n.
  sociology 122, 131
cognitivist model 119–20, 125–6, 129 n.
commodification 210, 216, 225
Communism 254–5
comparative social mobility 53, 61 n., 62
consequentialism 128
contractual hazards 213–14, 217, 225
convergence thesis 55, 179
correlation 266, 269–70, 277, 279, 290
cost–benefit analysis 128–9, 172–6, 184, 238 n.
credentialism 97, 141
crime 18, 263, 282–3
  rates 265, 272
criminology 5
Cuba 52 n.
cultural:
  capital 168–9, 248